SANSKRIT PLAY PRODUCTION IN ANCIENT INDIA

PERFORMING ARTS SERIES

General Editor

FARLEY P. RICHMOND

VOLUME V

Sanskrit Play Production in Ancient India

TARLA MEHTA

MOTILAL BANARSIDASS PUBLISHERS
PRIVATE LIMITED • DELHI

First Edition: Delhi, 1995

ISBN: 81-208-1057-0

Also available at:

MOTILAL BANARSIDASS

41 U.A. Bungalow Road, Jawahar Nagar, Delhi 110 007
120 Royapettah High Road, Mylapore, Madras 600 004
16 St. Mark's Road, Bangalore 560 001
Ashok Rajpath, Patna 800 004
Chowk, Varanasi 221 001

PRINTED IN INDIA

BY JAINENDRA PRAKASH JAIN AT SHRI JAINENDRA PRESS,
A-45 NARAINA, PHASE I, NEW DELHI 110 028
AND PUBLISHED BY NARENDRA PRAKASH JAIN FOR
MOTILAL BANARSIDASS PUBLISHERS PVT. LTD.,
JAWAHAR NAGAR, DELHI 110 007

To
Vipin
my brother
who was happy
to see me complete this study
and would have been
happier at its publication.

FOREWORD BY SERIES EDITOR

India is one of the great repositories of performing arts, particularly those of the classical, folk/popular, devotional and modern traditions. The sheer enormity and diversity of its cultural expressions in music, dance/drama and theatre are the envy of many nations around the world. This series intends to assemble some of the best books now available on these subjects.

Without exaggeration, a series such as this would not have been possible twenty years ago when I first began writing about Indian theatre. At that time little more than a few dozen books comprised the entire field of scholarship in the English language, not to mention the paucity of materials in regional Indian languages. Today that picture has radically changed. Numerous publishers have devoted precious press time to volumes of well-illustrated, detailed and, yes, sometimes even esoteric works on the multiple aspects of this fascinating subject. Comb any bookshop in Delhi or Madras, Bombay or Calcutta and you will regularly find new works appearing on the shelves. This represents a real area of growth. It is to the credit of Motilal Banarsidass Publishers Private Limited that there is now the potential of assembling numerous volumes together under one umbrella.

This book joins the ranks of a relatively few other works exclusively devoted to disseminating and deciphering the meaning of India's most famous text of dramaturgy. Dr. Mehta brings her own considerable background as a stage and screen actress—a practical person of the theatre—to the process of interpreting the complicated works of ancient Indian theatre to modern readers.

FARLEY P. RICHMOND

ACKNOWLEDGEMENTS

A long time has gone in preparing and publishing this work which has grown out of my Ph.D. thesis 'The Production Techniques of Sanskrit Dramas in Ancient India', submitted in 1981 and passed by the Bombay University in 1982. It would not be possible to mention all the scholars, Sanskrit pandits, theatre workers and dancer friends who have, with their knowledgeable help and sympathetic encouragement, contributed in the process of my research. To each one, I am grateful.

For special thanks I, first of all, wish to acknowledge late Prof. R.B. Athavale who inspired me for this work and made me relish the beauty of Sanskrit poetics and ancient Indian aesthetics.

Ms Prakriti Kashyap for the happy and fruitful hours she spent with me perusing and deciphering many interpretations offered in the commentary of Abhinavagupta on the Nāṭya Śāstra and her ever willing enthusiastic support for the cause of this work. Also Prakash Deshmukh.

Prof. Hrishikesh Pathak who often helped in clarifying my point of view whenever I was confronted with knotty problems either at the level of concept or expression.

Balvant K. Parekh Foundation for lending it's support to the cause of this publication. And also Shri Deepak Mehta who enthusiastically lent a helping hand during the long period of this publication from 1984 onwards.

Lastly I wish to remember the theatre workers and scholars, chief among them my sister Smt. Shanta Gandhi and Prof. G.H. Tarlekar who enjoyed the process of practical visualisations of some of the scenes of Sanskrit dramas with me and which creative experience I share with you.

518, Mahajani Marg
Bombay 400 019

TARLA MEHTA

FOREWORD

I have great pleasure in writing a foreword to this excellent book which gives a masterly survey of the theory and practice of Sanskrit play production in ancient India. Much has been written in India and abroad on the subject; but most of the writings are by scholars who had no direct experience of the stage and by artists and connoisseurs who had no intimate knowledge of the basic texts. The author of this book, Tarla Mehta, is a famous actress with mature experience on the stage and cinema; she is also a deep scholar who has studied carefully the available source material with discrimination and aesthetic vision. The book is written in a racy, fluent style with great clarity and penetration.

The most important work on Indian theatre and dramatic theory is the *Nāṭyaśāstra* ascribed to the legendary sage Bharata together with its elaborate and comprehensive commentary by Abhinavagupta; this is still in need of a critical and definitive edition. Later texts on dramaturgy like the *Daśarūpaka* of Dhanañjaya with Dhanika's commentary, references found scattered in literature as in the *Harivaṃśa* and the *Kuṭṭanimatam kāvyam*, and the facts revealed by a study of the available dramas themselves shed much useful light on the general nature of the Sanskrit plays on the stage. A comprehensive and comparative study of the living traditions of stage performances in different parts of India is also helpful in clarifying many problems regarding ancient practices.

The living *Kutiyattam* tradition of staging classical Sanskrit dramas as a temple art by hereditary communities in Kerala, which has a continuous history extending to more than a thousand years was unknown outside Kerala till very recently and had not received attention even in standard works on Indian theatre like those of Sylvain Levi, Sten Konow and A.B. Keith. Several stage manuals, called *Kramadīpikā* and *Aṭṭaprakāram* in Sanskrit and Malayalam, the former explaining the procedure to be adopted for the staging of plays and dealing with the songs, dance-steps, *rāgas* and stage directions; and the latter indicating the acting method, transforming the meaning of the passage to be enacted into a connected, continuously moving story, are not available in print for the students of the Sanskrit stage. The *Naṭāṅkuśa* of the mediaeval period attacking the *Kutiyattam* performance as often transgressing the rules of Bharata's *Nāṭyaśāstra* is also not yet printed. Even though the

Kutiyattam tradition of Kerala is an adaptation of the Sanskrit theatre for the Kerala stage with many innovations, it retains many ancient practices. Much more intensive study of the *Kutiyattam* is sure to help the student in having a clearer picture of the ancient, classical stage tradition in Kerala.

Sanskrit dramas formed an essential part of a highly evolved theatrical tradition. Unlike the Western dramas 'the internal conflict' of the individual character was not central to the dramatic action in India. The theory of *rasa* universally applied to Indian artistic traditions was evolved in the context of the theatre. The nature of this aesthetic experience of *rasa* is considered as one of the unalloyed pleasures and delights uncontaminated by any personal involvement and akin to the bliss of mystic experience of the ultimate reality. This is to be brought about by the performance of the story involving human relationship where emotions have a prominent place. The concept of *Sandhis* was formulated to explain the structure of the dramas. Indian dramas have been a combination of dance, music and mimetic representation, mainly intended to give pleasure and delight to the audience and often associated with an air of religious halo. The Indian drama was highly stylized and was not strictly realistic. The way of the stage (*Nāṭyadharmī*) and the way of the people (*Lokadharmī*) had to be combined harmoniously. The four types of Abhinaya: *āṅgika, vācika, āhārya* and *sāttvika* have been worked out elaborately by the theoreticians and practised by the performers. The *ekāhārya* technique in solo performance where the same actor enacts different roles without a change of costume or get-up was quite popular, though we find some criticism against it in the *Naṭāṅkuśa*. In the stage practice unity of place was not adhered to and regarding the unity of time the only rule was that the actions covered in one act should have taken place within one day. Any number of years could intervene between acts. Sometimes there is a deliberate slowing down of the time sense to suit the proper evocation of *rasa*. The dramatic technique of an exit and quick re-entry after the task is performed is often resorted to.

Besides making a clear exposition of the various features of ancient Indian play production, the author has also made a critical analysis of a dozen important classical plays, pointing out the salient features interesting from the point of view of production. According to the *Nāṭyaśāstra* the aim of play production was *Siddhi* or success in making the spectators experience the blissful *rasa* through the proper performance on the part of the actors. I am sure that this book will achieve real *Siddhi* by making the readers enlightened about Sanskrit play production in ancient India.

Adyar Library
Madras
22.1.1984

K. KUNJUNNI RAJA

CONTENTS

PART ONE

THE BACKDROP
(Spectator—Performer—Play-house)

PART TWO

THE PLAY-TEXT

PART THREE

THE PERFORMANCE

PART FOUR

EVIDENCE OF SURVIVAL

PART FIVE

Visualisations

LIST OF TABLES AND FRAMEWORKS

LIST OF ILLUSTRATIONS

LIST OF ABBREVIATIONS

Abh	:	Abhinavabhāratī
Abh. Sak	:	Abhijñāna Śākuntalam
ABORI	:	Annals of the Bhandarkar Oriental Research Institute
AD	:	Abhinaya Darpaṇa
AG	:	Abhinavagupta
ASIR	:	Archaeological Survey of India, Annual Report
Arth. dyo	:	Arthadyotanikā of Rāghavabhaṭṭa
Bh. P.	:	Śāradātanaya's Bhāvaprakāśana
DR	:	Daśarūpaka of Dhanañjaya
GOD	:	Gaekwad's Oriental Series
Haas	:	Haas's translation of Daśarūpaka
IHQ	:	Indian Historical Quarterly
JOI	:	Journal of Oriental Institute, Baroda
JOR	:	Journal of Oriental Research Institute, Madras
JMAM	:	Journal of Music Academy of Madras
JNCPA	:	Journal of National Centre of Performing Arts, Bombay
Ka	:	Kālidāsa
Kashi ed	:	The Kashi-Sanskrit-Series-NS (1929)
MAT	:	Mattavāraṇī
ND	:	Nāṭyadarpaṇa of Rāmacandra Guṇacandra
NLRK	:	Nāṭaka Lakṣaṇa Ratna Koṣa
NS	:	Nāṭyaśāstra
NSP	:	Nirṇaya Sāgar Press
RP	:	Raṅga Pītha
RS	:	Raṅgaśīrṣa
SD	:	Sāhityadarpaṇa
SR	:	Saṅgīta Ratnākara of Śāraṅgadeva
Sat	:	Saṭdāruka
TSS	:	Trivendram Sanskrit Series
Vdh. P.	:	Viṣṇudharmottara Purāṇa

INTRODUCTION

An attempt to visualise and understand the traditions of ancient Sanskrit play production must encounter two seemingly antithetical positions. One, over a long period of time these traditions in their original forms are not to be seen as living, dynamic traditions. Two, there are nevertheless a number of evidences with the help of which, one can almost reconstruct these traditions in a fairly comprehensive form.

It is often argued that in the absence of a living model of continuously evolving Sanskrit theatre, there cannot be a pet solution such as locating the handing over of traditions through generations of performing artistes (*gurus* of *gharānās*). Despite that, one may not take it for granted that the tradition is irretrievably lost. The Indian habit of conserving and piling up of trends of past traditions, compared by Jawaharlal Nehru to a palimpsest, has not allowed that to happen. In fact, like those ancient manuscripts written over and over again on preceding unwiped layers, the remnants of the ancient Sanskrit theatre design can still be gleaned in the present-day performances of the traditional and folk theatres of India.

Over and above that, a wealth of information regarding ancient Indian drama production—*prayoga vijñāna*—is preserved in the treatises of Sanskrit dramaturgy, the commentaries on Sanskrit dramas and the play texts themselves.

Rich Dramatic Literature

We have inherited a rich dramatic literature. We have more than five hundred and odd ancient Sanskrit plays, which were composed, without exception, as plays for production before an audience, with a set of techniques best suited to their staging. It is known that Aśvaghoṣa (c. 58 B.C.—A.D. 120) used to present his plays in Vārāṇasī. The fragments of manuscripts on palm leaves of his plays discovered at Turfan reflect a well developed and sophisticated style of playwriting for production.

Bharata's *Nāṭyaśāstra* (c. 200 B.C.—A.D. 200) with its several manuscripts found all over India, is a monumental encyclopaedia of the past theatre practices compiled by the later literate brahmin tradition. No one knows how far back these practices go. The earliest clear indication we get of them is in Pāṇini's *Aṣṭādhyāyī* which dates back to c. 500 B.C. Pāṇini refers to *Naṭa Sūtras* (Aphorisms for actors) and suggests an existence in his time of two schools of actors' sacred practices which were linked with the Vedic branches of Kṛśāśva and Śilālin.[1] This implication, apparently hints that the tradition of actor's art might lead back through the immense reaches of time to India's archaic past. *Nāṭyaśāstra* itself mentions many anonymous sources (referred to with such remarks as *Ācārya, tathā hi, anyc ca, atraucyate,* etc.). It also includes a list of Bharata's one hundred sons (or disciples) and ends with a reference to the subsequently lost treatise of Kohala.

As far as available works on dramaturgy are concerned, there is a long gap of more than eight centuries between *Nāṭyaśāstra* (c. 200 B.C.—A.D. 200) and *Abhinavabhāratī* (A.D. 980-1030) the illuminating commentary on *Nāṭyaśāstra* by the Kashmiri philosopher-aesthete Abhinavagupta. During this long interim period, we come across the names of a number of authorities[2] on ancient Indian drama, who are referred to in *Abhinavabhāratī Daśa rūpaka, Bhāva prakāśa, Nāṭaka lakṣaṇa ratna koṣa, Nāṭya darpaṇa* and other dramaturgical texts. Even when the original works of the ancient authorities like Kohala, Śāṇḍilya, Kīrtidhara, Mātṛgupta, Udbhaṭṭa, Śri Śaṅkuka, Lollaṭa, Bhaṭṭanāyaka and others are lost to us, the mention of their names, quotations and views indicates a lively thriving theatre activity, which formed a vital part of the life of the ancient Indian citizen. When this thriving performing tradition declined, and over a period almost disappeared around the 12th century, it however did not altogether vanish. The production design and the style of performance were carried forward via the *uparūpaka* (minor drama forms with emphasis on dance, songs, *abhinaya* and *sāhitya* where the stress on texts written by playwrights was practically non-existent) tradition in the regional traditional theatres. The present traditional theatres can find links with these.

Indigenous Theatre Idiom

As regards Sanskrit play texts, interest in them was revived after a lapse of centuries, with the translation of *Sakuntala* by William Jones in 1789. Attempts to assess the possibilities of their theatre worthiness began in India and abroad. But by then India had already come under the strong influence of Western ideals of art, literature and theatre. When implanted in the alien soil of a prosaic and all too naturalistic framework of the West-oriented theatre then in vogue, production of Sanskrit plays failed to make the desired impact on the mainstream theatre. As a result, they were confined, for all practical purposes, to the classrooms of Sanskrit poetics.

Nevertheless the play texts, their commentaries and treatises on dramaturgy continued to intrigue the scholars, both in India and abroad, who carried on ceaseless research to understand and decipher their theatre worthiness.

They had a formidable task before them. The *sūtra* style of writing of the ancient Indian treatises is often enigmatic. For example, *Nāṭyaśāstra* is a work which was primarily meant for the practising artistes of a bygone era, whose training was supplemented with practical demonstrations and oral instructions. The works of later commentators and theorists, while professing a faithful adherence to it, had often given alternative and self-contradictory opinions on many of the terms, practices and aphorisms (*sūtras*). This fact, when added to the confusion of general approach of a contemporary urbanite influenced by the Western norms, provided a bewildering reaction pattern to the indigenous theatre design. As a result, we, no doubt, have with us an enormous amount of invaluable research material on the subject but, more often than not, the material also baffles a student with a plethora of controversial interpretations offered on one and the same topic.

In recent years, after Independence, there has been a renewed endeavour to explore Sanskrit play production with a view to discovering a theatre idiom rooted in the Indian soil. A number of researchers and theatre workers, with an awareness of the indigenous staging techniques, have begun to offer various approaches to locate an acceptable framework of the ancient Indian play production. As a result, a relatively greater clarity has undoubtedly been achieved as regards the general concept. However, no consensus has been arrived at till to-day, regarding the problems of precisely working out the norms of Indian aesthetics in the context of Sanskrit plays and their style of production.

The exact understanding and practical application in the plays of concepts such as the following need to be examined.

Rasa and its experience

Bhāva-s and the systems of their representation

Sattva and its unfolding

Abhinaya and *Dharmī*-s in terms of the conventional and worldly practices of extended delineation through speech, body and mind (*vāc-aṅga-sattva*) of the performer aided by the physical supports (*āhārya*)

Vṛtti and *Pravṛtti*—the styles and regional modes of production

Vastu and *Netā*—the structure of play construction and character classification

Siddhi—perfect balance between the appreciative spectator and the skilled performer

Raṅga—variously shaped stages of the ancient Indian playhouses

Music and *Dance*—as integral strands in the fabric of a drama performance

These concepts must be examined in the light of what the play productions were meant to achieve, and what sort of audiences they might have hoped to satisfy.

The present study is an attempt to explore, understand and conceptualise the above aspects of Sanskrit play production in the context of their times and to examine the possibilities of their recreation. The idea is to rediscover an idiom of ancient theatre production for which Sanskrit plays were composed. It is based on seven years research which resulted in my doctoral thesis.

As it happens with various researchers, one and the same field is examined by many of them. In my own wanderings, I began to read the ancient Sanskrit play texts, works on dramaturgy—specially the *Nāṭyaśāstra*—and other relevant literature as a performer and a producer. After long searchings for answers in many places, I felt that the style of ancient Sanskrit play production can certainly be located, and many corresponding questions can be answered. Unfortunately, there is no set way of simply writing down the answers in the manner of theoretical text book definitions. The answers must really be worked out personally—in the process of practical performance and production. The thrust of my efforts is, therefore, mainly undertaken with *prayoga-pradhāna vṛtti* (the practice based approach).

A substantial section of this work is devoted to an exploration of the cultural contexts from which the purely practice-based techniques of indigenous production have emerged. I believe that a thorough understanding of the way our social and cultural ethos has evolved is necessary before one can tackle the purely practical problem of execution of an ancient art form. It is surprising how often the simple solutions arrived at in the past through necessity of a given circumstance, throw a whole new light on a problem which appears to be quite enigmatic in the contemporary context.

Cultural Contexts

The life of the ancient Indians, their magico-ritualistic ceremonies, their festivals, social organisations, the mythology and the concept of history, the social and cultural creativity of the common folk and the elite, the priests and the poets—in short the entire ethos was moulded by the basic national impulse and thought which put faith in such concepts as:

1. Man not an isolated being but a participant in the life of nature as a part of nature;
2. Basic unity beneath the diversity of nature; and
3. Threefold fundamental quality (*Triguṇātmaka prakṛti*) which envelopes every form of nature.

The aim and ideal of life was the realisation of reality as harmony through a blissful ecstasy as a result of the union of the personal (self) with the universal consciousness. The arts, among the other systems in ancient India, aimed to express this belief also. Concepts like the *rasa* realisation, *bhāva*-s and their representation, and *sattva* and its unfolding were intuitive perceptions which the arts set out to portray.

Thus, one finds that the sophisticated Sanskrit plays exhibit, among other things, a basic difference of attitude to life, which separates them from the plays of the West. They are the products of the ancient art of the all-inclusive indigenous theatre called *nāṭya* which is a comprehensive concept denoting the written play and its representation. It also forms a total assemblage assimilating all the ancient arts and crafts.[3] Sanskrit plays, thus, have an intimate relationship with other fine arts of ancient India like music, dance, painting, sculpture, architecture and other crafts.

Not only did the Sanskrit plays share the common norms of aesthetics of *rasa* realisation, but they also had many techniques of representation in common. The remarkable proclamation of *Viṣṇudharmottara Purāṇa* which says that the painting and the sculpture without a knowledge of the drama and the dance is incomprehensible and the drama and the dance, in their turn, require a knowledge of music and the songs which again is dependent upon a mastery over the languages—both Sanskrit and Prakrit with their prose and poetry, grammar and prosody and so on—

underlines the interdependence of techniques of these arts. The understanding of Sanskrit play production, therefore, would involve the understanding of the techniques of these allied fine arts also.

Puruṣārtha—The Life Ideal

The ideal set before the ancient Indian society regarded that achievement of a joyful consciousness of harmonious equipoise (*ānandamayī cetanā*) could be possible only after the fulfilment of one's worldly desires. Accordingly, enjoyment of wealth and prosperity (*artha*), love and pleasure (*kāma*) through righteous actions (*dharma*) were accepted as the three goals of human existence to attain the final equipoise (*mokṣa*). This ideal generally goes under the nomenclature of *caturvarga* or *trivarga sādhanā* or *puruṣārtha* and will be referred to as such in this work. The structure of Sanskrit plays was so designed that the fruition of the above threefold desires of the hero (*phalabhoktā netā*) could be depicted. A plot of a Sanskrit play, therefore, can be analysed by evaluating the hero and the object of his achievement.

The Integrated Form

The form of *nāṭya* was an amalgamation of stylised speech and movement, music and dance, *bhāva*-s and *rasa*-s, and the colour and the costumes presented in a balanced fusion. To conceptualise such a form of drama would require us to discard the West-oriented approach of modern theatre, because, in the West in the process of evolution, these elements have grown apart and assumed independent identities such as opera, ballet, realistic drama, poetic drama and so on. This is not so in the case of the Sanskrit play production. In essence, these ancient plays adhere to the most perfected form of *nāṭya*. In their production, the playwright's inner idea (*nāṭyārtha*) or the *rasa* content of the play was presented through *abhinaya* of *bhāva*-s by means of the actor's body, speech, mind and physical get-up in a specific acting area, with its architectural peculiarities, so as to pervade the responsive spectator with the blissful experience of a *rasa*. The whole concept of such a production was determined in a traditionally conceived design of conventional styles (*vṛtti*-s), regional modes (*pravṛtti*-s) and embellished by music, songs and dance. All these elements were intrinsically related in a production framework. The performance was dictated by strict convention of their execution. The aspect of spontaneity formed the part of the artiste's genius (*pratibhā*) which enabled him to innovate and improvise and yet remain within the boundary of traditional dictates. Just as in rendering of the classical music, for example, an artiste utilises the same set of minutely structured patterns of the techniques of his art to create an entirely new atmosphere of a known *rāga*; likewise in a Sanskrit play production, a creative genius would exploit the traditionally authorised set of rules and conventions of staging to generate a totally novel experience of a *rasa* in the spectator.

In the following chapters Sanskrit play production is explored against this background.

I have collected the data, material and the resources along the following lines.

Literary Sources

(1) The study of Sanskrit play texts, their stage directions and commentaries:
Plays of Bhāsa, Kālidāsa, Śūdraka, Śri Harṣa, Viśakhadatta, Bhaṭṭanārāyaṇa, Bhavabhūti, with two specimens of *prahasana* by Bodhāyana and Mahendra Vikrama Varmā and four specimens of *Bhāṇa-s—Caturbhāṇi* of Śūdraka, Vararuci, Syāmilaka and Īśvaradatta.

(2) Ancient Indian works on dramaturgy:
Bharata's *Nāṭyaśāstra,* Abhinavagupta's *Abhinavabhāratī,* Dhanañjaya's *Daśarūpaka,* Nandikeśvara's *Abhinaya darpaṇa,* Rāmacandra and Guṇacandra's *Nāṭyadarpaṇa,* Śāradātanaya's *Bhāvaprakāśa,* Sāgarnandī's *Nāṭaka lakṣaṇa ratna koṣa* and Viśvanātha's *Sāhitya darpaṇa.*

The texts of these Sanskrit plays, *Nāṭyaśāstra* and the later treatises on dramaturgy have helped develop among others, the first three parts of this work. I must also add that the Sanskrit plays as production scripts became more intelligible to me after my reading of the dramaturgical treatises and vice versa.

Empirical Findings

Empirical information connected with the present study includes my field-visits to cover the considerable remnants of the ancient Sanskrit theatre design as still being presented and practised in the traditional and village theatres of India and South-East Asia, China and Japan. Chief among them are Kudiyattam, Yaksagana, Kuchipudi, Kathakali and other South Indian forms, folk theatres such as Bhavai (Gujarat), Chau (West Bengal, Orissa and Bihar) and Manch (Malva) in India, besides the Chinese opera (China) and the Noh theatre (Japan).

As regards forms like Ankiya Nat (Assam) and Bhanda Jashana (Kashmir) and the traditional theatres of South-East Asian countries—which I have not personally witnessed—I have researched into the necessary data and information from several books, articles and reports, which have been published at various points of time. To the extent that they have helped me in my understanding of the survival of the style of the ancient Sanskrit play production, I have relied on them. I have, however, verified the deductions by personal discussions with the experts, viewing of films and photographs of the performances.

I should, at the same time, state that my understanding of the style of Sanskrit play production, with the knowledge of the above forms, is subjective. And it could admit of alternative interpretations at the hands of other person. But, I wish to add that being a performer myself, it has given me the strength to accept the subjective interpretation as a part of my field-work.

Before concluding certain points need to be clarified.

Choice of Bhāsa to Bavabhūti

The plays of Bhāsa to Bhavabhūti have been taken as main terms of reference in this work. It should be, however, pointed out that these plays are selected not so much as pieces of literary works but as play scripts to be produced and as illustrations to understand the validity and appropriateness of production techniques of ancient Sanskrit theatre. The plays cover roughly the time span of 200 B.C.—800 A.D., which can be considered to be the best phase when the principles of the ancient Indian theatre production were ably demonstrated.

Dates

As this study is restricted to the exploration and visualisation of the production style of the ancient Sanskrit plays, the controversies of the dates of the dramatists and the dramaturgists are bypassed. An attempt has been made, however, to maintain the chronological order of the playwrights and the other works.

Translation of Sanskrit Terms

It is difficult to translate many Sanskrit terms in exact English equivalents and convey the precise connotations of all that the terms imply. In such cases, either the Sanskrit term alone is used or it is placed in bracket with its nearest English equivalent. The reader may, however, refer to the glossary for clarification. Quotations from Sanskrit texts are generally translated. *Nāṭyaśāstra* quotations have been mostly taken from *Dr. Manmohan Ghosh's* translation of the treatise. Sanskrit-Prakrit words have been transliterated. But the names of the present-day traditional and village theatres of India, South-East Asia, China and Japan as well as the dramatic terminologies used there in have not been transliterated. The names of the works and the authors are, as a rule, not abbreviated, except in the notes on the chapters and in some chapters where it is specifically mentioned.

Sanskrit-Prakrit Plays

The plays referred to as Sanskrit plays are, in fact, multilingual plays. The languages of the plays consist of Sanskrit as well as a number of Prakrits spoken in the period of their composition. The use of the term 'Sanskrit plays' in this work necessarily implies 'Sanskrit-Prakrit plays'.

NOTES

1. Pāṇini—Pāṇini; Āṣṭādhyāyi, 4.3.10 cf. Agrawal V.S., India—as known to *Pāṇini*, pp. 338-39.

2.

Authorities	*Mentioned in works*		*By*	
	A. (Before NS)			
1. Śilālin	Aṣṭādhyāyi		Pāṇini	
2. Kṛśāśva	"		"	
	B. (Around the period of NS)			
3. Dattila	NS		Bharata	
4. Śāṇḍilya	"		"	
5. Vatsya	"	(also Abh. and Bh.P)	"	(Abhinavagupta Śāradātanaya)
6. Kohala	"	"	"	"
7. Sadāśiva	"	"	"	"
8. Padmabhū	"	"	"	"
9. Drohiṇi	"	"	"	"
10. Vyāsa	"	Bh.P	"	"
11. Vṛddha Bharata	"	"	"	"
12. Nandikeśvara (Taṇḍu)	Abh.			Abhinavagupta

	C. (After NS)	
13. Udbhaṭṭa	Abh.	Abhinavagupta
14. Śrī Śaṅkara	"	"
15. Lollaṭa	"	"
16. Bhaṭṭanāyaka	"	"
17. Kīrtidhara	"	"
18. Mātṛgupta	NRLK	Sāgarnandi
19. Aśmakuṭṭa	"	"
20. Bādarāyaṇa	"	"
21. Satkarṇi	"	"
22. Nakhakuṭṭa	"	"
23. Subandhu	Bh.P	Śāradātanaya
24. Abhaya and 27 others	Artha Dyo	Rāghavabhaṭṭa

3. NS I.113 (Kashi Ed.).

Once upon a time when the life on Jaṃbudvīpa became miserable because of evil passions and vulgar behaviour of people, the gods with the great Indra as their head approached Brahmā and said:

"We want an object of diversion, a playful thing (*krīḍāniyakam*) which is visible as well as audible. As the Vedas are not to be listened to by the śūdras, be pleased to create another Veda which can equally belong to all the coloured groups of people."

"Let it be so" said Lord Brahmā.

And he created a thing called "Nāṭya, dramatic art, and called it the fifth Veda—the Nāṭyaveda".

Nāṭya Śāstra, Chapter 1

PART ONE

THE BACKDROP

(Spectator—Performer—Play-house)

Tālapuṭṭa, the naṭagāmaṇi (a leader of actors), rose and asked a question to Lord Buddha at Rājagṛha. He asked: "An actor (naṭa) who on the stage (raṅga) or in the arena makes people laugh and cry with delight. What is his reward in the afterbirth? Does he get to be reborn in the company of laughing gods?

"Buddhist evidence for the early existence of drama" *I.H.Q.* Vol. XVII, pp. 196-206

CHAPTER 1

SANSKRIT PLAY PRODUCTION: A FRAMEWORK OF INTERDEPENDENCE

The Indian word for drama and its representation is *nāṭya* which is a composite art of Indian theatre covering all aspects of the ancient Indian play production. *Nāṭya* also includes a number of varied manifestations of spontaneous and studied expressions of many ancient Indian fine arts and crafts. In order to understand the distinctive style of Sanskrit play production, we have to comprehend the concept of *nāṭya* and everything that it connotes.

Saṅgraha Śloka

The best enumeration of all aspects covering an ancient play production is to be found in a brief digest of *Nāṭyaśāstra*, Chapter VI, verse 10. We get here a very definite and categorical picture of eleven essential components which constitute a *nāṭya*. It says:

रसा भावा ह्यभिनया धर्मिवृत्तिप्रवृत्तयः ।
सिद्धिस्स्वरास्तथातोद्यं गानं रंगं च संग्रहः ॥

The verse speaks of the arousal in the spectator of a pure state of joy (*rasa*) which is aesthetically aroused by the portrayal of universalised and super-sensual inner states of being (*bhāva*-s) through the medium of the actor's art of communication—through his body-speech-mind-physical get up (*abhinaya*)—delineated according to the two practices of performance (*dharmī*-s), in four styles (*vṛtti*-s), in four regional variations (*pravṛtti*-s) with accompanying vocal and instrumental music (*svara-gāna-ātodya*) in the playhouses (*raṅga*) for the success of production (*siddhi*). This description provides a comprehensive idea of a set of components which formed the whole framework of an ancient Sanskrit play production.

Interrelated Components

None of these components is mutually exclusive of the rest.

Each of them can be properly understood in the context of the others alone. This synergic interrelationship is at the core of the principles and practices of the ancient play production. In other words, the play, the character, the performance, its practices, the styles of production, their regional modes of presentation, the music, the playhouse, the spectators and above all the *rasa*-s pervading all these elements are mutually interdependent and interwoven in the fabric of a theatre production so intrinsically that a replacement of even one of them may disturb the harmony of the style of production.

A schematic representation as shown in Chart I demonstrates in totality the *rasa*-oriented combinations and inter-relationships between individual components of the ancient Indian play production.

Chart I
A schematic representation.

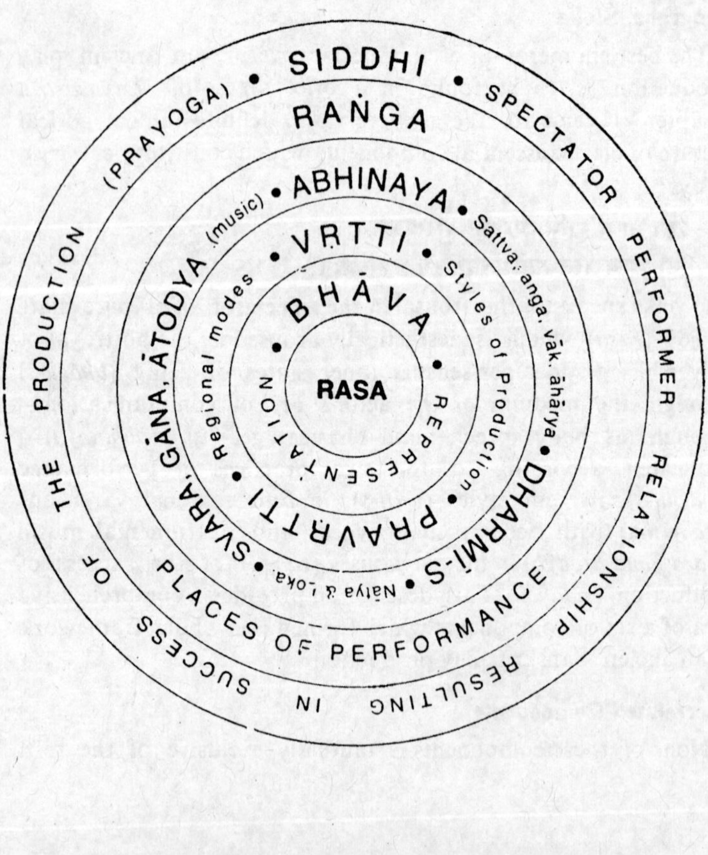

This interacting and interpenetrating system was found essential in a style of Sanskrit play production which did not strive for realism as we now understand the term, but presented a theatre of suggestion and convention for a fixed aesthetic principle of *rasa*. Its form was an all-inclusive total theatre.

All-inclusive Indigenous Theatre

Very different from the West-oriented theatre, based on the dictum of "no conflict, no drama", Sanskrit drama belongs to a group of ancient Indian fine arts which reflects the artistic ethos and aesthetics which considered art as a discipline to glorify the joyful consciousness (*rasa*) of every experience of life. Like the other allied fine arts, Sanskrit drama has emerged out of the indigenous culture of our soil. They were, however, later nurtured by the elitist upper classes of ancient India patronising mostly the palace courts and temple precincts. And so the Sanskrit play production developed a formalised idiom of sophisticated stylisation which could, at times, be intensely abstract but always remained deeply moving. In this, it was moulded by the traditional rules of dramaturgy which laid down a framework of play production through which *rasa* could be evoked in the responsive spectators. The *rasa* principle, thus, pervaded all the other components of the play production.

Sanskrit playwrights took the story material from epics, *Purāṇa*-s and *kathā* literature and refashioned the incidents according to the *rasa* that they wished to evoke. Their plots, while depicting the exploits of the beings of the three worlds, were latent with *rasa* just as a "piece of dry wood is latent with fire."[1] Unlike the plot progression of most of the action-based modern dramas, Sanskrit dramatists based their plots on the portrayal of inner states of being—*bhāva*-s—of characters placed in various situations (*avasthā*-s). The success, or otherwise, of the drama depended on whether or not it had succeeded in enkindling the intended *rasa* in the spectator.

The plot progression always depicted the achievement of the hero (*netā* or *nāyaka*) of one or more of the three-fold goals of human existence (*puruṣārtha* or *trivarga sādhanā*) as recognised by the ancient Indian society. The hero, heroine (*nāyaka*-s and *nāyikā*-s) and other dramatis personae were based in a fixed format of arche-types representing a particular state induced by a particular situation (*bhāvāvasthā*) to be presented and in whom particular qualities predominated. The spectators were familiar with the types. This familiarity helped them to identify with the hero and relish the entire *bhāva* presentation. It is interesting to note that the term *nāyaka* literary means one who leads to the inner meaning of the play.

Like the other ancient Indian fine arts, Sanskrit plays also have a richly textured structural pattern with minutely worked out units and sub-units of plot (*vastu*), hero (*netā*) and *rasa*. The combination in various degrees of these three elements give rise to a number of major and minor *genres* of Sanskrit plays called *rūpaka*-s and *uparūpaka*-s. Sanskrit play texts are to be understood in this context instead of the known Western divisions of tragedy, comedy, opera, melodrama, realistic drama etc.

According to *Nāṭyaśāstra*, a play is "a representation of the states of the three world"[2] when it is produced on the stage with the interplay of all the above mentioned relevant components employed in a harmonious balance. *Nāṭyaśāstra* has also laid down elaborate rules and conventions governing such a framework together with detailed instructions for carrying them out. Sanskrit playwrights have focused their attention on the prescribed guidelines of presentation and yet succeeded in providing plays which are freshly personal. Judging by the present day practices of the rendering of classical music and dance, one can visualise the possibility of the production of ancient Sanskrit plays, based on the traditional framework, having a stamp of individuality.

The Backdrop

This integrated framework of play production is India's own idiom of theatre. It is natural that one would be curious to decipher the maze of social and cultural context and influences which have gone into forming the concept of such a total theatre. Apart from the Indian world-view of synthesis which fits into the pattern of ideals, value system and objectives of the ancient Indian people, one would like an answer to a somewhat nebulous question of how far one should go into the matter of tracing the ultimate genesis, growth and continuity which would in some way explain the emergence of such a theatre idiom with its meticulously worked out system of practice. In the absence of a continuously evolving theatre and without a consensus of scholarly opinion regarding the origin and development of Indian theatre,[3] we can only have glimpses of a broad outline from the maze of evidences and influences which are to be found in our enormous ancient literature and in the bits of archaeological finds scattered across the Indian subcontinent.

The traces left by the prehistoric tribal and civilised cultures like the paintings at Bhimabetaka, Mirzapur in Vindhya hills and on rocks of Singhanpur in Madhya Pradesh show ritual representation of an animal hunt or a battle with figures in stylised poses and mask-like head-dresses in concentric outlines. The fertility rites with its worship of the mother goddesses of later agrarian communities and the archaeological finds of the Indus valley civilisation with the dancing girl, the mask and the musical instruments have been generally recognised as pointers to archaic magico-ritualistic practices by priestesses and priests before the initiated spectators.

It is not unlikely that from the interplay of a group rejoicing in wonder at the magic of life and its expression in religious rituals of various tribes and communities across the Indian subcontinent, with their attendant conventions and symbolism, arose strong popular cultural patterns. These patterns, while continuing their independent course of evolution, were also assimilated into the exclusive ritual performances of the original state of renderings of the priestly order. These practices, might have, subsequently developed into two parallel trends. One, connected with the ritualistic priestly ceremonials which was exclusive. The other, growing out of social festivities of tribal gatherings of different regions of India, which were popular 'outside' practices. These trends greatly influenced each other even as they maintained their separate identities. Consequently both the trends provided an atmosphere for the primitive drama to germinate.

Practices of Performance—Dharmī

In the Vedic period, the sacerdotal Aryan practice came to be known as exclusive (*ābhyantara*), divinely ordained path strictly for the initiated (*mārgī*) and the other non-Aryan practices were recognised as popular, exterior or outside (*bāhya*) and regional (*deśī*). These two practices went on side by side, often intermingling, interacting and enriching each other. *Nāṭyaśāstra*, later on, formalised them as theatre practices (*dharmī*-s). The exclusive was the source for the *nāṭyadharmī* practice, while the popular grew into *lokadharmī* practices. The growth and the development of the framework of ancient Indian theatre is a vast assimilative process of the intermixture of these two practices and the circumstances of their enactments in terms of occasions, places, performances and spectators.

The first glimpse of a record of some sort of the origin of drama is to be found in the legendary tale of origin of drama in *Nāṭyaśāstra*.[4] Even though written in the then prevalent brahmanic tradition, which usually emphasised the sacredness of all arts by tracing their descent from divine Brahmā in perfectly evolved form, the legend, nevertheless, has veiled references of certain factual details. According to the legend, when the gods grew tired of the "vulgar practices" of the people, they requested Lord Brahmā for an object of diversion, an audio-visual plaything which would act as an instrument of instruction as well as an entertainment for people comprising of all coloured-groups. Lord Brahmā responded by creating *nāṭya*, or the fifth Veda, by taking the elements of speech, music, *abhinaya* and *rasa* from the four Vedas. Here, *Nāṭyaśāstra* recognises a number of distinct early influences which provided the rudimentary format of Indian drama.

The Spoken Word (Pāṭhya): Beginning of Later Dramatic Literature

The speech of drama had roots in the precisely enunciated and intoned recitations of the Ṛgvedic hymns. The words in *mantra*-s, composed by poet-priests (*kavi*-s)[5] when chanted in a specified manner, were thought to be potent with magic power. Ṛgvedic hymn chanting employed the use of one raised note (*udātta svara*) throughout. The speech rendering in the dramas governed by the exclusive practice of the later days emphasised this style.

In addition, we have in the Ṛgvedic *Saṃhitā*-s, a number of hymns in the form of dialogues which have been recognised by many scholars as precursors of the later dramatic literature. Well-known mythical tales were unfolded by means of conversation between two or more persons like Yama and Yamī (10/86), Purūravas and Urvaśī (10/95), Indra and Nemābhārgava (8/10), Agatsya, Lopāmudrā and their son (1/76) and many others and this have led scholars like Max Müllar and A.B. Keith to conclude that the dialogue hymns were "acted out by two parties of priests", where "the priests assumed roles of gods and sages."[6] As a summary illustration, here is a tale from *Kātyāyana Śrota Śūtra*, in a dialogue form between a priest and a seller of Soma juice.[7] The dialogue goes like this:

> 'O Seller of *Soma*, will you sell the King *Soma*?'
> 'It will be sold.'
> 'It will be bought.'
> 'Take it.'
> 'I will give a portion of a cow for it.'
> 'King *Soma* deserves more.'
> 'A cow is no less important. She has sweet curd, milk, purified butter within her.'
> 'No, sir.'
> 'Well then, take eight portions of the cow.'
> 'No sir, King *Soma* deserves more.'
> 'Well then, take one-fourth of the cow.'
> 'No indeed, better price is required.'
> 'Alright brother, take the whole cow.'
> 'So be it, King *Soma* is sold'. . . .'

Such tales were recounted and enacted by the priests before the sacrificers around the open-air areas of sacrificial altars. Unquestionably, the seed of the later *nāṭya* literature is evident here.

The more popular exterior practices of the Ṛgvedic times were performed on the occasions of *samana*.[8] *Samana* was essentially a folk gathering where tribes from nearby villages gathered at the time of seasonal rites and festivities. Collective dancing, singing, poetry recitation, pantomimes by tribal entertainers with mimicry and mirth went on for several days and nights.

Although we have no records to tell us in one way or another of the manner in which the outside popular practices might have interacted with the exclusive sacerdotal enactments at the sacrificial grounds. we see the elements of singing and dancing of communal festivals slowly seeping in. This is particularly evident in the hymn recitals by the time of *Sāmaveda*.

Music: Svara, Gāna, Atodya

Music was derived from *Sāmaveda*. The exclusive practice

of chanting on one ascending note (*udātta svara*) had developed into a melodic musical scale with the inclusion of another descending note (*anudātta svara*), intra tones (*svarita*—in between notes) and the use of three voice registers. Separate groups of priests who chanted and narrated the Vedic *mantra*-s in the company of special *vīṇā*-playing priests, with players of different kinds of drums, wind pipes and cymbals had also emerged. Some interaction with the popular outside practice is registered in *Sāmaveda* where both *gāndharva* and *gāna* music as well as terms like *mārgī* and *deśī* occur. The roots of the *nāṭya* components of the note (*svara*), the song (*gāna*) and the musical instruments (*ātodya*) can be witnessed at this early stage.

The Performance: Abhinaya

Nāṭya abhinaya reflects its source in the ritual practices of *Yajurveda*. Ceremonial aspects of formalised action to express the import of the hymn recitals with the accompanying note, song and musical instrument was employed in liturgical practices of the priests. Stylised gestures of hands (*hasta mudrā*-s), the precise way of sitting and standing (*āsana*-s and *sthāna*-s), walking with prescribed gait, going round (*pradakṣiṇā*), changing of red turbans to white ones for special rituals signifying magic symbolism of colour and the ceremonies such as the chariot race, dice game, royal consecration and the mock fights became rituals demanding acts of great precision and stylisation. Luis Renou describes them as "a kind of drama, with its actors, dialogues, its portions set to music, its interludes and climaxes".

The intermingling of priest-performers of this exclusive vedic practice and the popular non-Aryan practitioners find corroboration in the reference in the third chapter of *Śukla Yajurveda* to the non-priestly castes of outsiders or popular entertainers like a *sūta* (a dancer-actor), a *śailūṣa* (a singer), a *kāri* (a jester), a vāmana (a dwarf-hunchbacked buffoon), a *vīṇā* player, a drum beater and a handclapper being invited for the entertainments at the sacrificial grounds.[9]

Another facet of exclusive entertainments, involving an intermix of performers were the rhapsodes (*ākhyānavid*-s)[10] who recounted stories of Aryan folklore and heroic legends to the priests and sacrificers gathered around the sacrificial ground. These early rhapsodes belonged to the Vedic tribes of *Bharata*-s. They were experts in Sanskrit recitation and eventually became "the actor proper" of the *nāṭya* troupe as described in *Nāṭyaśāstra*. The verbal style of drama presentation (*bhāratī vṛtti*) originated from these *Bharata*-s.

Rasa

It is extremely interesting to note that the concept of *rasa* goes back to our archaic past of pre-Vedic cultures in terms of its origin. Lying at the root of its concept is an assumption that life contains positive experiences of pleasure, worldly gratifications and ecstacy which should be cultivated and put to use because the full saturation of sensations and emotions alone are the most powerful motive forces of human existence. It is very likely that the concept of *rasa* had developed out of influences of the archaic cult of the *tantra*-s. Discussing the deeper meaning of the *rasa* experience as given by Abhinavagupta, who incidently was also a writer of a monumental work on *tantra*, Philip Rawson in "Art of Tantra" suggests that the state of tasting the *rasa* in which it transcends its emotive content is called the great *rasa*. . . . It is intrinsically not different from the great *rasa* or *mahārāga* of Tantra.[11] At another place he mentions that *tantra* is even referred to "as *Atharvaveda*, thus identifying it (*tantra*) as an aspect of the most ancient, sacred and orthodox literature of Hinduism."[12] It seems, therefore, quite plausible when *Nāṭyaśāstra* mentions that *rasa*-s have originated from *Atharvaveda*. Abhinavagupta in his commentary hints at the various *rasa*-s in the rudimentary magic rituals of charms and spells in *Atharvaveda*, performed for the wish-fulfilment of the four *puruṣārtha*-s of *dharma*, *artha*, *kāma* and *mokṣa*. Erotic and comic (*śṛṅgāra-hāsya*) *rasa*-s are said to have resulted from the rituals of gratification (*pauṣṭika karma*), pathetic and furious (*karuṇa-raudra*) *rasa*-s from those of destruction (*māraṇa karma*), heroic and marvellous (*vīra-adbhuta*) *rasa*-s resulted from the rituals of bewitching (*mohana karma*) while the terrible and odius (*bhayānaka-bībhatsa*) *rasa*-s are the consequents of the rituals of ruining one's enemy (*ucāṭana karma*).[13]

The Styles: Vṛtti-s

As mentioned earlier, the verbal style of production (*Bhāratī vṛtti*) was evolved in the initial stages of *nāṭya* performance with emphasis on Sanskrit recitation. The marvellous and pathetic *rasa*-s dominated in them. The subject-matter of these enactments was based on the semi-historical tales (*itihāsa*). *Itihāsa*, according to Indian tradition, is the account of the past events embellished with instructions about how the past heroes achieved three *puruṣārtha*-s. The mythical tales of legendary heroes (*netā*-s) constituted the plots (*vastu*-s). The incidents of drama, *itivṛtta*-s, as they were called, were selected to project the required *rasa*-s. The *nāṭya rūpaka*-s thus developed around such combinations of *netā*, *vastu* and *rasa*. The sublime and energetic styles (*sāttvatī* and *ārabhaṭī vṛtti*-s) evolved around the heroic episodes featured in *rūpaka*-s. Heroic, marvellous and furious *rasa*-s were predominant in the former, while terrible and odious *rasa*-s dominated the latter. The wrestling bouts which were a feature of the amusements at festivities also influenced the techniques of these styles.[14]

The dancing girls were included in the dramatic enactments at a later stage of development. Consequently, the graceful style (*kaiśikī vṛtti*) featuring female artists, erotic *rasa*, dances, songs and colourful costumes got evolved.

The Regional Modes: Pravṛtti

Regional modes of representations (*pravṛtti*-s) took roots with the staging of *nāṭya* before an audience of all classes at the festival time. At the time of the first ever mythical performance at the festival of Indra, Bharata cautioned his actors that they must assume their respective roles by observing and adopting the disposition appropriate to the characters.[15] Thus, a trend of appropriate modes of regional representation was seen in the formative stage of drama.

Playhouse, Spectator-Performer Relationship: Raṅga and Siddhi

Such rudimentary enactments were staged within a consecrated area (*maṇḍala*) demarcated for the purpose in the open air in the beginning. But soon after, the necessity for an enclosed playhouse was felt to keep away the outside disturbances, and to maintain a concentrated rapport between the actors and the spectators. This was a feature which was never lost sight of even in the later more developed playhouses of Bharata.

Unquestionably, this phase represents a creative and formative epoch in which well grounded foundations were laid of trends and tendancies which gradually evolved into the framework of a Sanskrit play production. With such a background, a play was accepted as a vehicle for entertainment and instruction and its seeds were sown and sprouted in the popular festivities and exclusive amusements at sacrificial grounds.[16–18]

This rudimentary framework of Indian drama evolved still further in a continuous process of growth with the rise of kingdoms, later empires, the growth of city centres and the subsequent stratification of society. We get an enormous amount of literary substantiation to understand how drama gradually became a vital part of the life of all stratas of ancient Indian society.

Change in Patronage

In the post-Vedic period, occasions of *nāṭya* performances shifted from the communal gatherings around the sacrificial grounds to separate environments of different segments of society. Kings adopted it as a part of the palace entertainment. So also, the temple precincts (Buddhist, Jain and Hindu) utilised drama for the religious edification of the devout. Rich citizens, following suit, had plays performed in their courtyards. While the town and village councils organised festive enactments of *nāṭya* as part of seasonal and religious celebrations.

Occasions of Performance

The celebrations of a victory of a king, his royal consecration, and his efforts for sovereignty as well as domestic celebrations such as a birth of a son, marriage, reception to a friend, and entry into a new house or a town were the occasions when a play would be performed.[17] Popular religious sacrifices and seasonal festivals in the form of pageants (*yātrās*) and amusements at village crossroads, on a hill top, a river bank or a sea shore were other circumstances for drama performances. *Harivaṃśa Purāṇa* tells a story of an actor named Bhadra, who so pleased the assembly gathered around the sacrificial grounds that he was rewarded with the power to assume any form at will and the ability of free movement in the sky.[19]

The epics, the *Bauddha–Jain* canons and other later literature are replete with instances of drama performances. We can get a clear idea from them of development of the playhouses, change in patronage, emergence of wide varieties of performers and the changing relationship between the performer and his patron.

Nāṭya at Special Palace Pavilions

The palace entertainments of kings took place in special pavilions (*maṇḍapa*-s) called *nāṭyaśālā*-s, *nāṭakaśālā*-s, *raṅgaśālā*-s, or *prekṣāgṛha*-s. Kings and princes surrounded by performing actors, dancers and musicians have often been depicted in sculptural friezes and fresco paintings.

A theatre with a stage and an auditorium is described in *Rājasuya Parvan* of the *Mahābhārata*. Jain Rāja praśnīya-āgama also details an enclosed pavilion—called *prekṣāgṛha maṇḍapa*.[20] Even *Mayamatam* of Mayamuni, considered by some scholars as our oldest extant work on architecture, has vague details of a dance pavilion.[21] A hazy picture of division of theatre space into stage, dressing room, auditorium with other details of decorations are available from these sources. Viśvakarmā's *Vāstuśāstra* gives a somewhat clearer picture of such a pavilion.[22] Let us look at some of the characteristic features of these ancient theatre pavilion as given there:

> Playhouses (*raṅgaśālā*-s) were constructed in the front portion of palaces or in the centre of the city or at crossroads or on a king's highway. The theatre space was divided into three portions: (1) *Daiva*, for the gods, (2) *Gāndharva*, for the celestial singers, (3) *Mānuṣa*, for human beings.
>
> (1) *Daiva* portion was in the back parts (dressing rooms) where deities were kept and worshipped before starting a performance.
> (2) *Gāndharva* portion was the stage proper where the performance took place.
> (3) *Mānuṣa* portion was the auditorium. The lengths assigned to the three portions were in the ratio of 1:2:3 respectively. Dimensions of the theatre were calculated in four to twenty *daṇḍas*. The place for the musicians on the stage was called *raṅgavedī*. The playhouse was adorned with latticed windows, paintings and *toraṇa*-s.

The *Rāmāyaṇa* mentions a playhouse of Rāvaṇa's queen Mandodari and describes the queen's proficiency in *nāṭyasaṅgīta*.[23]

Prince Bharata and his friends were entertained with humorous plays in a palace theatre.[24] The *Mahābhārata* provides many instances of *nāṭya* performance in palaces. Gods, kings, princes and princesses were proficient in the art. Arjuna learnt the art in the court of Indra and later taught it to princess Uttarā in the palace *nartana-śālā* (dance hall).[25]

Buddhist canons show that a drama performance was arranged by king Bimbisāra in his court in honour of two Nāga chieftains. The Jain work Rāja-praśnīya-āgama describes thirty two kinds of dramas performed before a prince named Meghakumāra.[26] One of them depicted the story of Mahāvīra from his conception to *nirvāṇa*, with actresses and actors forming a row.

Nāṭya in Buddhist Caitya

The Pali text Avadāna-śataka refers to many plays on the life of Buddha enacted in Buddhist temples. It is believed that Buddhists were the first to introduce written play texts.

Nāṭya in a Rich Patron's Courtyard

Suruci Jātaka describes a temporary erection of tier upon tier of a seating arrangement in a rich patron's courtyard, where a comedian-actor provided laughter with his body acting with "one hand, one foot, one eye, one tooth, dancing, throbbing, flickering to and fro. . . ." The actor acted in this manner while "the rest of the body stood still" and the crowds responded with laughter so hard that "they rolled over and over in the courtyard."[27]

Nāṭya in Popular Gatherings: Samāja, Pekkhā, Samāja Maṇḍala

Buddhist Pali literature gives picturesque descriptions of the popular entertainments with a variety of wandering entertainers presenting their shows at fairs, village crossroads and courtyards of rich patrons. Terms like *samāja*, *pekkhā*, *viśukadassana* denote such shows. Buddhaghoṣa refers to them quite simply as *naṭa samāja* because *naṭa*-s (actors) took a leading role in them. The arena-like acting area in them was known as *raṅga* or *samāja maṇḍala*. These *samāja*-s became so popular that they attracted censure from Buddha and, later, Aśoka.[28] There is an amusing story in *Vinaya piṭaka* of two Buddhist monks named Aśvajeet and Punarvasu getting caught by superior monks just when they were spreading their robes on the stage with a plea to the female dancer to dance on them with words like 'Please sister, please dance on our robes.'[29]

Stylisation in Nāṭya Enactment

There are many instances where *nāṭya* performances are described with stylisations (*nāṭyavidhi*) and *rasa*-s which give an insight to the nature of the gradual development of the dramatic art.

Sabhā Parvan in the *Mahābharāta* refers to plays with *hāsya* and *lāsya* in the royal courts.[30] *The Rāmāyaṇa* gives a vivid description of a *nāṭya* enactment organised by sage Bhārdvāja to entertain Bharata and his army by mentioning that in the performance Nārada sang, divine female actresses like Miśrakeṣī and Puṇḍarikā danced and dwarfs and hunchbacked comedians regaled the audience with laughter.[31] Jain *Bhagavatī Sūtra* describes details of thirtytwo *nāṭyavidhi*-s performed on the stage by a gorgeously costumed actress before an audience of thousands of people.[32]

Much later in Patañjali's *Mahābhāṣya* (*c.* 150 B.C.) we get a vague but significant reference to two performance—*Kaṃsa-vadha* and *Vāli-vadha*[33]—held in a theatre which had announcers (*ārambhaka*-s) who narrated and actors—mimics (*naṭa*-s), who performed in the company of their leaders (*sobhanika*-s) with reciters (*granthika*-s) reciting. Patañjali makes an interesting allusion to a male actor playing a female role (*bhṛkuṃśa*). There were plays exclusively performed by female artistes. *Arthaśāstra* gives instances of special shows put up by women for the women audience (*strī prekṣā*)[34] as well as special shows of men for men only (*puruṣa prekṣā*).

Performers

These long centuries of development of drama in different environments had generated an enormous variety of performers. These performers were either organised into professional groups who were retained by the royal courts and temple authorities or they were wandering groups of entertainers who performed for a fee at a rich patron's assembly or on a festival ground. There were also performers who continued the exclusive practices of *nāṭya* as a sacred vocation in teacher-disciple tradition.

Pāṇini (*c.* 500 B.C.) gives a glimpse of the well established continuity of the exclusive practices of actors who carried on their sacred practices. Of special significance is his reference to the training and transmission of the actor's aphorisms (*naṭasūtra*-s) through the generations of actors going back to the Ṛgvedic branches of Kṛśāśva and Śilālin.[35] These branches were most probably two schools of interpretations of Sanskrit *nāṭya* emphasising *abhinaya* and dance respectively.

As far as can be judged from the enormous amount of literary evidence available regarding the floating body of popular outside entertainers, a number of interesting and informative general statements can certainly be made.

As mentioned earlier, these professional groups were either retained by rich patrons or they were wandering entertainers who had flourished around popular festivals. They belonged to the lower strata of society and castes. The patrons had an ambivalent attitude towards them.

For example on the one hand, they were considered auspicious and essential parts of the palace and temple processions and amusements. In the *Śāntiparvan* of the *Mahābhārata*, Bhīṣma advises that actors, dancers and other entertainers should always adorn a city.[36] And a Jain source describes a king's royal procession for a meeting with Lord Mahāvīra, in which actors, jesters and musicians were the major revelers.[37] But at the same time many references are found where performers as a class, were looked down upon by the patrons—especially the actresses of easy virtue. In the same *Śāntiparvan* of the *Mahābhārata*, the very same Bhīṣma also cautions that one should not eat food prepared by actresses.[38] In the *Rāmāyaṇa*, Sītā taunts Rāma with words like: "Rāma is leaving me in strange hands, just like an actor would."[39] Patañjali also remarks about the lascivious manner of the actor's wives.[40]

Regardless of such shifting of attitudes of the patron's approach to the performers, it is very apparent that no communal or family occasion was complete without a *nāṭya* performance in ancient India. As a result, a large variety of performers had grown out of diverse environments and a pattern of arrangements of drama troupes had started forming around a set number of performers with different specialisations.

Each of these performers had imbibed his skill through hereditary family tradition. This fact is reflected in many Jātaka stories. Bodhisattva in many Jātaka tales has been described as taking up the family profession of an actor or a drummer. A story in Pālinikāya, an earlier Buddhist source, amusingly describes Tālapuṭṭa—the popular actor, comedian and a leader of actors often featured in Pāli literature—going up to Lord Buddha and asking him this question: "Does a comedian actor (*naṭa*), who makes people laugh with delight from the stage, get reborn in the company of the laughing gods?"[41] This Tālapuṭṭa is said to have acted and stagemanaged many *samāja*-s at Rājagṛha.[42]

Around such a stage manager a group of performers would gather for a show. Broadly speaking, a drama group would consist of:

1. *A leader of the troupe—naṭagāmaṇī/ārambhaka/sūtradhāra*

They were the reciters and leaders who organised the shows.

2. *An Actor—Naṭa*

There were many categories of them. There were actor-dancers, actor-mimics, actor-singers, actor-comedians and actors who were masters in the portrayal of *rasa*.

3. *A Jester*

The jester went through many phases and appeared under many names in his evolution as the *vidūṣaka* of Sanskrit plays. In Vedic times, he was known as a *kārī* (a bald jester) and a *vāmana* (a hunchbacked dwarf). In later Jain *āgamas* he was referred to as a comedian (*vailambiya*), a buffoon (*damakāra*) and a laughter-maker (*hāsakāra*).[43]

4. *An Actress—Naṭī or A Raṅgastrī*

The actress belonged to many categories. There were actresses who were actor's wives (*Naṭī/naṭṭiyā, nāṭakīyā, raṅgastrī* or *naṭa-bhāryā*), prostitutes (*gaṇikā, rūpajīvā*), female dancers (*nartakī, nacakī*) and those belonging to the palace harem (*nāṭakīyā*).[44]

5. *Musicians*

Male and female vocalists (*kuśīlavas* and *gāyikās*) and a wide variety of instrumentalists who played on *vīṇā*, wind pipes drums and cymbals (*gāndharva*-s and later *taurika*-s).

6. In addition, there were different categories of theatre craftsmen who were devoted to various crafts.

The Dramas produced by such groups were in Prakrit.[45] In an evolution, which must have lasted some centuries Sanskrit-

Prakrit play-texts with exalted characters speaking in Sanskrit and the others including female characters speaking in Prakrit finally emerged. The gradual intermixture, in a *nāṭya* troupe, of the popular performers with the exclusive Sanskrit speaking actors[46] may have been one of the reasons for Sanskrit-Prakrit play texts.

Connoisseur Citizen: Patron
Creed of Secular Śṛṅgāra

With the growth and popularity of dramas, the patron-spectator gradually emerged as a vital factor contributing and influencing the trends of a play production. *Kāmaśāstra* throws some light on this. By that time, cultivated appreciation of the dramatic art had become one of the important accomplishments of the cultured elites forming the sophisticated intimate gatherings (*goṣṭhī sabhā*-s). *Nāṭya* appreciation appeared in every list of the sixty-four arts, cultivated by the leisured upper classes in prosperous urban centres. Keen awareness of aesthetic and technical brilliance with fixed standards of appreciation was sought to be acquired by connoisseurs, the aesthetes and the citybred *nāgaraka*-s.

The tastes of these patrons belonging to the leisured upper classes subtly influenced the play writing and play production. For example, emphasis gradually shifted from play productions evoking the heroic and the marvellous *rasa*-s to the delineation of the erotic *rasa*. And in course of time, a subtle change took place even in the treatment of erotic *rasa*. Originally, *kāma* was considered an auspicious source of procreativity and gratification; later on, depiction of erotic play *kāma-krīḍā* became almost the playwright's creed obliging him to dwell on it in elaborate details. Plays portraying the lovers and beloveds in various stages of union and separation (*nāyaka-nāyikā-bheda*) gained ascendence. The amorous pastimes of a prince or a king or a citizen, his gentle beloved (*kulastrī*) or a courtesan, helped by a gallant expert in ways of the courtesan (*viṭa*), or a jester, expert in the ways of women (a *vidūṣaka-narma saciva*) were portrayed in minute details to evoke erotic *rasa* in the drama.

Nāṭyaśāstra Compilation

Around *c.* 200 B.C., the framework of play production had developed into an intense theatre activity with long traditions of conventions, dramatic rules and techniques covering each of the eleven mutually interdependent components. Thus, a perfected framework of Sanskrit play production was available in a major synthesis which *Nāṭyaśāstra* provided by *c*. 200 B.C. to 200 A.D.

It was precisely this combination of interrelated components which generated a large number of Sanskrit plays by playwrights of the succeeding centuries. One has only to glance through the play texts to see the continuity of this basic pattern.

Here, then, in its aspect of the continuity of long tradition born out of a specific ethos and passed down the generations from performer to performer, we approach the secret of the ancient Sanskrit theatre and also its difficulties. It was a communication of the most universal expression of human experiences in a most refined and suggestive conventional framework. It's strictly formulated techniques of suggestions, conventions, stylisation and symbolism, nevertheless, allowed the introduction of countless variations. These variations were bound equally by exposition of studied techniques and the inspired spontaneity in their usage by a playwright or a performer. The result of these two opposite forces is the key to the understanding of the Sanskrit play production.

It was a great moment when a performer executed a portrayal with skilful precision and flawless effortlessness, for that was the moment when the spectator had his supreme experience of joy. They were co-sharers of the joy that they had created together, one through his/her performance, the other through his/her response. That moment was the supreme moment because the creation of that joy was the basic *raison d'etre* of the art. This partaking or sharing (*siddhi*), therefore, constituted an essential component of the framework.

The Sanskrit play production, thus, was merely the deployment of the eleven interdependent components to aid and magnify the subtle art of communication of a heightened awareness of life's experiences.

Let us explore these components one by one.

NOTES

1. NS, VII, 7 (Kashi ed.).
2. NS, I, 103 (Kashi ed.).

3. There are different opinions regarding the origin of Indian drama, like:
   (i) NS—legendary account of nāṭya.
   (ii) Vedic origin—Vedic dialogues—M. M. P. V. Kane, Dr. Hertel, Prof. Schroeder, Prof. Levi, Max Müller, A. B. Keith.
   (iii) Origin from epic recitation—Macdonall.
   (iv) Secular origin: Hillenbrandt and Konow, Dr. Pischel (Puppet plays), Prof. Luders (Shadow Play).
   (v) Greek influence: Weber, Windisch.
   (vi) Origin from Sacred Dance: Dr. M. Ghosh, Dr. Oldenberg.
   (vii) Non-Aryan Origin: Indusekhar.
4. NS, I.
5. The word *kavi* in the Veda-s combined the idea of wisdom, poetic gift and the mystic power of *ṛcā* making sages.
   Pargiter, EE, Ancient Indian Historical tradition, p. 185, also p. 321.
6. A. B. Keith, *The Sanskrit Drama in its Origin, Development, Theory and Practice*, p. 16.
7. Soma plant was the most important ingredient in ancient sacrificial offerings.
8. *Ṛgveda*, 10, 18, 3.
9. Śukla *Yajurveda*, 30/6 Nṛtāya Sūta, Gitāya Śailūṣa.
10. Aitereya Brāmhaṇa, 3, 35, 1.
11. Philip, Rawson, *The Art of Tantra*, p. 109.
12. Ibid, p. 15.
13. Sastri Madhusudan, *NS* with the commentary of Abhinavagupta (in Hindi), I, p. 11.
14. V. Raghavan, *The Vṛttis*, *JOR*, Madras, Vol. VI, p. 41.
15. *NS*, 63-64 (Kashi ed.).
16. It is universally accepted that the drama in its formative stage was a part of festivals where different tribes gathered for communal rejoicing. These festivals were seasonal and magico-religious. There were many non-Aryan festivals like serpent festival, *Yakṣa* festival, river and ghost *yātras* etc. as well as festivals like *Kaumudī mahotsava, Madanotsava, Yava caturthī, Alola caturthī*, festivals to celebrate the sprouting of new leaves and flowers like *Aśokavasthī, Aśoka pāda prahāra* etc. A Jain canon, *Aupapātika Sūtra* describes the *Yakṣa* festival by saying that "it was haunted by actors, dancers, rope-walkers, wrestlers, jesters, ballad singers, story-tellers, pole-dancers picture show men (*mankha*), musicians and minstrels".
17. *NS*, IV, 262 (Kashi ed.).
18. *AS* 16.
19. *Harivaṃśa*, 2.91.26.
20. J. C. Jain, *Life in Ancient India* as Depicted in Jain Canons, ff. 189.
21. *Mayamatam of Mayamuni*, ed. by T. Ganapati Sastri (TSS-1919) Chapter 25, pp. 172-91.
22. *Viśvakarmā's Vāstuśāstra*, ed. by K. Vasudeva Sastri and N. B. Gadre (TSS-1958), Chapter on *Raṅgaśālā nirmāṇakarma*.

23. Gairola Vachaspati, *Bhāratīya Nāṭya Paramparā aur Abhinaya Darpaṇa*, p. 124.
24. *Rāmāyaṇa*, A. K. 2.6 : 4-5, p. 503.
25. *Mahābhārata*, Virata Parva, 4.2.23, p. 12.
26. J. C., Jain Op. cit. p. 184-85.
27. *Suruchi Jātaka* as translated in "Jataka-s or the stories of Buddha's former births" ed. E. B. Cowell, p. 363–73.
28. Bhandarkar D. R., —*Inscriptions of Asoka*, Indian Antiquary—October, 1913. B.K. 42 Part I, p. 255-56 (*na ca samajokatavyo bahukaṃ hi dosa samajamhi*).
29. *Vinaya Pitaka*, Culavagga.
30. *Mahābhārata*, Sabhā Parva, 2.5.107 p. 33, 46
31. *Rāmāyaṇa*, A. K. 2.91.44.47.
32. *Bhagavatī Sūtra*, 11/10.
33. Patañjali, *Mahābhāṣya*, 1.4.1.ff. also 1.4.29.
34. *Arthaśāstra*. 3.2.21.
35. Pāṇini, *Aṣṭādhyāyī*, 4.3.110-11.
36. *Mahābhārata*, *Śānti Parva*, 69–58.
37. *Aupapātika Sūtra*, Sūtra 31.
38. *Mahābhārata*, *Śānti Parva*, 37-22.
39. *Rāmāyaṇa*, A. K. 2.30.8.
40. Patañjali, *Mahābhāṣya* 1.4.1/2.
41. Vijesekhara, O.H. de A. *Buddhist evidence for the early existence of drama*, IHQ, Vol. XVII, pp. 196–206.
42. *Psalms of Brothren*, p. 369.
43. *Aupapātika Sūtra*, Sūtra 1.
44. Actresses belonged to the palace harem, and performed plays in the delicate (*sukumāra*) style. The productions were full of songs, dance, erotic *rasa* and gorgeous costumes. Women took the roles of men. Śri Harṣa's *Priyadarśikā* (III) shows such an exclusive reproduction by women. In Java and Cambodia plays performed exclusively by women are prevalent.
45. Winternitz M., *History of Indian Literature*, Vol. III, Part I, p. 197.
46. Sanskrit plays reflect reality of ancient Indian society in the use of Prakrits. Sanskrit was a language spoken by a few in society. It was spoken by the learned, cultured men, brahmins and those belonging to upper strata of society. Majority of the people used Prakrits spoken in different regions of the country.

    In the plays, gods, brahmins, king, men of noble rank and generals speak in Sanskrit. The rest, including women, (unless specially specified) use Prakrits of the period of composition.

    Śaurasani was the most commonly used Prakrit language in the plays.

CHAPTER 2

SIDDHI—SPECTATOR-PERFORMER-RAPPORT

An ancient Sanskrit play production was something more than a mere enactment, and a spectator was not just an onlooker. In fact, a performance of a play was often compared to a sacrificial ritual—a *yajña* with the performer as the ritual-performing priest and the spectator as the sacrificer who attained the final reward of a blissful *rasa* experience by complete self-identification with the rituals that were being performed. Establishment of such an intangible involvement of both the spectator and the performer, where each entered into the inner spirit of the performance on the basis of identification, was the objective of a play production. It culminated into the achievement of success of production (*siddhi*).

In order to achieve such a success (*siddhi*), the performer was required to cultivate mastery over the specialised skills of his art so that he could stage a play without any flaw or blemish, and communicate the inner meaning of the play to the spectator. The spectator at the same time, was also required to so identify with the performance that he might attain fulfilment of a blissful *rasa* experience. *Siddhi*, thus, was a process of mutuality and joint participation between the performer who presented and the spectator who relished. Familiarity with the plot, the characters and the codes of staging facilitated such a process. When the spectator had a responsive understanding and the performers performed their roles with precision, then alone the said participation was realised and the *siddhi* attained.

In course of time, *nāṭya* appreciation or an aesthetic proficiency formed a part of the accomplishment of a connoisseur citizen of ancient India. And the sophisticated drama production aimed to please such a connoisseur for attaining success or *siddhi*.

Siddhi—According to Nāṭyaśāstra, Abhinavagupta, Later Commentators and Sanskrit Play Texts

Nāṭyaśāstra attaches the highest degree of importance to *siddhi* and says that "the production of a play is wholly meant for attaining success in it."[1]

Abhinavagupta elaborates this by saying that attainment of mere 'tangible fruits' (*dṛṣṭaphala*)[2] like banners[3] or material rewards may not indicate success of a play production. The real success was achieved only when the play was performed with skilled precision, devoted faith and pure concentration in the manner of a priest performing rituals. Such a perfectly rendered faultless performance alone succeeded in immersing the spectator with pure joy of *rasa* experience. And that was the real act of merit—an achievement of 'intangible fruits'—or success for a performing troupe. The spectator, in this process, was compared to a sacrificer by Abhinavagupta. Absorbed with singleminded concentration in the performance, like one in a meditation,[4] the spectator took the role of an active partner in creating the *rasa* experience. His concentrated absorption and appreciation, thus, contributed equally to the success of a production.

Responsive Spectator—Sahṛdaya

In course of time, this idea of cultivated appreciation by the spectator assumed a primary position in the partnership. Abhinavagupta and later commentators maintained that a production should specially cater to the sophisticated, expert spectator who, with his refined taste and thorough knowledge of merits and demerits of a performance, contributed to the *rasa* communion. Such a spectator was a *sahṛdaya*—a person with an empathetic response in his heart for the art.

Abhinavagupta opined that even when a play production might lack in some particular aspect, a *sahṛdaya* spectator could counterbalance it with his responsive appreciation and knowledge of the art so that the *rasa* communion remained undisturbed.[5]

Daśarūpaka emphasised that responsive spectators, with their own enthusiasm and imagination, contributed to the play in the manner of "children playing with clay elephants".[6] *Sāhitya Darpaṇa* suggested that such an ability was inborn in the spectator and was the reward of his *vāsanā*-s (latent memories of past lives). Such a responsive spectator came to be variously described as a specialist expert, aesthete, connoisseur, taster of *rasa* (*rasika*), etc.

The prologues of Sanskrit plays make it clear that the production was aimed to satisfy these responsive spectators and thus attain success. As mentioned in the previous chapter, Sanskrit dramas were staged before various exclusive assemblies patronised by the palace, the temple, the *goṣṭhī sabhā*-s of rich citizens and gatherings organised by the town and village authorities. The laudations in prologues in Sanskrit plays refer to these assemblies and the *sahṛdayī* spectators in them with such praises as:

> "this assembly is honoured with the presence of scholars.... Indeed, today we have to please them with a new play"[8] or, "this assembly is made up of spectators who are appreciative of merits, and we are skilled in the dramatic art...."[9]

Abhinaya Darpaṇa compares such an assembly of connoisseurs with a wish-fulfilling tree which gratified the desires of the performers.[10]

Levels of Appreciation in an Assembly

We get a description of an ideal spectator (or an assessor) even as far back as *Nāṭyaśāstra* where, the account of the required qualifications are so exaggerated that Bharata himself admits that no single person can have so many attributes in one life-time. Instead, Bharata acknowledges an assembly made of spectators with different levels of tastes and appreciation who could enjoy a drama collectively but from different points of view. He says:

> "Young spectators are usually interested in the portrayal of love, devout in the philosophical and religious aspects, and the seekers of money enjoy dramas where prosperity is achieved. Again, heroic persons would delight in the terrible and odious *rasa*-s generated through scenes of battles and combats; old people select tales of virtue and *purāṇic* legends, while the common women, children and fools prefer comic situations, costumes and make up...."[11]

Over and above these he mentions also other types of spectators who with their cultivated tastes and expertise in deeper aspects of production formed another strata of appreciative audience. These were the connoisseurs and experts who were well-versed in the minutest details of the techniques and conventions of a performance. There were scholars who cared more about the correctness of the use of techniques. There were masters of dramatic art who critically observed the usage of skills (*guṇa*-s) and the absence of defects (*doṣa*-s). There were specialists, artists, accomplished courtesans and sophisticated savants in different aspects of dramatic art who relished the subtle nuances in the rendering of their specialised fields. Services of these experts were called for at the time of drama contests. They were asked to act as special assessors especially when differences of opinion occurred.

A chief patron headed such an assembly. It was he who presented a banner to the winning troupe and rewarded the troupes with appropriate remuneration. He generally bore the expenses for these stagings. The other spectators were honoured invitees. The spectators, however, shared part of expenses when town or village authorities arranged drama performances.

Sanskrit drama productions aimed to please these patrons, assessors and connoisseurs. But at the same time, different levels of audience appreciation were never lost sight of. There were elements in the production to appeal to every taste of the spectators.

Timing of a Drama Performance

Except for the time of prayers or meals, a play could be performed at any time of day and night—early morning, forenoon, afternoon and evening. As a rule, a performance was fixed at a period of day or night or even a season which was most appropriately suitable to communicate the mood and *rasa* impact of the play. For example, a play evoking pathetic *rasa* might be staged in the mornings, while one latent with erotic *rasa* might be presented in the evenings.[12] Of course, timings could always be changed to suit the convenience of the patron.

Standards of Critical Appreciation

It is very explicitly pointed out by the traditional treatises that the yardstick of judging or critically appreciating a production depended on the perfect execution of techniques and conventions by the skilled performers in a flawless performance. Competent and technically critical spectators approved or discouraged a production according to canonical standards. The list of merits and demerits of a production as given in *Nāṭyaśāstra* is quite illuminating. It gives an idea of the detailed manner in which each aspect of production was assessed. A few of the details are given below:

> Appropriate *abhinaya* of *bhāva*-s, correct use of music, notes, songs, drums, speech, recitation, intonation and movements executed in a correct pitch in a performance to evoke the latent *rasa* of the drama text with their suggestive import (*dhvani*), style (*vṛtti*) and appropriate regional mode (*pravṛtti*) constituted the merits of a performance.
>
> On the other hand, unnatural *abhinaya* of *bhāva*-s, wrong movements, defective playing of drums, unsuitability for a role, loss of concentration, forgetting the text, falling off of crowns and ornaments, shyness in speech, entering the stage without proper costume or a late entrance, not being able to take the right note (*svara*) or even foolishly reciting a *nāndī* prayer involving a deity other than the special deity of the patron were some of the defects of a performance.[13]

The above list makes it obvious that a play production was appreciated in terms of technical dexterity with which the known codes of staging were executed by skilled performers. The *rasa* impact or the inner idea of the playwright was conveyed through the creative use of codes of *abhinaya*, music, visual patterns and other conventional elements of the production by the genius of the performers. These got communicated at every level of the audience who responded from their own angle of appreciation. A connoisseur, on his part, understood the subtle nuances of the codes and stylisations and responded from his cultivated knowledge of techniques.

For example, in Kālidāsa's *Mālavikāgnimitra* (Act II) the lady recluse praises the *abhinaya* of the heroine Mālavikā by extensively commenting on the merits of the performance. She says:

> "Everything was blamelessly executed in accordance with the rules of the art. The meaning was suggested well by her limbs that were eloquently expressive. The movement of the feet was in perfect time, and she was thoroughly absorbed in various

rasa-s. The enactment was delicate—different transitory states (*vyabhicāri bhāva*-s) pertaining to the basic state of love or passion remained the same throughout" etc.

In the plays *Vikramorvāśīyam* of Kālidāsa (Act III) and *Priyadarśikā* of Śri Harṣa (Act III), the demerits of the performances of the heroines are related to their 'lack of concentration'. It can be readily seen from these examples that not only did a cultivated spectator display his thorough knowledge of the technical rules of the dramatic art in his appreciation, but his response was mainly based on the correct rendering of canonical rules of the performance. Even a *sahṛdayī* spectator who gradually became a contributory factor to the success of production fully based his responsive appreciation on his knowledge of the perfection of the codes of techniques, and their creative usage in a production.

Set Modes of Demonstration of Appreciation—
Vocal and Physical

It is interesting to note that with the long list of merits and demerits of a performance, the dramaturgical tradition had also worked out the physical and vocal manner in which a spectator may demonstrate his appreciation. Some of the gestures by which a spectator showed his appreciation were:

Different types of smiles:

A faint flicker of a smile (*smita*)
A smile (*ardhahāsa*)
Excessive laughter (*atihāsa*),

Different exclamations:

How wonderful! (*aho*)
How pathetic! (*kaṣṭam*)

As well as, tumultuous applause, horripilation, tears, rising from one's seat, presenting a part of one's dress or a ring,[14] etc.

Nāṭya Troupes for Sanskrit Play Production:
Its Composition and System of Transmission of Skills

Success of a production, thus, demanded performers who would cultivate mastery over techniques of their skills and their creative usage, so that a drama, without any flaw or blemish could be effortlessly staged according to the canonical rules in a properly conceived design of production.

As mentioned in the previous chapter, such a design had its genesis in the magico-ritualistic ceremonies of the ancient people which was essentially conventional and ideally determined with symbolism and stylisation forming the core of its communication. Generations of performing artists had sought to preserve and conserve the heritage through the teacher disciple tradition of transmission in the exclusive practice. It must be emphasised again that this exclusive trend was renewed time and again by incorporation of newer influences from the regional and the popular expressions of the outside entertainers whose skills were also imbibed by the family—hereditary transmissions.

By the time of *Nāṭyaśāstra*, this design of production had reached the stage where the techniques could be identified and codified into a *śāstra*. And rigorous training and concentrated discipline of performers had perfected the hereditary skills of various specialisations.

It is illuminating to note in this connection that the original drama troupe of Bharata and his hundred sons, as described in the legendary account of the origin of drama in *Nāṭyaśāstra*, consisted of performer-sages who were "skilfully learned, bold in speech and inured in hard work."[16] Not only did they learn *Nāṭya Veda* and put the dramatic art into practice, but most of them achieved a high degree of proficiency in their specialised area. The names of the hundred sons or disciples of Bharata include names of persons like Kohala, Dattila, Śālikarṇa, Piṅgaḷa, Bādarāyaṇa, Nakhakuṭṭa, Aṣmakuṭṭa and many others who were themselves recognised authorities on dramaturgy, dance, music, prosody, etc. in ancient India. Their works were quoted and referred to by the later commentators. It seems likely, therefore, that the ideal characteristics of each member of the drama troupe, as given in *Nāṭyaśāstra*, was based on the supposition that an ideal troupe consisted of members who were experts in their own ambit of specialisation.

The drama troupe of Bharata belonged to hereditary groups (*jāti*-s, castes) of performers, who in course of time came to be known as *naṭa*-s (actors) producing various types of plays. Each member of the troupe was a specialist in a particular area of production and learnt his skill through the teacher-disciple system of rigorous personal training and observation of the performance of the master.

Although we have no records to tell us about the manner in which the Vedic *Bharata*-s with *sūta, śailūṣa, naṭa, kārī, vāmana, raṅgastrī* and other artists might have combined to form a basic production unit of the ancient Indian theatre, we have with us a detailed description of the final full-fledged drama troupe as described by Bharata. Very likely it was a semi-permanent hereditary unit in terms of its members. Let us look at some of the characteristics of the main members in the light of the perfection of skills which was ideally required from them:

Nāṭya Troupe—As described by Bharata

(a)	Troupe leader	—*Sūtradhāra*
	His assistant	—*Pāripārśvaka*
(b)	A drama-maker (dramatist)	—*Nāṭyakāra*
(c)	Jester (comedian)	—*Vidūṣaka*
	Actor proper	—*Bharata*
	Actor dancer	—*Naṭa*
	Actress	—*Naṭī*
(d)	Experts in musical instruments	—*Taurika*
	Musicians	—*Kuśīlava*-s
(e)	Crown maker	—*Mukuṭakāra*
	Costumer	—*Veśakāra*
	Ornament maker	—*Ābharaṇakāra*
	Garland maker	—*Mālyakāra*
	Dyer	—*Rajaka*
	Painter	—*Citrakāra*
(f)	Craftmen who made stage property with lac, stones and metal	—*Kāruka, Śilpakāra*

Sūtradhāra

He was stage manager, teacher and the organiser of the troupe. He was required to be an expert in all arts and crafts covering a production, a master of "everything concerning the theatre"[16] —in terms of speech, rhythm, notes, musical instruments, conventions of gaits and movements, *rasa* and *bhāva abhinaya*, rules of prosody, allied arts and crafts as well as canons of *artha, kāma*, epics and *purāṇa*-s, names of royal descendants, etc. His duty was to utilise his knowledge for putting up a performance, assigning appropriate roles to actors and looking after their entire training. He had to have sharp memory, intelligence and charming manners.

Sūta

In the opinion of some scholars, *sūtradhāra* was the stage substitute of the *sūta*-s—the principal reciters—of Vedic times.[17] This opinion is quite credible. In the third chapter of *Śukla Yajurveda*, we find a *sūta*, who was an expert dancer, being specially invited to take part in the entertainments around sacrificial ceremonies.[18] A *sūta* was not a part of the priestly caste, but belonged to a caste which emerged out of the union of brahmins and *kṣatriya*-s. In the post-Vedic period *sūta* appeared as a charioteer of kings. In epics and *purāṇa*-s, he formed an important part of the king's entourage. His chief function was to herald the descent of royal kings, sages and gods.

In a play production, he featured as the troupe leader and stage manager—*sūtradhāra*. It is probable that in the initial stages of development of drama, he acted as a chief narrator of dramas. This style of narration stopped at a later stage when the playwrights started writing the narrative-linking scenes—like *praveśaka* and *viṣkambhaka*—which were enacted by actors.

From then onwards *sūtradhāra* appeared only in the prologues and at the time of the recitation of actor's benediction (*Bharata-vākya*) at the end of the play. The Sanskrit theatre declined after the 12th century. But the *sūtradhāra* has not vanished from the Indian theatre scene. He is seen even now as a *sūtakathākāra*, the chief narrator, stage manager and director in almost all the traditional theatre forms in India.

Pāripārśvaka—Sūtradhāra's Assistant

He was the assistant of *sūtradhāra*, his second-in-command. *Nāṭyaśāstra* describes him succinctly as the one who was similar to *sūtradhāra* but had slightly less qualifications.[19]

Nāṭyakāra—The Dramatist

It is significant to note that a dramatist or, literally, a 'drama maker' was considered an important member of a drama troupe from the earliest times in ancient India. His task was to write a play on any given theme according to the canonical rules of *nāṭya* presentation. Later on, the dramatists themselves became part of the connoisseur's assemblies of a king,[20] and got their plays produced by different drama troupes. We have instances of Aśvaghoṣa and Bhavabhūti organising the performance of their own plays.

Bharata—The Actor Proper

Bharata was the main actor acting many roles, playing many instruments and providing many accessories.[21]

At the risk of over simplification, one may suggest that he stands comparison with the Vedic *Bharata*-s, singers of ballads of *Bharata* tribe, who were experts in Sanskrit speech, originators of verbal style (*Bhāratī vṛtti*) and the leading actors of exclusive practices of earlier rudimentary drama *genres*.

Bharata, the actor proper in the later drama troupes, apparently performed more or less the same duties as did the *sūtradhāra*. It was perhaps quite possible that with the passage of time, *sūtradhāra* and the actor proper became one and the same principal actor of the troupe. Such a tradition persists in many traditional theatres in India, and also in the Noh theatre of Japan.

We have examples of *sūtradhāra* and his assistant assuming important roles in two plays of Bhavabhūti. Some scholars also believe that the reason why a *sūtradhāra* and the chief actor, the hero, never come face to face in a play is that mostly one actor assumed both responsibilities.

Naṭa—The Other Actor

Naṭa enacted stories of men with *abhinaya* which was latent with *rasa* and *sattva*. He was a master in performing a play according to canonical dictates of drama practice. He was acquainted with theatrical accessories and their uses and was also skilful in playing four kinds of instruments.[22]

Naṭa certainly had emerged from the outside popular practices of performances. He subsequently came to hold such an important position in the drama troupe that in course of time the entire troupe came to be known as a group of *naṭa*-s (*naṭamaṇḍalī*).

The Comedian—Vidūṣaka

He was another important member of the troupe who, according to *Nāṭyaśāstra*, looked after "the pleasures of the people".[23] He was an expert in pleasantry (*narma*—the ancient Indian system of pleasure connected with erotics). With his ready wit, he imitated the manners of people and censured the hypocrisy in society. He was an adept in mixing with women.

The Actress—Naṭī, Nāṭakīyā, Gaṇika

There were different categories of actresses.

The beautiful actress—sarvāṅgasundari[24]—was the *nāṭakīyā*. She was required to be an expert in playing drums, and had to be conversant with *bhāva abhinaya*, rhythm and tempo.

A courtesan (*gaṇikā*) was another category of an actress who was accomplished in sixty-four arts and crafts, skilful in amorous movements and *abhinaya* of *hāva*, *bhāva* and *helā* (gestures and expressions of stages of love).

Naṭī (or *naṭabhāryā*) was the actor's wife who usually featured in the prologues of the dramas.

One other category of actresses also referred to as *nāṭakīyā* (theatre women), belonged to the groupes patronised by the palace harem. They performed exclusively in all female performances in the theatres attached to the harem. Where they enacted the roles of men also. As Bharata says:

> "A delicate person's role is always to be taken up by women. Hence, women should impersonate gods, men and women of delicate nature. It is for this reason that the drama came to be established in heaven, in the court of Lord Indra, through celestial actresses like Rambhā, Urvaśī and others. Similar has been the case in a king's harem.... because want of fatigue in dance and music is always considered a quality of women."[25]

The Musicians: Taurika and Kuśilava-s

They formed the musical orchestra. *Taurika*-s were master musicians experts in all aspects of musical instruments. *Kuśīlava*-s were clever in singing and playing instruments.

The Craftmen

The craftmen of the drama troupe had perfected the skill of their craft in family tradition and were named after the things they made.

The members of such a drama troupe were expected to be experts in the areas of their specialisation. Each of them was traditionally trained with meticulous care through the teacher-disciple method following his hereditary-family system. A play was produced under the supervision of a teacher who was also the leader of the troupe (*sūtradhāra*, nāṭyācārya). Each member, under his guidance, employed his skills with traditional precision and widely understood codes of conventions.

The drama troupe knew these codes from inside and they used them in a way where each object, feeling, action and a facet of experience had an *abhinaya* technique to represent it. And where each technique was imbued with a deep symbolic significance according to fixed traditional dictates. Ideally, the enactment was not approached from the angle of just giving a performance. It was as if the performer was being engaged in a rite. It was like a ritual in which performance was supposed to be enacted with preordained dictates and without any blemishes. Success or *siddhi* was gained only after such an effort by the troupe.

The plays that were so performed were latent with *rasa*-s. Their plots were traditionally designed to present a state of final serenity achieved by the hero as a result of fulfilment of one of the three goals of human existence (*trivarga sādhanā*).

The traditional spectator generally referred to as a *sahṛdaya*, by complete identification with the hero achieved similar state of fulfilment and serenity at the end of the play. This self-identification with utmost concentration was taken still further by a *sahṛdayī* spectator who, with his inborn awareness of the absolute possibilities of *abhinaya* and its suggestive import, coutributed to the *rasa* communion. He relished the play in the manner of a mind expanding blissful experience (*ānadamayī cetanā*).

There is an obvious difference between this approach and that of the modern spectator. The modern spectator views the happenings on the stage with empathy but with an approach of impartiality. He can sympathise or wonder at the experience of a protogonist of a play, but he keeps his own identity and distance. Not so the traditional spectator. A sense of complete self-identification with the hero and his exploits enabled him to achieve a similar state of harmonious serenity which the hero attained at the end of a play.

The obvious difference of a modern and the traditional performer is apparent in their approach to a performance. The flow of a performance is usually generated by a modern actor by a process of his own unique personal expression of conscious involvement with the role. In the case of the traditional performer, however, there is a studied distance kept from the role. He interprets, improvises and presents the character with his own creativeness (*manodharma*) or genius (*pratibhā*) and awareness of the possibilities of his art as a connoisseur. He keeps his distance from the character in enactment while at the same time remaining within the fixed periphery of the canonical rules.

Such a presentation by the performer and the responsive understanding of the spectator to it was considered essential for the success (*siddhi*) of a play production in ancient India. In fact, this level of identification with the performance formed the foundation on which the entire structure of Sanskrit theatre of suggestions and conventions was based.

NOTES

1. NS. XXVII.1 (tr. M. Ghosh).
2. Abh. XXXIII.1.
3. NS, XXVII, 71 (Kashi ed.) Bhāsa is mentioned as a winner of many banners—*patākā-s*—by Bāṇa in his introduction of *Harṣacaritam.*
4. Abh. Vol. I, VI p. 676 ff.
5. Ibid, p. 681 ff.
6. DR. IV.50.
7. SD III, 8 and subsequent comments.
8. Ka, Abh. Sak. prologue.
9. Śri Harṣa, *Ratnāvali* prologue.
10. AD. 1/19.
11. NS. XXVII.61.
12. Ibid. 93–95.
13. Ibid. 24-25, 27-28, 32, 34-37, 41, 84-85.
14. Ibid. 5–15 (tr. M. Ghosh).
15. NS. I, 19-20 (tr. M. Ghosh)—(*grahaṇe, dhāraṇe, jñāne, prayoge*).
16. NS, XXXV, 65–74.
17. Deshpande G.T., *Sanskrit Drama*, Indian Drama, Pub. div. G.O.I., Nov. 1956.

18. *Śukla Yajurveda* 30.6, cif. Pargiter F. E., Op. cit. p. 16.
19. NS. XXXV, 74-75.
20. Most Sanskrit playwrights later on got the palace patronage and became members of a king's assembly. This can be seen as follows:

    Bhāsa is said to have been a protege of Rājasiṃha.
    Kālidāsa is said to have been a protege of Vikramāditya.
    Bhaṭṭanārāyaṇa is said to have been a protege of Ādisura.
    Bhavabhūti is said to have been a protege of Yaśovarman.
    Śūdraka, Śri Harṣa, Mahendra Vikrama Varmā were themselves royal patrons. So was probably Viśākhadatta who was a sāmanta.
21. NS. XXXV.91 (tr. M. Ghosh).
22. Ibid. 75-77, 95, 100.
23. Ibid. 92-93.
24. Ibid. 60-64, 79 (Kashi ed.).
25. Ibid. 21-22.

CHAPTER 3

RAṄGA—THE PLAYHOUSE

The ancient Indian playhouse—*Raṅga*—with its distinctive structure, formed an essential part of drama production in ancient India. This fact was recognised by the ancient Indian dramaturgists from Bharata onwards. Most of the staging practices of Sanskrit plays were created to suit the distinctive stage structures of ancient Indian playhouses and the performer-audience rapport provided by them. Sanskrit playwrights were well aware of those characteristic requirements and composed their plays accordingly. In fact, Sanskrit play texts, the practices of their performance, structure of the stages and the audience-performance juxtaposition in the ancient Indian playhouses were interrelated and mutually dependent.

Early Open-Air Enactments

The allusion to an open-air enactment in *Ṛgveda* and the rudimentary performances of the dialogue hymns at *Yajus* rituals give some idea of the open-air staging of these times. It was in the style of simple "arena staging" or "central staging". There was systematic space allocation for performing and viewing even when the boundaries were not demarcated physically in the earlier stages.

On the sites of sacrificial grounds, on top of a hill, a bank of a river, in parts of tree groves or even in pleasure gardens, the performer performed within specified areas.[1] The spectators watched the performance from all sides or, at times, from three open sides. This arrangement was most probably devised with ritual precision to yield maximum contact between the performer and the spectator and provide an atmosphere of participation. It was only when this atmosphere of rapport was disturbed that a need was felt to have some kind of an enclosure or a shelter.

The *Nāṭyaśāstra* legend of the origin of drama describes in detail how a need arose to have an enclosed structure around the acting area in the very early phase of its development.[2] As the tale goes, the first ever open-air play performance was given by Bharata and his troupe before an audience consisting of all the "coloured groups" of people at the festival of the victory of Indra. The play depicting the victory of gods over demons was disturbed by the angry demons in the audience. As a result, the need arose to have an enclosed structure around the acting area. This indicates that some sort of an enclosed theatre structure came into existence in the very early phase of development of Indian drama. The reason was a simple one: Prevention of disturbance from outside the acting area. The spectators may or may not have occupied the sheltered areas.

Two Kinds of Theatre Enclosures

Two kinds of enclosed theatre structures are indicated in our early literature.

Mahābhārata mentions an enclosed area demarcated with a special kind of a fence or a railing (*vedikā*) and refers to it as a *raṅgavāṭa*.[3] It was a cleared space of land encircled by a railing made of thorns and pieces of wood used for archery contest among the Pāṇḍava princes.[4] *Raṅgavāṭa* has been described as an enclosure in the style of 'central staging' with the spectators surrounding the area on all sides.

Early Theatre Pavilions: Raṅgamaṇḍapa

The second kind of enclosed area formed a part of the *maṇḍapa* structure and has been described as a *raṅgamaṇḍapa* or a *raṅgaśālā*. It was a pavilion-like structure with four pillars supporting a roof which was open on all sides or at least three sides.

P. K. Acharya (*Māṇasāra* series Vol. VI—*Maṇḍapavidhāna*) describes it as a "pavilion, a bower, a shed or an open hall", or as "detached building in the compound."[5] Percy Brown suggests that it could also have been "a portable kind having wooden pillars turned on a lathe, and lacquered and coloured, to be set up like tents."[6]

These types of theatre pavilions can be seen in a number of sculptural bas reliefs of ancient monuments. In Rani Gumpha at Udaigiri caves in Orissa, a sculptural relief of a drama or a dance performance is depicted within a rectangular pavilion. The bas relief is described by Dr. G. S. Ghurye as, "the earliest representation of human beings dancing in our country."[7] (Sketch No. 2 on page No. 42)

Different theatre pavilion can be seen in frescos and sculptural friezes at Ajanta, Bharhut, Sanchi and Amaravati. A wooden pavilion from the fresco at Ajanta of the period around 200 B.C. shows details of its structural construction.[8] (Sketch No. 1 on page No. 42). The cave No. 1 at Ajanta shows a theatre pavilion with a performer in a fresco scene from *Mahājanaka Jātaka*. In this painting the spectators are also shown seated in another pavilion. The close rapport between the spectators and performer is very evident in these frescos.

These pavilions were either temporary or permanent structures erected according to the strict rules of *maṇḍapa* construction.

It is interesting to note that the design of this early theatre pavilion continued to be preserved in the course of subsequent development of ancient Indian playhouses and remained its core acting area. Not only that but also its basic design of a bare stage with four poles and a roof has remained a part of the living theatre tradition to this day. The rough and ready theatre structures of traditional and folk forms in India, South East Asia and even China and Japan provide proof of its continuity.

Gradual Development into Later-Day Permanent Playhouses as Described by Bharata

The gradual emergence of the temporary or semi-permanent structures of theatres called *prekṣāgṛha* or *raṅga* is a process which is shrouded in the mist of time. No definite documentation or monumental evidence is available at present marking the various stages of its development.

However, the fact remains that the building art in India had made a steady advance under the encouraging stimulation of a succession of stabilising empires from 400 B.C. onwards. The subsequent growth of prosperous urban centres generated a number of progressive elaborations in the stylistic pattern of buildings in different parts of the country. It is more than likely that this developed art of building found a suitable reflection in the construction of playhouses which were patronised by the royal courts, prosperous temple authorities and the city and village administrations. In fact, it is quite possible that such playhouses which aimed to cater to the exclusive requirements of select and affluent groups of society, would exhibit a variety of construction designs of different sizes, shapes and ornamentations as per the prevalent fashions in architecture.

We get a number of references to ancient playhouses like palace—*nāṭakaśālā*-s, *-nāṭyaśālā*-s, *-raṅgaśālā*-s, temple-*nāṭya-maṇḍapa*-s, *-nāṭyamandira*-s as well as the city and village *prekṣāgṛha*-s and *raṅga*-s in pre- and post-Bharata literature. Although sketchy, some descriptions of their construction are also provided by these sources.

Among these, Bharata's description of the three types of ancient Indian playhouses is perhaps the longest and the most detailed. Although, the text of this particular chapter[9] of *Nāṭyaśāstra* suffers from obscure references to unspecified details, it nevertheless gives a fairly adequate picture of the general concept of these playhouses and the space allocation in them. It is written in a style giving general guidelines to enable the builders and architects[10] to build three types of playhouses in vogue at the time of the compilation of *Nāṭyaśāstra*. It is made amply clear in the beginning of the chapter that the playhouses described were to be constructed according to strict rules of *vāstuśāstra*. Says Bharata:

> "The creations of gods are a matter of their will, but a man's creation should be carefully guided by the canonical rules."[11]

Accordingly, Bharata has left the constructions of the theatre buildings in the hands of able architects and builders who would adhere to the strict rules of their profession. He has only specified the general requirements of a drama troupe and has used architectural terms, unfortunately without specifications, taking for granted that planners and builders understood what was meant by them.

This fact has proved to be a great handicap in our understanding of the precise structural designs of the ancient playhouses in the absence of any surviving monuments. Fortunately, we do possess relevant literary references, which throw some light on certain architectural details of ancient Indian building construction. Indeed, a long period of development is registered in these descriptions which are collated from epics, *Purāṇa*-s, Baudha-Jain sources, various texts of ancient Indian architecture as well as pre- and post-Bharata literature on dramaturgy and music.[12]

Certain general common features emerge from these sources regarding the ground plans of the playhouses, space allocated to the stage proper, the dressing room and the auditorium in them; as well as many distinct characteristics of small compact theatre buildings suitable for a drama performance.

For example, ancient Indian playhouses consisted of following sub-structures:

The Stage Proper—Raṅgamaṇḍapa

The stage was constructed as a pavilion with four or more pillars and an ornamental roof.
It was of varied sizes and shapes.
It faced the east.
It was slightly elevated.
There was a special place on it for musical orchestra.

The Dressing Room—Nepathyagṛha

The dressing room was in the back region of the stage.
Properties and costumes were stored there.
It was connected with the stage by a partition with two doors.

The Auditorium—Prekṣā

The auditorium had:
A polished floor for the spectators to sit on.
A prominent central seat for the chief patron was kept mainly in the front row.
Raised platforms and galleries with different enclosures for separate groups of spectators.

The Playhouses—Raṅga

The playhouses were of many shapes and sizes—square, rectangular, oblong, circular and triangular.
There were many ornamental pillars supporting the roofs with painted ceilings.
They had well plastered walls with fresco paintings.
There were many altars. And high windows, some of these windows were latticed and shaped like a cow's eye (*gavākṣa*).
The playhouses were built round the focal point of the stage proper and the seat of the chief patron.

Raṅgamaṇḍapa—Basic Stage Design

1

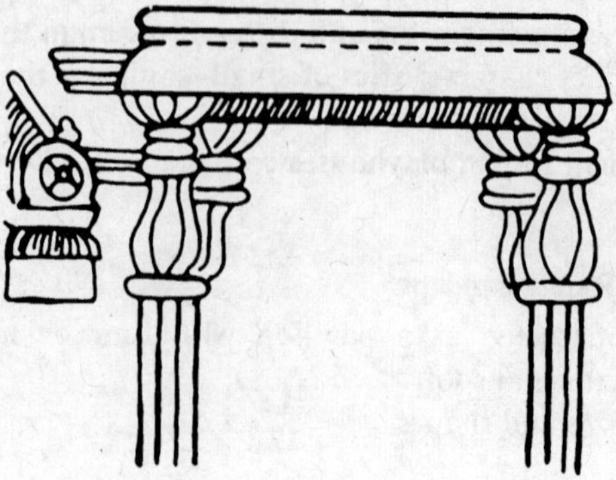

A wooden pavilion—from Ajanta [E.B. Havell, op cit. p. 24, pl. IV]

2

Khandagiri—Udaigiri Ranigumpha (200 B.C.) [Zimmer, op. cit., pl. 55]

3

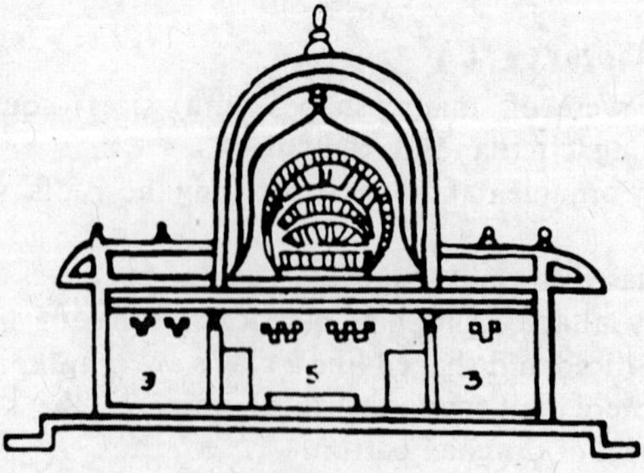

Bharatas Stage Elevated

Raṅgamaṇḍapa—Basic Stage Design

4

Kuttambalam stage —Trichur, Kerala

5

Kalamandalam—Kerala restructured stage design

6

Rough and ready stages of present day traditional theatres

They were small and intimate theatres catering to select assemblies.
The juxtaposition of the audience and performance was close and near.

When viewed against such a background of comparative similarity of designs of the other ancient Indian theatre buildings, many mistifying facets of Bharata's playhouses become somewhat easier to visualise.

Bharata's Playhouses

Bharata describes three types of playhouses and variously refers to them as *nāṭyaveśma*, *nāṭyamaṇḍapa*, *prekṣāgṛha* etc. They were of three shapes—rectangular, square and triangular. Each of these variously shaped playhouses were of three sizes also, viz. large, medium and small. The measurements were made either by the ancient method of '*hasta*-s' or '*daṇḍa*-s'.[13] (One hasta is equal to one and a half feet: 1 H = 1½'). The playhouses, according to their sizes and shapes in *hasta* measurement, were as follows:

Shape	*Sizes*		
	Large (*Jyeṣṭha*)	Medium (*Madhya*)	Small (*Avara*)
	E-W × N-S	E-W × N-S	E-W × N-S
Rectangular	162' × 81'	96' × 48'	48' × 24'
(*Vikṛṣṭa*)	108H × 54 H	64 H × 32 H	32 H × 16 H
Square	162' × 162'	96' × 96'	48' × 48'
(*Caturasra*)	108 H × 108 H	64 H × 64 H	32 H × 32 H
Triangular	Measurements not given.		
(*Trayasra*)			

Abhinavagupta in his commentary says that plays like *samavakāra* and *ḍima*, in *ārabhaṭi* style, dealing with a large number of characters of gods, demons and the like, needed large playhouses. *Nāṭaka*, *prakaraṇa* and *nāṭikā* dealing with a lesser number of characters as in a king's or a noble hero's stories required medium-sized playhouses. *Bhāṇa*, *prahasana* varieties of plays with smaller number of characters required small theatres.[14]

Bharata discouraged the use of large theatres measuring 108 H by mentioning that they were meant only for gods and not for mortals. On the other hand, he recommends medium theatres for most types of performances. He says:

> "It is the best because then you can hear the speech and also see the *bhāvābhinaya* in the best manner. If the stage is too far away then the *abhinaya* becomes indistinct and distorted."[15]

It is interesting to note here the recent findings of scientific studies which mention that for minute observation of expressive movements of the eyes a spectator should not sit farther than 52.5′ (35 H).[16] Bharata's recommendation places the farthest spectator at 48′ (32 H) away from the stage. In fact, *Nāṭyaśāstra* prohibits the connoisseurs and the assessors from sitting either too far or too near the stage. It states that they should sit not more than 18′ (12 H) away from the stage in order to adequately judge the merits and demerits of a performance. The intricacy of minute and subtle movements of major and minor limbs of the body, expressive glances of eyes and *sāttvikabhāva*-s like tears, slight tremor, sweat, blush or paleness on the face of a performer required close viewing in a small to medium sized theatre.

Bharata, therefore, describes the construction of a medium rectangular playhouse in detail. Small square theatre and triangular theatres are described by him in generalities. Significantly, he has not given any details of larger theatre varieties.

Description of Playhouses in the Context of Their Construction

Bharata describes the playhouses according to stages of their construction. He adopts the ancient Indian architectural maxim of providing comparative description of buildings to suit the construction of other similar structures.[17] Accordingly, he describes the stage proper in details in terms of construction of medium rectangular playhouses while providing details of the seating arrangement and erection of pillars and walls of the auditorium in terms of their construction in small square playhouses. His description of the selection of site, the measuring of ground plan, laying of foundation, raising of pillars and the decorative aspects are common for all the three playhouses.

The Selection of Site and the Measuring of Ground Plan

This was done according to strict rules of the ancient Indian building art. After selection of suitable site by an expert builder, the ground was to be cleaned, levelled, consecrated and demarcated with exact measurements by an appropriate measuring string, into a number of shapes and sizes such as a rectangle, a square or a triangle.

Such a sanctified ground (*bhūmi*) was then to be divided proportionately into similarly shaped and consecrated smaller areas (*maṅḍala*-s) each with a special presiding deity (*vāstudevatā*). The central shape or a central group of specific number of shapes was presided over by Lord Brahmā and was considered the most auspicious area of the building site. This diagramatic dimension of the ground plan was coterminus with the concept of a specially sanctified area of the cosmic being of the building (*vāstu puruṣa maṅḍala*). The cosmic being (*vāstu puruṣa*) was thought of as lying prostrate on the building site with different presiding deities occupying various parts of his body. These parts with their special deities made different sections of the building and the whole constituted its entire structural design. Ancient buildings were constructed on such a scheme of space division of various consecrated areas.[18] And Bharata's playhouses were to be erected in this pattern.

Medium Rectangular Playhouse of Bharata—Details of its Construction

A properly selected and consecrated piece of land with a plain, firm and hard soil, cleared and levelled with a plough, was to be measured to form a rectangular boundary of E-W 96′ × N-S 48′ (64 H × 32 H). This boundary was again to be divided breadthwise into two equal parts forming two square areas of 48′ × 48′ (32 H × 32 H). The square on the western side was the performance block, and that on the eastern side was allocated for the auditorium. This is shown in the sketch No. 3 on page p. 47.

The Performance Block

The performance block of 48′ × 48′ was to be further divided into two equal rectangular blocks of 24′ × 48′ each. The rear rectangle was allocated to the dressing room and the front one to

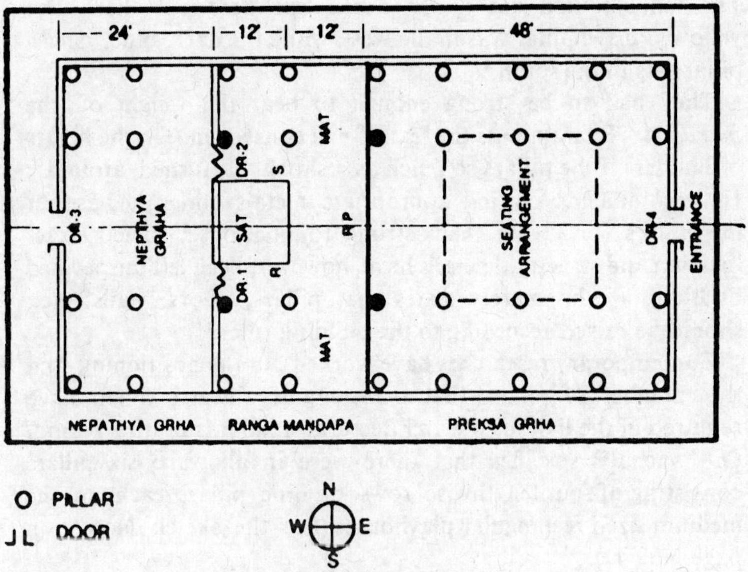

Sketch No. 3.
Medium Sized Rectangular Theatre.

the stage proper. The foundation was supposed to be done with proper ritual ceremonies at every stage of construction.[19]

Walls

After the foundation, the walls were to be built. The outer walls were constructed with well-burnt bricks very thickly set together.[20] The walls were then plastered, white washed and decorated with mural paintings depicting dance movements of men and women in amorous poses.[21]

Pillars

The importance of pillars inside the playhouse is demonstrated by the rituals attached to their erection. They were to be raised on appropriate foundation by the master of the dramatic art and the expert builder with accompanying auspicious music and chanting of *mantra*-s.

Four main pillars are mentioned here. They were wooden pillars representing four main caste groups of people of ancient India. A white pillar in the east was called the Brahmin pillar.

The red coloured one in the north was *Kṣatriya* pillar. The yellow, *Vaiśya* pillar was in the west, while the dark blue, *Śūdra* pillar was in the south.[22]

They had to be strong enough to bear the weight of the *maṇḍapa*. Bharata puts the fear of evil consequence in the hearts of builders if the pillars so much as "shock or turned around". He recommends putting appropriate metals under the bases of the pillars for giving them strong foundations.[23] Their exact location and structural details have, however, been left unspecified by Bharata who merely states that pillars, doors, walls, etc., should be raised according to the building rules.[24]

Contemporary researches have worked out the positioning and the number of pillars that a rectangular theatre might have required in the light of the architectural standards of the period. G. Panchal[25] specifies that there were in all thirty-six pillars consisting of four lengthwise rows of nine pillars each, in the medium sized rectangular playhouses (See the sketch No. 3 on page No. 47).

Out of these, two rows of half-pillars touched the insides of the walls of the theatre lengthwise. They were at equal distance from each other. The other two rows of pillars were placed opposite them, forming a corridor or an aisle of 12′ on either sides of the playhouse. A central vacant space of 24′ × 24′ therefore automatically provided seating space in the middle of the auditorium without any obstruction in viewing. The architecturally formed aisles on the sides might have facilitated the movements of the spectators also.

The pillars formed the parts of the stage area also. The stage proper had twelve pillars in all with four lengthwise rows of three pillars each on either side of the stage. Of these, two rows of half pillars touched the stage edge of walls at the extreme north and south sides. The inside two rows of three pillars each were at a distance of 12′ from the former. This arrangement provided a central rectangle as the main performance area in the middle of the stage with two corridor like structures formed by pillars on either side. (See sketch No. 3 on page No. 47.)

Roof or Roofs

The existence of so many pillars in the playhouse gives a definite indication that some sort of a roof was supported by them.

Although Bharata has not made any direct reference to the construction of a roof, or its size or proportion, he has nevertheless specified that a playhouse should resemble a cave[26] and the pillars in it should be strong enough to support the *maṇḍapa*[27] or the roof. He has, time and again, underlined the importance of maintaining proper acoustics[28] in the 'cave-like' theatre building.

A sloping vaulted roof supported by pillars and low walls, in all probability, gave the playhouse an appearance of a subterranean chamber or a cave. In addition to enhancing the tonal quality of the sound within, such a curving roof might also have given an impression of expansion and enlargement to the structure without disturbing the feeling of close intimacy between different working spaces. The cool and dark atmosphere that such an interior eminated has been described by Bharata.

Over and above this roof, another separate canopy like structure covered the stage area in the playhouse. This is more than certain because the design of a *raṅgamaṇḍapa* itself implies a roof. Besides maintaining the tonal quality of the performance, this roof also provided an ornate, colourful focal point in the playhouse.

In the absence of specific details, it is reasonable to suppose that their exterior facade were designed to suit different regional architectural fashions of the period around 200 B.C.-200 A.D.

Doors

Bharata makes categorical reference to two doors[29] on a wall which separated the dressing room from the stage proper. The actors made their entries and exists through them. (Doors 1 and 2 in the sketch on page No. 47). He also suggests one more door for the audience to come into the theatre. (Door 4 in the sketch).[30]

Abhinavagupta mentions another door for the actors and their families to enter into the dressing room from outside (door 3 in the sketch).[31]

It is more than likely that there were at least four doors in the playhouse. The ancient Indian works on architecture corroborate to the scheme of ancient buildings having four doors, one on each side of the building. They also suggest that there could be even four more doors in each corner of a building.[32]

Windows and Ventilators

Being mainly concerned with the performance, Bharata, time and again, emphasised the importance of proper acoustics in the playhouse. He forewarned the builders and the carpenters not to construct any pillars, pegs, windows or a door exactly facing an opening. He maintained that the windows should be small, placed high on the wall, to prevent cross ventilation. This was to ensure the acoustical quality of the playhouse.

We get a general description of three types of windows such as:

(i) Variously placed small latticed or intricately banded windows at a higher point in the walls.

(ii) Interior windows.[33]

(iii) Latticed ventilation in the theatre walls for the playhouse to be airy and yet sheltered and cave-like.[34]

It is quite possible that a highly placed larger window in the shape of cow's eyes (*gavākṣa*) on the eastern wall, also provided a lighting source for the day time performance. This is just a conjecture. But a conjecture based on the evidence of the usage of such windows in Buddhist cave temples where a sunlight beam passing through such a window falls straight on the stupa or the Buddha idol.

Auditorium

The auditorium was allocated half the area of the entire playhouse. Bharata gives a general idea of the auditorium in the square block of 48′ × 48′ on the eastern side of the medium rectangular playhouse. He does not indicate any special seating arrangement for the spectators, but gives details of tiered seats 'in the form of a staircase' in his description of the small square playhouse. Bharata says:

> "Thus between the pillars, seats are to be constructed in the form of a staircase by means of bricks and wood for the accommodation of spectators. Successive rows of seats should be made 1 *hasta* (1½′) higher than those preceding them. The lowest row of seats being 1 *hasta* higher than the floor."[35]

This type of seating arrangement would accommodate a larger number of spectators.[36] The audience could be seated all along the three sides of the stage in the square playhouse with facility for good viewing without hindrance. In the rectangular playhouse, however, the audience-performers juxtaposition might have been frontal.

Sāraṅgadeva in his *Sangīta Ratnākara*[37] describes another seating pattern for spectators in a royal theatre. He describes two levels of seating arrangement in a palace auditorium with the seat of the king on a high platform and members of his assembly sitting around him in precisely indicated positions. Most of the literary sources make special reference to the valuable throne on a decorated platform in a central high place on which the chief patron sat. This type of two-levelled arrangement can explain the concept of two levels or *dvibhūmi* in the auditorium. Bharata has vaguely implied this when he said that a "*nāṭyamaṇḍapa* should have two levels (*dvibhūmi*)".[38]

There is another possibility that the spectators just squatted or stood on the polished floor of the auditorium—as is the custom in the present day temple theatres in Kerala.

The seating arrangements thus varied according to the elaboration that different patrons belonging to various strata could afford. It is even possible that only royal palaces and other affluent patrons could afford to own the highly elaborate playhouses as described by Bharata. Common folk might have watched a performance squatting or standing around a simply constructed auditorium.

The Performance Block

This was to be constructed on the square space of 48′ × 48′ on the western side of the theatre stretching from wall to wall. Several divisions were formed on it structurally by four rows of pillars appearing lengthwise on the stage. This block was also divided into two equal rectangular sections of 24′ × 48′ by a stage wall, with two doors.

The Dressing Room—Nepathyagṛha

Bharata's instructions about the construction of the dressing room is very vague. He says "like the pillars, doors and walls, the dressing room should be built as per the rules of the building art."[39]

However, from sources other than *Nāṭyaśāstra* one gathers

that the dressing room was constructed on the extreme western edge of 24′ × 24′ rectangular space of the playhouse. Two doors (Dr. 1 and Dr. 2 in the sketch on page 47) on the back wall of the stage joined it to the stage proper. The stage wall might have been made of wood, built with bricks or just a plain cloth partition.

The actors did their make-up and rested between the entries in the dressing room. Occasionally noises off the stage, specially the divine voices (*divya vāṇi*) and the crowd noises (*hāhākāra*), were produced from there. It was also a storage place for costumes, properties and the musical instruments.[40] The first nine rituals of the preliminary ceremonies were also executed from here.

Bharata indicates that the dressing room had smooth, levelled floor filled with black clay. There is no mention of any kind of windows or separate enclosures for males and females in dressing room, but Abhinavagupta suggests a door on the extreme western wall of the playhouse for exclusive entry of the actor and his family in the dressing room.

It is significant that the dressing room area was assigned one-fourth space of the entire playhouse.

The Stage Proper—Raṅgamaṇḍapa
The Acting Area

The front rectangular area of 24′ × 48′ formed the performance block. It faced the auditorium in the east. The entire area was on a raised level of a plinth of 27″ (1½ *hasta*) high and was allocated one-fourth space of the playhouse. It was divided into a number of stage divisions which were known by specific names such as:

1. The main acting area : *Raṅgapīṭha* (RP)
2. The subsidiary areas : *Mattavāraṇī*-s (MAT-s)
3. The subsidiary acting areas : *Raṅgaśīrṣa* (RS)
4. The ornate structure formed by six wooden planks—a part of *Raṅgaśīrṣa*. : *Ṣaṭdāruka* (SAT)

(See the sketch on page no. 47)

(For the sake of convenience, the above abbreviations are used in this chapter.)

Bharata's text is very vague regarding the purpose, locations and dimensions of the above-mentioned areas. In the absence of an original model of Bharata's playhouse and because of probable disappearance of certain features of the stage for want of usability, one finds that even the earliest commentators on *Nāṭyaśāstra* have offered only conjectural interpretations regarding them. In reviewing these areas, various views have been considered and certain observations are offered in the following paragraphs with an aim to gain a clearer idea of the above terms as parts of the stage proper in the light of their specific usages during a performance. These areas are, at the same time, examined from a fresh perspective based on the principles of the building art in Bharata's period.

The Main Acting Area—Raṅgapīṭha (RP)

As shown in the sketch on page no. 47 this was the extreme downstage central front, rectangular area of 12′ × 24′ formed by horizontal division of the rectangular block of the stage proper (24′ × 48′). It faced the spectators sitting in the eastern block. The term 'pīṭha' itself suggests a plinth and RP had a height of 27″.

The main action of the Sanskrit play was mainly performed in this area. If the stage proper was divided horizontally into two strips of interior and exterior zones as per the *nāṭyadharmī abhinaya* of zonal division, RP would constitute the exterior zone.[41] The beginning prayer, the end-benediction and the main performance mostly took place in this section.

In the scheme of *vāstu puruṣa maṇḍala* where each diagramatic space of a building was fixed, placed, consecrated and named according to the parts and limbs of the body of the cosmic being the most auspicious smaller rectangular space of *Brahmā maṇḍala* would be in RP's extreme downstage centre.

The Subsidiary Acting Area—Raṅgaśīrṣā (RS)

As far as RS is concerned, there has been a divergence of opinion in regard to its dimension, position, usage, relationship to RP and SAT, because of ambiguity in the use of this term by Bharata. RS and RP have been used in place of each other in different editions of the *Nāṭyaśāstra*.

Abhinavagupta has explained the location and reasoning for

the name of RS (and in that context RP and SAT also) by referring to the scheme of the *vāstu puruṣa maṇḍala*, by visualising the entire playhouse structure in the form of the cosmic being lying on his back. He suggests that RS was the area where the cosmic being's head might be and RP was at a place where his back (*pīṭha*) might be placed.[42] The ornate SAT in the RS centre as a decorated head of the cosmic man can then be visualised.

The majority of scholars are also in agreement with Abhinavagupta's suggestion that RS region covered the interior rectangle or the upstage area of the stage proper which was either 48′ × 12′ or 24′ × 12′.[43] This part of the stage was connected at the back with the dressing room by two doors on extreme right and left edges of the stage wall. A wooden ornamental structure—SAT—of 12′ × 24′ was constructed on the RS between these two doors of the stage wall and the musical orchestra (*kutapa*) sat there during a performance. There might have been an elevation of this area. The 12′ × 12′ portions of RS, on either side of the musical orchestra, were used for entrances and exits of the characters. A character before and between his entries might have as well hidden behind an ornate pillar in this area of the stage instead of going back to the dressing room.[44]

RS certainly was a supplementary acting area. The voices from the backstage (noises off) at times came from the musical orchestra itself. Certain scenes depicting an interior of a mansion were enacted in the front portion of this slightly elevated area.

RS, in this way, formed the extreme upstage area of stage proper, of either 24′ × 12′ or 48′ × 12′ dimensions. It was connected with the dressing room by the two doors of the stage partition. The place for *kutapa* was reserved between these doors. The decorative structure of SAT also formed a part of its central region.

Ṣaṭdāruka (SAT)

This was a very ornamental structure, made of six wooden planks or pilasters in the central space of RS in between the two doors of the stage wall. Its function was to provide decoration for the stage area as well as to demarcate the musicians from the action of the drama proper. Occasionally its front part was also used as the interior zone in a play performance.

Bharata describes the decorative embellishments of this

structure in some details. He says that "It should be smooth and even like a mirror. It must not be convex, like the back of a tortoise or that of a fish"[45] but its woodwork should have many ornate and decorative carvings and structural embellishments. Many conjectural designs of SAT have been offered by various scholars. A theory has also been postulated that Bharata may have been describing the ornate roof of a canopy like structure formed by six wooden planks in the upstage area, similar in appearance to the base of the *kirita* complex of the later day temple architecture. Due to the paucity of records, we can be only certain of SAT's ornamental appearance and its location in the centre of the RS.

It seems more than likely that RP, RS and SAT were different performance areas of the same stage proper. It is quite possible to conjecture that they might have constituted the practical stage jargon or technical terminologies specifying different areas of the stage for the facility of the performers and architects in or before Bharata's time. Dr. M. Ghosh says in this connection that Bharata himself never made a distinction between these areas of the stage. When he described the separate presiding deities of the stage areas, only RP is mentioned—never the RS.[46] This is a significant point which corroborates with the surmise that the RP, RS and SAT were different intersections of the same stage proper.

Mattavaraṇī-s (MAT-s)

Mattavāraṇī-s are the areas of the stage which have remained unexplained despite a number of conjectures about them. Time and again, they have sparked off controversies involving distinguished scholars and theatre workers. Apparently, their practical usage in the stages or their nomenclature had ceased to provide any meaning by the time of Abhinavagupta, because, even in his commentary there are only a number of conjectures and inferences regarding their name, location and purpose in the ancient playhouses.

And, Bharata's remarks about them are really enigmatic. He refers to MAT-s in the following few lines:

"On each side of stage should be built the MAT-s and they should be furnished with four pillars, and they should be of equal length to the stage, and the plinth should be cubit and a half high (i.e. 27 inches)....The plinth of the stage proper should be equal in height as that of the two MAT-s."[47]

These are the only references to MAT-s made by Bharata in his description of medium rectangular playhouse.

What is the meaning of the term and what was the use to which the areas were put to in Bharata's playhouses? Bharata is silent on these points.

The word *mattavāraṇī* does not occur in any Sanskrit dictionary. A dictionary of Hindu Architecture by P.K. Acharya also does not explain the term. There is a word *Mattavāraṇa*, meaning "a turret or a small room on the top of a large building, a verandah, or a pavilion".[48] It has been suggested that it is a Prakrit word, a *deśī* term of *vāstuśāstra*, which has been later adopted in Sanskrit and that it means an architectural projection of a house, balcony or verandah—*kathedā* in Gujarati where one can sit.[49]

Without any positive evidence, apart from the above stray facts, only certain general conjectures can be made about the possible meaning, placement and the relationship of MAT-s with the other areas in the stage proper.

The Meaning

The architectural meaning suggests a balcony or a verandah like structure in the playhouse.

The Location

As indicated by Bharata himself, they were either 12′ × 12′ or 12′ × 24′ pavilions on both sides of the stage made by four gaily decorated pillars.

Their Use in Bharata's Stages/Playhouses

(i) The presence of such corridors or squares on either side of the stage formed by pillars would certainly provide interesting possibilities for the *nāṭyadharmī* stage technique of the zonal divisions. Actual physical divisions formed by the pillars would supply ample visual and psychological acceptance of separate zones on the same bare stage. Contemporary producers of Sanskrit plays have experimented with such

MAT-s in the shape of corridors or square pavilions on either side of the stage to indicate separate acting zones of stage.

In the present day, *svāṅg*, a folk theatre of north India, two structures, supported by four wooden pillars can be seen outside the entire stage block on either sides of the performance block. These structures are used for performance also. Some particular noises off the stage and speeches are made and certain special scenes are enacted in these structures.

It is interesting to note that the stage structure of the Noh theatre of Japan exhibits an uncanny resemblance to Bharata's square stage. In the former, there is a wooden passage, named *hashigakari* which connects the stage with the curtained door of the make-up room from where the main actor makes his entry. This passage becomes an important acting area right from the entrance of the actor. Scenes suggestive of bifocal and tri-focal zonal treatment of the Sanskrit theatre take place on this passage. This is something which is very similar to the corridor like structures of Bharata's MAT-s.

(ii) When the MAT-s are viewed as balcony or verandah like structures on the stage or in the theatre building one can well imagine their use for the seating of important spectators. Abhinavagupta suggests such a possibility.

In Kerala for instance, the chief patron like Zamorin of Calicut, had a seat in the gaily decorated balcony like side area of the stage itself. Even today, in the Kuttambalam temple theatre of Kerala, narrow strips, on either sides of the stage, are used as seating accommodations for special people among the audience. We have a literary evidence of theatres with special balconies for courtesans and ladies in *Harivaṃśa Purāṇa*.[50] In the absence of positive records one cannot be more specific than this regarding the usages of MAT-s in Bharata's playhouses. We can only surmise that they were:

(a) Two pavilion like square areas of 12′ × 12′ demarcated by four gaily ornate pillars on either sides of RP.
(b) It is possible that they were supplementary acting areas.
(c) They might have been used as sitting accommodation for special spectators also.

(d) It is quite possible that in the course of further development, MAT-s were superseded by newer arrangements in the playhouses and became obsolete. And only the term 'MAT-s' was still preserved by the *Śāstra*-s as a fossil.

(e) Contemporary producers of Sanskrit dramas have nevertheless utilised the two MAT-s as acting areas either in the form of two corridors or small pavilions on either side of the stage for *nāṭyadharmī* zonal divisions.

The Decorative Aspects of the Playhouses

The decorative aspects of the entire theatre building as well as the stage proper,—especially the SAT area are indicated by Bharata in his references to the woodwork and the mural paintings on the walls.

The Woodwork

The woodwork of the playhouses are intricate and highly polished. It covered the pillars, pilasters and ceilings of the stage proper, the SAT and the auditorium. Upper and lower portions of the wooden pillars were carved with decorative designs. Upper mouldings of the pillars were properly fastened with the roof. This part was carved with fillet like woodwork forming devecotes and wooden statues. A *śālabhañjikā* or *śālastrī* (a woman with the tree) motif has been mentioned in this context in the description of the small, square playhouse by Bharata. The upper parts of the pillars were connected by ornamental arches marked with leographs, cross-circles, projections and quadrangles in the ceiling by wooden joinery. Intricately designed, latticed, banded high windows shaped like cow's eyes formed parts of the woodwork design. Well moulded columns adorned the rows of pillars making aisles or pavements in the auditorium. The pedestals and railings on the stage and in the auditorium were constructed with richly carved woodwork.[51] So was the decorative SAT on the RS. The walls of playhouses were well-plastered, carefully white washed and painted with colourful murals. Such decorative, fillet-like woodwork and gaily coloured painted walls, polished floors with mirror-finish and the pillars adorned with festoons, flowers, garlands, perfumes and incense corroborate with the description of the ornamental playhouses gathered from other literary sources also.

The Functional Use of the Decorative Rows of Pillars on the Stage

In addition to supporting the stage roof, the decorative rows of pillars gave an ornamental and colourful appearance to the stage. They provided natural separation to the stage areas also. Such an arrangement aided the *nāṭyadharmī* zonal division, the tonal quality of the performance and the resonance and timbre of musical accompaniment. On many occasions, lamps were hung on these pillars for lighting the stage. The pillars themselves became part of the suggestive *nāṭyadharmī* settings during many a play performance.

Sketch of Small Square Playhouse

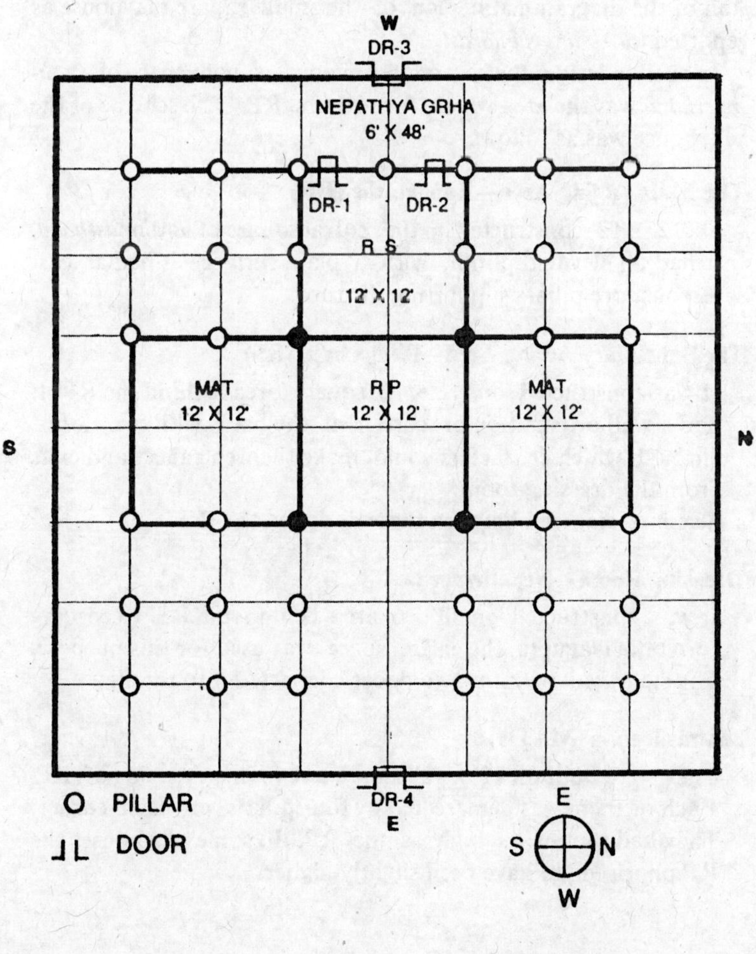

The Description of the Small Square Playhouse

A small square playhouse measured 48′ × 48′ (32 H × 32 H).

After proper selection, levelling and ritual consecration of the ground, the building site of 48′ × 48′ was demarcated lengthwise and breadthwise by eight equal straight lines which divided the entire area by 8′ × 8′ forming 64 squares–like a chessboard. The central space made up of four equal squares was the *maṇḍala* of Lord Brahmā.

Such a schematic area division of the building site was executed according to the rules of ancient Indian building art. This is substantiated by the information available in *Bṛhatsaṃhitā* of Varāhamihira (6th century A.D.) and Śri Śaṅkuka's interpretation of the diagrammatic plan of the small square playhouse as reported in *Abhinavabhāratī*.

In such a design, the central, auspicious, square space of *Brahmasthāna* was the area which formed the RP. The scheme of the playhouse was as follows:

The Main Acting Area—Raṅgapīṭha (RP)

Of 12′ × 12′ constructed on the central square of *Brahmasthāna*, it had an elevated plinth, with a plain surface. It had at least ten or more pillars supporting the roof.

The Subsidiary Acting Area—Raṅgaśīrṣa (RS)

It was constructed on 12′ × 12′ square area behind the RP. It had a wall or partition or curtain at the back with two doors, through which characters could make their entrances and exits from the dressing room.

The musicians sat between these doors on the RS.

Dressing Room—Nepathyagṛha

It was constructed on 48′ × 6′ area behind the RS. According to Abhinavagupta, the entire space was used for this purpose. The stage wall with the two doors connected it to the stage.

Mattavāraṇī-s (MAT-s)

They were built on 12′ × 12′ square area on either side of RP. Each of them was demarcated by four pillars on each corner. They had plinths as high as the RP. In some playhouses the RP plinth might have been slightly higher.

Auditorium—Prekṣā

Auditorium had tiered seating arrangement constructed with brick and wood, rising 1½′ (1 H) higher than the levelled surface of each preceding row covering three open sides of the RP. Firm walls of burnt bricks were built on the foundations. Several pillars were raised to support the roof. However, it is not very clear whether the auditorium was also covered by a roof or not. Bharata has, however, explicitly described ornately decorated pillars supporting the roof of the *raṅgamaṇḍapa.*[52]

The Description of the Triangular Playhouse—Trayasra

Bharata's remarks regarding the triangular playhouse are minimal. He specifies that the playhouse had a triangular shape, with a triangular RP in the middle, RS and the dressing room were also of triangular shape. Two doors have been mentioned. One in the western corner of the playhouse and the other at the back of the stage for the characters to enter from the dressing room on the stage. Abhinavagupta suggests that one more door on the eastern side of the triangle was there for the audience to enter the auditorium.[53]

Bharata has laid down that the playhouse was to be built by adhering strictly to the rules of building art for construction of triangular buildings. This helps us to visualise the scheme of such a playhouse and attempt to conjecture a possible design.

By forming a boundary of an equilateral triangle and dividing it again into eight equidistant sides, sixty four triangles could be formed by drawing lines from each dividing point, parallel to the corresponding sides. See the sketch on the page no. 62.

1. RP might have been constructed on the triangular area made of four triangles with its extreme down stage centre falling on the *brahmasthāna*.
2. RS could be visualised as placed behind the RP in either one or three triangles.
3. Dressing room would be behind the RS in one triangle.
4. Although Bharata does not mention any MAT-s, two MAT-s can be visualised on both sides of the RP, formed by three triangles each.
5. The audience might sit on the remaining three open sides.

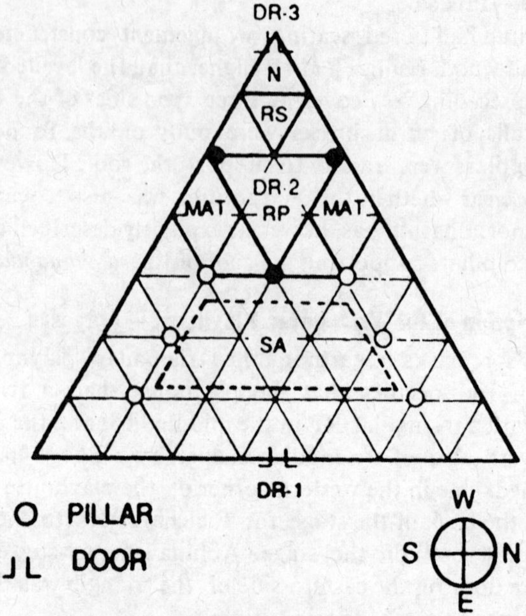

Sketch of Triangular Playhouse.

The Appearance of Bharata's Playhouses

How did these ancient playhouses look like? Bharata does not give us a clue.

Nevertheless, one remarkable fact that emerges from the above examination is that through long centuries of development and elaboration, ancient Indian playhouses appear to have retained an element of continuity in one particular aspect. They have remained enclosed structures essentially meant to aid and sustain the atmosphere of identification between the spectator and the performer. The stages were open and bare where the performer was the top man. The spectators were positioned in such a way that they could participate with the happenings on the stage totally.

For this purpose, the playhouses were enclosed buildings with a cave-like sloping roof, small high windows and cool, dark interiors conducive of dream-like visual experience of heightened consciousness. Their comparative smallness and compactness aided the sensory contact between the audience and the performance.

In this basic characteristic they contrast with other theatre buildings. For example, they were:

Distinct from Ancient Greek Amphitheatres

Ancient Indian playhouses differed in construction and atmosphere from ancient Greek amphitheatres in size, structure and in spectator-performer juxtaposition.

The latter were huge, open air theatres carved out of hills, accommodating about 20,000 to 30,000 people.[64] As against this, Indian playhouses as described by Bharata were small theatre buildings catering to not more than 400 spectators belonging to a particular segment of society. The medium-sized playhouse, which alone was preferred by Bharata for a play production, was only 96′ in length and 48′ in breadth.

In the large, spacious, open-air Greek amphitheatres the round orchestra circle with the *skēnē* stage behind, distanced the performer considerably from the farthest seats on the hill slope. In order to reach his audience, the Greek actor needed to amplify his performance with the aid of the masks, heightened stances and the declamatory speech. As against this, the stage-auditorium positioning in the ancient Indian playhouse provided maximum closeness and rapport between the performer and the spectator. The most minute and almost imperceptible variations of body movements, facial expressions and *sāttvika bhāva*-s like tears, sweat, etc. could easily be observed and understood by the spectators because of this.

Distinct from Present Day Theatre Buildings

In this essential characteristic of intimacy and the use of spaces, Bharata's playhouses differ from most of the west-oriented present day theatre buildings also. Unlike the latter, there were no 'picture behind the proscenium' frames with arches or a drop curtain or the side wings separating the spectator from the performer. Nor were there any settings or many artifices on the ancient stages to divert the spectator's attention from the actor.

Ancient stages were bare, open and pillared structures. The actor, mostly retaining his frontal position, created the settings and the scene transfers by the power of his suggestive *abhinaya*. This was easily communicated to the spectator who surrounded him and observed the performance by sitting closely on three open sides of the stage.

Distinctive Structures for Siddhi

The most striking features of the ancient Indian playhouses was that they were buildings specially designed to provide an atmosphere where a spectator could achieve a mind expanding experience through a close intimate rapport with the performer. The playhouses consistently remained powerful channels through which the instinctive and deeply rooted style of enactment operated. This can be clearly seen when their structural design is viewed in the comparative light of the arrangements of the ancient magicoritualistic sacrificial pavilions and the Buddhist cave temples around 200 B.C.-200 A.D. Let us briefly examine their similarities.

Arrangements of Sacrificial Pavilions and the Ancient Playhouses

(a) Both structures had the three basic shapes, viz., the square, the rectangular and triangular.

(b) The large Vedic altar and the *raṅgapīṭha* with the plinth were both enclosed sheltered places for the safety and success of the sacrifice or the performance.

(c) Both were consecrated spaces with the *Brahmamaṇḍala* forming the most auspicious area. Other presiding deities were also given honoured places on the stage. (Major part of pre-performance preliminaries—*pūrvaraṅga*—is devoted to the ritual consecration of stage deities.)

(d) The sacred sacrificial pavilion was protected by a flagstaff. Similarly Indra's banner staff (*jarjara*) was placed at a strategic position before a *nāṭya* performance began.

(e) The central place was given to the sacrificer or the chief patron in the viewer's area because the ritual or the performance was for his benefit. The same was the case in the ancient Indian playhouses. This is because the total identification between the priest-performer and the sacrificer-patron alone ensured success of the *yajña* or the *nāṭya yajña*.

Audience Performance Juxtaposition in Various Theatres.

1

Palace performance depicted in Amaravati medalion 2nd century A.D.

2

Theatres of Epidarous Greece, with full round dancing circle [from Sheldon C, op. cit. pl. 4]

3

Ajanta Cave—No. 1 —5th century A.D.

Audience Performance Juxtaposition in Various Theatres.

4

Italian architectural perspective setting with ornate proscenium frame [From sheldon C, op. cit. pl. 25, 304b] Adopted by Parsi Theatre in India.

5

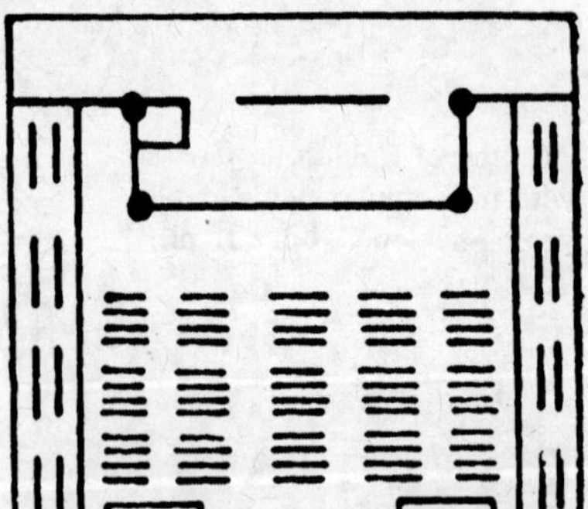

Chinese Opera Theatre in Shanghai with four pillared open stage and audience surrounding it.

6

Japanese Noh Stage with three open sides surrounded by spectator's seats. [Reconstructed at Bhabha auditorium, Bombay].

The Arrangement in Buddhist Cave Temples and in Bharata's Playhouses

(a) Both shared a cave-like shape and atmosphere.

(b) The halls of the Buddhist temples, as can be seen in the Karla and Bhaja caves, are vaulted rectangular halls hewn out of rocks and with an apsidal end where the *stūpa* is placed. Bharata's playhouse had RP at that focal point.

(c) Buddhist temple-halls are divided lengthwise by four rows of pillars forming two aisles on extreme north-south sides. A broad nave is thus formed in between the middle areas. The pillar position of Bharata's playhouse was possibly similar. The pillars in the playhouse also formed a central area for the audience to sit with the two extreme lengthwise corridors on either side.

(d) Buddhist halls in their construction were designed for providing perfect acoustic convenience for chanting. Bharata's playhouse also required structures providing perfect resonance of voice.

(e) Buddhist halls have a window shaped like a cow's eye high in the entrance wall. It functions as the main source of light. Bharata mentions such windows and probably they were used for similar purposes.

These structures were constructed according to the similar traditions of cosmographical ground plans with an aim to provide maximum concentration with the audio-visual rites or performance.

It is from such traditions that the distinctive design of the ancient Indian playhouse—*raṅga*—emerged giving a meaning and continuity to close identification between the performer and the spectator for success of a production. The special structure of their pillared stages generated many performing practices of *abhinaya* as a consequence. *Raṅga*, from this point of view, forms one of the essential components of ancient Indian play production.

NOTES

1. A 5th Century A.D. Gupta relief in Gwalior museum depicts an open-air performance of the *Yajña* ceremony of king Bali.
2. NS. I, 66-80 (Kashi ed.).

3. Brown Percy, *Indian Architecture* (Buddhist and Hindu periods), p. 3.
4. *Mahābhārata, Āraṇyaka Parvan*, 21–26. This kind of cleared, encircled, demarcated and consecrated area is to be seen in the present day Bhavai, a folk theatre in Gujarat where the boundary is called Paudha.
5. Acharya P. K., *Hindu Architecture*, India and Abroad Māṇasāra Series Vol. VI, Chap. 34, Maṇḍapa Vidhāna, p. 119.
6. Brown Percy, op. cit., p. 50.
7. Ghurye G. S., *Bharata Nātya and its Costume*, p. 29.
8. From Havel K. B., *Ancient and Mediaeval Architecture of India*, Pt. IV, p. 24.
9. NS. II.
10. The builders and architects were *sūtradhāra*-s and *sthapati-s*. *Sthapati* was a master builder, son of Viśvakarmā, knower of all Śāstra-s, and *ācārya*. *Sūtradhāra* was a draftsman, son of Maya, holder of the sūtra. This hints at a possible origin of *sthapati* as an āryan, Viśvakarmā's son and *sūtradhāra* as a non-āryan—Maya's son. Four types of artisans connected with the building art are mentioned in the ancient texts. They are *sthapati*—the chief architect, *sūtragrahi* or *sūtradhāra*—the draftsman; *vardhaki*, the painter and *takṣaka*, the jointer.
11. NS. II.5.
12. The literary sources are: Harivaṃśa, Rāja praśniya Āgama, Śilāpaḍḍikaram, Mayamatam, Viśvakarmā's Vāstuśāstra, Śilpa Ratna of Śrikumāra, Bhāsa's Pratimā nātaka, Vdh. P., Māṇasāra, Sangita Makaranda, S.R., Bh. P., Pre-and post-Bharata sources (up to 16th Century A.D.) are included because although compiled at a later date, they report practices of much earlier times.
13. NS. II.9.

    Bharata has given the measurements at some places in *Hasta*-s, at other places in *Daṇḍa*-s. He also gives the details of ancient units of measurements:

8 atoms	=	1 particle (*raja*)
8 particles	=	1 hair end (*vāla*)
8 hair ends	=	1 knit (*likṣā*)
8 knits	=	1 lice (*yukā*)
8 lices	=	1 barley (*yara*)
8 barlies	=	1 finger (*aṅgula*)
8 fingers	=	1 cubit (*hasta*)
4 cubits	=	1 staff (*daṇḍa*)
8 staffs	=	1 string (*raju*)

    Traditional measurement was an *aṅgula* which was equal to 17.86 mm. V dh P mentions that roughly twelve *aṅgula* make one *Tāla*.
14. Abh. II on 11–16, L 6 to 15.
15. NS. II.21-23 (Kashi ed.).
16. Kerala Kalamanḍalam brochure on *nāṭyagṛha*, p. 4.
17. Abh. II.95–106, L 1.
18. Stella Kramrisch—The Hindu Temple, Chapters 2 and 3, Bṛhat Saṃhitā of Varāhamihira—Ed. J.H. Athale (Marathi), Ratnagiri, 1974.
19. NS. II.24.

20. Ibid 90.
21. Ibid 85-86.
22. Ibid 45–56.
23. Ibid 50–57.
24. Ibid 63-54.
25. Panchal G., Kuttambalam and its link with Bharata's stages, INCPA, Vol. VI, March 1977, p. 30 cff. I have also consulted in this reference an unpublished article 'A note on the construction of the rectangular theatre described in NS' by Smt. Shanta Gandhi, whose model of Bharata's medium rectangular theatre is in Browder Mathews Museum of theatre arts at Columbia University, New York, U.S.A.
26. NS. II.81.
27. Ibid 91-95.
28. Ibid 81 (Dhira Śabda).
29. Ibid 95–100.
30. Ibid 98.
31. Abh. Vol. I, II, 95–106, L 57-58.
32. Acharya P. K. op. cit. Chapter 38 on *Dvāra Sthāna*.
33. NS II.78.
34. Ibid 81-82.
35. Ibid 86–92.
36. Mankad D.R., Ancient Indian Theatre (1960), p. 11 thinks that an auditorium would accommodate 500–600 spectators. Contemporary researchers like G. Panchal postulate that the seating space of 24′×24′ can only accommodate 250–300 spectators. Guttila Jātaka describes an open-air theatre with tier upon tier seating arrangement for a performance in a royal courtyard. It mentions its construction also, thereby indicating its temporary structure.
37. SR. Chapter VII, 1351–1361.
38. NS. II.81-82.

    The term "dvibhūmi" meaning two-levelled arrangement has aroused many controversies among present day researchers. Although there is insufficient indication in the chapter, the possibility of two storied playhouses or stages cannot be ruled out in this connection. The building art of ancient India was sufficiently advanced to have had multi-storied buildings. Such structure would then explain (1) the performance of multifocal scenes in Sanskrit plays (2) placement and usage of MATs and (3) decorative SAT area with ornate woodwork on the pilasters.
39. NS. 60–63 (tr. M. Ghosh).
40. Bhāsa: *Pratimā-nāṭaka*, Act I.
41. NS. XIV 8 (Kashi ed.).
42. Abh. Vol. I, Chapter II, 37–39, L-5 onwards.
43. Ibid L-6.
44. Ibid 73-75, L-11.
45. NS. II.72-74 (tr. M. Ghosh).
46. Ghosh M., The Hindu Theatre, IQH Vol. IX, Calcutta, 1933, pp. 391–594, p. 446.

47. NS. 63-65 (tr. M. Ghosh).
48. Sandesara B.J. and Shah U.P. *Parimāṇa Mañjarī* (in Gujarati) JOI, Vol. X., No. 4, June 1961, p. 62.
49. Ibid.
50. Harivaṃśa, Viṣṇu Parvan, A-29.
51. The meaning of the structural decorative terms have been taken from "A dictionary of Hindu Architecture" by P.K. Acharya, "A Sanskrit-English Dictionary" by Monier Williams and "The Students Sanskrit-English Dictionary" by V.S. Apte.
52. NS. II.92–95 (M. Ghosh).
53. Abh. Vol. I, Chapter II, 107–110.
54. Mankad D.R., Loc. cit., p. 11.

PART TWO

THE PLAY-TEXT

'A play is simply a collection of rasas. . . .
What is an actor, then?
He is just an instrument or a receptacle
(pātra) for the relish of the rasas.
That is why he is so called.'

Abhinavagupta, Abh. Ch. VI, pp. 684, 686

CHAPTER 4

RASA BHĀVA—ESSENCE OF SANSKRIT DRAMAS

Rasa evocation through *bhāva* presentation forms the quintessence of a Sanskrit play production. Sanskrit play texts, which were generally referred to as *nāṭya rūpaka*-s, were the vehicles through which a performing troupe with their *abhinaya* evoked a *rasa* experience in a responsive spectator. This was achieved through elaborately worked out plan of *bhāva* presentation which pervaded each element of a drama production individually and all the elements in various combinations evoked the *rasa* in its totality.

The Background

Lying at the root of the concept of a *rasa* experience were the rudimentary rituals for fulfilment of vows of ancient Indian people culminating into a trance state of ecstasy. It is suggested that the concept of *rasa*-s had taken root in *Atharvaveda* itself. From this magico-ritualistic beginning, in course of time, a highly sophisticated and controversial *rasa* theory pervaded the practice of Sanskrit dramas.

Rasa theory developed around the art aesthetics which glorified the achievement of heightened consciousness of the essential unity beneath diverse manifestations of life. The feeling of joy experienced at such a self-realisation was sought to be recorded and re-experienced by the people of ancient India in various fields: religion, philosophy, even the medical sciences (*āyurveda*) and the arts. The arts attempted to reflect this awareness of life through the portrayal of the 'essence' of existence beneath the complex of fragmented human experiences so as to arouse in the spectators a momentary consciousness of pure joy (*ānandamayī cetanā*) which rhetorician Māmmaṭa compared to the union with the divine and which Abhinavagupta described as a *rasa samādhi*.

Such a *rasa* evocation in the art of Sanskrit plays was accomplished by the representation of various inner states (*bhāva*) of the hero (*netā*) placed in different situations of the plot (*vastu*) of a play-text depicting his efforts to achieve the three-fold goals of human existence—*artha*, *kāma*, *dharma*; and his final attainment of a state of harmony as a result of fulfilment of his desires The spectator, by identifying with the hero, experienced the joyful relish of the similar state at a deeper (or perhaps, heightened level.

The hero (*netā*) and the plot (*vastu*), in this way are so interwoven with the *rasa-bhāva* presentation of Sanskrit play-texts, that the examination of the latter requires proper understanding of the minutely worked out traditional structures of the former two elements also. These three elements are, therefore, examined in the context of Sanskrit play-texts in the following sections:

Section 1—*Rasa-Bhāva*

The aesthetic principle governing the *bhāva* presentation of the subject matter.

Section 2—*Vastu* (*Plot*)

Adoption of the story to the fixed format of the plot structure to provide stimulus (*uddīpana*) in the scheme of *bhāva* presentation.

Section 3—*Netā* (*hero*)

Concept of the hero, as the principal beneficiary, leading towards the intrinsic meaning of the play—with traditional framework of dramatis personae as supports (*ālambana*) of the *bhāva* presentation.

Section 1

Rasa Bhāva

What is *rasa*? And, what constitutes the *bhava*-s? These terms cannot be easily translated, adapted or defined. Attempts have been made to translate these terms, into English, the former as 'flavour', 'relish', 'juice' or 'sentiment' and latter as 'feeling', 'mood', 'emotion' etc. But the connotations turn out to be either so broad and general or so narrow and limited that they are only true for a part of the actual meaning suggested. It is said that the concepts of *rasa* and *bhāva* cannot be put into words or explicitly expressed. They can only be obliquely suggested. This is because they are the experiences to be experienced by the experiencer. They can only be understood experientially, as they constitute a process of inner alchemy.

The concepts have acquired different connotations in the context of their use. For example, in the Vedas the term *rasa* is used to denote the relish of the essence or the juice produced by the mixture (union) of water, milk and *soma* leaves.[1] *Atharvaveda* indicates it as the state underlying the joy at the point of satiation of desires of human existence. The Upaniṣads compare *rasa* with Brahman itself,[2] the supreme giver of joy. The Sāṅkhya philosophy,[3] *tantra*-s,[4] Āyurveda[5] have all used *rasa-bhāva* concepts in their own contexts.

When Bharata in the *Nāṭyaśāstra* explains these terms in the context of a play production, he relies on the traditional heritage handed down by generations of performing practices and takes recourse to catechisms.

Rasa

While explaining the concept of *rasa* he pointedly asks:

"What is the meaning of the word *rasa*?"

And then quoting a traditional verse he answers:

"It is said it is so called because it is capable of being tasted (*āsvādyatvāt*)."

"How is rasa tasted?"

In answer to this question Bharata quotes two traditional verses which explain the concept of *nāṭyarasa*-s by taking the analogy of food. Briefly, the verses convey this:

"Just as eating of well-cooked food prepared with many spices and flavours gives pleasure and satisfaction to well-disposed persons, in the same way the *nāṭya-rasa*-s evoked by the presentation of the basic states of being suggestively represented by *abhinaya* are relished by the responsive spectators.[6]

Rasa, therefore, is the self-experience or relish (*āsvādana*) of the spectator in the receptive frame of mind.

Bhāva

The term *bhāva* is also explained by Bharata in a catechism. He asks:

"Why are *bhāva*-s so called?" and answers.

"*Bhāva*-s are so called because through words, the body, the colour of the face and *sattva* they pervade or infuse (*bhāvayanti*) in the spectators the inner idea of the playwright."

The term *bhāva*, in this way, conveys a process. It is a process through which the inner idea of the play is transformed into *nāṭya rasa*-s (for the relish of the spectators) with the aid of the four-fold *abhinaya* of the performer.

Bharata further adds that *bhāva* is an instrument of causation denoting something more than mere emotional states, moods, feelings or sentiments. In fact, the term suggests a process of wider or deeper self-awareness of an experience in the manner of an organic development of a seed into a fruit. As Yāska explains, the root of Sanskrit word *bhāva*, *bhū*, implies an extended process of being born, maturing, growing, decaying and dying. *Bhāvābhinaya* in a play would, therefore, connote a communication of extended savouring of the inner states of 'being and becoming'.

Sanskrit play texts are so composed and structured that they have in them *nāṭya-rasa*-s (*rasa*-s of drama) in a latent form, 'as fire is latent in a dry piece of wood' or as 'a fully grown tree, with fruits, is latent in a small, green seed'.[8] A catalytic agent is needed to evoke these latent *nāṭya-rasa*-s in the spectators. This is done through the *bhāvābhinaya* of performers. As D.K. Bedekar says, just as a stone statue gets the potency of divine power after proper consecration, so does the inner meaning of the play-text acquire the power to evoke *nāṭya-rasa*-s in the spectators when properly delineated through *abhinaya*.[9]

This inter-relationship of *rasa* and *bhāva* is also explained by Bharata in an analogy of 'seed power' (*bīja-śakti*). He says that "just as a tree grows from a seed and flowers and fruits from a tree, *rasa*-s are the roots of all *bhāva*-s, and, likewise, *bhāva*-s exist as the source of all *rasa*-s.

From this point of view, the inner idea of the play (*nāṭyārtha* or *rasa*) was a deliberate condition of experiences of a hero (*netā*) and other dramatis personae formulated in terms of a number of basic states of being (*sthāyi bhāva*-s) by the playwright in the body (plot, *vastu*) of the play-texts.

Traditional format of Sanskrit play texts offers eight basic states of being capable of evoking eight *nāṭya rasa*-s.

TABLE No. 1

Eight Nāṭya Rasa-s as per NS and later Dramaturgists

Rasa	*Sthāyi*[1] *Bhāva*	*Colour*[2]	*Presiding*[3] *Deity*	*Produced by*[4] *(Vibhāva)*	*In general represented by* *Anubhāva*[5] *Vyabhicāri* *Sāttvika*
1. *EROTIC* (ŚṚṄGĀRA) of three kinds : (a) The Union (Saṃbhoga) (b) Privation (Ayoga) (c) Separation (Vipralaṃbha)	Love (Rati)	(Śyāma)	Viṣṇu	(1) *Ālambana:* Youths, 'highborn and brightly attired' (2) *Uddipana:* (a) Favourable seasons, garlands, ornaments, beloved's company, music, poetry, garden, painting. (b) + (c) Separation from the beloved.	*Anubhāva:* (a) Joy in the eyes and face, pleasant glance, smiles and sweet words, rejoicing and pleasant movements. Clover movements of eyes (NS, VI. 45-46). (b) Self-disparagement indifference, depression, doubt, envy. (c) Langour, fear, jealousy, drowsiness, illness, excessive breathing, swoons, stupefications, etc. also Ten *Kāma Daśa*-s as illustrated in NS, XXIV, 94–98, 156-168 and 169-

1. NS, VI, 45–72, Kashi ed.
2. Ibid 42-43.
3. Ibid 44.
4. NS, VII, 8–27, also BhP., I, 27–34.
5. Ibid.

Rasa	Sthāyi Bhāva	Colour	Presiding Deity	Produced by (Vibhāva)	In general represented by	Anubhāva Vyabhicāri Sāttvika
						196. All the eight *Sāttvika bhāva*-s. *Vvabhicāri*-s: All except repugnance, ferocity and indolence.
2. *HEROIC* (VIRA) of two kinds: (1) Yuddhavira: (Valour in fight) (2) Dānavira: (Valour in philanthrony)	Enthusiasm or energy (Utsāha)	Reddish Yellowish (Gaura)	Mahendra	*Ālambana:* Superior characters who are valourous, adventurous, capable of using weapons and yet sacrificing. Full of *Sattva,* with presence of mind, optimism, diplomacy, discipline, aggresiveness etc.		*Anubhāva:* Firmness, patience, heroism, charity, diplomacy, etc. *Vyabhicāri-s:* Contentment, judgement, pride, agitation, energy, determination of purpose, indignation. (NS. VI, 66–68). *Sāttvika:* Horripilation, perspiration, change in colour.
3. *FURIOUS* (RAUDRA)	Anger	Red	Rudra	(1) *Ālambana:* Its origin from *Rākṣasa, Dānava* and such haughty men engaged in wars and similar acts. Many handed multifaced, white coloured, tyranical (krūra), wick-		*Anubhāva :* Red eyes, knitting of eye-brows, defiance, biting of lips, movement of the cheeks, pressing one hand with another. Action of beating, crushing, fighting, drawing of blood, etc.

Rasa	*Sthāyi Bhāva*	*Colour*	*Presiding Deity*	*Produced by (Vibhāva)*	*In general represented by* *Anubhāva Vyabhicāri Sāttvika*
				ed and evil men. (2) *Uddīpana* caused by anger, rape, abuse, insult, untrue alligation, threats, revengefulness, jealousy, etc.	*Vyabhicāri-s:* Presence of mind, determination, energy, indignation, restlessness, fury. *Sāttvika:* Perspiration, trembling, horripilation, choking of voice, etc.
4. *ODIOUS* (*BĪBHATSA*)	Disgust (Jugupsā)	Blue (Nila)	Mahākāla	(1) *Ālambana:* Disgusting shape, dress and behaviour, lepers, vampires etc. (2) *Uddīpana:* Hearing of unpleasant, offensive, impure, harmful things. Seeing and discussing them. Disgusting tastes, smells, touch, sight and sound, causing uneasiness.	*Anubhāva:* Stopping movement of all the limbs, narrowing down of the mouth, vomitting, spitting, shaking the limbs in disgust, covering the nose, bending down and walking imperceptibly. *Vyabhicāri-s:* Epiletic fit, delusion, agitation, fainting, sickness, and death. *Sāttvika:* Change of colour, choking of voice.
5. *COMIC* (*HĀSYA*) (Accompanies Erotic) of two kinds: (1) Self-centred (Atmastha)	Laughter (Hāsa)	White (Sita)	Pramatha	(1) *Ālambana:* Women and men of inferior types mostly with unseemly dress, ornaments and speech,	*Anubhāva:* Throbbing of the lips, nose, cheeks, opening the eyes wide and contracting them. Sweat. Humorous glances.

Rasa	*Sthāyi Bhāva*	*Colour*	*Presiding Deity*	*Produced by (Vibhāva)*	*In general represented by Anubhāva Vyabhicāri Sāttvika*
(2) Centred in others (Parastha) arising out of unseemly dress, limbs and words.				shrewd, cunning indulgence in imitating others and use of double entendre. (2) *Uddīpana:* Show of unseemly dress and ornament and speech, impudence, greediness, quarrel, defective limb, use of irregular words, etc.	*Vyabhicāri-s:* Indolence, drawsiness, sleep, dreaming, insomnia. *Sāttvika:* Horripilation, tears, trembling, change in colour, choking voice.
6. *MARVELLOUS* (ADBHCTA) (accompanies Heroic) of two kinds: (a) Celestial (b) Joyous happenings	Wonder (Vismaya)	Yellow (Pita)	Brahmā	(1) *Ālambana:* Words, characters, deeds, personal beauty, sight of heavenly beings, events, strange shapes, dress, behaviour. (2) *Uddīpana:* Attainment of desired objects. Entry into superior mansion, temples, assemblies seven, storied palace, illusory and magic acts.	*Anubhāva:* Gesture of feeling, sweet smell, joyful shaking of limbs, wide open eyes with fixed gaze, waving the end of dhoti or a sāri, uttering words Hā, Hā, Hā, making gifts, joy. *Vyabhicāri:* Hesitation, hurry, inactivity. *Sāttvika:* Horripilation, tears, perspiration, choking voice, tremer, etc.

Rasa	Sthāyi Bhāva	Colour	Presiding Deity	Produced by (Vibhāva)	In General Represented by Anubhāva Vyabhicāri Sāttvika
7. *PATHETIC* KARUṆA (accompanies furious) arising out of (a) Obstruction of lawful deeds (b) Loss of wealth (c) Bereavement	Sorrow (Śoka)	Gray (Kapota)	Yama	(1) *Ālambana:* Persons afflicted under a curse, separated from dear ones, facing misfortune, weak, sick, mentally unhappy, poor persons. (2) *Uddīpana:* Death, destruction and unpleasantness to loved ones, loss of wealth, captivity, accidents, destruction of established order.	*Anubhāva:* Shedding of tears, lamentation, fainting, dryness of mouth, loss of memory, being out of breath. *Vyabhicāri:* Indifference, anxiety, yearning, sadness, dejection, inactivity, epilepsy. *Sāttvika:* Change of colour, paralysis, tremor, tears, etc.
8. *TERRIBLE* BHAYĀNAKA (accompanies Odious) Arising out of: (a) feigned fear (b) wrong action (c) danger	Fear (Bhaya)	Black (Kṛṣṇa)	Kāla	(1) *Ālambana:* Mainly women and low born. (2) *Uddīpana:* Hideous noise, sight of ghosts, battles, entering an empty house or forest, offending one's superior or the king.	*Anubhāva:* Trembling of hands and feet, looking around with uneasiness, dryness of the lips and mouth. *Vyabhicāri:* Fear, stupification, dejection, restlessness, epilepsy, *Sāttvika:* Horripilation, change of voice and colour, paralysis, perspiration, choking voice, etc.

The Scheme of Eight Nāṭya Rasa-s

	Rasa-s of Drama (*Nāṭya Rasa-s*)	*Ba ic States of Being* (*Sthāyī Bhāva-s*)	
1. Erotic	*Śṛṅgāra*	Love	*Rati*
2. Heroic	*Vīra*	Energy	*Utsāha*
3. Furious	*Raudra*	Anger	*Krodha*
4. Odius	*Bībhatsa*	Disgust	*Jugupsā*
5. Comic	*Hāsya*	Laughter	*Hāsa*
6. Marvellous	*Adbhūta*	Wonder	*Vismaya*
7. Pathetic	*Karuṇa*	Sorrow	*Śoka*
8. Terrible	*Bhayānaka*	Fear	*Bhaya*

The first four are the main *rasa*-s. The last four are their respective concomitants.

Bharata does not offer any explanation for the scheme of eight *rasa*-s for the drama, but accepts them as the traditional heritage of the performing troupes. He elaborates on them, however, by giving details of (1) the corresponding basic states of being (*sthāyi bhāva*-s), (2) their presentation through stimuli—(*Vibhāva*-s) and representation through responses (*anubhāva-s*) and complimentary transitory states (*vyabhicāri-s*), (3) their colour, and (4) their presiding deities.

This scheme is given in the table 1 on pages 77-81. Abhinavagupta, the great exponent of Indian aesthetics, who belonged to the *pratyabhijña* (recognition) school of Kashmir monastic Śaivism, explains the scheme of *rasa*-s in a drama as emerging from the basic instincts that are inherited from the latent impressions of one's own experiences of past births—*vāsanā*-s. According to him, these genetic memories produced the basic states (*sthāyi bhāva*-s or *cittavṛtti*-s) in a being.[10] Adding *śāntarasa* with the basic mental state of quietitude (*śama*) to Bharata's scheme of eight *nāṭya rasa*-s, he explains that right from the moment of one's birth, the basic instinct of a being is attracted to pleasure and is repelled by pain. The instincts for pleasure are love, enthusiasm and energy, laughter and wonder. The instincts repelled by pain are anger, disgust, sorrow and fear. These instincts and their responses are parts of the states of consciousness of every being. When this inner reality of human experiences is organised in a pattern of a *rasa* design and communicated through traditionally worked out *abhinaya* of stimuli, responses and complementary transitory states, it becomes capable of being relished by the responsive spectator at a higher level of consciousness. The *rasa* design, as an experience of heightened state of consciousness, is now accepted, in a general sense, also by contemporary psychologists.[11]

Many modern scholars have tried to explore the origin of the *rasa* design from contemporary attitudes and approaches. Among those, D.K. Bedekar has, in a series of articles, offered very interesting views regarding the possible explanation for the emergence of the scheme of eight *nāṭya-rasa*-s. He suggests their genesis from the primitive drama of war between gods and demons performed around sacrificial rituals. He explains the design of the four principal *rasa*-s forming a quartet of twin notions of erotic and heroic as the divine elements and furious and odius as the equally powerful demonic elements. The subsidiary four *rasa*-s came as a consequence to these four primary elements.[12]

The Rasa Sūtra

The dramaturgical tradition of *Nāṭyaśāstra* presents a fully worked out system of presentation of the eight *nāṭya rasa*-s through a play production in a succint aphorism—the *rasa sūtra* of Bharata. Translated the aphorism reads:

"*Rasa* is produced by the combination of stimuli (*vibhāva*), responses (*anubhāva*) and complementary transitory states (*vyabhicāri*)."[13]

In order to understand the aphorism, let us take the case of Śri Harṣa's play *Ratnāvalī*. The play-text has the latent capacity of evoking erotic *rasa*. In order to immerse the spectator with the *rasa* the portrayal of the basic state of love is delineated with the aid of the following constituents:

VIBHĀVA—(The Support, cause or the stimulus for the *rasa* experience.)

They are presented through:

(a) *Ālambana Vibhāva*

Those components of the causation or stimuli on which the *rasa* realisation in a drama depends, such as hero, heroine and other dramatis personae in various relationships. (In the case of the drama Ratnâvalī, Udayana, Sâgarikâ and the other dramatis personae.)

(b) *Uddīpana Vibhāva*

The auxiliary causes or stimulating circumstances for the manifestation of the basic inner state, e.g., the appropriate time, circumstances and situations of the plot. (In case of the drama Ratnāvalī, the palace garden, the private meetings, etc.)

ANUBHĀVA—(Response)

The etymological meaning of the term is the "state of being which follows", i.e. the stimuli. They are physical and psycho-mental responses in the form of deliberate manifestations of speech, gestures, facial expressions and physical get up; in short, the suggestive techniques of *abhinaya*. They depict:

(1) *STHĀYI BHĀVA-s*—(The eight basic states of the eight *nāṭya rasa*-s)

Their portrayal is done with a conscious representation through traditionally formulated techniques of four fold *abhinaya* often with the aid of depiction of appropriate complementary transitory states. They do not comprise the actual states of the dramatis personae or the actors; they are presented, *suggestively*, and with a deliberate technique, for the purpose of generating aesthetic relish of the *rasa* among the audience.

(2) *SĀTTVIKA BHĀVA-s*—(Involuntary psycho-mental responses)

These are traditionally acknowledged eight involuntary responses to the outward stimuli by the concentrated inward activity of the performer. The responses are: pallour, tears, horripilation, choking, sweat, trembling, fainting and paralysis.

(3) *VYABHICĀRI BHĀVA-s*—(Complementary transitory states)

They are thirty three; their number was, in all probability, considered unspecificable; the number 'thirty three' was associated with them because it was considered auspicious. *Nāṭya-śāstra* gives typical stimuli-response for each *rasa* and enumerates the right transitory states which may be represented in connection with them.

In this way, we see that the *rasa* experience could only be evoked when a number of factors combined. The play-text with its plot and the hero had the capacity to evoke *rasa*, but in a latent form. So also the actors who had the capabilities to evoke *rasa*, but unmanifested within them until the moment of performance. Each by it or himself was of no account till they all came together in a play performance to pervade the spectator with the *rasa* experience.

In the years following the compilation of *Nāṭyaśāstra* the *rasa* theory of Bharata was discussed and interpreted by a number of dramaturgists and rhetoricians. Whose inner states—bhāva—were presented in the play? The actor's own or those of the characters? Who was the real beneficiary of the *rasa* experience? These and many such questions were raised and discussed threadbare. Abhinavagupta has thrown light on different constructions which were offered especially regarding the *bhāva* presentation in a play and the relish of the *nāṭya rasa*-s of a play. Of these, some interpretations which are relevant to the present study are given below.

Bhaṭṭanāyaka's Theory of Presentation of Universalised (sādharaṇīkṛta) and Supersensuous (lokottara) 'Bhāva'-s (Bhuktivāda)[14]

Bhaṭṭanāyaka (10 cen. A.D.) has offered an illuminating insight into the *bhāva* presentation in a drama from the point of view of Śāṇkhya philosophy. According to him, the spectator in his concentrated state, relished the *rasa* experience on a universalised and supersensuous impersonal level, and not as an individual experience. This could only happen when the *bhāva* presentation was universal and aesthetically impersonal. Such a portrayal was enjoyed mainly by the developed state of the spectator (*bhāvaka*) who relished neither the basic states of the actor playing Rāma, nor of the character called Rāma in a play. He relished the delineation of the universalised and supersensuous *Rāmatva* which was the essence of Rāma—and which could be part of the spectator's inner reality also. In this way, the pathetic and odius *rasa*-s would become relishable experiences.

Abhinavagupta, in his comments, presented the concept of aesthetic cognition in terms of the manner of the presentation of the basic states in a performance. He said that it was true that the inner idea of a play-text was presented by means of gestures, movements, speech, physical get-up and natural suitability of an actor for a role. But this fact alone could never lead one into falsely identifying the actor with the character because the *bhāva*-s presented in a play did not originate from actor's own experiences. The actor did not and could not exhibit his personal emotions in his performance. Abhinavagupta advanced many reasons for this. Some of them are:

(1) The actor and the character have different identities and can never be of the same mind.
(2) The actor and the character can never look similar as some twins do (sādṛṣya).
(3) No spectator in his right mind mistakes an actor enacting the role of Rāma for the real Rāma (āropita svarūpa).
(4) Nor is the spectator in the state of mind of a lover to whom the face of his beloved appears like a lotus or a moon (*utprekṣyamāna*). He cannot possibly mistake the character with the actor.
(5) There is neither a resemblance between the two as there is between oneself and one's portrait (pratikṛti); nor is there a case of imitative identification that exists between a pupil imitating his master (anukaraṇa).
(6) No magic is involved here, nor is there any hypnotism (*yukti*, etc.).

The actor recognised that the character had a separate identity and acted according to the dictates of the playwright—his creator. Distancing himself from the character, the actor, as a connoisseur and a skilled performer, represented the aesthetic responses of the character to the stimuli offered by the situations depicted in a play-text. The actor did not attempt to imitate (*anukaraṇa*); he only aimed to suggestively portray the character by a process of extended savouring of the latter's states (*bhāva*) in all possible shades (*anukīrtana*).

Abhinavagupta's Theory of Rasa Carvaṇā (Tasting of Rasa)

Abhinavagupta took the theatre experience on a different level. He emphasised that for *rasa* experience it was necessary that the spectator's sensibilities should be cultivated enough to respond to what is presented to him. The preliminary rituals, the music, the play performance—in short, the entire atmosphere of the theatre was so designed as to induce in a responsive spectator a state of heightened consciousness of pure joy. With perfect concentration (*tanmayībhāva*) and mental identification (*tādātmya*) with the happenings on the stage, the spectator forgot for a while his mundane pain and conflicts and blissfully experienced and recognised the variegated states of sorrow, love, anger, fear, etc. as the expressions of one and the same essence-rasa—the pure unbounded joy. Abhinavagupta maintained that the *nāṭya rasa*-s were tasted or chewed (*carvaṇā-āsvādana*) by the spectator alone, who was competent and to whom the relish came as a flash of wonder and delight of a *camatkāra*.

He gives a beautiful simile to emphasise the concept of tasting or chewing of *rasa* by the spectator. He compares the *rasa* of a drama with a fruit of a tree whose seed is the playwright's awareness of life, the play is the tree, the performance is the flower and the tasting or chewing by the spectator the final fruit. The entire tree is latent with the *rasa* but the juice of the fruit is full of it, and it is the spectator alone who relishes it. And so, he is the final benefactor.[15]

Rasa and Dhvani

Rasa-s in a drama were not directly presented but were suggested by a representation of a process of extended savouring of universalised states of being through *abhinaya*. Abhinavagupta and others maintained that the relish of the *rasa* of a drama came to a spectator in a sudden flash of delightful self-revealation. This was comparable to the sudden expansion of mind in wonder that the power of reverberation of the implied meaning of the words and their sounds (*dhvani*) invokes in a sensitive mind.

In the aesthetics of *dhvani*, the suggested meaning of the word and the process of overtones of its sound is more relevant than the literal meaning. Likewise, the relish of the *nāṭya rasa*-s. In a theatre performance, the implied and extended savourings of *bhāva-abhinaya* of a play alone induced in a spectator similar flash of sudden delight of a *rasa*-experience.

Propriety in Rasa Presentation—Aucitya

Only the appropriately dignified *rasa-bhāva* presentation was capable of giving relish to the spectator. The characters, the situations, the *abhinaya* were never to be presented which might give rise to contradictory and repungnant feelings in a spectator or disturb his *rasa*-experience.

Some Conventions of Rasa Presentation

A number of conventions grew around the manner of designing the *rasa* content of a play-text and its presentation in a production. Some of them are described below:

1. Although one principal *rasa* was sought to be communicated in a play, the manner of presenting it was done in a pattern of weaving many strands of different subordinate *rasa*-s as counterpoints to the principal *rasa*. *Daśarūpaka* compares this interrelationship of *rasa*-s to a "*guru* among his students" or a "king among the other men".[16] Contradictory *rasa*-s were often counterbalanced with one another to enhance the enjoyment of the principal *rasa*. For example, in Bhavabhūti's play *Mālatī-Mādhava*, the main *rasa* is erotic but as the play progresses various other *rasa*-s like comic, heroic, pathetic, odius, terrible and marvellous appear enabling the principal erotic *rasa* to stand out most forcefully.
2. The principal and concomitant *rasa*-s were generally depicted together. The hero in love (support of the erotic *rasa*) was often accompanied by the jester (support of the *hāsya-rasa*). The hero evoking pathetic *rasa* was always accompanied by a character evoking furious *rasa* as in Bhāsa's *Ūrubhaṅgam* and *Karṇabhāra*, where the heroes in the state of sorrow are shown together with Aśvatthāmā and king Śalya, respectively, in the state of fury.
3. In a *nāṭaka* genre of the Sanskrit dramas, marvellous *rasa* was always presented at the conclusion. This was mostly done by the device of divine intervention. In Śri Harṣa's *Nāgānanda*, for example, the almost dead hero is revived in the end by the appearance of a goddess and by such a contrivance marvellous *rasa* is evoked in the end.
4. The convention of a Sanskrit play ending on a happy note reflects the presentation of a serene state of contentment of the hero who had attained the goal of his desire and whose further desire could only be the wish for the wellbeing of all. The actor's benedictory verse (*Bharatavākya*) conventionally expressed this sentiment at the end of a play.

The ultimate end of a Sanskrit play was always positive and could not end with an unresolved conflict. The objective of a play was to attain success by enveloping the spectator in a blissful *rasa* experience. The whole traditional structure was designed with this end in view. The plot, the hero, and the *bhāva* presentation were employed to achieve the fruition of the desire of the hero to attain one or more of the three goals of human existence. Crisis, tension, conflicts and moods of indecision were always depicted as passing obstacles (*vighna*-s) which the hero of the plot overpowered by a concentrated resolve of his purpose and the faultless execution of his efforts. Just as a ritually performed sacrifice succeeds in the attainment of desires of the sacrificer, so did the Sanskrit plays. They ended on a happy note, depicting a serene state of the hero, who had achieved the goal of his desires and who had finally recovered "the *sattva* of his personality".[17]

5. The Concept of Pathetic (Karuṇa) Rasa in Sanskrit Dramas

In this background, the delineation of the pathetic *rasa* in Sanskrit plays provides an altogether separate orientation from the Grecian concepts of the tragedy and the tragic end with which the pathetic *rasa* is at times compared. The tragic heroes of Greek tragedies depict a fall of a noble hero. The shattering feeling of 'pity and fear' is excited in the audience who watch a noble figure of the hero, in sharp conflict with his surroundings, succumb and fall and thereby exhibit a flaw or 'error of frailty' in his character.[18] Such plays which end tragically in an atmosphere of unresolved conflict have no relevance in the scheme of Sanskrit plays. In fact, it is significant that *Nāṭyaśāstra* has no word to denote the term 'conflict'.[19] Resolution of all conflicts, satiation of all desires and attainment of a serene state of equipoise is the happy note on which all Sanskrit plays end. The spectator achieves the blissful state of a *rasa* experience by complete identification with the hero.

If one attempts to understand the pathetic *rasa* in the context of the *nāṭya rasa* framework, the traditional description of the pathetic *rasa* provides an enlightning insight.

Pathetic *rasa*, according to traditional sources reported in *Nāṭyaśāstra*, has sorrow as the basic state. The god of death—

Yama—is its presiding deity and it is a concomitant of furious *rasa*.

The basic state of sorrow (*sthāyi*) traditionally denotes a condition of despair as an outcome of either an affliction under a curse, loss of wealth, captivity and other misfortunes, or separation of dear ones. These are produced in two ways. Either as a result of the state of fury caused by fights of demons and haughty men[20] or as an effect of the condition of love in separation (*vipralambha śṛṅgāra*) depicted by the traditional framework of the ten stages of love (*kāmadaśā*).[21]

The Sanskrit plays delineate the pathetic *rasa* in this format only. The two exceptional plays of Bhāsa, which are at times put forward as examples of Sanskrit tragedies, faithfully adhere to the above traditional presentation of pathetic *rasa* where a very strongly delineated but a *passing* state of sorrow in the hero is depicted. Both the plays *Urubhaṅgam* and *Karṇabhāra* are no doubt unusual. They belong to the *Utsṛṣṭikāṅka* genre, which is strongly dominated by pathetic rasa. The plays also end, unusually, with the death of the heroes. In the former play, the hero dies on the stage. In the latter, the hero goes towards his certain death. Both plays start with a strong atmosphere of sorrow by presenting a condition of despair caused by misfortunes. The heroes are shown brooding over their past wrong deeds and in a state of gloom, anguish and other despondent moods. In *Urubhaṅgam*, furious Baladeva and Aśvatthāmā as well as the weeping queens with the defeated and wounded hero provide an incentive (support) for the pathetic. The play *Karṇabhāra* opens with Karṇa engulfed with doubtful premonitions of an impending doom.

But as the plays unfold and move towards the end, both the heroes gradually achieve a state of serene calm and resolution of their conflicting moods. They accept their certain deaths with a tranquil recognition that specific actions produce specific results (*karma* theory). In fact they almost welcome death with a serene conviction that they are dying in a heroic manner and are journeying to heaven which is the rightful abode of a hero dying on a battle-field. The plays, thus, end on a note of heroic *rasa*.

The spectator relishes this depiction of pathetic *rasa*, which, in the end imperceptibly but definitely transfers into an energetic heroic *rasa*, thereby enveloping the spectator in a sudden delight (*camatkāra*) of the *rasa* presentation.

Bhavabhūti's Uttararāmacaritam is intended to glorify the pathetic *rasa*. And he does it so expertly that the taste (*āsvādana*) of pathetic *rasa* depicting love in separation is actually enjoyed with a pleasurable relish.

(6) The Concept of Erotic Rasa—(Śṛṅgāra)

The traditional presentation of the erotic rasa in Sanskrit plays was worked out in great detail by the ancients. It had a complex and yet precisely defined method of depiction and delineation.

The rasa was evoked in the spectators through the presentation of the state of love—*rati bhāva*. The instinct of love or pleasure was recognised as the basic awareness of every being and was given the principal place in the *nāṭya rasa* design. The word *śṛṅga* itself connotes a pinnacle or a summit. In its inception, *śṛṅgārin* emphasised the pairing of a couple—*mithuna*—symbolising the source of creative energy and fertility. The terms *śṛṅga* or *śṛṅgāra* consequently were equated with the idea of auspiciousness suggesting a gratification, welfare, good fortune, happiness and prosperity of a community.

Nāṭyaśāstra describes erotic *rasa* in terms of a state of love of men and women in fullness of their youth. It says that the *śṛṅgāra rasa* takes its name from those elegantly dressed (*śṛṅgārin*) couples. Viṣṇu, the father of the god of love—Kāmadeva—is the presiding deity. The colour of the *rasa* is *śyāma*—shining, pure, bright and beautiful.[22]

The basic state of love with the pleasure of union as its foundation was caused by the stimulus of seasons, garlands, ornaments, unguents, attainment of the desired objects and lack of opposition. And it was portrayed by the responses of smiling face, sweet words, charming demeanour and so on.

With the change of patronage from the communal sacrificial rituals to the elitist gatherings of the royalty and the leisured classes, the angle of presentation of the erotic *rasa* changed its emphasis. Firstly, the *rasa* became very popular and imperceptibly superceded the heroic *rasa*. Secondly, its depiction was influenced by the then popular theory of pleasure, as an amusing past time for the men of rank of ancient society. Sex (*kāma*) as well as love-sports (*krīḍā*) and the activities of pleasure (*narma*) dominated its portrayal.

Two aspects of love dominated its portrayal. The love in union (*sambhoga śṛṅgāra*) and the separation in love (*vipralambha śṛṅgāra*). The latter was further divided into two stages of separation; the separation before the union and the separation after the union.

The *rasa* was supported by the portrayal of heroes (*nāyaka*-s) and heroines (*nāyikā*-s) in these traditionally worked out stages of love. Their union and separation were aided by a number of assistants who were called *kāma sahāyaka*-s or *narma saciva*-s.

Pleasure of the season, enjoyment of garlands, perfumes, ornaments, sensual objects, splendid mansions, meetings in gardens and in moonlight were the stimuli.

Love messages, favourable mind, unfavourable mind, winning of the beloved, agreement for union, various types of erotic affairs of kings and aristocrats with noble ladies or common courtesans; the expertise of the jester in the ways of women and of the gallants in the ways of courtesans; manifestation of love in men and women like personal omens, causes of jealousy, etc., have been described at length in all works of ancient Indian dramaturgy under the heading of erotic *rasa*.

The state of separation in love was elaborately formulated into the following system of ten stages of love (*kāmadaśā*):

> Longing for the beloved, anxiety, recollection, enumeration of merits, distress, lamentation, insanity, sickness, stupor and death.[23]

As regards the depiction of the state of love in union, scenes of explicit love-making on the stage were forbidden. These situations were to be depicted by appropriate songs with delicate (*sukumāra*) style of dance. *Nāṭyaśāstra* had its own reasons for this mandate. Says Bharata:

> "A drama is to be witnessed by the father and the son, the mother-in-law and and the daughter-in-law, all sitting together" and so "an expressive dance or a song describing the appropriate season and the nearness of the beloved should depict these situations."[24]

One notices an apparent overlapping in the description of erotic *rasa* in *Nāṭyaśāstra*. At some places, the erotic *rasa* is described in terms of the auspicious *kāma*—one of the goals of human existence. And at other places, it is equated with the system of pleasurable pastime (*krīḍā* and *narma*). It is interesting to note that the later dramaturgical works have only concentrated at length on the heroes and heroines in various states of love—*nāyaka-nāyikā bheda*—and the ten stages of love (*kāmadaśā*). Sanskrit playwrights who belonged to the elite assemblies of the rich patrons have faithfully reflected the prevailing tastes in their depiction of the erotic rasa—with Kālidāsa and Bhavabhūti reaching the heights of its refined delineation.

Section 2

The Plot—Vastu

"If *rasa* is the soul of the drama, the plot constitutes its body" says Bharata.[25] This is because the inner core of the *rasa* design lies in a latent form enveloped in the body of a plot composed of many incidents and episodes. The incidents of a Sanskrit play are taken from well-known sources like epics, the *Purāṇa*-s and *kathā* literature. The success or otherwise of a play depended to a large extent on whether the selection of the incidents and the scheme of presenting them in a tightly worked out structure of the plot and the performance had succeeded in immersing the spectator in the *rasa* presentation.

A Sanskrit play begins with a germ idea—or the seed (*bīja*)—of a desire in the mind of the *abhikarī* hero[26] (the principal beneficiary of the fruit of the action of a play) to attain one or more of the threefold goals of human existence. (As previously mentioned the threefold aims of life as recognised by the ancient Indian society were the desire for (1) wealth and prosperity—*Artha*, (2) love and pleasure—*Kāma* and (3) the righteous action—*Dharma*.)

The hero's efforts towards the fulfilment of these desires motivate the dramatic action of the principal plot. He is aided by other subsidiary characters of the sub-plots and faces many obstacles (*vighna*-s) which he successfully overcomes with his self-controlled perseverance and concentrated efforts. At the end of the play, he succeeds in attaining the fruits (*phala*) of his actions—and achieves a condition of serene contentment (*mokṣa*). The incidents of the story are fitted into this basic plot structure which is primarily divided into:

(i) *The Principal Plot*: (*Adhikārika vastu*)

Around the *adhikārī* hero and other dramatis personae like

the heroine and others who are concerned with and are the supports of the principal *rasa* of the play.

(ii) *The Subsidiary Plot/Plots*: (*Prāsaṅgika vastu*)
Around the subsidiary characters, who may have an interest of their own, but who are the supporters of the hero and the principal *rasa* as well. (The *patākā* and *prakarī* nāyaka-s and other dramatis personae who aid the hero.)

The plot progression in terms of the efforts of the hero for the achievement of his desire is, at the same time, split up in five divisions from the following three points of view:

I. *Five Successive Stages of the Hero's Action* (*Kāryāvasthā*)
There are five stages of situations (*avasthā*-s) of the deliberate efforts of the *adhikārī* hero and his supporters for the achievement of the fruit of the hero's desire. These stages indicate linear development. The first stage is the beginning (*prārambha*) of the desire in the hero. The second stage is the effort (*prayatna*) towards it. The third, fourth and fifth stages are the possibility of attainment (*prāptyāśa*), certainty of achievement (*niyatāpti*) and finally the attainment of the fruit (*phalayoga*). The obstacles are there but they are to be faced and overcome.

II. *Five Phases of the Development of the Inner Idea of the Plot* (*Arthaprakṛti*)
The literal meaning of the term—*arthaprakṛti*—is the nature (*prakṛti*) of the inner idea of the play (*artha*). It denotes the urges and drives which induce phases of the changes of *bhāva* presentation of the plot. This is an aspect of the plot progression which is not in a form of a linear movement, but appears to indicate the organic development of the germ idea and its gradual outward expansion.

In the case of the self-controlled, fully resolved hero they depict his inner states which carry him towards accomplishing the final fruit of his desire. The seed—*bīja*—or the idea for the achievement of the goal—*kārya*—is germinated initially in a very small form—*bindu*—in the mind of the hero where it sprouts. It is seen, off and on, during the progression of the plot, as a sign of continuity, 'like a drop of oil in water'.[27] Naturally these three phases of *bīja*, *bindu* and *kārya* are directly connected with the quality of the inner states of the hero.

Over and above these, there are two other situations involving secondary characters of the sub-plots which carry forward the inner idea of the play and thus help the hero's resolve. They are: (1) *Patākā*—or the episode which has a subsidiary character as a leader (*patākā nāyaka*) of the sub-plot and (2) *Prakarī*—the incident which has as its leader, a *prakarī nāyaka*, who appears briefly but nevertheless gives considerable support to the progression of the inner idea.

Bindu acts as a continuous outward moving thrust of the germ idea, often interrupting the merely informatory parts of the story or the sub-plots and resuming the thread of the seed development.

III. *Five Junctures (Sandhi-s)*

The junctures (*sandhi*-s) are sequences which ingeniously connect the five *arthaprakṛti*-s and *kāryāvasthā*-s and demonstrate the design of *bhāva* presentation through the plot structure. The opening (*mukha*), progression (*pratimukha*), development (*garbha*), pause (*vimarśa*) and conclusion (*nirvahaṇa*) are the five junctures. They indicate the points or sequences in the plot structure which reflect the movement of the hero's efforts towards the achievement of his desire and his inner states during this journey. These sequences, therefore, indicate a style of plot progression in terms of gradual linear motion of the situations, while at the same time exhibiting succesions of the organic growth of the seed or the germ idea of the play, "being sown, sprouted, developed, sought for and ripened into a fruit".[28]

Sub-units of the Junctures (Sandhyaṅga-s)

The *sandhi* sequences are further broken up into minute sub-units of 64/65 *sandhyaṅga*-s. They reflect an intricately worked out traditional schematic design of *bhāva* presentation in a play. Each of the sub-unit has an individual name, *rasa-bhāva* content and an intensity of mood and pitch. They can be compared to the smallest basic units of music (*śruti*-s) and dance (*karaṇa*-s). Their different combinations in a *sandhi* sequence provide an easy understanding of the *rasa-bhāva* import of the play. Their usage, number and order, in sequence, depend on the basic intent of the *bhāva* presentation.

The spectator, by this device, is made aware of what is intended to be achieved so that he can relish each stage of the development of the *bhāva* presentation.

Fixed Format of Representation of the Plot in a Production

1. The play opens with a prayer which is called a *nāndi śloka*.
2. The prologue follows the prayer with the *sūtradhāra*, his assistant, the actress and the jester introducing the play proper.
3. The plot of the play is presented through traditionally fixed number of acts—*aṅka*-s—which are connected by short scenes called linking devices (*arthopkṣepaka*-s).
4. The play ends on a happy note. It concludes with the hero achieving his desired goal and finishes with the actor's benedictary verse—*Bharata vākya*—wishing for the well-being of all.

Presentation of the Play Proper

The basic unit of a play is the act or an *aṅka*. Its presentation is done through continuous representation—narration style. Only those situations of the plot which are latent with *rasa* capable of portraying the *bhāvāvasthā*-s are represented in an *aṅka*. These are referred to as incidents latent with *rasa* (*sa rasa vastu*) by tradition. They are represented with extended *abhinaya* of the inner states by the performers.

The other incidents, which are without *rasa*, lengthy and forbidden by the tradition for portrayal,[29] but which are nevertheless important for providing links with the plot progression, are either simply narrated or hinted at. They are called incidents without *rasa* (*nīrasa vastu*). These narrations are presented by interesting devices of short, informatory, or explanatory, brisk, linking scenes called *arthopkṣepaka*-s by one/two/three subsidiary characters. The linking devices are:

(i) *The Supporting Scene* (*Viṣkambhaka*): Where middle (*madhyama prakṛti*) characters indicate the parts of the story that have happened or are about to happen in a condensed version; either in a monologue or in a brisk scene between two or three characters speaking in Prakrit or Sanskrit or both.

(ii) *The Introductory Scene* (*Praveśaka*): Which explains the happenings between the acts, often indicating a scene transfer, change of setting, time or season. They are enacted by the Prakrit speaking characters.

(iii) *The Intimating Speech* (*Cūlikā*): A speech from behind the curtain or the dressing room suggesting explanation of some vital matter.

(iv) *Transitional Scene* (*Aṅkāvatāra*): A narrative device by which the characters at the end of the scene anticipate the action or the setting of the following act.

(v) *An Anticipatory Scene* (*Aṅkamukha or Aṅkāsya*): A narrative device where a male or a female character, in the beginning of an act, indicates what is to follow in the act.

The format of the presentation of a plot of a Sanskrit play is, thus, that of a continuous narration—representation with an *aṅka* forming its basic unit. The main plot is always inducted by a *nāndi* prayer. The play ends on a happy note and is concluded by a verse suggesting an actor's benediction for the well-being of all. All the Sanskrit playwrights have used this traditional format as a vehicle through which their genius could create or suggest various states of being for *rasa* evocation.

Section 3

Netā—The Hero and Other Dramatis Personae

Like the fixed format of the plot, the dramatis personae in the Sanskrit plays are also classified by the ancient dramaturgical traditions as easily recognisable supports (*ālambana vibhāva*) who act as catalysts for the *rasa* realisation. In order to fully understand the classification, it is necessary to underline the point that the characters in Sanskrit plays are not individuals but universalised archetypes with a set of easily identifiable characteristics. They may be called conventional types or the idealised symbols utilised basically to establish impersonal moods or inner states of human experience. In fact these characters are referred to as 'vehicles' (*pātra*) acting as supporting stimuli of the latent states of being presented in the play-texts. When represented through *abhinaya* by the actors, the characters infuse the spectator with a delightful *rasa* experience. Each gesture, each inflexion, each reaction and attitude as well as each shade and shape of the disposition and outlook have suggestive implication and are traditionally predetermined to suit the basic nature (*prakṛti*) and the corresponding characteristics of the character types. The traditional classification and definitions of these characteristics are illuminating and it is necessary that a drama producer knows them.

The division is based on:

(1) emphasis on the qualities (*guṇa*-s), the states (*bhāva*-s) and the situations (*avasthā*-s) of the characters;

(2) Difference of *abhinaya*—(i) Body movements, (ii) Speech, voice and the manner of its usage, (iii) *Sattva*, psycho-mental states, (iv) *Āhārya*, physical get-up in the portrayal.

The traditional classification of the dramatis personae as supports of *rasa-bhāva* presentation, and the ideal characteristics of the actors of the drama troupe who could impersonate them are examined as under:

The Main Classification—Superior, Middle, Inferior (Uttama prakṛti, Madhyama prakṛti, Adhama prakṛti)

According to ancient Indian tradition "everyone is different with reference to one's basic nature (*prakṛti*) which one inherits at the time of one's birth."[30] And so, *Nāṭyaśāstra* classifies the dramatis personae into three main groups of superior, middle and inferior natures enumerating the qualities and the characteristic behaviour of men and women belonging to each group. We quote a few of these qualities here:

(1) *Superior Nature*: *Uttama Prakṛti*

Superior man: "He is a type with controlled senses, wise, skilled in arts and crafts, expert in enjoyment, grave, liberal, patient, munificient, one who brings consolation to the poor and is versed in the *śāstra*-s."

Superior woman is the woman "who is tender by nature, is unfickle and speaks smilingly. She is free from cruelty and is good mannered and endowed with natural beauty and nobility. She is [also] grave and patient."[31]

(2) *Middle Nature*: *Madhyama Prakṛti*

Middle type man is an "expert in the social graces, proficient in arts, crafts and the śāstra-s and is wise."

Middle type woman exhibits "all qualities of the superior type of woman, but in a lesser degree."

(3) *Inferior Nature*: *Adhama Prakṛti*

The qualities of both men and women of the inferior type are the same and so they are enumerated together. The description of such a person runs as follows:

"Harsh in word, ill-mannered, low spirited, criminally disposed, irascible and violent; can kill friends or anyone by torturing; prone to be engaged in useless things, mean, haughty, ungrateful, indolent, expert in insulting honoured persons, covetous of women, fond of quarrel, treachrous, doer of evil deeds, stealer of other's property, etc."

The Hero (Adhikāri Netā)

Whatever be the *rasa*, the one, who by his efforts achieves the final fruit, is the *adhikāri* hero or the *netā* or *nāyaka* or the *phalabhoktā*. It is the hero whose desire is finally fulfilled in a play and as such he is the focus of the spectator's concentration. The very name *nāyaka* implies that he is the one who leads towards the inner meaning of the play. The character of such a hero, with whom the spectator identifies for the *rasa* experience, is the most impressive. His essential quality is that of always being self-controlled (*dhīra*), unruffled in the face of adversities and of resolute mind (full of *sattva*) in his efforts.

Types of Heroes: *Nāyaka Bheda*[32]

Taking these characteristics as common to all types of heroes, their classification is based on:

(A) *Hero as per his conduct*

(1) *One who is self-controlled and exalted*: *Dhīrodātta*

"Ideal in constitution, noble and high souled, firm and forgiving, steadfast in action, of exceedingly harmonious mind."

(Rāma of the *Rāma*-plays and Jīmūtavāhana of *Nāgānanda*.)

(2) *One who is self-controlled and lighthearted*: *Dhīralalita*

"Soft, sportive, happy, humorous, drawn by harmless guiles and wiles, attached to arts, gentle and gay."

(Udayana of Bhāsa and Śri Harṣa; Agnimitra of *Mālavikāgnimitra*.)

(3) *One who is self-controlled and calm*: *Dhīrapraśānta*
"Fond of fine arts, elegant, a little serious, graceful." According to *Daśarūpaka*, he is either a brahmin or a merchant. He is an ordinary, common man, never a divine hero.
(Cārudatta in *Mṛcchakaṭikam*, Mādhava in *Mālati-Mādhava*.)

(4) *One who is self-controlled and vehement*: *Dhīroddhata*
"Full of pride, jealousy, clever in the use of delusive and illusive art, fickle and boastful."
(Duryodhana in Bhāsa's *Ūrubhaṅgam*.)

(B) *Hero as a Support of the Erotic Rasa*

In the ancient polygamous society, the hero as a lover is divided into four categories of—

(1) *Chivalrous hero*: *Dakṣiṇa*: One, who even when enamoured by another woman, remains kind to his previous love.
(Purūravas in *Vikramorvaśīyam*)

(2) *Deceitful hero*: *Śaṭha*: One, who hides his unfaithfulness.
(Udayana of Śri Harṣa)

(3) *Shameless hero*: *Dhṛṣṭa*: One, who lets the disfigurement of his body caused by the love play with another woman be seen by his previous love.

(4) *Faithful hero*: *Anukūla*: One, who has only one lady love.
(Rāma of *Rāma*-plays)

By permutations and a combinations of these characteristics 16 or 48 different varieties[33] of the hero-types are produced.

The *Nāṭyaśāstra* tradition has laid down axioms for the selection of the right actors for appropriate roles also. From that category.

The Type of Actors who would be given the Role of the Hero—Kings and Princes

"Actors of the best kind, who have beautiful eyes, eyebrows, and facial features, and who are tall, possessed of pleasant appearance, dignified gait, who are neither fat nor lean, are well-behaved, wise and steady in nature"[34] were found suitable for the role of the hero as a king or a prince.

Companions and Supporters of the Hero

They are *patākā* and *prakarī* leaders who aid the hero. The former is also called *anunāyaka*, the follower of the hero. According to *Nāṭyaśāstra* the *patākā* leader should be intelligent and possess qualities like a hero but in a lesser degree.[35]

In addition, there are assistants of the king-hero who are classified as under:

(1) King-hero's assistants in duty regarding righteous conduct (*dharma*): *Dharma saciva*-s
(2) King-hero's assistants in duty regarding wealth and property (*artha*): *Artha saciva*-s
(3) King-hero's assistants in duty regarding his conduct in love affairs (*kāma*): *Kāma saciva*-s like the jester, gallant-parasite, masseur (*Vidūṣaka, Viṭa, Pīṭhamarda*).

Types of Actors Suitable for these Roles

Actors with "well-formed limbs, distinctive speech, neither tall nor fat, heroic, brave, eloquent and with presence of mind were found to be suitable for the roles of the army leaders and the ministers"[36] by the *Nāṭyaśāstra* tradition.

The roles of priests, ascetics and seers were given to actors who were proficient in Sanskrit speech and expert in conducting rituals.

Role of a Jester or Vidūṣaka

The jester is the most important ally of the hero in his affairs of the heart. As a support of the comic (*hāsya*) *rasa*, he often goes hand in hand with the hero who is a support of *erotic rasa*. This is specially so during the delineation of hero's state of love in separation.

As an assistant of a king-hero in his love affairs in the *nāṭaka genre* of Sanskrit play-texts, the jester is shown as the wit of the court who is also a familiar figure in the royal harem. He is expert in conversation,[37] an adept in mixing with noble ladies, and a figure of fun everywhere. His excessive fondness for food makes him a glutton. He is a brahmin but speaks in Prakrit and exposes his lack of learning and finesse. With his funny manners and speech he invokes laughter.

He usually carries in his left hand a crooked staff with three bends (*kutilaka*). As a royal clown, he is dandily dressed. This is evident from the frescoes of Ajanta. In Sanskrit play-texts dealing with a king's love story, he is mostly depicted as a brahmin youth who is a buffoon and a prankster. Many instances are there of irate ladies of the harem ridiculing him as a 'wicked lad' or a 'young lad' (*duṣṭa baṭu* or *baṭuka*). In the plays of Kālidāsa, he is constantly referred to as a 'young boy'—*māṇavaka*.

Traditionally his name should suggest spring or some flower. In Śri Harṣa's plays he is called *Vasantaka* (meaning spring).

In the *prahasana* genre of popular social farces, the jester appears in an altogether different light. Four types of jesters are shown in the important roles of "sectarians or hypocritical godmen, their disciples, brahmins and other twice-born castes". By their sanctimonious behaviour, ludicrous posturing and pretentious manners they evoke laughter. Hediously dressed in rags and tatters with disfiguring marks of colirium, red chalk and ashes on their bodies, they look gross and ridiculous.

The character belongs to the middle type.

Actor who Plays the Role of a Jester

The principal comedian of the company who formed the nucleus of the five main actors of the *nāṭya* troupe enacted the role of the chief jester.

After presenting himself in the preliminary ritual of "the three men's talk", the chief comedian of the troupe, who specialised in enacting various types of jesters,[38] portrayed the role of the main jester of the play.

Gallant-Parasite or a Rake: Viṭa

The gallant parasite was another assistant to the hero in his love affairs. He was a cultured, shrewd but a depraved man, proficient in the ways of courtesans (*Vaiśika śāstra*).

The gallant was the 'has been', a married nāgaraka, who was no longer wealthy. (*Nāgaraka*-s were usually, affluent cultured citizens of ancient society.) He primarily functioned as a messenger or a friend of the hero in love. He was a man with a wide experience of human nature. He was an expert in polite and quick-witted conversation and flattery. The *nāgaraka* hero (in *Bhāṇa* genre of plays) commissions the gallant-parasite-*viṭa* specially to help him in his love affairs with courtesans.

Actor Playing the Role of the Gallant-parasite

The actor who played the role of the gallant parasite was one possessing all the qualities of the *sūtradhāra*, in regard to the theatrical production. According to *Nāṭyaśāstra* "The actor would be sweet, poetic, proficient in the meaning of the *śāstra*-s and in the knowledge of the courtesans; capable of seeing the positive and negative sides of any argument."[39]

Masseur: Pīṭhamarda

The masseur (*pīṭhamarda* or *anunāyaka*) was another helper of the hero in love. He was a bachelor, too poor to be a citizen (*nāgaraka*) but he was proficient in the art of pleasure. He had the skill of massaging and shampooing. The name, *pīṭhamarda*, was derived from a special stool (*pīṭha*) supported by a stick that he usually carried with him.

A Servant and a Woman Messenger: Ceṭa and the Dūtī

They were "important allies in the love affairs of the hero. Often they were experts in distinguishing between persons who were to be honoured. The *ceṭa*-s served under bondage. . ."[40]

Hero's Entourage

In the case of a king-hero there were characters like women body guards (*pratihārī*-s), chamberlain (*kañcukī*), bards (*vaitālika*-s and *māgadha*-s) who formed his entourage. Of these:

The Chamberlain—Kañcukī

He is depicted in Sanskrit play-texts as an old-infirm keeper of the royal harem, in charge of king's armour and crown. He is known by a loose gownlike dress—kañcuka—that he wears. He also holds a stick. *Nāṭyaśāstra* describes him as a man "truthful, learned, with deep knowledge, wisdom and free from sexual passion".[41] We have *kañcukī*-s in Sanskrit plays from Bhāsa onwards.

There was a character type—*prati-nāyaka* or the antagonist or obstacle, who was often employed as an adversary or a villain in the plays. There were female antagonists (obstacles) also-specially in *nāṭikā*.

Classification of Heroines: Nāyikā Bheda

The heroine or *nāyikā* was the total focal point (*āśraya*) of the hero's state of love; consequently she was given an important place in the scheme of *bhāva* presentation. In fact, in the plays evoking erotic *rasa*, the heroine more or less shared with the hero the status of the main support of the *rasa*.

The heroines in the Sanskrit plays were classified according to their qualities, age, class and behaviour in love. We find precisely enunciated classifications of the heroines in *Nāṭyaśāstra* which subsequently grew more complex in course of time.

Heroines Categorised according to their Class

Nāṭyaśāstra divided the heroines in four classes of:

Goddesses (*divyā*), queens (*bhavatī*), women of high family (*kulāṅganā*) and courtesans (*gaṇikā*).

Heroines Classified by their Qualification in Love

In addition to dividing heroines according to their class, they were also classified by their qualifications in love:

A self-controlled one (*dhīrā*), a light hearted one (*lalitā*), an exalted heroine (*uddātā*) and a modest heroine (*nibhṛtā*).[42]

Heroines Categorised according to Various Stages of Love Situations

The heroines were also classified according to their stages in love situation. The eight-fold division of heroines in love situation—the *Aṣṭa nāyikā bheda*—is reasonably well-known and can be witnessed in mediaeval paintings and classical dances even to this day. The classification according to *Nāṭyaśāstra* is given below:

Vāsakasajjā, one dressed up for union with the beloved,
Virahotkaṇṭhitā, one distressed by separation,
Svādhīnabhartṛkā, one having her husband as her slave,
Kalahāntaritā, one separated from her lover by a quarrel,
Khaṇḍitā, one annoyed with her lover,

Vipralabdhā, one deceived by her lover,
Proṣitabhartṛkā, one whose husband is away on a visit,
Abhisārikā, one who sets out to meet her lover.

Daśarūpaka and later theoreticians have further elaborated the classification of the *nāyikā-bheda*, reflecting the predominant position of erotic *rasa* in later plays and *kāvya* literature. With permutations and combinations, *nāyikā-bheda* came to 128 types of heroines.[43] Later rhetoricians gradually arrived at a grand total of 384 types.[44] Some even postulated that the varieties of heroines would compute up to 16,000, thus giving credence to the mythical notion of Śrī Kṛṣṇa having as many queens!

The Actress who should Play the Role of the Heroine

Nāṭyaśāstra is explicit about the actress who should play the role of the heroine. It says: "The actress should be endowed with a good physical form, good qualities, character and of young age; she should possess gold necklace and garlands; should be shining, affectionate, sweet and should possess (sic) charming words with a lovely voice; she should also be steady in exercise—yoga—and conversant with rhythm, tempo and *bhāva-sattva abhinaya*."[45]

Generally, "an actress should know all about playing of drums, rhythm, tempo and should be conversant with *rasa* and should be beautiful (*sarvāṅgasundarī*)".

Heroine's Entourage

In the play-texts the heroine has her own retinue of friends (*sakhī*-s) of equal age, messengers (*dūtī*-s), maids in waiting, the elderly ladies like a nurse (*dhātrī*), a female recluse (*parivrājikā*) and so on.

Other Female Characters

Besides the heroine, the female dramatis personae in Sanskrit plays dealing with a king's story include the chief queen, the other queens and their attendants. These characters sometimes act as obstacles in the way of the fulfilment of the desired end of the *dhīralalita* king hero.

Members of the Nāṭya Troupe in the Prologue of Drama

Apart from the dramatis personae, five main members of the

nāṭya troupe appeared as themselves in the prologues of the Sanskrit plays to induct the play proper. These members were the stage manager (*sūtradhāra*), his two assistants (*paripārśvaka*-s), the actress (*naṭī*) and the chief comedian (*vidūṣaka*). It was not essential that all five should appear together in the prologues. Usually two or three of them conducted the proceedings; in some instances, the *sūtradhāra* alone did the needful.

Rasa, the plot (*vastu*) and the hero (*netā*), in this manner, formed the intricately worked out structure of the ancient Sanskrit play-texts. The three elements were inseparable, each of them individually and in different combinations succeeded in presenting a basic state—*sthayi bhāva*—for evocation of appropriate *rasa* in the spectators.

The Sanskrit playwrights followed this traditional structure faithfully in their compositions. The *nāṭya* troupes aimed to work at such a play structure at a level of the performance. The lay spectator was at least conversant with the necessary and vital information regarding the structure of *rasa*, *vastu* and *netā*. The connoisseur relished the nuances of the plot weaving and character delineation for presentation of the *rasa* design. Each spectator appreciated and enjoyed at his own level of appreciation the genius and mastery (*pratibhā*) of the playwright and the performers who succeeded in offering a refreshingly individual presentation by improvising this traditional structure of the Sanskrit play-texts.

NOTES

1. Ṛgveda 9.80.1, 3.48.1.
2. Kr. Yajurveda, Tai Up., 7.
3. Bedekar D.K., Sahitya Vichar (Marathi), pp. 66–86.
4. Rawson Philip, The Art of Tantra, p. 109.
5. Sen Ranendrakumar, Background in Ayurveda and Bharata's Vyabhichari bhava-s, IHQ, V. 30, Issue 1, 1954–2.
6. NS, VI, 31 prose lines and L 7-19 (Kashi ed.).
7. NS, VII, Prose line 2–4 (Kashi ed.).
8. The Interrelationship of Rasa and Bhāva is explained by Bharata as *bija-śakti*.
9. Bedekar, D.K., op. cit. p. 79.
10. Abh. Vol. 1, VI, p. 665, also p. 612.
11. Gupta Rakesh, Psychological Studies in Rasa, Aligarh, 1950.
12. Bedekar D.K., op. cit. 32 ff.
13. NS, 31, L-6-8 (Tr. M. Ghosh).

14. Abh. Vol. I, VI, pp. 641–49.
15. Ibid., pp. 646-58.
16. DR.IV.45.
17. Pandey K.C., Comparative Aesthetics, Vol. 1 (1950), p. 283.
18. Butcher S. H., "Aristotle's Theory of Poetry and Fine Arts" (London, 1907), p. 45.
19. Dalal Minakshi, Conflict in Sanskrit Dramas, p. 279.
20. NS, VI, 61–65 prose lines.
21. Ibid, 45, L-19.26.
22. Ibid, 45, L-9, also Abh. p. 702.
23. NS, XXIV, 169–71.
24. Ibid, 291–96, also IV 313, 314, 320.
25. NS, XXI, 1.
26. The germ idea can emerge in the mind of the chief assistant of the hero also. For example, Yaugandharāyaṇa in the play Pratijñā Yaugandharāyaṇa and Svapna Vāsavadattā and Cāṇakya in Mudrā Rākṣasa. However, the one who attains the fruit at the end is the *adhikārī phalabhoktā* hero.
27. DR.I.26 "Bindu" interrupts the secondary matter and resumes the thread of the seed development.
28. NLRK, II, 141–43.
29. NS, XX, 20.22, Actions forbidden on the stage are: curses, marriage ceremony, commencement of a miracle and its actual occurrence, a battle, a loss of kingdom, a death or a seige of a city, the killings of a hero and his flight, his capture, a treaty, a long journey, revolt, eating, bathing, intercourse, annoiting of a body, putting on clothes, etc.
30. NS, XXXIV, 1, 2 (Tr. M. Ghosh).
31. Ibid. 3, 4.
32. Dr. M. Ghosh's translation has been used to indicate the *Nāyaka-Nāyika bheda*-s. Specifications of DR. Bh.P., SD have also been incorporated.
33. Since each of the sixteen varieties may be superior, middle and inferior, there can be forty-eight varieties of *Nāyaka*—as per the dictates of DR.II, p. 44.
34. NS, XXXV, 9–11 (tr. M. Ghosh).
35. Ibid, 42.
36. Ibid, 36.
37. NS, XXXV, 21-22.
38. In Kudiyattam of Kerala, a *vidūṣaka's* role is next in importance to that of a *sūtradhāra*. An actor masters the *sūtradhāra*'s role first and then that of the *vidūṣaka*.
39. NS, XXXV, 76-77 (tr. M. Ghosh).
40. Ibid, 80.
41. Ibid, 75–78.
42. Ibid, 25–27.
43. DR. (Tr. Haas) II, 45, Notes on p. 40–58 of SD, III, 87, p. 81.
44. DR. (Tr. Haas), II, 45, Notes on p. 40–58.
45. NS, XXXV, 79–86 (tr. M. Ghosh).

CHAPTER 5

VṚTTI—PRAVṚTTI

The Styles and Regional Modes of Production of Sanskrit Plays

As seen in the previous chapter, the skilful blending of the three elements of the plot, the hero and the *rasa* constituted the structure of Sanskrit dramas.

Vṛtti connoted the style with which each of these elements were projected in a play to bring into focus a special mood and atmosphere of its *rasa* content.

Pravṛtti dealt with the purely physical framing of such a presentation. The plot and the hero of a play were always placed in a suitable regional mode, a local background with appropriate language, costumes, behaviour pattern of a specified milieu in order to fascilitate an easy communion of the *rasa* content of the play.

The styles and the regional modes provided, in this way, the basic mood and the physical mounting of the inner idea of the Sanskrit plays. They were traditionally defined, were necessarily interwoven and in their interrelationship they were a forceful source for various combinations of *rasa-vastu-netā* structure of Sanskrit plays. In fact, the genres of Sanskrit dramas, known by the nomenclature of *Daśarūpaka*, were determined by them.

Let us first examine the traditional concept of the styles—*vṛtti*-s—at length.

The Styles—Vṛtti

The styles had very ancient roots and have been linked up with the Indian drama from the beginning. Bharata describes them as "the mothers of *nāṭya*".[1] *Nāṭya Darpaṇa* goes further than that and says that the styles were "the mothers of all actions in *nāṭya* pertaining to *rasa*, *bhāva* and *abhinaya*."[2] The commentary of *Daśarūpuka* says that "the style of the procedure based on the hero's nature is *vṛtti*."[3]

All human activities were systematised by the ancient Indians into three categories, viz., of the mind, voice and body. *Vṛtti*-s denoted the styles of these activities in terms of the hero, plot and *rasa* dominating in a play.

Four Styles—Vṛtti-s—of Sanskrit Dramas

According to the legend of the origin of drama in *Nāṭyaśāstra*, the three main styles such as the verbal style (*bhāratī*) with an emphasis on speech, sublime style (*sāttvatī*) with an emphasis on mind and the energetic style (*ārabhaṭi*) with an emphasis on body originated at the time of the creation of *Nāṭya Veda* itself. This implies that these styles were the essential aspects of the rudimentary forms of earlier enactments of what later became Sanskrit *nāṭya-rūpaka*-s. The fourth—*kaiśikī*—or graceful style was incorporated later on when, for the first time, the actresses, as supports of erotic *rasa* and dance, were introduced in the drama.[4]

Verbal Style (Bhāratī Vṛtti)

This was a style of drama presentation with predominance of speech with Sanskrit recitations by the male performers. As its name indicates, the style was associated with *Bharata*-s who were the original rhapsodes reciting epic tales and who were proficient in Sanskrit speech and recitation. *Nāṭyaśāstra* says that, the style was "used by eponymous *Bharata*-s (actors) as *Bhāratī* (verbal)."[5]

It pervaded those plays which were latent with marvellous and pathetic *rasa*-s.

Sublime Style (Sāttvatī Vṛtti)

This was a style which was dominated by the expression of the concentrated conflict-free mind—*sattva*—and as a consequence was full of joy and was without any dejection.[6] Plays in this style dealt with plenty of heroic action undertaken for righteous purpose.

It was employed in plays which were latent with the heroic, marvellous and furious *rasa*-s.

Energetic Style (Ārabhaṭī Vṛtti)

This style displayed excitement of combats and fights with many vigorous body movements of jumping, falling down, different ways of fighting, deeds of magic and conjuring tricks.

Nāṭya Darpaṇa explains the name of this style by suggesting that "it indicates warriors (*bhaṭa*) who are as sharp as a whip (*āra*)."[7] *Nāṭyaśāstra*, on the other hand, says that "the style is so called because it characterises a bold person (*ārabhaṭa*) who is boastful, deceptive, false and loquacious."[8]

Bāṇa in *Harṣacarita* described a performance of *ārabhaṭī* actors performing with their hair blowing about due to their vigorous movements. The style was used to evoke the terrible, odious and furious *rasa*-s.

Graceful Style (Kaiśikī Vṛtti)

This was a graceful style with pleasing costumes, songs, dances and many female characters, evoking erotic feelings. It contained many elements of the subtle art of pleasure (*narma*). Plays with erotic and comic *rasa*-s exhibited the graceful style.[9]

The names of these four styles are also identified with the names of four tribes of ancient India. V.S. Agrawal and V. Raghavan have suggested this association.[10] Table 2 shows such an identification of styles with the characteristic behaviour pattern of the four ancient tribes from different parts of India.

Table No. 2

Style (*Vṛtti*)	*Tribe*	*Region*
Ārabhaṭī	Aribatas	South Baluchistan; between Indus and Baluchistan.
Sāttvatī	Yadavas	Gujarat, Saurashtra.
Kaiśikī	Kru Kaiśika	Vidarbha
Bhāratī	Bharata Janapada	Kurukshetra

The Regional Modes: Pravṛtti

While the styles dealt mainly with the bearing and the disposition of the three elements (*rasa-vastu-netā*) of Sanskrit drama structure as a whole, the regional modes—or *pravṛtti*-s—covered purely their physical characteristics. Appropriate mode of behaviour, costumes and get-up, the colour of the skin, the manner of hair-dressing, speech and mannerism of the dramatis personae were dictated by different regional and local usages.[11]

And the plots of the dramas were quite scrupulously presented in their appropriate milieu.

Four regional modes representing four broadbased zones of ancient India were taken into consideration and were named as follows:

(i) Pāñcālī: denoting the northern region.
(ii) Āvantī: denoting the central-western region.
(iii) Oḍra-Māgadhi: denoting the eastern region.
(iv) Dākṣiṇātyā: denoting the southern region.

These regional modes will be discussed in greater details later on when we examine the physical get up—*āhārya abhinaya*—especially the costumes and other physical aids of the dramatis personae.

The interrelationship of the styles (*vṛtti*-s) and the regional modes (*pravṛtti*-s) with reference to the local characteristics of the four groups of people coming from four different regions of ancient India is given in the following table:

Table No. 3

No.	Regional mades (*Pravṛtti*-s)	Countries	Region	Dominent styles (*vṛtti*-s) of the people
1.	*Oḍra-māgadhī*	Aṅga, Baṅga Kaliṅga	Eastern	Bhāratī and Kaiśikī
2.	*Āvantī*	Avanti, Vidiśa, Saurāṣṭra, Mālva, Sindhu	Western	*Sāttvatī* and *Kaiśikī*
3.	*Dākṣinātya*	Southern coastal areas and Vindhyas	Southern	Abundance of *Kaiśikī* (*Sukumāra—delicate style of production*)
4.	*Pāñcālī*	Pañcāla, Śūrasena, Kāśmīra, Hastināpur, Himālaya	Northern	*Sāttvatī* and *Ārabhaṭī* (*Āviddha—vigorous style of production*)

Suggested Development of the Genres of Sanskrit Plays on the Basis of the Styles of their Presentation

Sanskrit plays or *nāṭya rūpaka*-s as they were called, denote the audio-visual variety of Sanskrit poetical compositions. Perhaps, it may not be farfetched to propose that *rūpaka*-s might have gradually emerged as the development of *nāṭya* when the written texts were supplied by the playwrights. The *rūpaka* variety of Sanskrit dramas listed by *Nāṭyaśāstra* presupposes a process of presentation, assimilation and evolution. They reflect a development of a long period of transmission of earlier traditions by generations of practising *nāṭya* troupes and the playwrights attached to them. It is probably because of this that in the *Nāṭyaśāstra*, we find a lot of overlapping in case of some genres, not to mention the existence of assimilated features of earlier genres in the body of the later more perfected and fully formed (*pūrṇa vṛtti*) *rūpaka*-s.

This may be one of the reasons why despite acknowledging the nomenclature of *Daśarūpaka* (or ten *rupaka*-s), the dramaturgical tradition lists more than ten genres of Sanskrit plays. *Nāṭyadarpaṇa* enumerates twelve, *Bhāvaprakāśa* records some thirty. Even the earlier *Nāṭyaśāstra* tradition describes eleven genres of Sanskrit dramas. They are:

(1) *Nāṭaka*, (2) *Prakarṇa*, (3) *Nāṭikā*, (4) *Bhāṇa*, (5) *Prahasana*, (6) *Vīthī*, (7) *Samavakāra*, (8) *Ḍima*, (9) *Īhāmṛga*, (10) *Vyāyoga*, (11) *Utsṛṣṭikāṅka* or *Aṅka*.

These genres of plays, with their predominent styles, had evolved around different cultural and social settings representing diverse patronage. The presentation of *rasa-vastu-netā* in them differed accordingly.

We have seen that Sanskrit dramas had their roots in the primitive performances of ritual magic. Earlier *nāṭya* varieties had emerged out of two practices of such rudimentary enactments. One, out of the exclusive enactment of mythical tales around sacrificial grounds and the other from the acts of mimcry and mirth in the gatherings at tribal festivals. *Nāṭyaśāstra* gives broad hints to these primitive and rudimentary forms of earlier *nāṭya rūpaka*-s when it says that the exclusive tradition of *nāṭya* performance emerged when the *nāṭya veda* was brought down to earth in order to restrict the vulgar ways of the 'outside' popular performances, i.e. '*bāhyika grāmya dharma*' or *prahasana* types of plays. These primitive enactments of the popular, external variety depicted the foibles of common people and had worldly (*lokānusārī*) dramatis personae. The *rasa* evoked was comic. *Prakaraṇa* genre was the culmination which developed out of such enactments.

As against this, a parallel development emerged around the exclusive *nāṭya* enactments where the priest performers portrayed the legendary vedic tales of divine and semi-divine heroes in their heroic exploits. The verbal style with emphasis on Sanskrit speech followed by energetic and sublime styles evolved around these exclusive *nāṭya* enactments. These performances were more stylised and systematically learnt and transmitted. The *rasa*-s evoked were primarily heroic, furious and marvellous. *Nāṭya-śāstra* speaks of a vigorous (*āviddha*) mode of production which was adopted for these performances.

In the course of time, erotic *rasa* with female dramatis personae and the stories with heroes in delicate (*sukumāra*) mode of production came into vogue. The difference between the vigorous and delicate styles of production was that in the former there were only three styles while in the latter all the four styles featured with the graceful style dominating.[12] A group of play genres including the full-fledged *nāṭaka* with all the four styles evolved around this exclusive trend.

V. Raghavan has described these two trends as 'social' and 'heroic'.[13] It must be pointed out, however, that both these parallel developments were mutually interacting streams which adapted and adopted many features of each other. Let us examine the development and characteristics of Sanskrit drama genres against this background.

Earlier Plays in the Heroic Mould: Vīthī, Samavakāra, Ḍima, Īhāmṛga

These genres of plays were products of enactments of exclusive practice around sacrificial grounds and religious festivities. It is quite possible that these early genres did not have any written scripts. No ancient specimen of such plays exist. And yet, all the dramaturgic texts have faithfully described their characteristic features in detail.

Vīthī

Vīthī is considered by many contemporary scholars as our earliest incipient form[14] of the exclusive *nāṭya* enactments. Episodic representation of mythical tales were presented in this genre by the clever use of dialogues by one or two actors at the time of ritualistic religious entertainments and processions. The name suggests an avenue or a street corner. It is possible that such enactments were for the edification and entertainment of congregations of people around the sacrificial grounds and religious processions. In later time, *vīthī*-s were enacted around temple processions also.

It was a one-act, word-based play, dominated by the verbal style. Heroic, marvellous and all the other *rasa*-s, with the exception of erotic, were evoked through *vīthī*. The plot formation had only two junctures (*sandhi*-s) such as opening and the conclusion. The verbal style in *vīthī* later extended into ingenuous employment of the different manners of speaking of the dialogues. So much so that when eventually the genre disappeared, its style of witty exchange of dialogues gradually got assimilated into the prologues of the more evolved drama varieties.[15]

Samavakāra

Samavakāra was a drama genre in which different, loosely related episodes were strung together in three acts. In its representation it might fall under the category of vigorous production (*āviddha prayoga*) because it was a variety of drama with fights, combats and excitement generated through the depiction of battle, flood, storm, fire or a seige of a city. Well-known vedic tales of gods, demons and humans were portrayed with one exalted hero amongst twelve subsidiary heroes (*patākā nāyaka*-s). The progression of the plot had four junctures (*sandhi*-s) and three acts. The principle *rasa* was heroic. The entire duration of the play was eighteen *nāḍikā*-s (i.e. 7 hours and 20 minutes). It is interesting to note that the description given in *Nāṭyaśāstra* of the first drama staged by Bharata and his sons, depicting the war between the gods and the demons bears a striking resemblance to this type of play.[16] The next play of Bharata titled "the churning of the sea" is specifically named as a *samavakāra*.[17] This suggests that such a genre belonged to the earliest expression of drama in India.

Ḍima

Ḍima was another variety of the vigorous style of drama production. The name itself suggests a fight or 'injuring'. Well-known tales with many fights, duels, deeds of magic and sorcery, with eclipses, earthquakes and falling moteors were depicted. There were sixteen heroes and subsidiary heroes—most of them gods, *asura*-s and other supernatural beings like *rākṣasa*-s, *gandharva*-s and others. It presented all *rasa*-s—excepting erotic and comic. The furious *rasa*, however, predominated.

A *ḍima* titled 'Tripuradāha' was performed in the open air by Bharata and his sons in front of Lord Śiva, according to the legendary tale of *Nāṭyaśāstra*.[18] This places *ḍima* in the earlier stages of evolution of *nāṭya-rūpaka*-s.

Īhāmṛga

This was another variety of the production of vigorous plays at a later stage of development. Such plays were a mixture of known legends which were adapted to feature a divine or a human self-controlled and vehement (*dhīroddhatta*) hero. A divine heroine also made her first appearance with the introduction of erotic *rasa* as a principal *rasa*.

As the name suggests, the story apparently revolved around the scheming and planning of a hero in pursuit of a divine woman as eluding as a gazelle (*mṛga*). A divine subsidiary hero (*patākā-nāyaka*) played a major role. The plot progression had three junctures (*sandhi*-s) and was divided into either one or four acts. In the plot a battle was to be avoided at the point of killing.

Further Development of the Heroic Genres of Sanskrit Plays with the Verbal, Sublime and Energetic Styles

With drama troupes finding the court and temple patronage and the playwrights specially composing the play-texts, more mature and heroic plays like *vyāyoga* and *aṅka* were evolved. We have the specimen of these plays with us. Some of the plays written by Bhāsa fall under the category of these two genres.

Vyāyoga

It is a one act play depicting an incident of a single day. It delineates the furious or heroic *rasa* in the vigorous style of production and a renowned plot with three junctures—*sandhi*-s. A superior self-controlled and vehement (*dhīroddhata*) human hero confronts another male character in a duel. There are very few female characters in this genre which depicts a combat of many men. That is the reason for the name *vyāyoga*—(which literally means; where contentious struggle of many men is depicted).[19] Bhāsa's *Madhyama Vyāyoga, Dūta Ghaṭotkaccha* and *Dūta Vākyam* are examples of this genre.

Utṛṣṭikāṅka—Aṅka

This genre depicts strong shades of the pathetic *rasa* while evoking the heroic at the end. The plot is either renowned or devised. The story is set against a background of an end of a battle or a violent fight. As the name suggests, it is a one act play with two junctures—*sandhi*-s—the opening and the conclusion. It has all the styles except *kaiśikī* (graceful).

The hero is a superior type of a vehement (*uddhata*) human who has lost a battle. It includes appearance of lamenting women.

Bhāsa's *Ūrubhaṅgam* and *Karṇabhāra* are plays of this genre.

Earliest Plays in Popular Mould: Bhāṇa and Prahasana

As mentioned before, these early drama genres had come out of the popular entertainments of common people and were part of the outside (bāhya) practices. *Nāṭyaśāstra* tradition frequently ridiculed them, "as those plays which amuse women and fools"[20] but their popularity remained consistent all through the centuries. They remained in vogue as independent genres of drama until the decline of Sanskrit theatre set in.

Bhāṇa

It is a single act play with two junctures—*sandhi-s*—the opening and the conclusion. It is a drama where a single actor creates a number of characters and episodes by his mono-acting.

The plot is invented and usually deals with a gallant-parasite (*viṭa*) who goes on an errand to appease a courtesan ladylove of his noble friend. Happenings around the quarters of the prostitutes and rakes are enacted and narrated with the ingenious techniques of *ekāhārya abhinaya* (*abhinaya* without the *āropaṇa* of *āhārya*, or the adoption of characters without the change of costumes or get-up). He resorts to the stage convention of "speech in the air" (*ākaśa bhāṣita*) to hold forth conversations with imaginary characters who are not seen on the stage.

In the opinion of D.R. Mankad, *bhāṇa* genre is the most primitive *nāṭya* form.[21] There are four extant specimen of *bhāṇa* genre.

Prahasana

Prahasana is a farce or a bawdy satire of one or two acts, ridiculing the hypocrisy in society. The *rasa* evoked is comic. The plots are invented and have two junctures—*sandhi*-s—the opening and the conclusion. The dramatis personae belong to the group of religious ascetics like *bhāgavata*, *tāpasa*, *bhikṣu* and other secterians and hangers-on in a pure *prahasana*. The mixed *prahasana* has courtesans, servants, gallant-parasites (*viṭa*) and female messengers, etc. This genre has all the four styles.

Fully Formed Sanskrit Drama Genres with all the Styles—Nāṭaka, Prakaraṇa

Nāṭaka and *prakaraṇa* are fully developed varieties of drama with all the four styles (pūrṇa-*vṛtti rūpaka*) presented in delicate production style (*sukumāra prayoga*). *Nāṭaka* had evolved out of the heroic mould of drama genres and *prakaraṇa* had evolved from the social mould. Many popular features of the earlier genres were assimilated by them. The Sanskrit playwrights from Bhāsa onwards have composed both these genres of plays.

There are many similarities between them. Both have four styles (*vṛtti*-s), five junctures (*sandhi*-s) and five to seven acts. And yet they differ in their choice of the plot, the hero and the *rasa*. This is because they have developed around different sets of circumstances of patronage.

Perfected Heroic Play—Nāṭaka

It is a perfected heroic play and delineates both the heroic and erotic *rasa*-s. The plot is woven around well-known stories from the epics and *purāṇa*-s.

The hero is a celebrated person, of exalted nature, a superior type, usually a well-known king.[22] The heroine is either divine, royal or a woman of noble family. The other dramatis personae include the subsidiary—*patākā*, prakarī leaders, jester and the other assistants of the hero (*artha-dharma-kāma saciva*-s). The hero's entourage includes a chamberlain (*kañcukī*), female messengers (*pratīhārī*), servants and bards. In some plays there are adversaries (*pratināyaka*-s) of the hero.

Perfected Social Play—Prakaraṇa

Popular patronage is reflected in the choice of the plots, characters and *rasa* depictions in a *prakaraṇa* genre. It has stories derived from popular tales usually adopted from *kathā* literature. The hero is a self-controlled and calm (*dhīrapraśānta*) superior type who is either a brahmin, a merchant, a minister, a caravan leader or a priest but never a king. The heroine is either a woman of good family (*kulastrī*) or a courtesan (*veśastrī*). Other dramatis personae include traders, bankers, servants, gallant-parasites and others who are found in society but are not part of the royal court. The jester in a *prakaraṇa* is not a court jester but a friend of the hero. The *rasa* dipicted is always erotic.

The earliest extant specimen of *prakaraṇa* is Aśvaghoṣa's *Śārīputra Prakaraṇa*.[22]

Later Development—Harem Culture

Nāṭikā

In the atmosphere of king's palaces and harems, an altogether different set of royal amusements brought about a new genre of light romantic plays featuring a number of female characters with plots interspersed with many songs and dances. These play genres were called *nāṭikā*-s which mixed ingredients of a devised plot of a *prakaraṇa* and a known royal hero of a *nāṭaka*. The plot usually centred around a self-controlled and light-hearted (*dhīralalita*) king-hero in a light romantic escapade with a young heroine—usually from a noble family but belonging to the harem.

Nāṭikā genre has four acts, all the junctures and a dominant *kaiśikī* style. These plays were mostly performed by women in a royal harem for the pleasure of the king. Singing, dancing, display of costumes, graceful manners and lyrical movements were essential for its delicate (*sukumāra*) mode of production.

In the mediaeval times, this genre became very popular with royal assemblies of connoisseurs, and thereafter composition of a *nāṭikā* became a vogue among playwrights who belonged to these assemblies.

In the following table the basis of the classification of *Daśarūpaka* is enumerated.

Table No. 4

GENRES OF DĀŚARŪPAKA

No.	Name	Acts	Plot	Hero	Juncture (*Sandhi*)	Stages of action (avasthā)	*Rasa*	Style (*Vṛtti*)
1	*Nāṭaka*	5 to 10	Renowned	Celebrated or exalted (*udātta*)	Five	Five	Eight	Four
2	*Prakaṇa*	5 to 10	Devised	Nobleman who is not a king (*Dhīra praśānta*)	Five	Five	Eight	Four
3	*Nāṭikā*	4	Devised	Celebrated king	Five	Five	Erotic and comic	Four
4	*Samavakāra*	3	Well-known	Exhalted (12)	Four (opening, progression, development, conclusion	Beginning, effort	Heroic, Furious	Three no kaiśikī (graceful style)
5	*Ihāmṛga*	4 (or) 1	Well-known or devised	Divine vehement	Three (opening, progression, conclusion)	Beginning, effort attainment	Furious erotic	,,

No.	Name	Acts	Plot	Hero	Juncture (*Sandhi*)	Stages of action (*avasthā*)	*Rasa*	Style (*Vṛtti*)
6	*Ḍima*	4	Well-known	Known & vehement (*Uddhāta*)	Four (opening, progression, development, conclusion)	Beginning, effort, possibility of attainment, attainment.	All exeept erotic and comic	Three no *kaiśikī* (graceful style)
7	*Vyāyoga*	1	Well-known	Known & vehement (*Uddhata*)	Three (opening, progression, conclusion)	Beginning, Effort, Attainment	All except erotic and comic	„
8	*Utsṛṣṭikāṅka*	1	Well-known (some times devised)	Human Heroes who are known and vehement	Two (opening, conclusion)	Beginning, attainment	Pathetic, Heroic	Verbal (predominant)
9	*Prahasana*	1 or 2	Devised	Human heroes of either different religious sects or gallants and others	„	„	Erotic Comic	„
10	*Bhāṇa*	1	Devised	Men about town	Two (opening, conclusion)	Beginning, attainment	Erotic	„

No.	Name	Acts	Plot	Hero	Juncture (*Sandhi*)	Stages of action (*avasthā*)	*Rasa*	Style (*Vṛtti*)
11	*Vīthī*	1	Devised	All characters types, superior, middle, low.	Two (opening, conclusion)	Beginning, attainment	Eight	Verbal

It becomes apparent that the difference between various genres point to a gradual growth and evolution of Sanskrit *nāṭya rūpaka* from earlier simpler varieties with one or two styles (*vṛtti*-s) which finally culminated into the complete—*pūrṇa vṛtti*—genres like *nāṭaka* and *prakaraṇa*. At different stages, a particular variety of a play had come into being, developed and either got absorbed into a more mature variety or disappeared altogether. There was, thus, much overlapping and interpenetration. So much so that later fully formed genres like *nāṭaka*, *prakaraṇa* and *nāṭikā* exhibit many popular features of earlier variety of plays.

In this context a few interesting and curious points must be noted. The earliest genre from the exclusive enactments was *vīthī*, with its popular feature of witty dialogue and repartee. This feature of *vīthī* has been totally accepted as a part of the prologues of *nāṭaka* and *prakaraṇa*. Many of its subdivisions like accidental interpretation (*udghātya*), three men's tale (*trigata*), enigma (*nālikā*), repartee (*vākakelī*), etc., became integral parts of the prologues by the time of *Nāṭyaśāstra*. The rest of the subdivisions formed part of the units of junctures (*sandhi*-s) called *sandhyāṅga*-s which are the smallest linking units in the plot structure of a drama. And so, *vīthī* genre with its popular subdivisions got absorbed into *nāṭaka*, *prakaraṇa* and other *rūpaka* genres of Sanskrit plays. Even *prahasana* incorporated many elements of *vīthī*.

Certain aspects of *prahasana* itself were assimilated in *nāṭaka* and *prakaraṇa*. The *ekāhārya abhinaya* of the *bhāṇa* genre with its conventions of "Speech in the air" technique of carrying on dialogues with imaginary characters was adopted by all later *rūpaka*-s.

In this way, features of the Sanskrit plays reacted upon each other, overlapped and out of such interaction more complex varieties of Sanskrit plays were evolved.

The basic framework of *rasa*, plot and the hero remained the same. The changing tastes of patrons left a strong imprint on the style in which these three elements were presented. The styles of their production, vigorous or delicate, and the choice of the genres were affected only due to these changing tastes. Heroic plays, social plays, harem plays demonstrated variations of the styles of presentations of *rasa*, plot and the hero structure like patterns formed by a keleidoscope.

Here the Sanskrit plays exhibit similarities with their South Asian counterparts, especially the Noh play of Japan with its categories of god-plays, warrior-plays, demon-plays, woman-plays, etc. and the Chinese opera repertoire of military plays, civilian plays and so on which emphasise the style in which the hero and the plot are presented and accordingly named.

This chapter is concluded with a framework categorising the plays of Bhāsa to Bhavabhūti and evaluating them on the basis of the above discussion. The attempt is to develop a conceptual framework which, among other things, makes Sanskrit play scripts more intelligible in the context of their production. Only when the analysis and classification of each play is done from the angle of its style (*vṛtti*), *rasa*, plot, hero, junctures (*sandhi*-s) of the plot and acts—in short, in the accepted norms of the practice of the period—that the required practical evaluation of Sanskrit play-texts as scripts for production becomes possible.

Framework 1

SANSKRIT DRAMAS—AS SCRIPTS FOR PRODUCTION

Playwright	Nāṭya-Rūpaka	Genre	Rasa		Plot (Vastu)	Hero (Netā)	Act	Junctures	Styles
			Main	Subsidiary					
BHĀSA	1 Ūru Bhanga	Utsṛṣṭikāṅka	Heroic	Strong pathetic	Renowned	Duryodhana	1	2-Mukha 4–Nirvahaṇa	All three except Kaiśiki
	2 Karṇa Bhāra	„	„	„	„	Karṇa	1	„	„
	3 Dūta Ghaṭotkacha	Vyāyoga	Heroic	Raudra	„	Ghaṭotkacha	1	„	„
	4 Dūta Vākya	„	„	Strong Raudra	„	Kṛṣṇa	1	„	„
	5 Madhyama Vyāyoga	„	„	Raudra	„	Bhima	1	„	„
	6 Pañcarātra	Samavakāra	„		„	All Pāṇḍavas including Abhimanyu.	3		„
	7 Bāla Carita	Nāṭaka	„	Marvellous Bhayānaka	„	Kṛṣṇa	5	5	4
	8 Avimāraka	„	Erotic	Comic Marvellous	„[2]	Avimāraka	6	5	4
	9 Cārudatta	Prakaraṇa[3]	„	Comic	„	Carudatta	4	5	4

Playwright	Nāṭya-Rūpaka	Genre	Rasa		Plot (Vastu)	Hero (Netā)	Acts	Junctures	Styles
			Main	Subsidiary					
BHĀSA (*Contd.*)	10 Pratimā	Nāṭaka	Heroic	Marvellous Pathetic Erotic	Renowned	Rama/ Patākā nāyaka, Bharata.	7	5	4
	11 Abhiśeka	,,	,,	,, Furious	,,	Rāma/ Patākā Nāyaka Sugrīva.	6	,,	,,
	12 Pratijñā, Y.	Nāṭaka[4]	,,	Comic Pathetic	,,[5]	Udayana	4	5	3 (no Kai-śikī)
	13 Svapna Vāsavadattā	Nāṭaka	Erotic	Comic	,,	Udayana	6	5	4
KĀLIDĀSA	1 Mālavikā-Agnimitra	Nāṭaka	,,	,,	,,	Agni-mitra	5	5	4
	2 Vikramor-vaśiya	,, (Toṭaka)	,,	,, Marvellous	,,	Purūravas	,,	,,	,,
	3 Abhijñāna Śākuntala	Nāṭaka	,,	,,	,,	Duṣyanta	7	,,	,,
ŚŪDRAKA	1 Mṛccha-kaṭika	Prakaraṇa	,,	Comic	,,	Cāru-datta	10	,,	,,
ŚRI HARṢA	1 Priya-	Nāṭikā	,,	,,	Re-	Udayana	4	5	Kaiśiki

Playwright	Nātya Rūpaka	Genre	Rasa		Plot (Vastu)	Hero (Netā)	Acts	Junctures	Styles
			Main	Subsidiary					
ŚRI HARṢA (*Contd*).	–darśini	Naṭika	Erotic	Comic	Renowned/ Invented	Udayana	4	5	Kaiśiki
	2 Ratnāvali	,,	2	,,	,,	,,	,,	,,	,,
	3 Nāgānanda	Nāṭaka	Heroic	Erotic Marvellous	,,	Jimūta-vāhana	5	,,	4
VIŚĀKHA DAṬṬA	Mudrā Rākṣasa	,,[6]	,,	Raudra	,,	Candra-gupta	7	5	Three except Kai-śiki
BHATTA NĀRĀYAṆA	Veṇi Samhāra	,,	,,	Raudra Pathetic	,,	Bhima-sena	6	5	4
BHAVABHŪTI	1 Mahāvira Carita	,,	,,	Erotic	,, Invented	Rāma		,,	,,
	2 Mālati Mādhava	Prakaraṇa	Erotic	Rest of the seven	,,	Mādhava	10	,,	,,
	3 Uttara Rāma Carita	Nāṭaka	Karuṇa	Erotic Marvellous	Re-nowned	Rāma	7	,,	,,
MAHENDRA VV	Matta Vilāsa	Prahasana	Comic	Odious	Invented	Kāpālika	1	2	Bhā-rati
BODHĀYANA	Bhagavada Ajjukā	,,	,,	Erotic	,,	Bhaga-vata	1	,,	Bhārati and Kaiśiki

Playwright	Nāṭya-Rūpaka	Genre	Rasa		Plot (Vastu)	Hero (Netā)	Act	Junctures	Styles
			Main	Subsidiary					
VARARUCI	Ubhayābhi-sārikā	Bhāṇa	Erotic	Comic	Invented	Kubera-datta[7]	1	2	Bhārati and Kaiśikī
ŚŪDRAKA	Padma-prabhṛtaka	„	„	„	„	Karṇi-pūtra	„	„	„
ŚYĀMILAKA	Pādatāḍika	„	Comic	Odious	„	Viṭa	„	„	„
IŚVARADATTA	Dhūrta Vita Saṃvāda	„	„	„	„	„	„	„	„

1. Dr. Keith, op. cit., p. 346, p. 97 — he points out that in this play there are many heroes.
2. The story is taken from Bṛhatkathā.
3. The play has only four acts, but in all the other respects it satisfies the requirements of a prakaraṇa.
4. This particular play does not fit into any of the Daśarūpaka category—Dr. Keith thinks it to be a Prakaraṇa
   Winternitz/G. Shastri think it to be a Nāṭikā
   Banerjee Shastri ed. think it to be a Ihāmṛga
   Shanta Gandhi thinks it to be a Nāṭaka duology.
5. From Kathas of Udayana stories.
6. For details Infra Pt. V, Chapter 12, pp. 347-48. The play can be termed as a Nāṭaka when taken as a Nāṭaka-duology-with "Devi Candragupta" of Viśākhadatta.
7. The absent Kuberadatta is the hero. Viṭa is only Kāma sahāyaka.

NOTES

1. NS, XXII, 64.
2. ND, p. 135.
3. DR.
4. NS.
5. NS, XXII, 25 (tr. M. Ghosh).
6. Ibid, 38
7. ND, p. 140.
8. NS, XXII, 55.
9. A number of Sanskrit plays, especially *nāṭikā*-s have graceful style with the subdivisions of—
   (1) Pleasantry (*Narma*),
   (2) Beginning of pleasantry (*Narma sphūrja*),
   (3) Unfolding of pleasure (*Narmasphoṭa*),
   (4) Covert pleasure (*Narmagarbha*).
10. Raghavan V., Vṛtti-s, J.O.R. Madras Vol. VII, p. 40.
    Agarwala V.S., Indian as known to Pāṇini, p. 34.
11. NS, XIV, 36, L-12.
12. NS, IV, 10.
13. Raghavan V., The Social Play in Sanskrit, p. 2.
14. Raghavan V., Vṛtti-s, p. 281.
15. The specimen of old *vīthī* is not with us. But these street play genres written from 16th century onwards are popularly performed to this day in Andhra Pradesh, Tamilnadu and Kerala, where they are known as *Vīthī* or *Vidhi nāṭakam*.
16. NS, I, 59.
17. NS, IV, 3.
18. Ibid, 10.
19. DR. III, After 55, L-1.
20. NS, XXVII, 61 (tr. M. Ghosh).
21. Mankad D.R., op. cit. p. 78. C.F. Ketkar Godavari, Bharatiya Natya-sastra (Marathi), p. 351.
22. *Prakaraṇa* types were fully evolved around the pre-Christian era. As H. Winternitz says, "Buddhists were the first to introduce drama into literature". Plays with prose and verse in Sanskrit and Prakrits, divisions into acts and *vidūṣaka* as a lover of dainty dishes evoking comic rasa are seen in Aśvaghoṣa's plays.

PART THREE

THE PERFORMANCE

The costume should be decided in accord with the age (of the character). Movements, gestures—the entire gait should go with the costume. The gait follows the purport of the play. And the performance (abhinaya) should correspond to this aim.

Viṣṇu Dharmottara Purāṇa 3.29.39

CHAPTER 6

PERFORMANCE—ABHINAYA

Abhinaya was the traditionally formulated technique of performance where the actor through his body, speech, *sattva* and get-up, evoked in the spectator the *rasa* experience latent within the play-text.

The term *abhinaya* is explained by Bharata etymologically. He says that "that which carries the performance towards the spectator is *abhinaya*."[1] He elaborates further and adds that, "by proper gestures and postures, it explains the essential meaning of the play to the spectator."[2] Viśvanātha elucidates further by saying that "It is that, where the actor through his body, mind, speech and other physical aids imitates (*anukaraṇa*) the states of being (*avasthā*) of the characters on the stage."[3] Abhinavagupta goes still deeper and adds another dimension when he emphasises that *abhinaya* is not a mere imitation (*anukaraṇa*) of a character, but it is an interpretative exploration (*anukīrtana*) conveying a series of related meanings to the text of the play.[4]

An actor, through his *abhinaya*, then portrays the extended interpretations or savourings of the states of being of a character placed in a situation during the progression of the plot. In order to do this, an actor has to precisely manipulate a fixed format of *abhinaya* techniques representing a number of responses to various stimuli corresponding to different situations in a play.

The term *abhinaya* thus has a wider meaning than the term 'acting' with which it is generally associated in a modern-day usage.

Abhinaya and Acting

One of the most revealing distinctions between the two terms is the manner in which each term expresses the process of the actor's art of communication.

The modern spectator is largely conditioned to think of dramas in terms of the spoken words. And this way of approach to acting is understood in the contemporary parlance to mean a communication where an actor suitably represents the words of the playwright taking them as an artistic unity complete in itself with appropriately spontaneous (and in most instances, realistic) gestures, movements, facial expressions and the use of voice and speech.

Abhinaya, on the other hand, connotes a much more complex process of an actor's art which was highly systematised and precisely worked out. The codes of *abhinaya* must have been systematised prior to *Nāṭyaśāstra* (200 B.C.—200 A.D.) because we find in it a well established and minutely defined sets of rules and conventions of *abhinaya* in not less than fifteen chapters.

On a stage devoid of physical aids like scenery, furniture, fixtures or a drop curtain, the ancient actor confronted the spectator in his total presence. With skilful use of his body (*āṅga*), voice and speech (*vāc*), inward concentrated mind (*sāttva*) and colour, costume and hand-held properties (*āhārya*), the actor gave expression to the inner idea of the playwright's script in an exploratory improvisational style. Such a communication in its four aspects go under the name of the four-fold *abhinaya*. Fixed codes governed *abhinaya*. Each body movement, gesture, facial expression, intonation of voice, inflexion of speech, use of costume, colour (body paint) and hand properties as well as the portrayal of inner states—*bhāva*-s—had precise, traditional formulations. Such a communication conveyed layers of meanings leading to different interpretations and the exploration of the play-text. An actor had to acquire mastery over it through years of rigorous training. In this aspect, *abhinaya* in Sanskrit plays was classical in its most formal sense. Its codified structure and the manner of its exposition stands comparison with the classical Indian arts like music and dance, rather than with the realistic, dialogue-based modern theatre.

In fact, the *āṅgika abhinaya* of Sanskrit dramas (*nāṭya abhinaya*) and that of the classical dance (*nṛtya abhinaya*) utilise the same set of traditional *abhinaya* techniques, albeit with a different purpose. They sometimes appear so similar to the unintiated spectator that very often *nāṭya abhinaya* seems to be all dance to him. (This is the case with Asian theatre also. So much so that the theatre in Cambodia is known as 'the dance house'.) Nevertheless, a distinct difference does exist between the two. And it is pointed out by commentators like Dhanañjaya and others[6] which is well worth considering. Let us look at some of the points of distinction.

Āṅgika Abhinaya in Sanskrit Play Performance (Nāṭya) and Classical Dance (Nṛtya)

Abhinaya in Sanskrit Play Performance	*Abhinaya in Classical Dance*
(1) aims at evocation of the *rasa*.	(1) aims at evocation of the *bhāva*.
(2) depicts suggestively the implied meaning of the entire sentence (or a dialogue) (*rasārtha abhinaya*).	(2) elaborately delineates the meaning of each word in a song (*padārtha abhinaya*).
(3) employs subtle body movements (*spandana*) with emphasis on the *sāttvika abhinaya*.	(3) does this through larger movements of various limbs of the dancer's body (*gātravikṣepa*).

Thus we see that the same techniques of *abhinaya* were used in Sanskrit drama and the classical dance but with distinctly separate emphasis, dependence and aim.

The Four-fold Abhinaya in Sanskrit Dramas

The actor in Sanskrit dramas created the entire performance through the employment of:

(1) *Āṅgika Abhinaya*: Actor's communication through his body

This was further divided into:
Movements of the major limbs (*Aṅga*) such as head, chest, sides, waist, hands and feet.
Movements of the minor limbs (*Pratyāṅga*-s) such as neck, arms, back, belly, thighs, knees.
Movements of the parts of the limbs (*Upāṅga*-s) such as eyes, eyebrows, nose, cheeks, lower lips, chin.

For *abhinaya* in a drama, the *āṅgika ceṣṭā* of the entire body, the body postures and movements (*sthiti* and *gati*), the gestures of the hands (*hasta abhinaya*) and movements of the face (*mukhaja abhinaya*) were important.

(2) *Vācika Abhinaya*: Actor's communication through his voice and speech

The use of right notes of the three voice registers (*saptaka*-s with seven *svara*-s each).

Four ways of uttering and giving accent to the notes (*varṇa*-s).

Two ways of intonation (*kāku*-s).

Six ways of recitation of notes (*alaṃkāra*-s).

Six ways of enunciation of a sentence (*aṅga*-s).

Three kinds of time-measure (*laya*).

Pause (*virāma*).

Use of languages, Sanskrit, Prakrit (*deśi* dialects).

(3) *Sāttvika Abhinaya*: Actor's communication through inward concentration of pure mind-*sattva*

Representation of the latent *rasa*-s in a play text through the portrayal of eight basic states of being (*anubhāva*-s), subsequent transitory states (*vyabhicāri-bhāva*-s) and pure involuntary impulses (*sāttvika bhāva*-s).

(4) *Āhārya Abhinaya*: Actor's communication through his physical get up, colour of costumes, accessories, body paints, hand props.

A Fixed Terminology indicating employment of Abhinaya in Sanskrit Play Texts

The Sanskrit play texts, their stage directions and the commentaries written on them give an insight in the use of four-fold *abhinaya* in a play performance. The stage directions in the play texts, especially the ones preceding the spoken words, employ fixed terminologies like *nāṭayati*, *rūpayati*, *abhinita*, *rūpayitvā*, etc. When literally translated, the terms approximate to the English word 'gesticulation' which gives just a general idea which is only true for a part of the actual meaning suggested. The implied meaning of these Sanskrit terms is the visual representation through *abhinaya* of the written text. Or, as D. R. Mankad says, these terms, "when used in the stage directions mean to act so as to represent visibly a particular situation or an emotion".[6] (For the purpose of this study, the

English word 'enactment' is generally used to convey this meaning.)

The manner in which the fourfold *abhinaya* was employed in the audio-visual representation of the written text was traditionally worked out. The order in which the representation by the actor preceded, accompanied and followed the spoken word was conventionally approached by six ways:

(1) *Vākyam*: Suggests recitation and speech in Sanskrit and Prakrit verse and prose in the text. Fixed rules of voice and speech (*vācika abhinaya*) governed the rendering to indicate meanings evoking appropriate *rasa*-s.

(2) *Sūcā*: Suggests the delineation through *sāttvika abhinaya*, specially of the eyes and other facial expressions with subtle body movements, vibrations (*spandana*) of the implied meaning or *bhāva*-s of the speech. *Sūcā* was delineated before the words were spoken.

(3) *Aṅkura*: Implies the eepression of subtle body movement (*aṅga sattva abhinaya*) of the inner states (*bhāva*) emerging in one's heart as a result of the situations in a play, skilfully represented by hand gestures (*hasta*-s) and the facial expressions through subtle movements of the minor limbs. Like *sūcā*, *aṅkura abhinaya* might also be delineated before the spoken words.

(4) *Śākhā*: The body movements (*āngika*) made in due order by the hands, face, shanks, thighs and feet in the manner of branches of a tree. Kātyavema in his commentary on Kālidāsa's *Malāvikāgnimitra* defines *śākhā* as "gesticulation by means of movements of hands corresponding to the musical time measures."[7] This indicates stylised hand and arm movements, as is seen in the *abhinaya* of classical dance.

(5) *Nāṭyāyita*: There are four explanations offered for this term:

(i) One group of actors approaching and meeting other group of actors in the *nāṭyadharmī* zonal divisions of the stage.[8]

(ii) *Abhinaya* of a *dhruvā* song.

(iii) *Abhinaya* during the first entry of an important character (*pātrapraveśa*).

(iv) *Abhinaya* of a play within play.

(v) *Nivṛtyāṅkura*: Implied *abhinaya* of one actor through *sūcā* representing the meaning of the words spoken by another actor and vice-versa.

We get innumerable instances of all the above mentioned styles of the use of four-fold *abhinaya* in the stage directions of the Sanskrit play-texts. In the following four sections the stage directions are examined in terms of the audio-visual representation of the written text.

Section I

Āṅgika Abhinaya: Actor's Communication through his body

(As reflected in the stage directions of the Sanskrit play-texts.)

The body movements employed in Sanskrit dramas were not conceptualised for realistic acting or for spontaneous actions of the performer (not even in *lokadharmī abhinaya*). A highly stylised manipulation of different parts of the body in repose (*sthiti*) and in movement (*gati*) was meticulously worked out to be performed according to traditional rules. This was indicated in the stage directions of the Sanskrit play-texts in the following ways:

(1) The character types standing, sitting, reclining in various states and situations.

(2) The gaits and stage walks indicating entries, exits, going around, the combats and other stage actions.

(3) The varied representation of different objects and activities through specified movements.

Body in Repose (or sthiti)

Well worked out postures or stances of standing, sitting and reclining on the stage by different character types in various moods and situations—*bhāvāvasthā*-s—indicated the use of the body in repose. The proportions or stage stances worked out by ancient artists can be seen in the classical Indian sculptures and at times glimpsed in the performance of classical dance today. These were also shared by the rules of the perfectly balanced postures, stances, *karaṇa*-s and *hasta-mudrā*-s of the classical theatre.

The precision and technical meticulousness with which such stances were worked out by tradition can be illustrated by just one example of *SAUṢṬHAVA*: The basic stance of superior type—*uttama prakṛti*.

Superior types of characters in a Sanskrit play would maintain a basic posture of the body under all situations unless specifically mentioned to be without it. That basic stance was known as *sauṣṭhava*. Bharata describes it in this way:

> "The chest raised, the shoulders at rest and not raised much, the neck as graceful as that of a peacock, the shoulders eight *aṅgulas* apart from the ears, the chin four *aṅgulas* apart from the breast, the two hands, the right and the left, respectively at the navel and at the left hip."
>
> "The interval between the two feet should be two *tālas* and a half."

Apart from this, *sauṣṭhava* had to have the body free from shaking and tremor and straight ('unbent'). The posture was to be relaxed and still. The waist, ears, elbows, shoulders and head had to be in the natural position (*sama*) and the chest raised.[10]

This is the way in which the basic stance of the chief dramatis personae is detailed by tradition. Bharata also adds that, "the limbs without *sauṣṭhava* create no beauty (literally, do not shine) in a drama or a dance."[11]

Sūtradhāra, a superior character, maintained this posture. Non-maintenance of *sauṣṭhava* was considered to be a defect by the connoisseurs. Only in situations of separation in love (*vipralaṃbha* of *kāmadaśā*) such a stance was not maintained.

The Character-Types: Standing, Sitting, Reclining in various States and Situations (Sthāna-Āsana-Śayana)

There were fixed postures of standing, sitting and reclining in various states and situations (*bhāvāvasthā*-s) of different characters. By manipulating different positions of legs and feet (*vikṛṣṭa*, *trayaśra*, *caturaśra*) an actor gave a specific bend (*bhaṅgi*) to the body and expressed various actions, moods and *bhāva*-s.

The Standing Postures of Characters (Sthāna-s)

There were separate standing postures for men and women. The postures varied according to different situations, basic states, transitory states and *sāttvika bhāvas*.

The six standing postures for men were (1) *Vaiṣṇava*, (2) *Samapāda*, (3) *Vaiśākha*, (4) *Maṇḍala*, (5) *Ālīḍha*, (6) *Pratyālīḍha*.[11] The three standing postures for women were (1) *Āyata*, (2) *Avahittha*, (3) *Aśvakrāntā*.[12]

Vaiṣṇava posture for men and āyata and *avahittha* postures for women were recommended for general use. The sketches of these postures are given on page 139.

Stage directions like the "heroine stands with a downcast face" or "the hero stands lost in thought" would indicate fixed standing postures in many variations of "states and situations".

Sitting Postures of Characters (Āsana-s)

Eight sitting postures with variations of situations, moods and the body manipulations were common to men and women. They did not go under specific names but the difference was emphasised by the different states and situations, like sitting at ease, sitting in a thoughtful mood, sitting in sorrow, sitting in shame or asleep, sitting intoxicated or in a faint, sitting during a ceremonial occasion, sitting in worship, sitting for pacifying a beloved, etc.[14] The sketches of these postures are given on page 140.

Stage directions like "Then enters Vasantasenā, occupying a seat in a love sick state" or "then enters the king in a pensive mood" would indicate sitting postures in variations of states and situations.

Reclining Postures of Characters (Śayana)

Six reclining positions of men and women are described in *Nāṭyaśāstra*, with specific names. They are "*akuñcita*", lying down with limbs narrowed; "*sama*", reclining in deep sleep, "*prasārita*", reclining in a sleep of happiness; "*vivartita*", reclining posture after being wounded or intoxicated; "*udvāhita*", reclining with the head resting on the hand and knees; "*nata*", reclining in laziness, fatigue or distress.[15] These postures are vaguely described as far as the positioning of different limbs are concerned. They appear to be in a *lokadharmī* style.

Basic Standing Postures—Sthana-s—of an actor in Sanskrit theatre [As per NS]

FOR MEN

1. Samapāda [NS, XI, 57-60]

2. Vaiṣṇava [NS, XI, 51-5]

3. Vaiśākha [NS, XI, 61-2]

4. Maṇḍala [NS, XI, 63-5]

5. Āliḍha [NS, XI, 66-8]

6. Pratyāliḍha [NS, XI, 69]

FOR WOMEN Walking and speaking to others.

7. Āyāta [NS, XIII, 159]

8. Avahitta [NS, XIII, 163]

9. Aśvakrāntā [NS, XIII, 168]

Basic Sitting Positions—Āsanas—of an actor in Sanskrit theatre [as per NS]

10. Setting at ease [NS, XIII, 194]

11. Sitting in a pensive mood. [NS, XIII, 195]

12. Sitting in sorrow [NS, XIII, 196]

13. Sitting in faint, intoxication etc. [NS, XIII, 197]

14. Sitting in shame, sleep etc. [NS, XIII, 198]

15. Sitting on ceremonial occasion [NS, XIII, 199]

16. Sitting worshipping a deity [NS, XIII, 202-03]

17. Sitting pacifying a beloved woman [NS, XIII, 200-01]

The reclining postures are suggested by the stage directions like "Then enters Vasantasenā, in bed with her body covered up" or "Then appears Śakuntalā lying down on a slab of a stone attended by her friends", etc.

Body in Motion (Gati)

Stylised Stage-walk and Gait of different Characters Types (Cārī and Gati pracāra)

Stylised Stage Walks—(Cārī-s)

Cārī-s were stylised stage walks indicative of different stage actions. There was simultaneous movement of feet, shanks and hips in a stage walk (cārī) with the movement of one single foot predominating. Like *hasta abhinaya* where a movement of one hand suggests different ideas, in a stage walk—*cārī*—movement of a single foot was utilised to suggest different actions while the other foot remained planted firmly on the floor. Cārī always began with a standing stance (*sthāna*) and ended in one, and so the maintenance of proper stance or posture was vital in a *cārī*. Bharata suggests this when he says that "*Cārī* should be performed. . .with the *sauṣṭhava* and accompanied by music with (proper) tempo and time-measure."[16] Bharata also connotes a *cārī* movement with the term *vyāyāma* indicating stretching out of the foot.[17]

A combined movement of *cārī*-s with two feet alternating was called a *karaṇa*. Three *karaṇa*-s made a *khaṇḍa*. Three or four *khaṇḍa*-s made a *maṇḍala*.[18]

Stylised stage walks (*cārī*) suggested different actions like a chariot ride, use of bow and arrow, stage combats and fights and going around the stage to establish *nāṭyadharmī* zonal divisions (*parikramā*).

Both *cārī*-s and *maṇḍala*-s were used to establish two kinds of stage walks:

(1) Earthly stage walks (*bhaumikī cārī*-s) for actions like combats and other specified activities.
(2) Aerial stage walks (*ākāśikī cārī*-s) for missiles or walking in "heavenly abode" and other specified actions.

Nāṭyaśāstra describes thirty-two *cārī*-s. Later works on

dramaturgy and music have added to this list. *Maṇḍala*-s according to *Nāṭyaśāstra*, are twenty in number.

Gati Pracāra (Gaits)

Gaits were different styles of walking, prescribed for different character-types, set to a fixed tempo and time beat. They varied according to the proportions of the stages of the theatres. For example, in a rectangular stage, the foot movement could be large and in square and triangular stages the movements were squarish or triangular (*caturaśra* and *trayaśra*) respectively.[19] They also varied to suit the states, situations, place, occasion; in short, *bhāva*-s.[20]

Gaits had foot movements where both the feet were given equal importance and as such, *cārī*, which emphasised a movement of a single foot, led to a gait as a matter of course. The gait of the superior types was to be in a steady slow tempo, the middle types walked with medium tempo, while the low types walked with fast, speedy steps. In a sense, therefore, the gaits, *cārī*-s and *maṇḍala*-s were interrelated and were integral parts of the stage movements in a drama performance. Bharata has emphasised this again and again by saying that "except by a *cārī*, there shall be no movement in a play."[21] The entries and exits of dramatis personae, the going around (*parikramā*), the specified walks on the stage as well as the fights and combats made use of them. Each of them had measured steps, fixed rules of tempo and were generally accompanied by music—especially the drums. A few examples of *cārī*-s, *maṇḍala*-s and gaits as indicated in the stage directions of the play-texts are given below:

Different Gaits of Dramatis Personae

The Stage Directions

The different gaits of characters in a play are indicated in stage directions[22] like:

"Then enters the king surrounded by female *yavanīs* with bows in hand,"

"Then enters *Irāvatī*, in an intoxicated state,"

"Then enters the maid, Māgadhikā, with a basket in hand,"

"Then enters the jester,"

"Then enters the chamberlain", and so on.

The following gaits for the above stage directions are suggested by *Nāṭyaśāstra* tradition:

In the first instance, the king, in the lovelorn state would walk with the tempo of four to two *kalā*-s (time measure indicating *laya*). The attendant would "walk with steps of one kalā."[23] The king would walk with "graceful steps in a slow tempo with proper *sauṣṭhava*"[24] in the aerial *atikrāntā cārī* where "a *kuñcita* foot is thrown up, put forward and caused to fall on the ground."[25]

In the second instance, Irāvatī would "walk with dragging feet . . .", "sometimes going backward" . . . "with delicately faltering movements trying to grasp something (lit. the sky), rolling of eyes, uttering indistinct words and shaking of limbs"[26] to indicate her intoxicated state.

In the third instance, Māgadhikā as a maid would walk "with a slightly raised body and flourishing of arms, after assuming *avahittha sthāna* with the left hand pointing downwards and the right hand showing the *kaṭakāmukha* hand held at the navel."[27] This is a general direction regarding the gait of a handmaid. In the above case, the maid would have a basket in her hand. The *avahittha* posture indicates, "the left foot in *sama* and the right foot in *trayaśra* and left hip raised up."[28]

In the case of the jester, his gait would be with "feet raised high in the medium tempo." He would "carry the *kuṭilaka* in his left hand and show *catura hasta* with his right hand. He would lower each of his sides and hands by turn, observing proper tempo and *kalā*."[29] In the *catura hasta* "the four fingers are stretched and the thumb is bent near the middle finger."

In the case of a chamberlain, his gait would vary according to his age and condition. If he is not old and infirm, he would "walk with his feet raised half a tāla high and with simple steps walking as if he is treading on mud. If old, he would walk with "trembling body and (would) raise (his) feet slowly with deep breathing at every step."[30]

Obstruction in Gait

Rāghavabhaṭṭa describes the execution of the "obstruction in walk" of Śakuntalā through *udvṛttā cārī*.[31]

Cārīs Suggestive of different Actions

The Walk Around—Parikramā

This oft-repeated terminology in the stage directions, indicating *nāṭyadharmī* zonal division has been discussed in detail in the next chapter. Here we examine only the body movements, *cārī*-s and gaits of a walk around briefly.

In the play *Veṇīsaṃhāra* (Act II) the king and the chamberlain establish, through *cārī*-s and the gaits, a location of a palace park by simply moving around on the bare stage. Nearing the end of the sequence, they enact climbing up a hill in a park during a whirlwind only by going around on the stage, with the appropriate *cārī*-s and gaits accompanied by the audio-visual *abhinaya*. The locale of the park is established by their *āṅgika-vācika* and *sāttvika abhinaya* representing the fragrant breeze, the scent of flowers, warbling of cuckoos, humming of honeybees, aroma of ripe fruits, etc. Later they would employ *atikrānta* cārī to enact the ascending of the hill.

In a similar fashion a hermitage, a city street, a courtesan's mansion were conveyed through the stylised stage walks with other *aṅga—sattva abhinaya* accompanying the words. Aerial flights, ascents and descent from the sky were executed by this technique. It is interesting to note that earthly and aerial *cārī*-s distinguished the locales of hermitages of Kaṇva on earth and Mārīca in heaven in Kālidāsa's *Abhijñāna Śākuntala*.

Representation of Combats and Stage Battles

Although the tradition of Sanskrit dramas forebade the depiction of battles or combats on the stage and actual piercing, striking and flow of blood were also prohibited, earlier dramatists like Bhāsa, had scenes of combats in their plays. In his plays the fights were indicated by the stage directions using words like

"All are engaged in a combat."

Specific *cārī*-s and *maṇḍala*-s were employed in such combats and fights which were accompanied by the use of suggestive gestures, postures, music and rhythm.

This tradition still survives in the traditional theatres of India and South East Asia where scenes of combat are depicted with proper tempo, rhythm and stylised stage walks.

Varied representation of different activities through hand gesture, facial expression and body movement—Citrābhinaya

Many actions as well as animate and inanimate objects in the Sanskrit plays were simply suggested by the stylised movements

Framework No. 2

CITRĀBHINAYA EMPLOYED IN SANSKRIT DRAMAS

The Stage Direction (denoting gesticulates)	The Āngika Abhinaya as per NS, later authorities like AD. (Rāghavabhatta's ARTHA DYO. is also referred to wherever applicable)	
1. *Gathering of flowers*	*The hand gestures*: Kaṭakamukha[1] (plucking of flowers). Padmakośa[2] (small flowers) Bhramara[3] (plucking of flowers of long stems like lotus and water lily). Samdamśa (plucking of flowers). Any of these hand gestures with appropriate body movements. *Act IV*—Praveśaka: (Then enter two friends gesticulating as though gathering flowers) with left hand in arāla hasta with palm up, right hand in the side with hamsāsya hasta.	(Artha Dyo. p. 24)
2. *Troubled by a bee*	*Act I*—20, *L*-3 (Sakuntalā acts as though troubled by a bee). Artha Dyo describes vidhuta head movement with trembling lips, bringing of patākā hasta to one's face, which then is quickly turned away.	(Ibid. 24)
3. *Acts as though watering the trees*	*Act I*—16, *L*-10 (Acts as though watering the trees). Padmakośa hastas brought near the shoulder with vidhuta head; the movement is up and down.	(P. 20)
4. *Gesticulates painting of the feet*	Kartarimukha hands pointing downwards.[5]	N.A.
5. *Gesticulates pujā of the king*	*Use of hand gestures*: Tripatākā and Swastika.[6] Also to be indicated with Kaṭakavardhamāna or kapota hands touching the head.[7]	N.A.
6. *Gesticulates fixing of an arrow*	*The body postures*: Maṇḍala or Āliḍha Sthāna. Three out of four acts (Nyāya) relating to the bows, viz. preparing (Parimārjana) taking an arrow (Ādāna), taking an aim (Sandhāna) to be employed.[8]	N.A.
7. *Gesticulates the speed of a chariot*	*To be represented with the Sthāna and Gait*: (*a*) Sampāda sthāna is to be assumed. With short steps mime the movement of the chariot. Mime taking, of the pole of a chariot in one hand, also mime	

The Stage Direction (denoting gesticulation)	The Āngika Abhinaya as per NS, later authorities like AD. (Rāghavabhatta's ARTHA DYO. is also referred to wherever applicable)	
	taking a bow in another. The charioteer should ramain busy with the whips and the reins; and enter the stage with quick easy steps.[9]	N.A.
	(*b*) One who has to mount and move his body up, with the face looking up.[10]	N.A.
8. *Gesticulates flight in the sky or in a aerial car*	The gait of the character moving through the sky includes the aerial cāris and looking downwards. One moves first from the Samapāda sthāna in short steps with straight and wide or high and low or irregular and round about steps.[11]	N.A.
9. *Falling down from the sky*	Gaits of one who descends from the sky is also of this kind.[12] Gait of one who falls from the sky includes Apaviddha arms, scattering ends of clothes, with eyes set on the ground below.[13] With Kartarimukha hasta with its middle fingers bent backwards.[14]	N.A.
10. *Gesticulates ascent*	In ascending the stairs of a palace, a tree, or a hill or any other hight object, a person should move the feet in Atikarāntā cāri and with the body held up he should put forward his steps on (the flight of stairs). In case of hills, the limbs are to be thrown up. The climbing of trees need Atikrāntā, Sūci, Apakrāntā and Pārśvakānta cāri-s.[15]	N.A.
11. *Gesticulates descent*	In descending, the body should be slightly bent with one foot in Atikrāntā cāri, and the other in Ancita movement.[16]	N.A.
12. *Crossing over a river*	Gait of a person moving in a river will be according to the depth of water. In shallow water, with tucking of one's clothes and in deep (water) with the throwing out of hands one is to move with the fore part of one's body slightly bent. In case of a person being carried away by a current he is to stretch out his arms and push forward in water repeatedly and during this movement all his limbs are to be busily engaged with mouth filled up (with water).[17]	N.A.

The Stage Direction denoting gesticulation	The Āngika Abhinaya as per NS, later authorities like AD. (Rāghavabhatta's ARTHA DYO. is also referred to wherever applicable)	
13. *Gesticulates the whirl wind*	To indicate hot wind, heat from the sky, warding off dust, rains, insects and bees one should cover one's face.[18]	N.A.
14. *Parrots, sārikā-s, small birds*	To be indicated by two moving fingers in the Tripatākā hands (NS, XXVI, 65).	N.A.
15. *Big birds and animals*	To be indicated by proper recaka and angahāra the movements of the birds and animals with gaits and gestures suitable to them (NS, XXVI, 66).	N.A.
16. *Elephant, horse and other conveyance*	Elephant riding is to be represented by taking up a goad, the horse by a bridle, and other conveyance by a whip (NS, XIII, 106–107).	N.A.
17. *Entrance through a zonal door*	To be indicated by two Tripatākā hasta-s held like a Swastika facing each other. This would represent a door.	N.A.
18. *To indicate sound or listening attentively*	Is to be gesticulated by making a side-long glance, bending the head side ways and putting the hand near the ear.[19]	N.A.
19. *To indicate touch or gesticulation or feel of the touch*	Is to be done by slightly narrowing down the eyes, raising the eyebrows in the like manner as well as by touching the shoulder and cheek (in some cases).[20]	N.A.
20. *To indicate agreeable taste and smell or inhaling fragrance*	By slightly narrowing down the eyes and expanding the nostrils and in the same breath.[21]	N.A.

Notes

(1) NS, IX, 54–57. (Kashi ed.). (2) Ibid, 74–76. (3) NS, IX, 95-96. (4) Ibid, 104–106. Ibid, 38–40 (M. Ghosh); (5) NS, XXVI, 19, (6) NS, XXXVI, 71–73. (7) NS, XIII, 88–92 (tr. M. Ghosh), Ibid, Wherever decisive references of Artha Dyo. on a particular aspect have not been found, I have indicated this with N.A. (8) NS, XIII, 92-95. (9) NS, XIII, 92–95; NS, IX, 38–40 (M. Ghosh). (10) NS, XXVI, 19, also 96-100, An entire air journey from Lanka to Ayodhya is depicted in Bhavabhūti's Mahāviracaritam. (11) NS, XI, 30–45 (tr. M. Ghosh); also XIII, 92–95. (12) Ibid. (13) NS, XIII, 92–95. (14) NS, IX, 38–40. (15) NS, XI, 30–34–31–32. (16) NS, XIII, 96–98. (17) Ibid, also 101, 104 (tr. M. Ghosh). (18) NS, XXVI, 17. (19) NS, XXIV, 81. (20) Ibid, 82. (21) Ibid, 84.

of hands, face and body. Such a systematic use of the body movements was called *citrābhinaya.* Through this *ābhinaya*, the actor could convey aspects of nature like day, night, morning, evening, seasons, clouds, wide expanse of water, planets, stars, forests, tall trees, moonlight, heat, wind, rainy night, lightning, sun, dust, smoke, air, animals, birds, sight of pleasant and repugnant objects and beings, expressions of happiness, joy, anger, jealousy, sorrow, fear, love, intoxication, death, effects of poisoning, dreams, senses of sight, touch and smell, darkness, cold, vision of gods, ghosts, goblins, etc.

The spectators understood the implied meanings and convention of *citrābhinaya*. The performers made free use of this style and the playwrights indicated it in their stage directions simply by using the terms: *nāṭayati, rūpayati*, etc. which can be roughly translated as "he enacts".

In the framework on page 145 an attempt has been made to show the systematic relationship between the stage directions in Sanskrit play-texts indicating the *citrābhinaya* as per *Nāṭyaśāstra* and substantiating the same, wherever possible, by the directions of the performance suggested by Rāghavabhaṭṭa's commentary on *Abhijñāna Śākuntala*.

Section 2

Vācika Abhinaya—Actor's Communication Through His Voice and Speech

Potency of the word power—*śabda-śakti*—was recognized in India from ancient times when the precise utterance of a *mantra* or a prayer was believed to result in infinite energy. The words of Sanskrit play-texts and their proper rendering by the actors were given similar importance by dramaturgical treatises.

Says Bharata:

> "The *śāstra*-s are made up of words and rest on words, and hence there is nothing beyond words and words are the source of everything."[32]

And again,

> "One should take care of words. Gestures, costumes, make-up and acting of *sattva* merely clarify the meaning of words."[33]

The appropriate rendering of the words of the play-texts by an actor was given, thus, the supreme place of importance in a performance. The use of speech and voice was stylised and was meant to be utilised according to the traditional set of rules.

The play-texts were composed in Sanskrit and a number of Prakrits in an interesting mixture of prose dialogues and verse couplets in metres. Their rendering by the actors had to be technically perfect. Speech sounds, intonation of vowels, articulation of consonants, enunciation of compound words of both Sanskrit and Prakrit words were some of the things which had to be mastered.

The entertaining and instructive dialogue rendering or the art of conversation (*saṃvāda*) was a meticulously cultivated skill which had evolved with long centuries of oral tradition. This is readily understandable because conversation (*saṃvāda*) was an art developed over long centuries of training in oral tradition. Another name by which *Veda*-s are known is *śruti* which literally means "that which was heard". The style of ancient Indian literature was in the form of dialogues which were transmitted by precise oral rendering by generations of masters of speech and vocal intonation.

Prose dialogues were employed in Sanskrit play-texts with a feel for the right speech pattern and correct rhythm. The prologues of plays contained dialogues with witty humour, repartee, play on words and occasional double entendres adopted from the sub-divisions of *vīthi* requiring masterful control on the spoken word. It is significant that the main actors of the *nāṭya* troupe like the *sūtradhāra* his assistants and the jester, who featured in the prologues, were experts in dialogue delivery. Over and above the dexterous diction, the words were also skilfully employed in four connotations of—(1) the literal meaning (*abhidhā*), (2) indicated meaning (*lakṣaṇā*), (3) suggested meaning realised by sphoṭa or dhvani (*vyañjanā*) and (4) intended meaning of what was left unsaid (*tātparya*).

The sound pattern of Sanskrit theatre was dominated by the notes of *vāṇi* (speech), *viṇā* (lute) and veṇu (flute). Human voice was compared to a lute and an actor's voice, accordingly, was trained to bring out the right notes of the three pitches of voice register—viz. high, medium and low.

The Sanskrit-Prakrit verses were composed in a number of metres starting from *anuṣṭubha* to *vasantatilakā*. The verses were chanted or sung. Their recitation in high, excited, grave, low, fast and slow notes (*alaṃkāra*-s) reached a high degree of sophistication and was rendered to suit different states of being and situations to evoke appropriate *rasa*-s.

Words (*pada*-s) were used either freely in prose or systematically combined in metrical patterns of verse formed by long and short (*guru-laghu*) syllables. Pronunciation, accent and elongation of words were consciously understood and rigorously learnt. Recitation in proper time beat (*laya*) and tempo with exact accent (*varṇa*-s), elongation of vowels, timing of the pause (*virāma*) and two types of voice modulation to bring out the dramatic meaning of the speech (*kākus*) were utilised to suggest various shades of meaning to the written text.

It was understood that the words of the text became capable of evoking *rasa*-s only when they were delivered with the right intonation, modulation, pronunciation, accent and tempo indicative of the *rasa*-s latent in them. The use of the right note, time beat, *kāku* and other elements were the vocal means by which a skilled performer achieved that end.

As in the case of body movements (*āṅgika*), the use of speech and voice (*vācika*) was an integral part of the stylisation of performance. In fact it was the speech which separated the Sanskrit theatre (*nāṭya*) from the dance. Bharata compares the dramatic words to the body of the *nāṭya* and says again and again that the other facets of *abhinaya* were there merely to illustrate and help the relish of the full meaning of the words.

Vācika abhinaya was, in this way, equivalent to the rendering of the spoken word, *vākyam* or the recitation and enunciation of Sanskrit-Prakrit verse and prose of the play-text. It formed the base for the unfolding of the other three aspects of *abhinaya*. The indications connected with *vācika* in the stage directions thus necessarily correspond to *aṅga-sattva abhinaya* as well as the suggestive use of the stage speeches for *nāṭyadharmī* enactments:

(1) Stage directions indicating conventions of speech.

(2) Stage directions indicating speech behind the curtain—*nepathye*.

(3) Enactment of long, verbal passages.

Stage directions indicating conventions of speech

Sanskrit play-texts had certain conventions regarding speeches which were accepted by the playwright, the performer and the spectator as part of the *nāṭyadharmī* convention. Most of the stage speeches were meant to be heard by all characters on the stage (*sarvaśrāvya*). But there were some speeches also which were supposed to be heard by a limited number of characters (*nīyataśrāvya*). Then again, there were the speeches which were meant to be heard by none other than the character who spoke them (*aśrāvya*).

The distinction between these speeches was explicitly manipulated by special body gestures and movements which accompanied the speeches. The subtle interpretation conveyed by the movements and the speech were accepted by all as part of the stage conventions.

These stage techniques have become part of the theatre conventions and most of them have been retained in practice to this day in theatres all over the world. The table on page 153 gives an idea of the way in which *Nāṭyaśāstra* and later dramaturgical works formulated them. They are examined in the context of the modifications of their practices in the present day theatres.

The speech behind the curtain: Nepathye

In the audio-pattern of Sanskrit theatre 'the noises off the stage' or 'the speech behind the curtain' was employed when something relevant to the plot was linked, suggested or reported from behind the curtain. In most cases, such a speech became a major contributing factor to the progression of the plot. *Nāṭaka Lakṣana Ratna Koṣa* identifies the speech behind the curtain —*Nepathye*—with the linking device named *Cūlikā*.[34]

Such speeches or noises off the stage were either delivered from the place of musical orchestra on the stage or from the backstage area. They were used for many theatrical purposes like the following:

(1) Suggestive sentences uttered at dramatic moments from behind the curtain (*patākā sthāna*-s).
(2) The speech of important character heard first from behind the curtain thereby raising a sense of expectancy. After

that, the character entered the stage uttering the same speech.

(3) Happenings of important incidents behind the stage were indicated by such speeches.

(4) Dramatic atmosphere of a war or a gathering of people at public functions and festivals was established by such a device. The stage direction *Nepathye kalakala* or *Nepathye hāhākāra* usually indicated such noises from the background.

(5) Indication of time and scene transfers, when bards behind the curtain chanted the eulogy of kings.

Long verbal passages in Sanskrit dramas and their abhinaya

In almost all Sanskrit plays one comes across long verbal descriptive passages enunciated by one character,—at times by a group of three—depicting happenings involving others like a war, a battle, a sacrifice, a street scene, a night in a city, activities in a mansion, an aerial journey, etc. In Bhāsa's *Dūta Vākyam*, the entire Kaurava court is suggested by such a description.

Although there are no specific instructions to be found in the dramaturgical treatises for the techniques employed for such enactments, it is reasonably certain that the technique of mono-acting (*ekāhārya* or *ekapātra* abhinaya) was utilised.[36] This was the *abhinaya* technique where an actor enacted a number of roles, without change of costume or get up, by sheer brilliance of suggestive acting.

These long descriptive passages in Sanskrit plays were generally delivered by middle type characters who were expected to be experts in vigorous body movements also (*āṅgika abhinaya*). The rendering would resemble the enactment of *bhāṇa* genre of *rūpaka*-s where a solo middle type actor—a gallant-parasite—suggestively displayed a variety of incidents and situations involving more than one characters by expert use of body movements, gestures, expressions (*aṅga-sattva abhinaya*) and dexterous use of speech and voice (*vācika*).

The *vācika abhinaya* of long verbal passages can also be visualised in the light of the expert recitals of story tellers, ballad singers, *harikathākāra*-s and *māṇabhaṭṭa*-s of the present day folk theatres.

TABLE No. 5

The Stage Direction	The Description in the NS	Present Day Uasge
(1) *Aśrāvya*		
(a) *Speaking to self* (Ātmagata)	To be used when overwhelmed with excessive joy, intoxication, madness, fit of passion, repugnance, fear, astonishment, anger and sorrow. The words are spoken out which are in one's mind[1] and which are heard by oneself alone.	In folk as well as modern theatre this technique is profusely used and goes under the name of soliloquy.
(b) *Speaking aside* (Svagata)	Again, when something within one's self which is a matter of deliberation and feeling is spoken out it is called speaking aside.[2]	In folk as well as modern theatre this technique goes under the name of soliloquy ormonologue.
(2) *Speaking to the sky* (or in the air) (Ākāśabhāṣita or Ākāśe)	Addressing someone at a distance or not appearing in person, or indirectly addressing some one who is not closeby. This mode of speaking will present a dialogue by means of replies related to various (imaginary) questions which may arise. The questions are asked by the sentence.[3] "What do you say?" (*kim bravīśi* or *kim bhaṇasi*). This technique frequents in Bhana form of Daśarūpaka.	This technique of speech is to be found in the folk theatres. And, has been commonly adopted by certain modern dramas.
: *Concealed speaking* Niyata Śravya (Apavāritaka)	Related to some secret thought (*Nigūḍhabhāva*) which the character conveys to the spectator.[4] NS is not very explicit here. Later dramaturgists have offered different interpretations. told to *DR*: It imparts a confidence	If we interpret this convention with the technique of deliberate exchange of confidence with the audience or character, then this technique is frequently to be found in usage in the folk drama

The Stage Direction	The Description in the NS	Present Day Usage
	another by turning aside (*Parāvṛtta.*[5]) *SD*: A confidence told and then the actor takes a turn.[6] *ND*: A confidence told to only one character—not to be heard by other characters who may be on the stage.[7] *NRLK*: *Apavāritaka* is that which is not said as an aside[8] (*Parivārtika*). *N.B. Purohit*: "The speaker comes forward and speaks to the audience. He is interested in laughing, appreciating and grieving with the audience." *Apavārya* need not be addressed to some character in particular. But it is a deliberate confidence and a care has to be taken that the others do not hear.[9] *G.K. Bhat*: Character confides and then takes a turn around.[10]	as well as the theatre of the present day which has revived and adopted many of the traditional techniques.
(4) *Private Personal Feelings* (Janāntikam) or	"When out of necessity persons standing close by are (supposed) not to hear what is spoken to someone else." It should be indicated by the *Tripatākā* hand covering the speaker. NS does not mention where the *Tripatāka* hand has to be kept.[11]	This technique without the use of *Tripatākā* hand is to be seen in the folk as well as occasionally in the modern theatre.
Private Personal Address (Janāntikam)	*DR*: Mutual conversation in the presence of others by shutting them out by the gesture of the	

The Stage Direction	The Description in the NS	Present Day Usage
	hand with three fingers (except *Anāmikā*) raised.[12] *N.D.*: A conversation hidden from one person only—and generally told to the others by taking the *Tripatākā* hand near the mouth.[13] *NLRK*:[14] Ignoring one when two people talk to each other is *Janāntika*. It should be done with a hand with three fingers raised.	From the above examination, we may deduce that: (a) The term: *Apavāritakam*: refers to a mode of *Niyata Śrāvya* convention, where the character comes forward, imparts a confidence to the audience, and then turns round. This style of speech convention is frequently to be seen in the present day theatres also. (b) The term: *Janāntika*: refers to the *Niyata Śrāvya* convention where a character imparts a confidence with another character standing close by. The other characters on the stage are not supposed to be hearing the conversation. The one, who speaks indicates this convention by taking a *Tripatākā* hand

<table>
<tr><th>The Stage Direction</th><th>The Description in the NS</th><th>Present Day Usage</th></tr>
<tr><td></td><td></td><td>to his mouth. This style of speech without the Hasta gesture—is often to be seen in the present day theatres.</td></tr>
<tr><td colspan="3">A Note: These conventions of the speech have been used with some confusion regarding their special differentiations by the dramatists from Bhāsa onwards.
Bhāsa, Kālidāsa and Bhavabhūti use Janāntikam for private personal conversation with other character and Apavārya as imparting a confidence to the audience. Śri Harṣa does not use Jannātikam. But uses Apavārya for both purposes.
Śūdraka and Bhaṭṭa Nārāyaṇa use the terms without specific clarity.</td></tr>
<tr><td>Speaking in one's ears (Karṇe or Karṇe Evam Evam)</td><td>Words in a play connected with secrecy were to be spoken in one's ears preceded by words "Evam Evam". Also, for avoiding repetition of something which had occurred/or had been said earlier.[15]</td><td>Frequently seen in the folk theatres.</td></tr>
<tr><td>Speech during sleep (Svapnavākyam)</td><td>A speech with a slow voice with some words distinct other indistinct. The speaking should recollect the past.[16] This was a purely lokadharmi style of rendering.</td><td>NS description is lokadharmi—such realistic rendering is to be witnessed, in the present day theatre.</td></tr>
<tr><td>Dying Speech (also speech in a swoon)</td><td>Indistinct speaking at the time of dying or in a swoon was made with syllables produced by relaxed and heavy speech with a fluttering voice accompanied by hiccups, and hard breathing.[17]</td><td>-do-</td></tr>
</table>

1. NS, XXVI, 85–87 (Tr. M. Ghosh).
2. NS, XXVI, 89 (Tr. M. Ghosh).
3. DR, I, 67.
4. NS, XXVI, 82 (Kashi ed.).
5. DR, I, 127.
6. SD, VI, 138.
7. ND, I, 12.
8. NLRK, 2269 (ed. Dillon).
9. Purohit; N.B., "The Apavāritaspeech is Sanskrit Drama" AIOC, 1937, pp. 433–35.
10. Bhat G.K., In talks with him.
11. 7. NS, XXVI, 88-89.
12. DR, I, 126.
13. ND, I, 13, p. 28.
14. NLRK, 2267-68.
15. NS, XXVI, 89-90 (Tr. M. Ghosh).
16. NS, XXVI, 99 (Tr. M. Ghosh).
17. Ibid, 101-02.

Section 3

Sāttvika Abhinaya—Actor's communication through his inward concentration of pure mind

Abhinaya Darpaṇa of Nandikeśvara begins with a verse describing the four fold *abhinaya* in the form of Lord Śiva.

"The movement (*āṅgika*) of whose body is the world,
Whose speech (*vācika*) the sum of all language,
Whose jewels (*āhārya*) the moon and the stars,
To that pure (*sāttvika*) Śiva I bow."[36]

Here, he associates the *sāttvika* with Lord Śiva himself and emphasises the importance of various manifestations of *sattva* in the scheme of *abhinaya*.

The term *sattva* is another word which defies translation. It cannot be easily grasped by the English equivalents. The term can, however, be described as the essential pure quality or the central equipoise or the state of pure existence (*sat*) of every being. It can be explained in terms of the concept of '*triguṇātmaka prakṛti*' of *Sāṃkhya* philosophy which maintains that all aspects of the universe are made up of various combinations of three qualities, viz., the quality of great activity (*rajas*), of darkness and ignorance (*tamas*) and that of purity (*sattva*). This quality of purity is the core point—*bindu*—of one's being and remains so in the constantly rotating wheel of life. When this pure state of a being is shaken by the pleasure and pain of life's experiences, various *bhāva*-s are produced. These *bhāva*-s can be described as the inner states of a being, *cittavṛttis*, or simply as the states. Representation through *abhinaya* of these inner states cover the area of *sāttvika abhinaya* which literally means *abhinaya* with *sattva*. In fact, *sāttvika abhinaya* forms the foundation on which the edifice of the other three aspects of *abhinaya* is built. It denotes the subtle psycho-mental responses of the pure mind to various outside stimuli. These responses (*anubhāva*-s) are a combination of eight basic states (*sthāyi bhāva*-s), thirty-three transitory states (*vyabhicāri bhāva*-s) and eight *sāttvika* states.

The stage directions

The responses governing the *sāttvika abhinaya* in a play are suggested by three kinds of stage directions which generally precede the spoken words. They are:

(1) *Those indicating eight basic states*: *Sthāyi bhāva-s*

The eight basic states such as love, laughter, sorrow, fear, anger, energy, disgust and wonder are indicated by the stage directions like *sakāmam*, *sahāsyam*, *saśokam*, *sakrodham*, *sabhayam* and *vismayam naṭayati etc*.

Nāṭyaśāstra gives detailed instructions of delineating these states in the manner of *sūcā abhinaya*. The instructions are often *lokadharmī*, mostly dealing with facial expressions and glances induced by *sattva*.

(2) *Those indicating thirty-three transitory states*: *Vyabhicāri Bhāva-s*

They are indicated by as many stage directions preceding the speech in Sanskrit play-texts and are indicated by stage directions which prefix the written words as follows: *lajjām nāṭayati*, *cintām nāṭayati*, *sanirvedam*, *sāṭopam*, *viśādam nāṭayati*, *sākūtam nāṭayati*, *sakaruṇām*, *sāudvegam*, *sakautukam*, *sasambhramam*, etc. Among these, a stage direction indicating an effort to hide one's feelings: *samāvaraṇam nāṭayati* is an innovation often used by Bhavabhūti. The rules of their performance are generally suggested in Chapter VII in verses 28 to 91 of *Nāṭyaśāstra*.

(3) *Those indicating eight sattvika states*

Swoon	:	*Mūrcchām nāṭayati* or *mohamupagata*.
Perspiration	:	*Sasvedam*.
Tears	:	*Sabāṣpam* or *sāsram*.
Horripilation	:	*Saromāncam*, *sparśa sukham nāṭayati pulakam darśayati*.
Paralysis	:	*Stambham* nāṭayati.
Tremor	:	*Saspandam* (*vāmākṣi spandanam*).
Choking	:	*Gadgad*.
Change of Colour	:	*Svābhāvika*, *prasanna*, *rakta*, *śyāma* etc.

These *sāttvika* states were to be represented as natural and involuntary body responses to various situations by the actor's inward concentration or understanding of a character's essential pure quality.

However, Abhinavagupta suggests that they might also be

induced technically by the control of breath (*prāṇa*)[37] by an able actor in the following manner:

An actor could stimulate	paralysis	by concentration of breath	between the eyebrows
"	tears	"	"
"	perspiration	"	in the heart
"	change of colour	"	in the face
"	horripilation	"	in the throat
"	choking	"	in the head
"	swoon	"	in the nose

The dramaturgical treatises have listed involuntary (*ayatnaja*) and natural graces of young men and women which an actor could observe, absorb and imitate. The enactment of *sāttvika abhinaya* of the heroes and the heroines was based on these traditional specifications. The involuntary graces of men were:

Brilliant character, graceful bearing, self-possession, steadiness, gravity, sportiveness, nobility and spirit.

The involuntary graces of women were:

Beauty, charm, delicacy, radiance, self-control, courage and dignity.

Although traditionally formulated, these graces of young men and women as well as the *sāttvika* states were represented by the actors realistically by the observation of people and depended on the actor's identification with the universalised and super-sensual essence of the character. The enactment was mostly in *lokadharmī* style with occasional stylisations of the *sāttvika* states with *nāṭyadharmī* gestures. One can witness such *nāṭya-dharmī* representation in the present day classical dance and in the enactment of Noh plays of Japan where the tremor and the tears are represented with symbolic gestures.

Of the *sāttvika* states, we shall just take an example of the swoon and give details of it's *lokadharmī* representation.

The Swoon

The swoon is a frequently used device by the Sanskrit play-wrights. Probably, it provided a dramatic pause, a silence, a sudden cessation of action which had a theatrical impact.

A swooning character was usually accompanied by another actor, and the swoon was traditionally represented by the actor in a gradual process of "inaction, motionlessness, imperceptible breathing and finally falling on the ground."[38] The accompanying actor uttered consoling words like 'take heart' etc., and gave necessary support to the swooning actor. The manner of speech leading up to the swoon is described on page 156. There are extremely interesting situations in a play where a group of characters fall into a swoon altogether in a common shock as in Nāgānanda (Act V).

This technique of swooning by an actor with an assistant for support is seen in the performance of the Chinese Opera also.

The Stage Directions Suggesting Death—Maraṇa

Although it is generally understood that the representation of death was forbidden in the ancient Indian theatre, we have plays of Bhāsa, where the death scenes are enacted on the stage. Śri Harṣa's *Nāgānanda* depicts the death of the hero who later on revives with the aid of divine intervention. In Śūdraka's *Mṛccha-kaṭikam* the heroine Vasantasenā almost dies on the stage.

In the plays of Bhāsa, the deaths as depicted are due to various causes. In *Pratimānāṭaka* the death occurs after a prolonged and incurable state of separation from the loved ones (Daśaratha's death scene); in *Ūrubhaṅgam* and *Abhiśeka*, deaths of Duryodhana and Vālin are the results of mortal combats. In *Bālacarita* deaths are depicted on the stage as resulting from fatal violence or killings of Caṇura, Kaṃsa and others.

Abhinaya of Death

Nāṭyaśāstra has described the *abhinaya* of death in different chapters in no fewer than fourteen verses. The descriptions pertain to deaths as a result of either sickness or injury caused by fights, weapons, snake bites, poison, attack of animals and so on. It has also given a traditional verse describing the stages of death due to poison and its representation,[39] leading one to surmise that there may not have been any ban on death scenes in the plays in the earlier period.

Let us examine the *abhinaya* of death as described by *Nāṭya-śāstra*. Death from disease was to be represented on the stage by "looseness of the body, motionlessness of limbs, closed eyes, hiccups, deep breathing, looking for family members, speaking indistinct words and the like."[40] Death due to injury or wounds by weapons was to be represented by suitable words, gestures and movements and finally with responses such as "suddenly falling down on the ground" or "by absence of any further movements of the body." (Rendering of the dying speech is given on page 156.)

Very likely, the representation of death from different conditions was to be of different nature. At times the *sāttvika* state of paralysis was employed; at other times that of the swoon was used and always the final moment of the death scene was enacted by "closing of eyes". *Rasa-Gaṅgādhara* enumerates the premortem features of death like rolling in bed, ghastly looks, blackening of face and nails, moistening of nose, jolting, quiver, convulsions, senselessness, stupor etc.

In this connection, it should perhaps be mentioned that in the opinion of Abhinavagupta *maraṇa* as the last stage of ten *kāma daśā* was to be represented on the stage in the manner of a "swoon or a miserable depression where there was always a strong hope of revival".[41]

The Enactment of Erotic—Śṛṅgāra

The harmonious use of the four-fold *abhinaya* with a stress on the *sāttvika* was conventionally formulated and used to enact the state of love for evoking erotic *rasa*. Heroes and heroines (*nāyaka* and *nāyikā*) of various ages, situations, their physical, natural and involuntary graces in different stages of love were elaborately worked out by the dramaturgical treatises. The playwrights corroborated with the traditional rules and depicted the love situations accordingly. As mentioned before, progression of the basic state of love (*ratibhāva*) was delineated in two ways—as the love in union (*saṃbhoga*) and as the love in separation (*vipralaṃbha*). The latter was, again, sub-divided into two distinct types of representation:

(1) Yearning for the beloved before the union: *Ayoga* or *Pūrvarāga*.

(2) Separation from the beloved after the union: *Vipralaṃbha* or *Viprayoga*.

This state was caused by two situations, viz.

(i) A state of voluntary separation due to a journey, pride, jealousy, etc. (human cause)
(ii) A state of involuntary separation due to a curse, confusion, etc. (divine cause)

Stage Directions

Stage directions like *Śṛṅgāra-bhāvam nāṭayati, Madanāvasthām nāṭayati, Madanabādhām nirūpayati, Śṛṅgāra lajjāṃ rūpayati, Viyogadukhaṃ rūpayati, Madanakātaryaṃ rūpayati*, etc., indicate the performing techniques of states of love in specific contexts.

Conventional—Nāṭyadharmī—Ṛendering of Falling in Love

Representation of falling in love and showing signs of love, yearning for a meeting etc. were conventionally detailed for enactment. For example, the depiction of feeling of love of the heroines was minutely worked out in three stages:

(1) Beginning of love with excessive feelings (bhāva) was to be represented merely through expressive glances (*Dṛṣṭi*-s).
(2) The beginning of the expression of feelings (*bhāva*) was to be enacted with circular movements (*recaka*-s) of the eyebrows and the neck.
(3) The graceful expression of the state of love (*helā*) had ten graces like—
sportive mimicry, amorous gestures, dishabille, confusion, hysterical mood, manifestation of affection, pretended anger, affected coldness, lolling and want of response.[42]

Conventional Rendering of Love in Union

Love in sexual union was to be enacted with the *nāṭyadharmī* convention of rendering a graceful dance with a song. All transitory states except indolence, cruelty and disgust were to be used in such situations.

Conventional Rendering of Love in Separation

The ten stages of love—*kāmadaśās* depicted the love in separation.

In order to examine the techniques which governed the traditional *nāṭyadharmī aṅga-sattva abhinaya* of the play-texts, a framework delineating the sequence of progression of erotic *rasa* in Kālidāsa's *Abhijñāna Śākuntala* is given on page 165.

Section 4

Āhārya Abhinaya: Actor's communication through his get-up and the physical aids

Like the other three aspects of *abhinaya*, *āhārya* was also integral to the whole scheme of *rasa* evocation in Sanskrit theatre. The colour, the costume and the other aids were used as adornments of the support (*ālambana vibhāva*) in the form of dramatis personae to be presented for realisation of *rasa* and the traditional rules and conventions governing them were mainly motivated from this angle. Mere decorative purpose was not an important part of the scheme of *āhārya*. Long magico-symbolic traditions dictated its subtle communication. The colours of the body paint, the costumes and the head-dresses signified meanings which were relevant to the remote reaches of ancient rites and ceremonies. Each colour evoked a memory, a mood and a *rasa* and was utilised accordingly. Abhinavagupta compares *āhārya* to a constant thread (*sthāyī-sūtra*) used in a pattern of schematic relationship with the main design of *rasa* evocation. He says that the costumes of the character were so integrally woven in the *rasa* pattern that "even when the character passed through different situations and circumstances in the course of a play, his basic costume remained the same. Only his *abhinaya* changed, not the costume."[43] At the most, suggestive and symbolic use of a small piece of apparel or an ornament was made to imply the change of circumstances. For example in a play situation, when a lover went to meet his beloved after a long separation he merely picked up a flower or a garland to suggest a decorative dress.[44]

It was also believed that through *āhārya* an actor succeeded in assuming another character by entering as if into another's body (*parakāyāpraveśa*).[45] In this connection, Bharata makes some interesting observations *catechetically*. He asks "How can an actor who does not even possess more than one dress assume the qualities of a king?" And then answers:

Framework 3

SEQUENCES OF ŚṚṄGĀRA PROGRESSION IN KĀLIDĀSA'S ABHIJNĀNA ŚĀKUNTALAM

Stage Direction/Speech Vākyam	Types and Stages of Śṛṇgāra	In Ref. to	Anga–Sattva Abhinaya
Act I—Pūrva Rāga—Attraction—Abhilāṣā Ver. 20			
Parinyāsa—a *sandhyaṅga* meaning the kindling of love with *aucitya* "Without doubt she is fit to be married by a Kṣatriya, as my noble heart desires for her (*abhilāṣi me manaḥ*)" etc.	Icchā—desire	in the king (hero) Duṣyanta for Śakuntalā who is endowed with all seven involuntary graces.[2]	Representation by the hero of the favourable mind towards the desired (iṣṭa) by harmonious movements of limbs, horripilation, the opening of the mouth and a happy face[1] with *Kāmyā* and lalita glances.
Śakuntalā: 'Oh, heart, do not be impatient' etc. (Ver. 22, L-34-35)	Hāva Laksaṇa Vikāra	in Śakuntalā being attracted by the qualities of Duṣyanta.[4]	*Hāva* is the feeling (*Bhāva*) which arises from the *Sattva* and its ordinary expression (NS, XXIV, 7).[3] This is to be depicted through changes of eyebrows, the *recaka* of the neck etc. (NS, XXIV, 10). It is a very clear expression of one's emotion (in erotic) through various gestures. (ND, p. 204)
Śakuntalā (*Śṛngāra lajjām rūpayati*) gesticulates bashfulness. (Ver. 22, L-41)	Helā Laksaṇa Vikāra	in Śakuntalā	*Helā* is a graceful expression of feeling (*Bhāva*) (NS, XXIV, 11). It is a definite expression (*Artha Dyo*, p. 27). The heroine turns the head in bashfulness and with a shy glance. (Ibid,

Stage Direction/Speech Vākyam	Types and Stage of Śṛṅgāra	In Ref. to	Anga-Sattva Abhinaya
			p. 27) (*Lajjānvitā dṛṣṭi*); the eyelashes are slightly bent, upper eyelid is discending; eyeballs are lowered due to shame in *lalitābhinaya*. (NS, VIII, 65) horripilation, change of colour.
Ver. 28 *Prāpti*-Sandhyaṅga—Realisation of the barest fringe of the goal of the hero—beginning with the line of the hero "Can it be that just as we are towards her she is (inclined) towards us. Or, my desire has obtained scope"...	The display of Vilāsa (Amourous gesture)	In Mugdhānāyikā	Change in posture of standing, sitting, gait, movement of hands, eyebrows and eyes at the sight of the beloved. (NS, XXIV, 15)
	also *Madanodaya* kindling of *Anurāga* (love)	do	Change in facial and eye expression, respectful attention to the beloved's words, looking at him under pretext, etc. (*Artha Dyo.* p. 33)
ACT II. Ayoga Śṛṅgāra—Praudha Pūrva Rāga (love in its unfulfilled stages)			
Ver. 1	*Lālasā* (a strong passion, anxiety (*cintā*). His own *abhilasā* for *rati* rāga (*Artha Dyo*—On II, Sl. 1)	in the king Duṣyanta	Impatience (*Autsukya*), sighs, thinking with downcast face, dull drowsiness of the body, etc. and heavy breaths (NS, VII, 69, L-1-3) horripilation, pallour, trembling.
Ver. 2	*Smṛti* (or anusmaraṇa—rememberance of differ-	do	With looking down, rising of the eyebrows, quiver in the body, restlessness and pallour. (NS, VII, 63, L-1-3)[6]

Stage Direction/Speech Vākyam	Types and Stages of Śṛṅgāra	In Ref. to	Anga-Sattva Abhinaya
	-ent aspects and activities of be-loved.		
Ver. 3, 9, ,10, 11, 12	*Guṇakīrtana* (enumeration of merits gradually increasing in in tensity.)	in the king Duṣyanta	By thrill and horripilation, choking of voice in the throat and stammering voice.[6] (NS, XXIV, 179)
ACT III. Ayoga Śṛṅgāra (Love in the unfulfilled state)			
(Then enters the king in a love sick state) (*tataḥ praviśati kāmāyamānāvastho* rājā) or (madanabādhām nirūpya). Ver. 2	*Ādhi/or Cintā* (anxiety) unfulfil-ment of love and lovelorn state	in the king	*Lolita* head, *Dola hasta* and *Śūnya dṛṣṭi*. (*Artha Dyo*, p. 50) (Head moving on all sides loosely, hanging hands with open *patākā hastas*, vacant look.)
Śakuntalā's entrance on a stone slab attended by friends (L-5 after Ver. 6)	Lovelorn state Ud-vega (distress).	in Śakuntalā	Lying sleepless with sighs and attended by and "speaking to (*Dūtī*) *Sakhī*-s words such as, by what it means and in what manner there will be the union, with half closed eyes, handles the bangle, and touches nivi, navel and thighs."[7] Very weak voice, lustre-less eyes, pale face, slow gait, want of energy, thinness of body, change of colour etc. Restless,[8] with, deep breaths, utters
Ver. 8	Glāni, udvega and Vyādhi	do	
Ver. 10, L-2	Nirveda and Jaḍatā	do	
Ver. 14	Unmāda	do	

Stage Direction/Speech Vākyam	Types and Stages of Śṛṅgāra	In Ref. to	Anga-Sattva Abhinaya
			the response of 'Hum' at wrong place. Sitting and crying without any reason, horripilation, pallour, trembling, tears.
Love in the union—Sambhoga Śṛṅgāra			
(From the stage direction—"the king approaches suddenly" to the stage direction "Śakuntalā gesticulates as though preventing the king's embrace" L-2 after Ver. 14–L-1 after Ver. 22.)			
Brief union—(Saṅkṣipta)			
When the two meet for a short while, and the pleasure is 'limited by initial reserve' (*Sādhvasa*).			
Vipralambha			
ACT IV—Vipralambha Due to Curse			
Ver. 1 Durvāsā's Śāpa	Separation due to Curse (Śāpa Vipralambha).		
ACT V			
Ver. 1 and 2 and 31	Rememberance of *rati* or attachment	by the king	
ACT VI			
Ver. 5 to 22 after recognition of the ring	All the stages of *Vipralambha Kāmadaśā*—From *Udvega*, *Vilāpa* to *Unmāda*.	by the king	All characteristics enumerated in the footnote 5—with *Asauṣṭhava* of the body. Representation of heart, burning, sighs, lassitude, speaking sorrowful words, at times looking with a steadfast gaze, sometimes absorbed within oneself, weeping, pallour, tears.

Stage Direction/Speech Vākyam	Types and Stage of Śṛṅgāra	In Ref. to	Anga-Sattva Abhinaya
ACT VII			
Ver. 21, L-7, "Even cruelty practised by me has brought forth the desired end" etc.	*Sambhoga* : Union in love.	The king and Śakuntalā.	"Young man and woman unite, see and touch each other in pleasant surroundings and in freedom." At that time, the ten natural graces (*Alaṅkāra*) of the young heroine are revealed in the graceful movements (*lalitābhinaya*) in this context. The *Alaṅkāra*-s are (1) Sportive mimicry (*līlā*), (2) Amourous gesture (Vilāsa), (3) Dishabille (*Vicchitti*), (4) Confusion (*Vibhrama*), (5) Hysterical mood (*Kilkiñcitam*), (6) Manifestation of affection (*Moṭṭāyitam*), (7) Pretended anger (*Kuṭṭamitam*), (8) Affected coldness (*Bivvoka*), (9) Lolling (*lalita*), (10) Want of response (*Vihṛtam*) (NS, XXIV, 12-13—tr. M. Ghosh)

1. NS, XXIV, 83–85 (Kashi ed.) also 160 162 (Tr. M. Ghosh).
2. The involuntary graces (*Ayatnaja*) of women: Refer Chapter VI, Section C, p.
3. NS, XXX, 7 (Kashi ed.) : Refer Cha. VI. Section C, p. 160.
4. Eight aspects of *Sattva* in a hero. NS, XXIV, 31.
5. *Kāmadaśā*-s of men and women in *Vipralambha* are: anxiety, excessive breathing, lassitude, pain in the body, remembering the beloved's conduct, or looking at the beloved's path, gazing vacantly at the sky, talking pathetically, touching and twisting some objects or clinging to some support. NS, XXIV, 194–96 (tr. M. Ghosh)
6. *Artha Dyo.* also gives similar details of representation.
7. NS, XXIV, 174-75 (tr. M. Ghosh).
8. Ibid, 187

> "Through conventional *āhārya*, the actor, covered with paints and decorated with ornaments, reveals the signs of kingship. He should move his limbs on the stage only after he has been covered with paints"...because then alone "has the actor become the king."[46]

This highly escoteric concept of assumption of another's spirit was emphasised by auspicious rites accompanying every stage of make up and get up of the actor. Special rituals accompanied the moment when the actor put on the crown because it was believed that the spirit of the character entered the actor from the moment he covered his body with paints and adorned his head with a crown. Significantly the crown always occupied a special place in the dressing room.

The importance of *āhārya* in Sanskrit theatre was underlined by the fact that one-fourth of the total area of Bharata's playhouse was allocated to the dressing room.

The costumes were traditionally designed and the body paint, other accessories and the hand held properties conventionally suggestive. The actor in his gorgeous get up confronted the spectator on the bare stage as the most colourful focal point of identification. The spectator was given the first familiar signs of the nature, period and the states—*bhāvāvasthā*-s of the character[47] on the very first entry because of easily identifiable conventional costumes and get up. It is in this context that Abhinavagupta compares the *āhārya abhinaya* to 'a base wall on which the painting of the entire performance is depicted.'[48]

Sanskrit plays told the tales of the happenings of the beings of the three worlds and their texts give suggestions regarding *āhārya* of such beings in the stage directions. The shining costume of a courtesan,[49] the blue green dress of a divine nymph going for a meeting with her lover,[50] the coiffure with a single braid suggesting a heroine in separation from her beloved,[51] a blood-curdling appearance of furious Bhīmasena[52] are indicated in the stage directions. *Āhārya* of the superhuman beings and that of the personified allegorical ideas, weapons, natural phenomena etc. were stylised. The regional peculiarities and local usages (*pravṛtti*-s) were, however, adhered to as far as possible in case of human characters.

The playwrights have apparently abided by the traditional

dictates governing the painting of the limbs with colours by conventional symbolic colour scheme as well as the decoration of the body with flowers, ornaments, costumes, hair styles and head-dresses. As a result, their suggestive values have succeeded in presenting a certain definite meaning, which was recognised and relished at various levels of appreciation by the spectators, as well as providing one of the most powerful visual elements of aesthetic pleasure.

The Colour—Aṅgaracanā

The belief in the magical properties of the colours, the anointing of the body with appropriate hues and colouring and painting decorative designs on the face, cheeks and shoulders were part of the toilet of the ancient Indians from the days of the Indus Valley Civilisation. Dr. Moti Chandra while evaluating the magico-historical and social implications of the body painting, has said that the use of yellow (haldi), red (kumkum), red lead (sindūra), black (kajala) and yellowish white (sandlewood paste) as common cosmetics for both men and women was prevalent in India from the ancient days. So also were lac-dyes for the lips, black, white and red colours for drawing designs on the face, forehead, cheeks; the *tilaka* of different shapes painted on the forehead, sandlewood paste and musk for designs on the arms, temples and breasts; as well as collyrium for the eyes.[63]

Following this tradition, *Nāṭyaśāstra* has laid down the principles of painting the limbs of the dramatis personae. By using the original colours of black, blue, red and yellow with a variety of hues made out of the mixtures of these colours the divine, human and demonic characters were painted.[64]

The Costume—Alaṃkāra

The dress, in ancient India, formed only a part of the total ensemble of attire which included flowers, jewels, costumes, hairstyles and hairdresses.

G.S. Ghurye, in this reference, comments that "Costume pure and simple was a very small part of any art, and it figures with garland etc. as one aspect of it. Arranging an attire is rightly interpreted to mean the art of beautifying one's person with garments, garlands and ornaments."[65]

The costumes of the male and the female, during 200 B.C.—800 A.D. had a definite general pattern, such as:

Female Costume

(1) Upper garment (*uttarāsaṅga, uttariyavāsana, udarāṃśuka, stanāṃśuka*)
(2) Bodice, jacket (*kañcuka, kurpāśaka*)
(3) Lower garment which was tucked up in gathers or a knot called *nivi* (*ambara, aṃśuka, antariya, vāsana, vastram*)
(4) Girdle (*kaṭisūtra, kāñci, mekhalā, rasanā*)
(5) Veil (optional) (*avaguṇṭhana, śirovastra*).

Male Costume

(1) Head-dress (*uṣṇiṣa, kiriṭa, paṭṭa, veṣṭana, veṣṭanapaṭṭa*)
(2) Upper garment (*uttariya*)
(3) Lower garment (*antariyavāsana, jātipaṭṭikā, nivāsana, paṭṭa, vāsana*)
(4) Long coat, jacket (*kañcuka, colaka*)
(5) Mantle (*prāvaraṇa*)

This shows a very general pattern of male and female dress. The variations were mainly achieved by different styles of draping and the texture of the garments. In modern times, too, infinite variations can be seen in the manner of draping a *sāri*, a *dhoti*, a turban or a *dupaṭṭā*.

The Colour of the Costume

The costumes were divided under three varieties of colour: white, variegated and soiled (*malina*). Several conventions regarding the colours of the costumes and ornaments as well as the usage of particular colours to symbolise particular *rasa*-s were traditionally laid down:

(1) Śyāma[56] to suggest the erotic *rasa*
(2) White to suggest the comic *rasa*
(3) Dove-grey to suggest the pathetic *rasa*
(4) Red to suggest the furious *rasa*
(5) *Gaura* (reddish yellow) to suggest the heroic *rasa*
(6) Black to suggest the terrible *rasa*
(7) Blue to suggest the odius *rasa*
(8) Yellow to suggest the marvellous *rasa*.

Other Accessories

Different patterns of footwears—covering just the feet (*pādukā*) or half of the shanks (*puṭabaddha*) made of different metals, leather, wood, bamboo or palm leaves were also worn. Different styles of waistbands were used.[67]

Nāṭyaśāstra gives an enormous list of ornaments for different dramatis personae to be worn according to their regional peculiarities, local usage, basic nature, period and the state of mind (*pravṛtti, prakṛti, deśakāla* and *avasthā*).[68]

Fortunately, one can get enough supportive material regarding *āhārya* from available evidence of the cave paintings of Bagh and Ajanta, and other sculptural representations covering the period. Another source is valuable information supplied in *Citrasūtra* of *Viṣṇu Dharmottara Purāṇa*.

All of these have been referred to in the following examination of *āhārya* of the dramas of Bhāsa to Bhavabhūti.

A—The Male Dramatis Personae: Their Dresses and Colour

(1) *The Hero*

The heroes and their basic four divisions showed four different varieties of dresses and make-up. The *dhiroddhatta* hero, who was divine, was painted with reddish-yellow colour (*gaura varṇa*) and wore variegated dress with any of the three types of crowns: cylindrical (*pārśvagata*), conical (*kirīṭi*) or a crown made to suit the knotted hair (*mastaki*).

Citrasūtra suggests that he wore garish costumes and accessories.

The *dhīralalita* king-hero was painted with lotus colour which was made up of white and red or dark blue or reddish yellow colour. His dress was multi-coloured and the crown, *mastaki* type. He was always dressed in a delicately pleasing, fashion. Udayana, Agnimitra would be costumed in this manner.

The *dhīrodātta* hero was to be coloured reddish yellow (*gaura*). His dress was more pronounced than a *dhīralalita* hero's but not too loud. He might wear a *mastaki* crown according to his status, never other types of crowns, unless he was a divine hero.

The *dhīrapraśānta* hero: If he was a brahmin, a merchant (*Cārudatta*) or a noble man (Mādhava), he was to be painted with reddish yellow colour and was to be dressed generally in white. He might not wear any crown, but might wear a turban indicative of his profession. Such characters were decked with appropriate jewellery and at times had smartly turned out beards also.

These are a set of conventions of dresses for the heroes. But *Nāṭyaśāstra* also keeps a provision when the situations, conditions, habitations, birth and age of an actor's or a producer's preference could change the colour scheme.

(2) *The Jester: Vidūṣaka*

The jester of the *prahasana* genre of plays was well-known for his hideous dress, bald head, tawny hair and beard, dwarfish appearance with prominent teeth, reddish eyes and a hunchback. He usually carried on his left hand a crooked staff with three bends (*kuṭilaka*) [See the sketch 4 on p. no. 391]

On the other hand, the jester featuring as a king-hero's assistant in love affair was always dandily dressed. Being a brahmin, he was painted in reddish yellow colour and wore a white dress. The design on his face, arms and chest was done with white paint dotted with red.

We have two illustrations of court-jesters at Ajanta. In the first, he is wearing a full sleeved tunic and a *paṭaka* with both ends tied. In the second, he is wearing a *dhoti* like lower garment and an loose upper garment (*uttariya*) [Visualisation on page no. 387, fig. 2].

(3) *Masseurs, Ministers, Priests, Army Generals and Crown Princes*

Brahmins and *kṣatriyas* among them were given reddish-yellow complexion while the *vaiśya*s were painted with dark and deep blue colours. Their costumes were white or of varied colours. The ministers and priests were moderately bejewelled and wore turbans. The costume of a masseur was rather elaborate. Army generals were provided with varied weapons like armours with quivers attached and bows. *Citrasūtra* suggests that in paintings they were depicted with "knit brows, rather loud in their apparel and looking sharp." The crown princes had body paint and dresses similar to a king except that they did not wear crowns. Their hairstyle, however, was fashionable.

(4) *Gallant-parasite: Viṭa*

He was dressed in a variegated dress, with a body paint according to his caste. He might have curly, well-dressed hair, at times he might also don a turban. (One of these types is seen in the Kushan freeze (Circa 1st century A.D.) at Mathura National Museum). [See page no. 398]

(5) *Śakāra*

Śakāra was a character in Sanskrit plays who appeared in a ridiculous role of a brother-in-law of a king. (In fact he was the brother of the king's concubine.) He was vain, proud and raised to undeserving power by reason of his dubious relationship to the king.

His body paint would be "almost reddish yellow" with "foppish gaudy dress." Śakāra wears a turban (*veṣṭana*) in Śūdraka's *Mṛcchakaṭikam.*

He can be partially seen in a sculpture of Kuśāna period (1st century A.D.) in Mathura National Museum.

(6) *Chamberlain or Kañcukī*

He was chamberlain of the harem, usually an old man who was named after the dress he wore—a long loose, sleeved tunic of dark red (kaśāya) colour. That his tunic was loose and long is proved by a reference in *Ratnāvalī* when a dwarf is referred to as hiding underneath the tunic of the chamberlain. He kept a cane staff in his hand. *Nāṭyaśāstra* refers to a *pratiśirṣa* made of a piece of cloth tied around his head like a turban.

(In a harem scene from Ajanta, Cave 1, a chamberlain is painted. See Vakataka 5th century A.D. See Fig. 3 on page no. 389).

(7) *Retinue of Servants*

Various attendants, companions and servants of the king, queen, nobleman and courtesan formed this retinue. The dresses and ornaments of these men and women varied according to their places of origin. Lamp bearers, cauri bearers, fan and umbrella holders are frequently mentioned in Sanskrit plays and are represented in sculptures and frescoes. The dwarfs and hunchbacks among them wore variegated dresses. Old women were usually in white and were greyhaired. The bards according to *Citrasūtra* were "pompous in dress, with veins showing on their necks as they announce entry in the field of battle and loudly sing praises of the warriors skilled in warfare."[59]

(8) *The Daitya-s, Dānava-s, Rākṣasa-s and Their Wives*

They are generally referred to as demons but it is quite possible that each group belonged to early non-Aryan tribes of India. Their colour was painted as dark blue and their costumes were variegated. Their hair, eye colour, moustache were tawny. And those among them who were superior types wore cylindrical crowns. According to *Citrasūtra*, they were to be depicted as having "knit brows, gobular eyes and frightful faces." *Rāksaṣa*-s had their "hair straightened and jutting up on their heads."[60]

Their wives were to be presented as "very beautiful" and attended by ladies-in-waiting. The *Rākṣasa* women wore sapphire ornaments, black dresses and had very white teeth.

However, the demonesses like Śūrpaṇakhā and Vāsagandhā appeared in hedious dresses. Their appearance could also vary according to situations.

(9) *Semi divine mythical beings (Yakṣa, Gandharva, Nāga, Vidyādhara and Their Women)*

They were supernatural beings. Their body paint was of various colours and the dresses were variegated. They wore crowns. Vidyādhara-s, a class of demigods among them, usually appeared with their consorts with garlands, rich ornaments and short swords tucked in belts. If bearded, their beards were to be smartly done, their women had hair tied in top-knots decorated with strings of pearls. They wore white dresses. *Yakṣa* women, the fairy attendants of Kubera, the god of wealth, had ornaments suggestive of jewels, and wore top-knots. The ornaments of *Nāga* women, semidivine creatures having the face of women and the tail of serpants, suggested pearls and jewels with hoods. The *Gandharva* women, the celestial singers, wore ornaments suggestive mostly of rubies, and jewels and carried lutes in their hands. They wore saffron coloured clothes.

(1) *The Seers, Ascetics and Brahmins*

The colour of their skin was determined by the regions that

they belonged to. The body paint of the sages, however, was uniform. They were to be painted in a colour of a plum which had gradually changed into brown. This was to show them as observing penances. Their beards were to be 'bushy' and looks matted. Their dresses were generally white.

The ascetics might wear tattered clothes, bark and skins. Wandering ascetics, sages and Buddhist monks wore dark red (*kaṣāya*) clothes. Those following *paśupata* doctrine wore variegated dresses. Brahmins, in general, wore white with loose tuffs of hair on the crown of the heads (śikhā).

(2) *Prominent Citizens and Village Folks*

Their skin paint and costumes followed the regional characteristics, age, habitation, status and tribal origin. Males had ornaments for the head, ear, neck, fingers, forearms, wrists, elbows, chest and waist.

B—The Female Dramatis Personae: Their Costumes and Colour

Like the males, the female characters were also made-up according to the regional and tribal peculiarities in the case of humans and according to the predetermined conventions in the case of celestials, beings of the nether world and such others. Their body colours, dress colours, the styles of draping the costumes, hairstyles and jewellery had infinite variety. The main decoration consisted of jewellery from head to toes (*nakha-śikha*). Four kinds of garlands, body paints, cosmetics, hair styles, head dresses and the dresses varied according to different habitation, age, status and situations of characters.

(1) **The Heroine**

(a) *Celestials, Apsarās* (*Water Nymphs*): *Divyā Nāyikā*

They were painted reddish yellow. The celestial women had ornaments suggestive of lapis lazuli and pearls. Their dresses were of bright shining colours with the colour green of the shade of a "parrot's tail" predominating. On some occasions, their dresses were white.

The *Apsarās* in particular had ornaments suggestive of different gems. They were elaborately coiffured and at times donned turbans also (as depicted in reliefs and frescoes of Ajanta, e.g. Cave 17)

(b) *Human Heroines*

Their apparel and skin colour varied according to the regional peculiarities and local usages. To take a few examples, the women of Avanti had curly hair, tied in a top knot or braids. The Ābhīra women had two braids and blue dresses. The women of the north-east tied their hair in śikhaṇḍa, while women of the south had tatoos of different shapes on their foreheads.

Heroine from a Noble family: Kulajā

They were decorated with restraint and modesty. At times, they veiled themselves in public[61] specially on the occasion of marriage. This was done by covering the head or the face with a special *duppaṭṭā*-like cloth. Unmarried girls usually went without the veil. Mālavikā and Mālati provide such examples ('Mālavikāgnimitra', V Act, 'Mālatī Mādhava', VI Act).

Courtesans

They were opulently and flamboyantly costumed and coiffured. They also veiled themselves on occasions; as in the case of Vasantasenā in V Act of *Mṛcchakaṭikam.*

Daughter of a Sage

She was dressed simply with a single hairplait or a hairknot on head.

The mode of female decorations changed with situations, conditions and basic states. For example, a heroine in separation from her beloved wore dirty attire. A *vāsakasajjā* was elaborately attired and an *abhisārikā* set out in dark blue or shining garments to meet her lover.

A special white wedding dress was worn as per the regional fashion of the time. Mālatī's wedding dress was of a white silk and fine red cloth. Śakuntalā's wedding dress was of white silk with a veil. The dancing costume of Mālavikā was shimmering and transparent; and Vāsavadattā for her worship of the god of love wore a garment with its border dyed with red and orange. On the border of Sītā's upper garment Anasuyā's name was written. Queen Dhāriṇī's *pūjā* dress was made of pure white silk.

These garments were generally unstitched except for the stitched garments like jackets (*colaka*) or tunics (*kañcuka*). The unstitched garments were draped around the body in different styles. The upper garment was loosely draped. The breast cloth was tied in different ways. The lower garment was pleated in different styles. Either it was tied in a knot or in gathers (*nīvi*) and secured by a single girdle on the top. Vasantasenā's girdle of pearls is pictorially described by the gallant-parasite.[62] Irāvatī makes a beautiful frieze when she sets out to throw her golden girdle at king Agnimitra.[63]

C—Representation of Rivers, Mountains, Weapons, etc. In Human Forms

Rivers and streams were represented in female forms. The representation of rivers is frequently found in friezes and frescoes. Rivers Muralā, Tamasā and Gaṅgā (Bhāgīrathī) were adorned accordingly when they appeared as characters in a play. River Gaṅgā was represented in white colour. Mountains were conceived as male figures. The *Himālaya* was depicted in a white male form. Personified weapons had their respective symbols in their hands.[64] Their representation in friezes is frequent and they could be visualised as dramatis personae accordingly.

The forest spirit (vāsantī) was presented in a female form as can be seen in *Uttararāmacarita*. Indra, Varuṇa, the stars and the ocean were presented in white colour.

In case of characters with many arms, heads or animal heads, appropriate imitation arms and heads were made with grass, mat, clay, wood, lac and leather.[65]

Such were the conventions governing the colour of body paint, costumes and accessories of characters in the Sanskrit plays. The performer selected his get up from this basic scheme. Infinite variety was possible. The main criterion of traditional selection was that the āhārya was to be used as a vehicle to augment the *rasa* realisation. At the same time practical convenience of an actor was stressed again and again by the dramaturgical treatises. *Nāṭyaśāstra* forbids heavy ornamentation; which would hamper easy manipulation of the body by the performing actor. That is why the crowns and other accessories had to be light-weight as far as possible.

The conventional *āhārya* made the characters of Sanskrit theatre easily recognizable. Spectators, at all levels, understood who the character was on its very first appearance. This aided the spectator's identification with the character and consequently the relish of the *rasa*.

Property (Upakaraṇa) and its use

If the elaborate settings were disposed with in the scheme of the ancient Indian theatre, the usage of the small hand-held properties was made all the more frequent, theatrical and dramatically important.

Rings, garlands, paintings, canvass boards with accessories; letters, scrolls of Yama (yamapaṭa), painting boards, water pots, weapons, umbrellas and cowries, the plate with prayer accessories, bird's cages, upper garments, ornaments, *vīṇā* and other instruments were used as devices to help the momentum of the plot.

The ring in *Abhijñāna Śākuntala* and *Mudrā Rākṣasa*, the ornaments and the toy cart in *Mṛcchakaṭika*, the dress made of bark (*valkala*) in *Pratimā* and the painting board with accessories in a number of plays were the ingenious usages of the physical properties to aid and regulate the movement of the plots and subsequently the *bhāva* presentation.

Stage properties were made with cane, leather, cloth, bamboo, lac, hay, cork, wax, jute, leaves, wood, etc. Their lightness enabled an actor to easily manipulate a piece of property without any hindrance to his performance. The playwrights, in their turn, took care that these hand-held properties were brought on the stage by the actor himself and eventually taken back stage by the actors again in the course of the action of the play.

Just to take an example of the significant use of a hand-held property in a play, let us consider Śri Harṣa's play *Ratnāvalī*. In the second act of the play, Sāgarikā, the heroine, enters with a painting canvas and a box of brushes and paints. She paints a portrait of the king and her friend Susaṅgatā paints Sāgarikā's portrait on the same canvas. After a while both run away in fright leaving the painting board in the pleasure garden. The king and the jester, later on, find the canvas with the portraits. When the heroine and her friend return to get the canvas board they are confronted with the love-lorn king. The painting, thus, aids in the lover's meeting and mutual confession of love. Later on the lovers are caught by the chief queen due to the same painting board. At the end of the act, the canvas board is taken backstage by the jester. In this way the entire second act revolves around a handprop of the painting board.

Model Work: Pusta

Although, the limitation of realism was realised by the ancient Indian theatre in its avoidance of full-fledged settings and painted scenery, usage of model work was not altogether ruled out. Small and light suggestive cutouts (*pusta*) of objects like hills, chariots, carts, aerial cars, palaces, elephants, horses, peaks of mountains and houses were often utilised in a production.

Three kinds of model work were used on the stage: (a) Joined (*sandhima*) cutouts made of mat, cloth or skin wrapped around a framework; and coloured appropriately with exquisite colours to suggest various *bhāvāvasthā*-s, (b) Model work with mechanical contrivance of levers, wires and ropes (*vyājima*), (c) Moving objects made by wrappings on a framework (*ceṣṭima*).

It must be mentioned here that although the use of hand-held, light weight properties such as shields, armour, banner staff, as well as umbrellas, Indra's staff, jester's stick with the three bends, the imitation legs, hands, heads and skins are frequently witnessed in Sanskrit play-texts, use of mechanical contrivance and moving objects is not very evident in them.

Seats—Āsana-s

Seats were definitely used on Bharata's stage. All plays from Bhāsa to Bhavabhūti refer to a seat or seats. *Nāṭyaśāstra* also elaborately describes different kinds of seats with or without cushions and conventions of the use of these seats by different characters.

Sanskrit play-texts make frequent references to characters sitting and reclining on a seat. The play-texts maintain certain protocol regarding the seating arrangements when there are more than one characters on stage. Seats are almost ceremoniously asked for and the etiquette of sitting is pointedly observed with such sentences like:

"Please bring a seat"
"Here is a seat. Please be seated", etc.

One Seat—Possibly the Only Piece of Furniture

It is quite possible that more than one seat were utilized in a play performance and they were theatrically brought on the stage from the dressing room and taken back; whilst one seat remained on the stage throughout the performance. Although the dramaturgical treatises do not mention this anywhere, such a possibility cannot be ruled out. A permanently kept seat on a bare stage might have been symbolically accepted as a throne, a garden seat, a couch or a bed as the situation of the place and time required. Such a device is to be seen frequently in almost all the extant traditional theatre forms and the folk plays. The legendary account of Viṣṇu giving Bharata and his sons the gift of a lion seat for the stage also gives broad hints to the ancient stage having at least one seat as a permanent furniture. (See the sketch 7 on page 388)

The Creative Moment—Pratibhā

We have examined, in this chapter, the concept of the fourfold *abhinaya* by which the performer in the Sanskrit theatre communicated the inner idea of the play-text to the spectator. However, before concluding the chapter, it is worthwhile noting the ideals and the system by which the performer equipped himself for the task. The techniques of *abhinaya* were imbibed by him through years of rigorous training which required a teaching ambience under a watchful eye of a teacher in the master-disciple training. Not only was the performer expected to master the techniques but the essential requirement of a successful training was to awaken the creative genius in him so that he could improvise, explore and elaborate his medium to communicate the *rasa* content of a given situation in a play at a heightened point of performance. This ability of intuitive selection of the right techniques to create an original performance was known as the performer's "creative genius" or *pratibhā* or *manodharma*.

Ancient Indian dramaturgists from Bharata onwards put a great stress on this ability and said again and again that a performance was created not just by mechanical rendering of *abhinaya* techniques but through their skilful selection by the concentrated self-discipline of the performer in an inspired moment. Such a performance alone was considered "one without blemish". The creative artistes were classified by the Indian rhetoricians into two categories of born artistes (*sahaja*) and trained artistes (*abhyasta*). For a perfect 'blemishless' enactment, a performer needed to have creative genius (*pratibhā*) which was natural (*naisargika*) spontaneous (*sahaja*) and inspired or supersensual (*lokottara*) to leave the stamp of his individuality on the performance.[66]

Abhinavagupta has made an interesting observation in this context. He says that the stimuli (*vibhāva*-s) or the situation in a play are created by the playwrights, the physical and psychomental responses (*anubhāva*) or the fourfold *abhinaya* techniques are imbibed by the training with a drama teacher but the skilful usage of the thirty-three transitory states (*vyabhicāri*) *bhāva*-s depend on the performer's creative genius (*pratibhā*) alone.

Notes

1. NS, VIII, 6.
2. Ibid, 7—"*śākhā-aṅga-upāṅga* saṃyukta abhinaya".
3. SD, VI, 2 and its commentary.
4. Abh. I, 1, Sl.107, L-67, p. 125.
5. DR I, 10-12 (Haas), Bh. P. VII, 1-9. Bh. P. describes Nṛtta as *rasāśrayī*.
6. Mankad D.R., "Types of Sanskrit drama" pp. 28–36.
7. Kale M.R., ed. Mālavikāgnimitram, p. 55.5 Cf. NS, XXXIV, 46.
8. From talks with Dr. G.H. Tarlekar; *Nāṭyadharmī* zonal divisions are examined in detail in Chapter VII.
9. NS, XXIV, 46-47.
10. NS, XIII, 4–7, (tr. M. Ghosh), XI, 89–92 (GOS) 1 tala = 12 *aṅgula:* i.e. roughly 12".
11. NS, XI 89.92 (tr. M. Ghosh).
12. NS, II, 48–69 (Kashi ed.).
13. NS, XIII, 158-59 (Kashi ed).
14. Ibid, 193–204.
15. Ibid, 219–25.
16. NS, XI, 87, also XIII, 4–14 (tr. M. Ghosh).
17. Ibid, 2.
18. Ibid, 3-4. This *karaṇa* is different from *nṛtta karaṇa*. Abhinavagupta elaborates by saying that three *khaṇḍa*-s in *trayasra tāla* and four *khaṇḍa*-s in *caturasra* tāla make a *maṇḍala*. *Caturasra* indicates a *tāla* with sixteen beats, *trayasra* with twelve beats. For further details see page 230.
19. NS, XIII, 20.
20. Abh. Vol. II, XIII (XII) p. 1030, Sl. 14.

21. NS, XI, 5.
22. Abh. Sak., III, 3, L-2, *Mālavikāgnimitram*, VI, 12, L-3, Bhāsa's *Avimāraka*, IV, L-1; Abh. Sak. II, L-1; Ibid, V, 2, L-3.
23. NS, XIII, 22.
24. Ibid, 40–44.
25. NS, XI, 30.
26. NS, XIII, 121, also NS XXVI, 6, 62 (tr. M. Ghosh).
27. Ibid, 181–83.
28. Ibid, 164-65 (See fig. 8, in chart on page no. 139).
29. NS, XIII, 137–46; I, 58, 51 (M. Ghosh) XIII 143–46 and XXIII 179–90; IX, 92.
    Kuṭilaka is a crooked stick with three bends which a jester carries. It is also called *Daṇḍakāṣṭha* (See the sketch 4 on page 388).
30. NS, XIII, 112–14.
31. NS, XI, 22. Artha. Dyo, op. cit. 0.76. *Udvṛtta cārī* : Tala *sañcāra* foot placed onwards, one shank slightly bent and thigh turned up.
32. Ibid, 3.
33. Ibid, 3.
34. NLRK, 412 (ed. N. Dillon, 1937) NLRK specially mentions that generally *Sūta*, *Māgadha* and *Vandi*-s indicate the 'noises off' in *cūlikā* and only occasionally other leading characters resort to this.
35. NS, XX, 112, 137.
36. Coomaraswamy A.K., The Mirror of Gestures, p. 13.
37. Abh. Vol. I, p. 73.
38. NS, VII, 106 (tr. M. Ghosh).
39. NS, VII, 85 90. *Maraṇa* here is taken as *vyabhicārī* of love in separation also.
40. Ibid, 86 (tr. M. Ghosh).
41. Abh. VI, pp. 271, 708 onwards.
42. NS XXIV, 7–13 (tr. M. Ghosh).
43. Ibid, 5.
44. NS, XXXIV, 242.
45. NS, XXXV, 26-27.
46. NS, XXXIV, 57-63 (tr. M. Ghosh).
47. Abh. XXIII, 4.
48. Ibid.
49. *Mṛcchakaṭikam* (Act V) Vasantasenā's dress—*Ujjavalaveśā*.
50. *Vikramorvaśīyam* (Act II) Nilāṃśuka, Urvaṣī's dress.
51. Abh. Śāk. (Act VII)—*Ekaveṇidhārā*.
52. *Veṇi Saṃhāram* (Act VI).
53. Dr. Motichandra, Costumes, Textiles and Coiffure in Ancient and Mediaeval India, pp. 181–84.
54. NS, XXIII, 73–75, Vdh. P. (*Citrasūtra*) adds white and green to the NS list of four basic colours. With the mixture of these, an infinite variety of derivative colours, tones and hues can be produced.
55. Ghurye G.S., Indian Costume, p. 18.
56. There is no consensus of opinion regarding the *śyāma* colour. Various views have been offered. Dr. Ghosh thinks it is deep blue. Present-day

traditional theatres of South India (Kathakali, Kudiyattam) take *śyāma* to mean as green colour. Others have suggested dark deep bluish-green or purple of the rain clouds or a dark brown.

57. Dr. Motichandra, *Prācīna Bhāratīya Veśabhūṣā* (Hindi) pp. 38–41.
58. NS, XXIII, 11–68.
59. Vdh. P. 3.42, 31–41 (tr. C. Sivaramamurti).
60. Ibid, 3.42, 71 also 15–19.
61. Bhāsa's *Pratimānāṭakam*, 14, L-7.
62. *Mṛcchakaṭikam*, I, 27.
63. *Mālavikāgnimitram*, II, 21.
64. In Sesasayi Pancha Frieze from Deogarh, 5 Century A.D., personified weapons are depicted.
65. NS, XXIII, 206-07, XXXV 22-24.
56. De S.K., Sanskrit Poetics, pp. 53, 369.
67. Abh. Vol. 1, VI, p. 625.

CHAPTER 7

DHARMĪ-S—PRACTICES OF STAGING

Through a long period of continuous evolution, the *abhinaya* techniques of staging of Sanskrit plays had evolved into two identifiable practices of enactment: (1) exclusive practice emphasising esoteric stage conventions called *nāṭyadharmī, ābhyantara* or *mārgī* and (2) popular practices emulating the ways of the world called lokadharmī, bāhya or deśī. While these can be identified with two different streams of practices emerging out of separate circumstances, occasions and places, as was seen in Chapter I, in practice, the two traditions interacted, intermingled and merged with each other to form a variegated and complex design of *abhinaya* techniques governing the performances of Sanskrit plays.

Nāṭyadharmī practice was highly abstract and probably contained adaptions from very ancient and powerful esoteric conventions, assimilated over the years, of magico-ritualistic traditions of the olden times. They were sacrosanct, considered exclusive (*ābhyantara*) and not everyone was allowed to practise them. A zealous effort to maintain the original purity and guard its proper and pure rendering by a select few was attempted. This was done by oral transmission of *nāṭasūtra*-s (actor's aphorisms) by generations of hereditary groups of performers who were initiated into the practice through the teacher-disciple tradition. Later the *sūtra*-s were codified into a *śāstra*. Sophisticated connoisseurs thoroughly appreciated this practice.

At the same time, on the other hand, the vast subcontinent of India had also generated a number of popular, exterior (*bāhya*) performing practices which had their genesis in the creative expressions of the people from different regions of the country. Such practices emphasised *sādṛaśya abhinaya*—literally meaning 'that which resembles'—which were based on the observation of the worldly ways (*lokānusārī*) of the people. Regional modes of behaviour (*pravṛtti*), local customs and the nature (*prakṛti*), period (*deśakāla*) and cultural disposition of people were incorporated into this practice. This resulted in a variety of conventions and styles of *abhinaya* which were taken to the length and breadth of the country by roaming groups of hereditary entertainers. These exterior practices were termed *lokadharmī*. The term *loka* suggests worldly ways of the people from different regions and not the folk arts.

Difference Between Two Practices of Performance

The difference between the two practices was not so much of social strata or of high or low environments but that of the attitude of the practitioners towards the hereditary art. Nāṭyadharmī performers acquired it through rigorous teacher-disciple tradition and practised it with an aim to maintain its immaculate purity in the manner of a traditionally ordained ritual. Its conventions were of a highly specialised nature and were understood by or meant specially for only the select and erudite connoisseurs. The *lokadharmī* practices were not as sacred and inviolable and were not learnt according to the maxims of the *śāstra*-s but were acquired, nevertheless, as hereditary skills. They certainly had a repertoire of conventions based on the observation of local practices, customs and usages easily understood by spectators.

Indeed, in the course of long years of evolution, each practice interreacted, enriched and imbibed many aspects of the other. Consequently, the staging practices of Sanskrit plays exhibited a rich amalgam of suggestions and conventions gathered from both.

Traditional Description of Nāṭyadharmī Practices

As already mentioned, the *nāṭyadharmī* practice was codified and preserved, at first, in the *sūtra* system of hereditary transmission which were referred to as *nāṭyasūtra*-s as early as Pāṇini's time who mentioned them as sacred practices of actors (*naṭa*-s). In the considered opinion of scholars like V.S. Agarwal, this tradition was later incorporated into the *Nāṭyaśāstra*.[1]

Genres of Sanskrit plays like *nāṭaka*, *utsṛṣṭikāñka*, *nāṭikā*, *samavakāra*, *vyāyoga*, *īhāmṛga* and *ḍima*, dealing with the exploits of beings from the three worlds, were mainly performed in this practice. Divine beings, supernatural energies, natural forces like rivers, forest spirits, hills, armours, conveyance, banner staffs and even a curse appeared on the stage in human forms as characters in these plays.

The stage area was imaginatively divided into various zones depicting different locales through suggestive *abhinaya*. This was termed as the convention of zonal divisions or *kakṣyāvibhāga*.

Highly stylised hand gestures (*hasta*-s); sculpturesque stances of standing, sitting and reclining (*sthāna-āsana-śayana*); dance-like movements (*karaṇa*-s and *aṅgahāra*-s), walks and facial expressions especially of the eyes (*cārī*-s and *dṛṣṭi*-s); make-up and costumes with magico-ritualistic undertones were used as a code language suggesting implied meanings to the spoken word.[2] The stylised, intoned and accented speech, chants and songs monologues, asides, speech in the air, and concealed speech as well as the stylisation of *sāttvika*, were parts of this highly symbolic and abstract form of *nāṭyadharmī* theatrical practice.[3] V. Raghavan describes this practice as an "Idealism of Bharata's stage."[4] The responsive spectator who relished the rich nuances of this practice of suggestion and implication, was of course, a vital part for its success.

Traditional Description of Lokadharmī Practice

This convention, termed as "realistic practice" by the scholars, dealt with the "natural conditions of the things in the world"[5] as against the highly stylised *nāṭyadharmī* practice.

Prakaraṇa, prahasana, bhāṇa type of Sanskrit plays mainly emphasise this practice of performance because they deal with "the professions and activities of the people." According to *Nāṭyaśāstra* the practice had "no playful flourish of limbs and depended on men and women of different types found in the society."[6] Performers behaved, moved and spoke in accordance with the nature, position, culture and regional characteristics of the character types that they portrayed.

However, it must be pointed out here that this practice, often translated in English as "realistic", was nowhere similar to the modern concept of realistic or naturalistic theatre. *Lokadharmī* practice being an assimilation of the ways of the world, might not have been as dependent on rigorous specialisation as the *nāṭyadharmī* system and was comparatively less formal. But it was definitely performed according to the *lokadharmī* hereditary traditions governing the fourfold *abhinaya*.

Kallinātha, in his commentary on *Saṅgītaratnākara*, vividly underlines the difference between the *nāṭyadharmī* and *lokadharmī* practices, when he says:

> "In these practices, words are not merely used as in the way of common practice of the world . . . Both practices of dharmi-s indicate *āṅgikka abhinaya* which accompany the words. Only the enunciation of a sentence with the appropriate *abhinaya* (*vākyābhinaya*) is *lokadharmī*. The rendering of the sentence with intonation (*rāgayukta*) is *nāṭyadharmī*. In *āhārya abhinaya* also, the wearing of necklaces, armlets and ornaments is *lokadharmī*, while suggesting (by *abhinaya* alone) a banner or a car is *nāṭyadharmī*. Even in *sāttvika abhinaya* paralysis etc., when shown in their original nature, is *lokadharmī*. When gesticulated with hand gestures, they are *nāṭyadharmī*."[7]

Bharata gives equal importance to both practices in a drama production. He emphatically declares that "a play should always be produced with *nāṭyadharmī* practice, for without acting through gestures etc. no feeling is invoked (in the spectators)."[8] At the same time, he also repeats that "whatever is not in the *śāstra* has to be learnt through the observation of the ways of the world."[9]

The Use of the Two Practices in Sanskrit Plays

There appears to be no strict compartmentalisation in their usage in a play production. Both were employed according to the situations so that we get an unending variety of both practices of staging in the context of the Sanskrit plays.

The traditional production design for a Sanskrit play performance scrupulously followed by the playwrights was as follows:

(1) Preliminaries — *Pūrvaraṅga*
(2) Prayer — *Nāndī*
(3) Prologue — *Prastāvanā*
(4) Play text — In verse or *śloka* (*kāvya*) or prose (*vākya*), in acting units of an act (an *aṅka*) joined with linking devices
(5) Actor's benedictory verse — *Bharata vākya*

This format was represented by harmonious (*sāmānya*) and varied (*citra*) usage of the fourfold *abhinaya*, through both *nāṭyadharmī* and *lokadharmī* practices of staging.

The characteristics of the playhouses described by Bharata, the arrangement of the auditorium vis-a-vis the stage proper and the architectural distribution of the spaces in the stage area with its peculiarities and limitations also influenced the staging practices.

It may be recapitulated that the main acting areas in Bharata's stages were as follows:

(1) The stage proper (acting area) in the three types of playhouses was a precisely allocated space facing east, possibly at a different level from the audience.

(2) The acting zones of the stage itself were located and specifically named. In the context of the medium rectangular playhouse, they were as follows:

(a) The main acting area in the downstage centre—The *rangapīṭha* (RP)
(b) The acting area in the upstage behind the RP and/or the two *mattavāraṇī*-s—The *raṅgasīrṣa* (RS)
(c) Two extensions on either sides of the RP formed by pillars —*Mattavāraṇī*-s (MAT-s)
(d) The two doors (DRs) on either side of the stage wall dividing the stage from the dressing room.
(e) *Kutapa* (KUT)—The place for the music orchestra. The space between the two DRs probably elevated to form a platform (*pīṭha*) and/or with a railing (*vedikā*).
(f) The dressing room—A specified space behind the stage wall forming the dressing room.

(In the following paragraphs mostly the abbreviations of the above terms are used.)

A set of conventional practices of staging generated by the peculiarities of the ancient Indian theatre construction is as follows:

(a) Direct and frontal communication between the actor and the spectator.
(b) The style of continuous narration—representation.
(c) The zonal divisions of the stage (*kakṣyāvibhāga*)—a *nāṭyadharmī* technique which culminated in the bifocal and trifocal scenes in play-texts suggesting various locations and multiple actions with minimum or no use of setting.

(d) The curtain—the conventions governing its use.
(e) The conventions of entrances and exits.
(f) Lighting.
(g) Acoustic.

Each of the above is examined separately in the following sections:

Section a

Direct and frontal communication between the actor and the spectator

In Bharata's playhouses the stages confronted the audience directly without any dividing structures like proscenium arched framings or such impediments. Moreover, they catered mainly to the needs of small intimate gatherings of not more than five to six hundred spectators. The spectators sat either

(i) on seats facing the stage as in rectangular playhouses,
(ii) on 'tier upon tier' seating arrangement which surrounded the stage on the three open sides as in the square playhouses,
(iii) sat or stood around the stage on three sides, with the patron's ornate seat facing the peformers as in the royal playhouses.

The performer was predominant in such an arrangement of intimate juxtaposition. Right from his entrance the performer confronted the spectators frontally. The peculiarities of the ancient playhouse constructions which had the two doors (DR) for actor's entry at the stage back-wall aided him in this. In the intimacy of the small auditoria, he faced the three open sides of the stage where the spectators sat, presented himself frontally and maintaining the position, performed. The convention of repeating the *bhāvābhinaya* thrice probably arose from this practice.

The reason for the maintenance of the face-to-face representation can be deduced from the insight offered by Stella Kramrisch for such frontal juxtapositions in ancient Indian art. Commenting on such an arrangement between the image and devotee in the context of images in sculpture, she says, "The frontal image fulfills the function of an instrument of concentration . . . to facilitate (this) concentration and simultaneous fixation, the image has to confront the devotee in its entire presence unbroken by the third dimension."[10] If we substitute the words "image" and "devotee" with "the performer" and "the spectator", the principal idea behind the frontal positioning of the ancient actors becomes clear. It was to help the process of spectator's concentration and identification with the character which facilitated his *rasa* realisation.

Not only was the presentation frontal, but it was direct face-to-face communication with the spectator. There was neither structural nor imaginary barrier in the manner of "the fourth wall concept" dividing the performance from the spectators. In Sanskrit plays, right from the prologues, the *sūtradhāra* and other actors of the troupe establish direct dialogue with the spectators. They welcome and praise the assembly, introduce the playwright and the play and converse with them throughout. Like in the plays of Bhavabhūti,[11] the *sūtradhāra* announces with a flourish his assumption of an important role in the play proper like this: "So, now I am Kāmandakī" or "So, I now become a citizen of Ayodhyā" etc.

In this manner, many conventions of actor's direct communication of confidential exchanges with the audience through the performance were established from the very outset. They were as follows:

(i) direct announcement of the character's intention at the time of his entry, in the context of zonal division (*ātmanivedanam*),
(ii) monologues,
(iii) asides,
(iv) the direct relay of the comments and double entendre, specially by the jester,
(v) the detailed description of the states and situations (*bhāvāvasthā*) on the entry of a character.

It is interesting to note that the conventions of direct communication with the audience, frontal positioning of the performers and their frontal entries still survive in most of the traditional and folk theatres like Kudiyattam, Kathakali, Yaksagana, Kuchipudi, etc. It is interesting to note that the costumes are also designed with the frontal position in view so much so that a Kudiyattam actor appears half dressed when viewed from the sides or the rear. The technique of repeating the *abhinaya*—albeit with variations of the vyabhicāri bhāva-s—three times in three directions are still found in the present day *Jātra* and classical dance recitals even when the latter are performed in the modern day enclosed stages with side wings.

Section b

Continuous Narration—Representations

The Sanskrit play performance was continuous—without any audio-visual breaks. Choreographic design of such a continuous performance was ingeniously broken up into scenes of representation and scenes of narration varying in pace, rhythm and tempo. The performance progressed through:

(a) *Scenes of Representations*

These scenes comprised of sequences and situations latent with *rasa* (*sarasa vastu*) presented through extended *bhāvābhinaya* by the principal characters like the Sanskrit speaking hero, his aides, assistants and the heroine and her retinue speaking in Prakrit. With the verbal and the graceful styles dominating in the delicate (*sukumāra*) productions and the energetic, the sublime and the verbal styles dominant in the violent (*āviddha*) productions, these scenes were represented with full display of styles.

(b) *Scenes of Narration*

These scenes consisted of brisk linking devices of essential narration (*ni-rasa vastu*) presented with small connecting scenes. The incidents were concisely narrated with the insertion of the germ idea (*bīja-bindu*) indicating what is to follow in these scenes. This was done by one or more middle or low characters in brisk conversation or a monologue. The beginning and the end of the acts were mostly indicated by stock speeches by stock characters like chamberlain, bards etc.

The Conventions Regarding the Beginning and the End of Acts

Ancient Indian stages did not have any front or drop curtain to indicate the ending of an act similar to what we see in modern theatres. *Sāhitya Darpaṇa* mentions a theatre tradition saying that all characters took their exits from the stage at the end of an act.[12] Sanskrit play-texts provide more or less a common stage direction indicating the end of an act like. 'Then they all depart'—'End of act' and so on. At such moments the spectators were momentarily confronted with a bare stage occupied by the musicians providing the musical interlude leading to the mood of the next act. Also, certain types of characters got conventionalised into performing as links between two acts. The spectators understood the special purpose which these characters accomplished and accepted them as useful vehicles for the forward movement of the play. For example, the bard usually ended a sequence of a *nāṭaka* by the announcement of the period—time-of the day. Description of the season in which the play was set was also introduced in the prologues by the *sūtradhāra* and the actress. And the beginning of the act or a scene, as seen before, was accomplished by one or two minor characters. A chamberlain in a heroic play like *nāṭaka* had the same set of speech indicating his age, position and duties. The spectators were familiar with both the character and his speech. They expected him to disclose the whereabouts of the royal characters, especially the king-hero and his *bhāvāvasthā*.

In this connection, Dr. V. Raghavan sheds an interesting light. He states the possibility of a single act of a play taking up a whole night, while the performance of an entire play might have taken a series of night performances. The tradition of giving special names to each act by some of the playwrights and the Kerala Chakyara tradition of performing only a single act give credence to this view.

This framework of continuous narration—representation is presented in the context of Kālidāsa's Mālavikāgnimitra on pp. 198-200.

While maintaining the continuous progression of the performance through the technique of narration-representation, the main consideration was to sustain the rasa impact. Sanskrit theatre differed in this respect from the Greek concept of the three unities of the time, place and action.

The sequences and scenes in the plot progression were so arranged that they provided an atmosphere for the maximum *rasa* realisation. No impediment of space, time or even action was allowed to act as a break in this atmosphere.

Concept of Place and Action

With the themes based on epics, *purāṇa*-s and *kathā* literature the scope for the place and action changes in Sanskrit dramas is immense. Episodes covering a number of locales are depicted in one and the same act. The action can shift from heaven to earth and vice-versa (*Vikramorvaśīyam, Abhijñānaśākuntalam*), from one part of India to another (*Abhiṣeka Nāṭaka*) or from different areas of the city street to the terraces of the palaces (*Avīmāraka*) with ease in a single act.

These swift scene transfers were executed not by any physical means. But they were performed by suggestive *nāṭyadharmī abhinaya* of zonal divisions, the brisk introductory linking scenes like *praveśaka*-s and the use of the hand-held curtain. In addition, poetic descriptions of the surroundings was always supplied in the drama texts.

Concept of Time and Action

Similarly, time was condensed and elaborated to suit the aim of *rasa* evocation. Incidents of a single day were depicted in a single act, as per the traditional rules. But years could elapse between two acts. In Bhavabhūti's Uttararāmacarita, there is a lapse of twelve years between Act I and Act II. This passage of time is simply indicated by a single sentence in a brisk supporting linking scene (*viṣkambhaka*). At the same time the delineation of Rāma's state of love in separation is executed with appropriate extension of savouring of his *bhāvāvasthā*-s,[13] to evoke the erotic *rasa* in the spectator. This type of rendering, necessary for *rasa* experience, stretched out the moments of duration with a deliberate slowing down of time sense. Unnecessary actions, from the *rasa*-evocation point of view, were treated with a dramatic compression wherein a character made his exit and reappeared with his task done in a twinkling of an eye. Bhāsa makes very frequent use of this convention of an 'exit' and a 'quick re-entry' (*niṣkramya praveśya*). Often in a play, a piece of property or a character are called for and they appear within a split second. This gives the entire proceedings the air of the "montage technique" or the cinematic "jump cut" or "efficient shorthand" as aptly described by H. W. Wells.[14]

These exits and re-entries, however, were systematically

Framework 4

KĀLIDĀSA'S MĀLAVIKĀGNIMITRAM

Act	Narration/Representation	Characters	Speech	Purport	Remarks
ACT I	Nāndi with the prologue	Sūtradhāra and Co-actor (*Paripārśvaka*)	Sanskrit	Introduction of the playwright, the theme and its germ idea *Bija-Bindu*.	By leading members of *Nātya* troupes themselves. (For details of performance, see Infra, Chap. 8, pp. 238-40. Section on the prayer and prologues).
Narration	Miśra Viṣkambhaka	Two maids of the queen and *Guṇadāsa*	Sanskrit plus Prakrit	Gives the background of the beauty and the status of the heroine states in narration the attraction—(pūrva rāga) and kindling of love in the king after seeing Mālavikā in a picture. The displeasure of the queen (obstacle) is also hinted.	The main seed, the desire for *Kāma* (also) artha is introduced in brisk dialogues—hinting at its purpose, situation and the beginning (Prārambha) of the *Ratibhāva*, the state of love.
Representation	Main scene	King, Minister, *Viduṣaka*, two *Nāṭyācārya*-s, Queen and the female ascetic	Sanskrit plus Prakrit	(1) Conversation between the king and ministers. (2) Display of kindling of love—*Icchā*—in the king in the scene with the Vidūṣaka—*Erotic and Hāsya*.	The seed is well sown of love (*Rati*)—(Erotic *rasa*). The stage is prepared for the meeting of the hero and heroine—the *ālambana* of *śṛṅgāra*, the support of erotic *rasā*.

Act	Narration/Rep-representation	Characters	Speech	Purport	Remarks
				(3) Efforts (*Prayatna*) by the king and his *Narma saciva*—jester—for a meeting under the excuse to pacify the two quarrelling *nāṭyācāryas* by the suggestion to have a contest.	
The act ends with all the characters leaving the stage. The device of *Aṅkāvatāra* is made use of as a linking device between I and II act. It is through this device that the setting as well as the proposed action in the following set is indicated.					
ACT II					
Representation	The scene in the palace theatre (*Prekṣāgṛha*)	Most of the main characters including Mālavikā	Sanskrit plus Prakrit	The dance of the heroine, kindling of Anurāga in the king and the heroine, who displays amourous gestures (*Vilāsa*) with *bhāva*, *hāva* and *helā* under the excuse of the dance.	The seed of love develops between the hero and the heroine (*ālambana* of *śṛṅgāra*) aided by the jester (*alambana* of *Hāsya*).
The act ends with the introduction of *Cūlikā* in the form of the time indication by the bard from behind the curtain.					
ACT III					
Narration	*Praveśaka* in the royal garden	Three maids	Prakrit	The narration informs the progression of *Śṛṅgāra* between the king and the heroine.	The setting and the development of the germ is indicated by brisk dialogues giving the information.

Act	Narration Representation	Characters	Speech	Purport	Remarks
Representation	Main scene in the garden in bifocal and trifocal techniques	King, *Vidūṣaka*, Mālavikā, Sakhī, Irāvatī, Sakhī	Sanskrit and Prakrit	Representation of *Ayoga Śṛṅgāra* (a) by the king and Mālavikā (b) possibility of successful fulfilment *Prāptyāśā* (c) Disturbed by the appearance of an obstacle (*Vighna*) in the form of queen Irāvatī.	Elaborate scope for *bhāvānukīrtana* of *Ayoga Śṛṅgāra* viz., *lālasā*, *smṛti*, *guṇakīrtana*, *cintā*, etc. by the king. The same displayed in a subdued way by the heroine. And furious *rasa* by Irāvatī.

The act ends on a note of a pause/suspense in the form of Gargha Sandhi.

ACT IV					
Representation	Main scene	King, *Vidūṣaka*, Queen, the female ascetic, Mālavikā, Sakhī, Irāvatī, Sakhī	Sanskrit plus Prakrit	(a) Further efforts by the jester (b) meeting of the lovers in the *Samudragṛha* (c) Further disturbance by the arrival of Irāvatī. The possibility of success momentarily nullified by strong obstacle in the form of Irāvatī.	*Bhāvābhinaya* of all stages of *Vipralambha Śṛṅgāra* (or separation after a brief union) by both the hero and the heroine—molified in the company of *Hāsya* (Jester).

The act ends with an announcement (*Cūlikā*) from behind the curtain.

ACT V					
Narration	Praveśaka	The female gardner,	Prakrit	(a) Informs about political	All the loose trends are

Act	Narration Representation	Characters	Speech	Purport	Remarks
	Main scene	hunchback—Sārasaka All dramatis personae	Prakrit plus Sanskrit	Victory over Vidarbha. (b) Resolution gradually of the *vighna*-s by the arrival of the two maids sent by the king of Vidarbha, who unravel the status and the background of the heroine. (c) All obstacles are removed from the path of the hero and the heroine —Nirvahaṇa.	neatly wound up with the goal of *Kāma* and *Artha* achieved by the hero—Agnimitra

This act ends with the Bharata Vākya—by the actor playing the king—with a wish for the well-being of all.

The continuous progression of the plot is cleverly broken up by small scenes of narration by the use of the linking devices like Viṣkambhaka, Praveśaka, Cūlikā, Ankāvatara (with minor characters, speaking Prakrit and Sanskrit in brisk dialogues.).

The scenes of representation where the main characters are shown in different phases, states and situations of the sthāyibhāva of rati (love), concomitant hāsya (comic) and other rasa-s.

governed by the rules of conventions of practices and were to be executed according to the time beats of two *kalā*-s.[15]

Section c

The Zonal Division—Kakṣyā Vibhāga

A bare stage, without a front curtain, with ornate rows of pillars supporting the roof, and a stage wall at the back, with two doors on either side: This was the permanent setting of the ancient Sanskrit theatre. Plays dealing with the stories of the beings of the three worlds were enacted on such a stage in a continuous performance.

Suggestive settings, indicative of various locales of the dramatic narrative were imaginatively created by the stylised movements and *abhinaya* of the performers against this neutral background of the stage. For this, movements were meticulously worked out in a highly systematised *nāṭyadharmī* stage convention of zonal division known as *kakṣyā-vibhāga*.

The word 'kakṣyā' is translated by Dr. M. Ghosh as a 'zone'. Others understood it as *nāṭyadharmī* sub-division of scenes into different locales. Abhinavagupta explains *kakṣyā* as an activity which takes a character from one locale to another.[16] Bharata is more specific. He says:

> "Kakṣyā is to be indicated by going about (*parikramā*) on the stage. Such a going about will change the locale into another (locale) when a character moves out of it, or completes the going about."[17]

In short, by varying the movements of "going around" (*parikramā*) on the same stage area different locales or zones were imaginatively suggested to the spectators without taking recourse to any physical aids like change of scenery or settings.

By this purely *nāṭyadharmī* technique, the Sanskrit plays could depict with ease many scenes on different locations in a continuous sequence without any loss of tempo, pace or rasa impact. This was achieved in two ways:

(i) By the *nāṭyadharmī* body *abhinaya* of stage walks (*cārī-s*) and gaits (*gati*-s) used in the movement of "going around" (*parikramā*) on the same stage area.

(ii) By the *nāṭyadharmī* convention of entries, exits and

approaches in the imaginatively established zones on the stage (*praveśa, niṣkramaṇa, apasāraṇa*).

The body movements (āṅgika) were always accompanied by either vocal (vācika) descriptions or specific drum beats or both. The techniques governing its enactment were meticulously worked out. They were:

Different Stage Walks (Cārī-s)—Indicating Different Locales

The use of different suggestive stage walks (*cārī*-s) during "the going around" (*parikramā*) automatically indicated to the spectators a new locale. For example, aerial stage walks were employed to indicate locales in the sky or in the heaven. An *atikrāntā cārī* suggested an ascent to a locale on a higher level.

Distance and Nearness of a Locate

This was conveyed by the number of times "the going around" was enacted on the stage. If the number was lesser, a short distance was implied. If it was larger, a longer distance was suggested.

Indication of Interior (Ābhyantara), Exterior (Bāhya) and in Between (Madhya) Areas of an Established Locale

Another set of conventions suggested whether a character was in the interior, exterior or in between regions of an imaginatively established locale.

(i) *The Interior* (*ābhyantara*) *of a Locale*

This was established by the characters who had entered the stage earlier, and by moving around the stage had already suggested a locale and placed themselves inside.[18] For example, in Śūdraka's Mṛcchakaṭika, Cārudatta and Maitreya establish the interior of Cārudatta's house by occupying a zone on the stage in Act I, by their movements accompanying their speech after the prologue up to the verse 17.

(ii) *The Exterior* (*bāhya*) *of a Locale*

This was suggested by characters who entered the stage later and established another zone outside the one which had earlier been suggested as an interior of a locale. For example, Vasantasenā indicates the exterior of the Cārudatta's house by referring to a side door in the wall with a sentence "This is, indeed, a side door, I can feel the wall", etc.

Self Report (Ātmanivedanam) of a Character

A character wishing to enter the interior of a zone from the exterior region, or on entry from the dressing room desiring to convey his intention of seeing those who were in the interior zone, expressed his intention of doing so by turning to his left side and making an announcement of his intention.[19] A special term *ātmanivedanam* denotes this convention. It is translated in English as a character's "Self report".

In Act I of Mudrā Rākṣasa the spy enters the stage with a scroll (*yamapaṭa*) in his hand, after the interior of Cāṇakya's house has been established. He makes his entry from a separate zone and indicates his intention by turning on his left and making his self report by saying:

> "So after entering this house and exhibiting the *yamapaṭa*, I shall be singing songs" etc.

The spy would then start moving around the stage to suggest that he is about to enter the house of Cāṇakya.

(iii) *The In-Between Area of the Locale* (*Madhya*)

When a character enters the interior zone from the exterior zone or vice-versa, the in-between zonal locale is established which, in practice, is temporary and forms part of the movement of entering and approaching the suggested locale (*kakṣyā*). Stage directions like "then he enters" or "then he approaches" (*praviśya, upsṛtya*) denote this activity. For example, in *Mudrā Rākṣasa* Act I when the spy finally enters the interior of Cāṇakya's house he indicates the in-between zone by saying,

> "Here I enter" (entering and approaching)
> "Hail, Sir" etc.

In the enactment, the first sentence: "Here I enter" is the spy's "self-report" from a separate exterior zone. His action of approaching and entering the interior zone is indicated by the stage direction "entering and approaching". When he greets Cāṇakya with "Hail Sir". . .it is established that he is inside the interior of Cāṇakya's house.

This *nāṭyadharmī* convention of zonal division made choreographic representation of multiple action-time-place based scenes of Sanskrit plays very popular. Playwrights from Bhāsa to Bhavabhūti made ample use of this practice. Not only could the stories of the beings of the three worlds be easily depicted by this convention, but the flow of continuous performance could also go on without any break. There was no need to have any physical aids like settings to indicate the change of scenery. The transfer of scenes could be established by suggestive *abhinaya* on the same bare stage. With the aid of this *nāṭyadharmī* staging concept, the locales shifted from heaven to earth and back,[20] from the city streets to the terraces or the interiors of palaces,[21] from the top of the Himalayas to a sea beach[22] from the forest to the Laṅkā Island,[23] and from one locale of a garden to another.[24] Long journeys, crossing a river, groping around in dark locales from brighter sunlit exteriors could be easily indicated on the same bare stage without any break in movement or tempo of the continuous performance. To take one example:

In a sequence in Act III of Kālidāsa's *Vikramorvaśīya*, transfer of scenes is suggested with action shifting from separate levels of locales of a palace garden, terrace of the palace and aerial zones by this technique of zonal division as follows:

The chamberlain enters and establishes a zone symbolising a palace garden on the stage. He does this after his "self-report" of declaring his intention of seeing king Pururavas for whom he has a message from the chief queen. He moves around and describes the fragrance and the beauty of the palace garden. He also observes the activities around the palace at evening time (Ver. 2). This popular *abhinaya* convention to establish the location of a place with multifarious scenic varieties is frequently used in Sanskrit plays. After he has established the zone A, he describes the processional entry of the king surrounded by the lamp bearing maids and the jester (Ver. 3) in another area of the stage zone B.

Zone B

The chamberlain then approaches and enters the zone B, established by the king's group (Ver. 4-L-1). He delivers the message from the queen for a meeting on the terrace of the crystal palace from the interior of zone B.

Zone C

The king's group moves around on the stage enacting ascent. The terrace and the moonlit night are established through verbal description of the moonrise (Ver. 6-7). The maids with lamps descend, i.e. move around the same stage area by enacting the stage walk suggesting descent and exit from the stage. The ascent and descent would be suggested by moving around (*parikramā*) in appropriate stage walks (*cārī*-s).[25]

Zone D

The celestial nymphs Urvaśī and Citralekhā enter in an aerial car. This again would be indicated by the *āṅgika abhinaya* of a cārī.[26] A separate area on the stage would be established as a sky zone.

Zone E

When the nymphs descend from the aerial car, they would establish yet another independent zone on the terrace which separates them from the king's group.

Zone F

Processional entry of the chief queen, the worship in the moonlight and her exit with her retinue are established by yet another zone F by the same convention of performance. After the exit of the queen, the heroine Urvaśī and Citralekhā approach and enter the zone D.

Thus, six locales are presented in one sequence on the same bare stage by *nāṭyadharmī* technique of zonal division.

Such arrangements of multiple scenes in Sanskrit plays, often referred to as the bifocal and trifocal scenes, had their genesis in the extensive and effective use of the *nāṭyadharmī* convention of the zonal divisions. Many interesting variations of staging emanated from this practice.

For example, the *nivṛtyānkura* style which Bharata mentions. In this style of enactment, one or more actors, established in one zone delineated the *bhāva* presented by the situation in the play mainly through their speech while the other group of actors, in another zone, expressed the same *bhāva*-s through their movements alone (*āṅgika*).

Another variation of such simultaneous or parallel enactment was presented by two or three groups of characters, establishing two or three separate zones, conducting two or three sets of actions on the same bare stage in an interesting audio-visual choreographic pattern.

Let us examine this staging concept by taking a few examples from Sanskrit plays.

Nivṛtyānkura Style of Presentation
Play: Abhijñāna Śākuntala, Act I and II

King Duṣyanta in one zone (This zone can be termed as the exterior of the tree groves.) describes Śakuntalā and her friends who are watering the plants. The latter group is in the interior zone. These two groups may be placed in any part of the stage.

The two sets of actions or subsequences continue intermitantly on a parallel level. At times, the king describes the heroine and her actions and at other times, he represents his reaction (*bhāvāvasthā*) to the heroine's actions in *nivṛtynākura* style of *abhinaya*. All the while the scene of the heroine and her friends continue.

Simultaneous Parallel Enactments
Bifocal Scenes

At times, a pictorial freeze by one group was enacted when the other group was performing. For instance in *Mālatī Mādhav*, Act II—

(i) The heroine Mālatī and her friend are in a zone which suggests an upper floor of the palace.
(ii) Kāmandakī and Avalokitā enter the exterior of the zone and enact a scene, quite oblivious of the first group.

Till *Kāmandakī*'s scene is finished, the former group would resort to a beautiful pictorial freeze with the lovesick heroine in a swoon.

Trifocal Scenes
Play: Mālavikāgnimitra, Act II

(Separate zones in one common location of a royal park)

(i) The king-hero with the jester in a zone of the royal park.
(ii) Mālavikā, the heroine, enters the park but establishes another zone.

Both groups walk around in separate zones oblivious of each other, enacting separate scenes. After a while the king's group notices the heroine who is being decorated for the ceremony of the striking of the aśoka tree with her foot. The king's group comments as well as reacts to the activities of the first group.

(iii) Irāvatī, the queen, enters in an intoxicated condition and establishes a separate zone in the park. She watches both the groups.

In this way three separate scenes are enacted simultaneously in an intermittant fashion in a continuous sequence without a break in action.

At one point the king's group enters the locale of Zone No. 2 where the heroine is. Irāvatī watches this. In this way a trifocal scene is converted into a bifocal arrangement. In the end Irāvatī also joins the interior group and thereby establishes a single zonal unit.

Such a *nāṭyadharmī* staging practice brings to one's mind the 'quick cutting' of the present day cinema where a series of short montages of different locales are put together to form an entire sequence. Such enactments in Sanskrit theatre served similar purpose. They enabled the performers/playwright to give a choreographic design to the representation of *bhāvāvasthā*-s by accentuating, when needed, the speech, the movement or the expressive moments in different locales to build up a continuous sequence of a heightened impact of a *rasa* experience.

The Use of Pillars

It would be interesting to conjecture here on the part that the ornamental pillars of Bharata's stage might have played in the visual impact in the zonal division.

We have already seen in Chapter 3 that the ancient Indian stages had pillars supporting a roof. These were four lengthwise rows of pillars—with two rows of three pillars on either side of the stage. These pillars architecturally formed a separate areas on the stage which could be utilised in the presentation of zonal divisions. Fresco paintings of Ajanta and Bagh show human figures *vis-a-vis* pillars in artistically suggestive compositions. The separate areas formed by the pillars on Bharata's stages offer possibilities of establishing various locales.

A pillar could be used as a tree against which a heroine, Mālavikā, for example, could do the act of striking the tree with her foot or under which Vāsavadattā could perform her worship to the love god or king Purūravas enact Act IV of *Vikramorvaśīya*.

One point needs to be noted in this connection. This *nāṭyadharmī* convention of zonal division did not altogether rule out the use of the *lokadharmī* physical aids. *Nāṭyaśāstra* does mention the usage of accessories (*upakaraṇa*) in a play production. These were small and light pieces of scenic cut-outs of a hill, a palace, forest, chariot, etc.[27] However, *Nāṭyaśāstra* shows its marked preference for the convention of suggestive scene transfers through *abhinaya* alone when it says again and again that—

> "A play should always be produced with the *nāṭyadharmī* conventions."[28]

Section d

The Curtain

Another physical aid cited in the *Nāṭyaśāstra* and in the Sanskrit play-texts is the curtain. Although the ancient Indian stages did not have any drop curtains, many terms denoting a curtain-like arrangement are to be found in the Sanskrit play-texts as well as works on dramaturgy. These terms are: *yavanikā, javanikā, tiraskariṇi, citrayavanikā, paṭa-apaṭa, paṭi-apaṭi* and *nepathye*. Significantly, these terms are all translated in English as a curtain.

Yavanikā is mentioned in *Nāṭyaśāstra* to mean curtain in the context of pre-performance ritual preliminaries. There were some rituals in the preliminaries which were performed behind the *yavanikā* and some were performed in front of it.[29] *Nāṭyaśāstra* also mentions *paṭa-apaṭa* to suggest a curtain, while referring to the end of a *dhruvā* song or a *geyapada* when the curtain was drawn aside to reveal a character. These terms are also named to describe a sudden unannounced entry of a character who entered with a 'toss of a curtain' with an explanation that such entries (*paṭakṣepeṇa, apaṭikṣepeṇa*) were made by a character "in a state of excessive joy, sorrow or anger to a playing of drums."[30] Interestingly Abhinavagupta's commentary does not make any distinction between the uses of the terms *paṭa* and *apaṭa* and *yavanikā* and frequently employs one for the other.

The Sanskrit play-texts provide innumerable instances of the usage of these terms in connection with the entries of the dramatis personae. Major characters usually enter behind either a *yavanikā* or *javanikā* or a *citrayavanikā*. *Tiraskariṇī* is named to suggest an arrangement behind which a character stood unrevealed to other characters on the stage. Entries with a 'toss of a *paṭa* or *apaṭa*' are frequently found in the stage directions. It is more than likely that the above terms were used by different playwrights to mean one and the same thing—a curtain arrangement.

Some sort of curtain arrangement for the entries of the dramatis personae and for the swift scene transfers in the continuous performance seem to be more than evident in Sanskrit play production. It is more than likely that this curtain was not permanently fixed but was movable. A mobile curtain, under various regional names, including *javanikā* is seen to be effectively used by the traditional and folk theatres in India to this day for similar purposes. From the continuity in usage of a movable curtain one can make a fair assumption regarding the curtains and their employment in the ancient stages.

The Curtain Used in Sanskrit Play: The Description

A rectangular piece of cloth, gaily coloured and decorated, hand-held by two stage assistants, making its appearance at the right moment during the progression of the play was brought on the stage to indicate a swift transfer of the scene in the manner of *nāṭyadharmī* establishment of a separate acting zone. The characters entered behind this curtain unseen by the spectators. It could be withdrawn at the opportune moment and even removed from the stage by the two stage attendants when not required. A character or a group of characters could, in this way, make an entrance while in a sitting (*āsana*), reclining (*śayana*) or a standing (*sthāna*) positions. They could even make their entry while 'engaged in some activity'.

A number of such curtains were employed to symbolically enhance the *bhāva* presentation of different situations of the plot in a continuous performance.

The shape and the use of this kind of stage curtains can be easily confirmed by its continuity and popularity in almost all present day traditional and folk theatres in India.

The Colour of the Curtain

In the ancient stages the colours of the curtain were suggestive of the *rasa-bhāva* presentation of a play and the dramatis personae. An annonymous Sanskrit verse describes such curtains and their colours. It says:

> 'A curtain (*yavanikā*) is to be made of fine garment without any hole and should be held by beautiful women at the time of the respective entries.
>
> It should be shining or bright coloured. Shining (*śubhra*) for erotic, yellow for heroic, smoky grey for pathetic, variegated for comic, deep blue for terrible, tawnish dusty for odious, red for furious and black for marvellous.
>
> This is the view of the ancients. However, reddish (*aruṇa*) *yavanikā* may be used for all the *rasa*-s, in the opinion of the learned.[32]

The Usages of Curtains

The entrances of characters in a Sanskrit play were announced with vivid description of their states, moods and activities. A dramaturgical dictum laid down that, "no character is to enter or exit without proper announcement of his state, situation and activity."[33] Such a prior information was given either by a dramatis personae already present on the stage or by a *dhruvā* song sung by the musician or by the character himself. This was necessary for aiding the process of *rasa* realisation of the spectator.

Such entries were usually made behind a curtain referred to as *yavanikā*, *citrayavanikā*, *tiraskariṇī* and *javanikā*. A number of stage directions in Sanskrit play-texts employ these terms to announce the entrance of a character or a group of characters behind the curtains. The entries are usually prefixed by the same or similar words in the stage directions like 'then enters *as described* so and so...' There were many ways in which these curtains were used in the conventional staging practices. Here are a few examples from the Sanskrit play-texts.

For an Entry of an Important Character (Pātrapraveśa)

When the curtain was used for the entry of an important

character, a *dhruvā* song describing the state and the situation of the character was generally sung prior to the entry. For instance, in *Uttararāmacarita* (Act I), the entrance of Rāma is first announced by Ātreyī in the supporting scene, giving a graphic background of Rāma's *bhāvāvasthā.* Then only Rāma enters behind a *yavanikā*—curtain—hand-held by two assistants. An accompanying entrance song (prāveśikī dhruvā) introducing Rāma—his state, situations, etc. is sung by the musicians. At the right moment, the curtain may be lowered or dropped and removed altogether to reveal Rāma. This would create an extremely powerful impact by focusing the attention of the spectators on Rāma, his state and the situation.

Deliberate revealing of essential elements of the character such as briefly showing the head or part of the hair-dressing or only the hand or the feet or sometimes only the voice can be witnessed in the present day traditional theatres. Especially Kudiyattam, Kathakali, Yaksagana, Kuchipudi style of theatres make a very effective use of this technique. The underscoring of the disposition and the style (*vṛtti*) in which the character is being presented in the play is made, in this way, at his very first entry with sheer theatricality.

Entry of Seated and Reclining Characters
Play: Nāgānanda (I, 13, L-11)

The hero and the jester are wandering in the hermitage. They hear a song being sung by the heroine Malayāvatī while playing a *vīṇā.* They describe the merits of the well sung song.

A hand-held *javanikā*—curtain—appears on the stage, with the heroine and her maid behind it. After a while the curtain is removed, and the spectators who are already made familiar with the states and the activity are confronted with the pictorial composition of the heroine with her maid seated and playing a *vīṇā.*

Entries of seated reclining characters engaged in various activities were executed in a flash with the aid of such handheld curtains.

Graphic Previous Indication of the States and Situations of Characters

Play: Abhijñāna Śākuntala (III 6 L-5)

Duṣyanta in a state of love before the union (*ayoga śṛṅgāra*) is moving around in Kaṇva's hermitage. He enacts as if he is suddenly seeing Śakuntalā who is not on the stage. He first describes her as reclining in a love-lorn state being helped by her friends. He says:

"Ah! The bliss of my eye is obtained. Here is the beloved one of my desire, lying down on a slab of stone, covered with flowers and attended by her friends . . ."

The entry of the heroine is executed behind a *yavanikā*—curtain—after this announcement. The stage direction for this entry simply says: "then enters Śakuntalā acting as described . . ."

Pictorial Tableau

Play: Pratimānāṭaka (VII 10-1-2)

There is a pictorial tableau of a sudden reappearance of Rāma with his retinue after his coronation.

Rāma has taken the blessings of his mother for coronation and has just left the stage.

With the beating of drums and accompanying music Rāma with his retinue re-enters behind a *yavanikā*—curtain. And, after the *dhruvā* song, he is revealed with his retinue already coronated, in a sculpturesque tableau. These pictorial entries can be visualised in the comparative light of the *Jhānki*-s[34] as performed by some traditional theatre forms in present times.

For the Exit of the Characters

On occasions of the death of a character on stage or the fall after a combat, a curtain was brought on the stage so that the actor could make his exit in concealment.

Bhāsa uses this device on two occasions when he delineates death scenes in his plays and he uses the word *yavanikā* in his stage directions on both occasions.

Dramatic Use of a Flexible Hand-held Curtain

A highly dramatic use of *yavanikā* is made in *Mudrā Rākṣasa* (VII. 5, 1-15), where Cāṇakya enters a scene, fully covered by the *yavanikā*, with only his face left uncovered. He remains covered like this during most of the scene and at the climax he himself removes the curtain (*yavanikā*) and approaches other characters.

Unannounced Entry with "A Toss of the Curtain"

Entries with a toss of a curtain point to yet another kind of curtain arrangement located near the place of the entries of the characters. This could be the two doors on the stage wall connecting the acting area with the dressing room. Many contemporary theatre researchers suggest a possibility of these doors having curtains. A character could then make his entry either by "a toss of a curtain" (*vighātya*) or gently "drawing it aside" (*apasāraṇa*). Curtains on doors are frequently seen in the fresco paintings of Ajanta demonstrating their common usage during the period. In the Japanese Noh theatre, the door through which the main actor enters has a curtain which can be rolled up and down.

Sanskrit plays provide many instances of characters "in a hurry" or "in a state of excessive joy, sorrow or anger" entering unannounced with "a toss of a curtain". These entries generally include minor characters like a girl friend or a servant. There are a few examples of major characters like Rākṣasa's sudden and unannounced entry on the stage with a toss of a curtain in a state of anger at a very dramatic moment in Act III of *Mudrā Rākṣasa*.

In this manner, hand-held curtains were made use of in the ancient Sanskrit theatre to indicate a sudden change of locale in a continuous performance. At the same time, they were symbolically used in various ways to focus the attention of the spectators on the required details of the *bhāvāvasthā*-s for *rasa* evocation.

Section e

The Entries and Exits

The entries and exits of characters, especially their entries, assumed a significantly theatrical importance in this style of continuous play performance.

Fixed conventions and rules governed the entrances and exits. *Nāṭyaśāstra* tradition has tabulated them and the Sanskrit playwrights have faithfully followed them.

Two Doors of the Stage Back Wall

The two doors of the stage back wall which connected the dressing room with the stage proper were provided for entries and exits of the dramatis personae. It should be noted that these doors were always considered to be a part of the theatre building and were never used as any dramatic locale or parts of settings in a performance. They just provided a neutral background and facilitated the entries and exits of characters on the acting zones and gave scope for frontal theatrical entrances.

Entries Always Faced the East

Entrances were always made facing the eastern direction. Generally the stages of ancient playhouses always faced the east.[35] But if that was not the case in some patron's *raṅgaśālā*, the direction which the musical orchestra faced or the place where the patron sat was considered the eastern direction.

Four Kinds of Entrances

1. *Entry-exit from the Two Doors*: (*Praveśa-Niṣkramaṇa*)

There were definite *nāṭyadharmī* conventions for the usage of the two doors of the back wall of the stage for entry-exits.

If a character had entered through a stage-door and needed to make an exit, he always used the same door through which he had entered.[36] In case, after his exit, he had to return into a zone established by other characters who had entered after his exit, he entered by the same door through which they had entered.[37]

Regional modes of *lokadharmī* performance practices (*pravṛtti*-s) also affected the stage conventions of entries and exits. In *Dākṣiṇātya* and *Āvantī* regional modes, the door on the extreme north side of the stage wall was used for the entries. In *Pāñcālī* and *Auḍramāgadhī* regional modes, the door on the extreme south side of the stage wall was employed.[38]

As mentioned before, the split second exits and re-entries (*niṣkramya-praveśya*) were to be completed within a fixed time-measure of two *kalā*-s.[39] These were the entries where the characters made quick exit and immediately reappeared. Special drum-beats accompanied these exits and re-entries.

2. *Entrances from Behind the Javanikā* (*Curtain*): (*Pātrapraveśa*)

The special entrance of an important character was always preceded and accompanied by instrumental music and the singing of the entrance song (*prāveśikī dhruvā*). The song depicted "the states, seasons, age, locality, time and the situation of the character."[40]

The actor aimed to achieve the proper posture (*sauṣṭhava*), deep inward concentration of the states and right tempo and correct bearing according to his basic type (superior, middle, inferior) on his very first appearance. The actor conveyed his correlation in the main context of *rasa* that the character, and through the character, the play aimed at evoking in the spectator.

This entry behind the *javanikā*, therefore, was important. The actor, aided by the entrance song, his costume, get up and posture had full scope to present the style (*vṛtti*) of the character to the spectator on his very first entry.

Such entries of characters varied in keeping with the style of the play. For example characters like Duryodhana, Rāma, Karṇa and others would adopt postures, stances and states to suit the situations presented by the style of the play to be performed and not the generalised understanding of their characters *per se*. The entrance of Karṇa in *Karṇabhāra* might differ basically from that of Karṇa in *Veṇīsaṃhāra*.

3. *Processional Entries*

Another way of dramatically focusing the attention of the spectator on the entrance of a group of characters was the processional entry. Important characters of rank usually entered the stage surrounded by their retinue, each walking in the gait appropriate to their basic nature, rank and status in time with the beating of the drum. Such entries had an impact of a spectacle.

Conventional rules that governed the enactment of such entries were:

The king, queen and such other characters of rank entered the stage surrounded by their retinue of servants, handmaids, jester, girl friends, etc. Each character surrounded the major character in order of his rank and status. The major character walked side by side with his equals while others of inferior rank walked surrounding them. The handmaids always preceded the major character.[41]

The characters in the processional entry, walked in gaits which suited their character types in time with the tempo, rhythm and the time-measure. This provided deliberate variations in the styles of walk. A superior character kept a slow tempo (of four *kalā*-s) the medium character kept medium tempo (of two *kalā*-s) while the inferior characters walked with short quick steps (of one *kalā*).[42]

The very pictorial entry of the princess Padmāvatī playing with a ball accompanied by Vāsavadattā and the retinue,[43] the impressive entrance of Duṣyanta preceded by *yavana* girls bearing the bows,[44] the entrance of king Purūravas preceded by the lamp-bearing maidens[45] and the processional entrance of Cārudatta[46] and Candanadāsa[47] being taken for their execution are some of the examples of the processional entries in the Sanskrit play-texts.

4. *Entries Through Doors in Imaginary Nāṭyadharmī Zones*

As mentioned before, the two doors at the stage back wall were parts of the theatre architecture. They did not constitute any part of staging. When a door or doors are mentioned in the play-texts with a sentence like "so here is the door. I shall enter"... the 'door' in the sentence does not mean the doors on the stage wall. But it indicates an imaginary 'door' of *nāṭyadharmī* zonal division (*kakṣyā*). A set of rules of *abhinaya* suggests an entry through such a door which was to be enacted by conventional gestures of *hasta-abhinaya* or *citrābhinaya* of two *tripatākā* hands facing each other.[48]

It is significant to note here that even the Japanese Noh, Chinese Opera and Kerala Kudiyattam theatres use the stage doors only as parts of the theatre buildings and not as parts of the stage settings.

Section f

Lighting

As seen in Chapter 3, the ancient Indian playhouses were cave-shaped theatre buildings. The dim and darkened interiors of such buildings needed some source of illumination to light up the performers on the stage and also spill some brightness in the auditorium.

Nāṭyaśāstra briefly refers to illuminations of the stage proper and the auditorium in the context of the consecration of the theatre buildings when it says that "lighting should be of such strength that it should illuminate the performer as well as the patron."[49] This makes it evident that some illumination was stratagically placed between the performer and the patron which threw light on both of them.

The types of lights mentioned by *Nāṭyaśāstra* are: (a) a torch (*ulkā*) and (b) a lamp (*dīpikā*). The torches and lamps have been utilised as lights in India from ancient times. The flickering lights, at times hand-carried in the form of torches or placed as stratagic frontal light sources in the form of lamps (*dipa*) in the dim and dark cave-like interiors of our ancient theatres, is not very difficult to imagine.

Although we do not have any evidence of such light placings in the ancient theatres, two factors give a strong clue to the lighting pattern in ancient playhouses:

(i) We have established a similarity between the dim and dark atmosphere of the cave temples and the cave-like theatre buildings. It is interesting to note in this reference the remark of Le Corbussieur comparing the structure of a cave to "a machine for acquiring various modalities of consciousness."[50] Dazzling impact of strong but flickering frontal lights, either through torches or lamps, on the colours and contours of temple deities induce a sharp sensory perception in a viewer. We know that similar reaction was intended to be evoked in the spectator in the Sanskrit theatres. The dark, dim interiors of ancient stages with a dazzling flickering frontal light projecting the characters might have succeeded in aiding the spectator's concentration and induced his total participation with the performance without any distraction.

(ii) In the Kerala Kuttambalam theatres, performers in their colourful costumes and shimmering make-up face a huge well-lit brass lamp placed frontally on the downstage centre edge and create similar impact on the audience.

After witnessing the atmosphere created by such strong frontal flickering lighting in a dark interior one cannot but conclude that such an arrangement must have its link with the past traditions which expected the illumination in the theatre to "enhance the brilliance of the performer as well as the patron."

The sunlight streaking through the highly placed *gavākṣa* window on eastern side of the playhouse might have been one other source of light during the daytime performance.

Section g

Acoustic

One of the reasons for the traditional preference for a play performance in medium sized theatre buildings was that they provided facility for proper acoustics. Ancient playhouses had highly placed small latticed windows and the stage roofs and pillars with broken surfaces for this very purpose. Care was always taken to ensure that an actor was distinctly heard.

A connoisseur, a patron or an assessor were supposed to sit within the distance of six yards from the stage. This was because they were required to fully relish various tonalities and levels of speech offered in a play performance.

Indeed, the sound pattern of Sanskrit theatre offered a homogenous expression of various notes, accent and resonance. Sanskrit and Prakrit prose and verse either chanted or sung; stage whispers, off stage noises with the speeches of characters occasionally heard from the dressing room prior to their entries on the stage; songs, chants and instrumental music from the musical orchestra; even the *nāṭyadharmī* "speech in the air" technique where a character standing on the stage carried on conversation with imaginary characters—were the variety of sounds which were skilfully combined to present an audio rendering which needed the right acoustic facility which the cave-like theatres and stages with roofs provided.

To sum up, both *nāṭyadharmī* and *lokadharmī* practices of Sanskrit play performance were interdependent and connected with the peculiar constructions of ancient theatre buildings (*raṅga*). The entire performance was deliberately designed to induce total identification and participation of the spectator. Once the convention of both practices were understood, accepted and relished by the spectator, he was ready to be immersed in the delightful experience of *rasa* realisation. Sanskrit theatre, thus, was a threefold experience. It consisted in the performance which depicted the inner states of the hero in various situations in a plot, the sensory presentation of an audiovisual *abhinaya* and the impact of a state of heightened consciousness in the spectator which signified the success (*siddhi*) of the play production.

NOTES

1. Agarwal V.S., India as known to Panini, p. 167 ff.
2. NA, XIV, 72–82.
3. NS, XXVI, 83–89.
4. Raghavan V. Nāṭyadharmi and Lokadharmi, JOR, Madras, Vol. VII, pp. 359–75.
5. NS, XIV, 62-63 (tr. M. Ghosh).
6. Ibid.
7. Kallinātha, SR. (Adyar, Madras), Vol. IV, Chapter 7, p. 11.
8. NS, XIV, NS (Dr. M. Ghosh), also Raghavan V., loc. cit.
9. NS, XXVI, 111–19.
10. Bhavabhūti's *Mālatī Mādhava, Uttararāmacaritam* prologues.
11. Kramarisch Stella, Indian Sculpture, p. 94-95.
12. SD, VI, 19, p. 172.
13. DR, II, 41.
14. Wells H.W. 'The Classical Dramas of India' 1963. Chapter 10, p. 108.
15. Bh. P. VII, 85.
16. Abh. Vol. II, XIII, Sl. 1, L-16.
17. NS, XIV, 3 (tr. M. Ghosh).
18. NS, XIV, 9.
19. Ibid, 10—NS says that a character turns on the *right* side and does his self-report (*dakṣiṇāmukham* etc.). It is not very specific about whose right-side is to be considered here, the actor's or the spectators? Abhinavagupta discusses this point at length and concludes that it should be the spectator's right. That would mean that the actor turns towards his left, i.e. the northern direction.
20. *Vikramorvaśīyam*, I, III; Abh. Sak. VI, VII.
21. *Avimāraka*, III, IV.
22. *Nāgānanda*, V.
23. *Abhiṣeka*, II, *Praveśaka* and the following act.
24. *Mālavikāgnimitram*, III, *Ratnāvalī*, II.
25. Supra, Chap. 6, p. 145 Frame work no. 2.
26. Supra, Chap. 6, p. 145 Frame work no. 2.
27. NS XIII, 87.
28. Ibid, 74(a).
29. NS, V, 11, 12.
30. NS, XIII, 3, 13, XXXI, 485, XXXII 438 also XXXIII, 211-L-33.
31. Abh. V, 11-15, 1-1-4.
32. Anonymous verse quoted by S.H. Tagore, Eight Principal Rasa-s of Hindu-s, p. 50.
33. Neither NS or Abh. make a mention of such a convention, nor do DR,

Bh. P. or SD. NLRK is the source which refers to such a convention by quoting an anonymous authority, viz.:

"*asūcitasya pātrasya praveśo naiva vidyate*"

(NLRK, II, 330-31)

Sanskrit dramatists have followed this convention. *Artha Dyo* and Ranganātha's commentary on *Vikramorvaśīyam* give the convention a slightly different reading like, '*nāsūcitasya pātrasya praveśo nirgamo pi ca*' (*Artha Dyo* pp. 133–92).

34. *Jhankī*-s are tableau like groupings accompanied by singing, music or at times by recited text. They are seen in certain traditional temple theatre forms like *Rāsalīlā*.
35. NS, XIV, XIII, 11 and Abh. Vol. II, XIII, XII, 11-L-3.
36. NS, XIV, 11 (Kashi ed.).
37. Ibid, 12.
38. Ibid, 54.
39. Bh. P. VII, 85. Kalā was a musical beat, a measure of time. It was a measure arising out of a group of *mātrās* (i.e. 5 *nimiṣa*=1 mātrā NS, XXI, 3). Nimish,—twinkling of the eyes,—was counted as a measure of time.
40. NS, XXXII, 400 (tr. M. Ghosh).
41. NS, XIV, 16.
42. NS, XIII, 10-11 and 21-22.
43. Bhāsa, *Svapna Vāsavadattā*, II, L-1, after *praveśaka*.
44. Ka's Abh. Sak. II, L-1, after *praveśaka*.
45. Ka's *Vikramorvaśīyam*, III, 3, L-2.
46. Śūdraka's *Mṛcchakaṭikam*, X, 6.
47. *Mudrā Rākṣasa*, VII, 2, L-14.
48. NS, IX, 32–37.
49. NS, III, 82–85.
50. Lannoy R., The Speaking Tree, Part I, Chapter 2, p. 44ff. The author describes in detail the effect of strong flickering light on the bright colours and forms of the cave frescoes in the context of the dim interiors of Ajanta Caves.

CHAPTER 8

SVARA, GĀNA, ĀTODYA

(The Note, the Song, the Musical Instrument)

Nowhere does the truism of Sanskrit play production being something more than mere enactment of the spoken word of the play-text gets more emphasised than in its use of the songs, the musical instruments and the dance.

From ancient times in India, the vocal as well as instrumental music (*gīta-vādītra*) went hand in hand with *nāṭya* enactment. Soon afterwards, pure dance (*nṛtta*) got imperceptibly absorbed in the former two elements to form a trio of interwoven arts (*trividhaṃ śilpa*).[1] Later on all the three arts went under a common nomenclature of *Saṅgīta*,[2] as *Saṅgīta Ratnākara* says: *Saṅgīta* constitutes songs, dance and musical instruments.

Although each art retained its individual identity, there was such an intermixture in the all inclusive drama performance that these arts became inseparable from each other in the play production. Bharata describes this blending with a simile. He says:

> "The song, the instrumental music and the *nāṭya* having different kinds of appeal, should be made use of by the producers of a play like a brilliant entity formed by a lighted torch revolving and appearing as a single undivided circle (*ālāta cakra pratimā*)."[3]

Saṅgīta, in this way, became an integral component of a Sanskrit play production right from its inception. It established the tone, pace and the atmosphere within which the entire performance was created. A musical orchestra consisting of minimum ten musicians occupied the most decorative area of the ancient stages. Ritual arrangement of the musical instruments, their tuning and singing in unison with them covered the first nine rituals of the auspicious pre-performance ceremonies by the drama troupe. The progression of the plot was continuously accentuated with the rhythm of the drums and cymbals, singing of songs and playing of *viṇā* and flutes. The end of the play was announced by the chanting or singing of the benedictory verse (*Bharata vākya*) and ritual beating of drums. Special songs and dance situations were introduced in the play to enhance "the strength and ripeness of the meaning of the words by expressing things which cannot be expressed in speech."[4] Truly, music in Sanskrit plays provided possibilities, unrivalled by the spoken word, to convey the extended and amplified experiences of various states of being.

This highly systematic use of music in a Sanskrit play production is examined in the following pages, especially in the contexts of:

(1) The musical orchestra (*kutapa*) its organisation, application, and the seating arrangement.
(2) Preliminaries, the prayer and the prologue.
(3) *Dhruvā* songs, song and dance situations and the actor's benedictory verse.

Section 1

The Musical Orchestra, its Organisation, Application and the Seating Arrangement

A special place was permanently earmarked for the musical orchestra in the ornate Śatdāruka area of ancient stages between the two doors of the stage wall. This place was probably elevated at times. The term kutapa[5] is generally used to connote the musical orchestra and its place on the stage.

The musical orchestra consisted of four kinds of musical instruments, viz., Drums (covered), *Viṇā* (stringed), Flute (hollow), Cymbals (solid) and male and female vocalists. Every instrumentalist and vocalist had his traditionally fixed place to sit. The order of the seating arrangement was important because the orchestra constituted a continuous musical accompaniment which needed the correct maintenance of proper resonance. Additionally, it provided a permanent visual background to a performance.

(I) The Seating Arrangement: (Kutapa or Bhāṇḍa Vinyāsa)

1. *Mṛdanga* player
2. *Paṇava* player
3. *Dardura* player

} (a) Drums

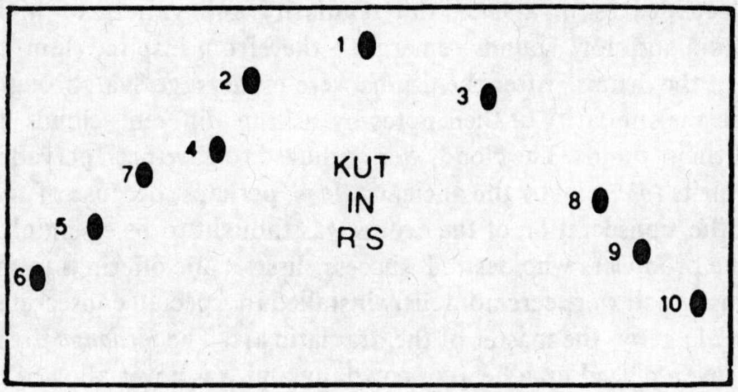

4. Viṇā player 5. Viṇā player	(b) Viṇā
6. Flute player 7. Flute player	(c) Flute
8. Tāla	(d) Cymbals
9. Female vocalist 10. Male vocalist *or/and* 11. Female vocalist 12. Female vocalist	(e) Vocalist

(II) Organisation and Application of Music in a Play Production

(a) *Drums : The Covered Instruments* (*Avanaddha*) :

There were three kinds of drums:

(1) *Muraja* (Mṛdanga): A drum with two heads, with its body formed with clay.

(2) *Paṇava*: A drum with two heads, thin in the middle part.

(3) *Dardura*: A drum with one face shaped like a pitcher (ghaṭa).

These drums were covered (*avanaddha*) instruments which were described as "the basis of the performance" by Bharata.

A legendary tale describes the origin of the drums. One day when the sage Svāti was observing the torrential rains falling on the lotus leaves in a lake, the regularity and variety of high, medium and low sounds emerging therefrom inspired him to invent the drums. After the drums were made, sage Svāti brought about the similarity of their notes by asking different clouds to lend their sounds. The clouds were believed to have been pervaded by spirits (*bhūta-s*) by the ancients. It is, perhaps, because of this that the consecration of the drums was thought to be essential.

The producers who desired success, first made offerings to the drums which were ceremoniously installed in special consecrated *maṇḍala*-s by the master of the dramatic art. The *mṛdanga* drum was even placed on a heap of cowdung and was never allowed to touch the ground. *Nāṭyaśāstra* describes the installation of the drums in no less than twenty-five verses (NS, XXXIII, 259-84).

Drumming involved the complex technique of producing regular notes (*svara-s*), minor patterns of rhythm (*karaṇa*-s) and the ancient melodies made up of notes (*jāti*-s) through different ways of playing the drums. This needed expert drummers who had mastered the techniques of playing them.

Different styles of drumming with suitable changes in tempo, rhythm and pitch were executed to suit the situations and the states (*Bhāvāvasthā*-s) and the basic nature (*prakrti*) of a character. The entrances (*praveśa*), the gaits (*gatipracāra*), the stage-walks (*cārī*-s), the going around (*parikramā*) and the exits (*niṣkramaṇa*) as well as different *āṅgika* movements of the character on stage were determinded and differentiated by the beats of the drums. The drums predominated right from the preliminaries onwards to the final benedictory verse (*Bharata vākya*). The playing of drums was stopped during the delineation of subtle *abhinaya*. But for the beginning of a *dhruvā* song, clear drumming was needed. The drum players sat facing the audience in the centre of the *kutapa*.

(b) *Vīṇā* (*Lute*): *The Stringed Instrument* (*Tat*)

Vīṇā was a stringed (*tat*) instrument. It was the principal instrument dominating the musical orchestra. Two kinds of *Vīṇā*-s are mentioned in *Nāṭyasāstra*: vipañcī and citrā. The former had nine strings and was played with a plektrum. The latter had seven strings and was probably played with the strokes of the fingers.

Ascending, descending and constant variation of notes (*varṇa*-s), their different combination (*alaṃkāra*-s), the sounds produced by different styles of stroking the strings (*dhātu*-s), their amplification (*vistāra*), the styles of playing (*vṛtti*-s) gave rise to the ancient mode of *jāti* music. Although there is lacuna about the exact nature of the ancient *jāti* music, it is generally accepted that it was perhaps a mode of melody music which was the precursor of later *rāga*-s and *rāginī*-s.

The first nine rituals of pre-performance preliminary ceremonies had *vīṇā* music as an overture to set up the appropriate atmosphere for the play. During the progression of the plot the *vīṇā* playing enhanced the mood and the atmospheres of different situations in a play. It's notes formed the basis of the human notes (*svara*-s) that were adopted in the recitation of the spoken words also.

Special notes (*svara*-s) dominated the *jāti*-s and the recitations and evoked particular *rasa*-s:

Rasa	*Notes (Svara-s)*	
Erotic, comic	*Madhyama* and *Pañcama*	(Ma, Pa)
Heroic, Furious, Marvellous	*Ṣaḍja* and *Ṛṣabha*	(Sā, Ri)
Pathetic	*Gāndhāra, Niṣāda*	(Ga, Ni)
Odious, Terrible	*Dhaivata*	(Dha)

The base of these musical notes were the *śruti*-s which were systematically derived exclusively from the wooden *vīṇā*. The *śruti*-s or the quarter tones were produced by marking the musical interval inbetween the two notes of the scales (*saptaka*-s) of three registers of seven notes each in different pitches—high (*tāra*), medium (*madhya*) and low (*mandra*). Arrangement of *śruti*-s assigned to each note in a scale were called *grāma*-s. Indian music had three *grāma*-s: *Śaḍja*, *Madhyama* and *Gāndhāra*.

The notes of *Vīṇā*, in this way, formed the very backbone of the music in a play production.

One *Vīṇā* player was assigned a seat on the left side of the male vocalist while the other was placed on the right side of the female vocalist.

(c) *Flutes: The Hollow Instruments—Suṣira*

A flute is considered the oldest Indian instrument. Originally it was made of bamboo (*vaṃśa*) and that is why it was called *vaṃśa* or *vaṃśa vādya* (later bansī or bānsurī) or simply *veṇu.* In later times flutes were made of horn, wood, metal and ivory also.

The notes and the *śruti*-s of the flute were categorised by the way in which they were produced. Corresponding *śruti*-s were produced by the manner in which fingers on the holes of a flute were shaken—(*kampita*), kept half-open (*ardha mukta*) or fully open (*vyakta-mukta*).

The flutes were secondary instruments to *vīṇā* and the human voice because they depended on the notes taken by the latter. The vocalist was necessarily accompanied by the flutist who sat on the right side of the male vocalist.

A conch shell was also one of the musical instruments.

(d) *Cymbals: Solid Instruments—Tāla* (*Ghana*)

The cymbals were simply referred to as *tāla.* The word probably came from the keeping of time by clapping of hands in the early days (*tāla* means the palm of hand). The *Tāla*-s of the musical instruments were the cymbals of the solid (*ghana*) variety. The cymbal player kept the proper time beat (*kalā*) with the tempo (*laya*). Three types of *tāla*-s determined the tempo and pace of the performance: quick (*drut*), medium (*madhya*) and slow (*vilambita*).

The cymbal player sat near the female vocalist.

(e) *Vocal Music: The Human Body as Vīṇā*

The three musical scales or voice registers determined the pitch of intoning and singing. The notes from the chest (*ura*-s) corresponded to the *mandra saptaka,* those from the throat (*kaṇṭha*) to the *madhya saptaka* and those from the head (*śira*-s) to the *tāra saptaka.* A note overlapping two reigsters *kākalī niśāda* has been mentioned by *Nāṭyaśāstra.* We have examples from Sanskrit dramas where the connoisseurs admired the *Kākalī* note in the music.

Systematic grouping of these notes formed ancient Indian *jāti*-s. As mentioned earlier, the *jāti*-s were the incipient, melodic music about which there is very little knowledge. What we know is that the songs in Sanskrit plays were based on the *jāti* music with appropriate metres, tempo, *tāla* and words. The songs (*gāna*) were either written or indicated by the dramatists in their texts. Or, they were dramatic songs (*dhruvā*-s) which were incorporated by the master of dramatic art from the repertoire of the drama to enhance the presentation of *bhāvāvasthā*-s and to carry forward the tightly structured progression of the plot. The song situations were most traditionally categorised and generally drama troupes had their own repertoire of such songs which was either handed down by family tradition or specially composed by the performing company.

The male vocalist sat facing the north side of the playhouse. He generally intoned the recitations. The female vocalists sat facing the south side of the playhouse. They usually sang the songs.

The General Application of Music (Sangita) in a Play Production

The unison of the human voice, the *vīṇā* and the flute formed the music of the Sanskrit play production. The appropriate unison of the notes—*svara*-s of the *vāṇī*, *vīṇā* and *veṇu* were specially praised in a performance. It is interesting to note that *Nāṭyaśāstra* often refers to the human voice (*vāṇī*) as the "*vīṇā* of the human body."[6] The rhythms and the tempo provided by the drums and cymbals were compared to a 'bed of *nāṭya*' (*śaiyā hi nātyasya*)[7] and the percussion instruments like cymbals (*tāla*) were considered the foundation of a *nāṭya* performance. Even *nṛtta*, the pure dance, which reflected the rhythmic patterns through the instrument of the human body was considered a part of music as a medium of the visual depiction of rhythm.

Gāndharva and Gāna Music in Sanskrit Play Production

These were the two kinds of music employed in Sanskrit theatre. The term *Gāndharva* denoted the mārgī music of the ancient times and originated from the exclusive rendering of the metrical hymns of *Sāmaveda* (*Sāma ṛcā*-s) with emphasis on the correct pitch and intonation of the notes (*svara*), the time beat (*tāla*) and the words (*pada*). The *Gāna* variety probably emerged out of the intermixture of popular (*bāhya*) rendering of different regions with less formally structured music.

Both types of music had common constituents like the note,

the time beat and the words but they differed in their formal structure.[8] The purpose and the nature of their employment in drama also differed. The purpose of the employment of *gāndharva* music was for the unseen award (or reward for the meritorious deeds done in this life for carrying forward in the next one) for the *nāṭya* troupe. The music, therefore, was employed in the pre-performance preliminaries which were the ritual prayers of the drama troupe for their own benefit and for the success of the production. The *gāna* music was aimed at the immediate objective of pleasing the spectators and thereby gaining a reward of cash or an award. The *gāna* music (*dhruvā*-s and songs) was used during the play proper to enhance the enjoyment of the audience.

Both types differed in their practice and observance (*dharma*) also. In *gāndharva* music, words were less important than *svara* and *tāla*. In the *gāna* music, words were more important than *svara* and *tāla*. The *gāndharva* music was equated with divine music of *gāndharva*-s who were the celestial musicians. It accompanied the sacral rites and was sung with gestures. Its word content had either a hymn element or *nirgīta* element. (*Nirgīta* was a systematised musical combination of intricate *tāla* patterns accompanied by meaningless syllables.) In fact, it was a sacrosanct *mārgī* music for exclusive (*ābhyantara*) tradition and was meant to be preserved in its original purity. It is believed that the *gāndharva* music was codified in the *Gandharvaveda*. The music was closed and rule-bound. As a result, it gradually disappeared.

The *gāna* (*deśi*) music was made up of the songs which were sung during the play performance. Poetic content and clarity of diction were more important in their rendering than the rigid adherence to the nuances of the notes by splitting of words. As Abhinavagupta says: "Importance here (*gāna* music) is on the words and the meaning."

Different Levels of Appreciation of Music

The *Nāṭyaśāstra* tradition, however, considered *dhruvā* singing, in comparison to the *gāndharva* music, as a music which was inferior and which was only "capable of creating the interest in the auditorium full of women and common people."[9] It should perhaps be made clear, here, that this comment is made in connection with different levels of appreciation of music that is taken into account by *Nāṭyaśāstra* when it says that "masters like a harmonious closure, the scholars, precise enunciation of words (*pada*); women, a sweetness of voice in the singers and the rest of the audience a full-throated, loud singing.[10]

Section 2

Preliminaries, Prayer Prologue--(Pūrvaraṅga, Nāndī, Prastāvanā)

The pre-performance preliminaries, the prayer śloka and the prologue took place before the play proper commenced. Music was an important feature of these items.

The Preliminaries: Pūrvaraṅga

The preliminaries were the essential preamble to a play performance which consisted of ritual ceremonies of the drama troupe entailing the propitiation of the gods and appeasement of obstacles for the successful completion of the play performance.

The entire troupe participated in the nineteen auspicious rites. The musicians and the four or five chief members of the troupe like the *sūtradhāra*, his assistants, the actress and the jester were main performers of the ceremonies during which the musical instruments and different areas of the stage were purified, consecrated and their presiding deities as well as those of the different spheres (*digpāla-lokapāla*) were ritually worshipped. The preliminary performance or *pūrvaraṅga* was not a part of the written play-text but as Bharata says "it was so called because it was performed before the beginning (*pūrvam*) on the stage (*raṅgam*) before the play performance."[11] The rituals were performed with full employment of *saṅgīta* viz., the *gāndharva* music, songs, pure dance (*nṛtta*) and *abhinaya*.

The music and the dance attracted the spectators and made them curious to witness the performance. For the connoisseurs among them, an atmosphere was created which enabled them to focus attention on the happenings on the stage. As Abhinavagupta comments, "Bharatamuni conceived of this item with music etc. to lift the spectators above mundane feelings and emotions. At the same time, while the *sūtradhāra* and others entertained the audience with music dance and repartee, the main actors got ready for the drama performance.[12]

Three Kinds of Preliminaries (Pūrvaraṅga)

In the *Nāṭyaśāstra*, Bharata devotes an entire chapter (Chapter V)—and parts of the Chapters XXIX and XXXI to describe three kinds of preliminary rituals and their performances according to the conventions of his time. With the passage of time, these got shortened. However, certain essential items like ritual *pūjā* (*puṣpañjali*) of the stage, the worship of the musical instruments and the recitation of *nāndī* prayer have surprisingly remained in traditional theatre forms up to the present time.

Three kinds of pūrvaraṅga were:

(1) Pure variety conducted in *caturasra tāla*[13] called *śuddha pūrvaraṅga*.

(2) Pure variety conducted with *trayasra tāla*.[14] This was more abridged in comparison to the first variety.

(3) Mixed variety—*citra pūrvaraṅga* which had items like pure dance (*nṛtta*) by female dancers who appeared with "resounding sounds of drums" at a particular juncture of the ceremonies (eleventh ritual of Utthāpanā during the singing of Utthāpani *dhruvā*). Dressed as godesses, the female dancers scattered white flowers on the stage while dancing with *piṇḍibandha*-s, recaka-s and *aṅgahāra*-s.[15]

The pure variety had nineteen stages which are described below from the view point of convention and techniques of staging.

First Nine Stages of Śuddha Pūrvaraṅga: Bahirgīta

The first nine rites of the *pūrvaraṅga* were to be performed behind the *yavanikā* curtain (*bahirgīta*). They were executed behind the hand held curtain, *yavanikā*, before the *kutapa*, i.e. the place where the musicians sat on the stage. As Abhinavagupta says: "the curtain *yavanikā* is held between *raṅgapīṭha* and the centre of *raṅgaśirṣa*"[16] on the stage.

In the present day traditional theatres and *yātrā*-s the same practice is followed.

The procedure of the first nine rites basically dealt with: (1) the occupation of special seats by the orchestra, (2) tuning of the musical instruments and (3) the beginning (*ārambha*) with a variety of *nirgīta*[17] or *bahirgīta*.

These nine rituals were:

(1) The ritual arrangement of the musical instruments (*Pratyāhāra*).

(2) The seating of the singers in their specified places (*Avataraṇa*). [See the sketch on page 223]

(3) The commencement of vocal exercises for singing, tuning of *viṇā*, drums and other instruments (*Ārambha*).

(4) The tuning of musical instruments in one unison by the *nirgīta* (*Āśrāvaṇā*). Mixing of the notes (*svara milavuṭa*) of different instruments was done by playing the same note of two *mandra* (low) and *tāra* (high) registers alternately in the extended nature of *vīṇā* playing (*vistāra dhātu*).

(5) Rehearsing different types (*vṛtti*-s)[18] of musical instruments (*Vaktrapāṇī*). *Bhāvaprakāśa* explains that different instruments were divided according to the manner with which they were played in this rite—flute (*veṇu*) played with the mouth and drums and *vīṇā* played with hands and fingers and so on.[19]

(6) The adjustment of the strings of the instruments (*Parighaṭṭanā*). *Saṅgīta Ratnākara* mentions that this was to be done with *nirgīta* or *śuṣkagīta* with a variety of styles of playing on *vīṇā* with strokes of fingers or a plektrum.

(7) Rehearsal of different hand signs (to indicate the time beat) by the *vīṇā* and the drum players (*Saṃghoṭana*).

(8) Playing together of the *vīṇā* and other instruments with drums in harmony with one another (*Mārgasārita*). This was also performed by taking recourse of *śuṣkākṣara* (meaningless words) *gītā*.

(9) The practice of division of *tāla* structure in increasing meaningless words (*Āsārita*).

[Āsārita was a name of certain components forming the time measure (*tāla*) structure in gradually ascending tempo (*Vardhamānaka*). This was assumed to have been performed by taking recourse to *nirgīta* or *śuṣkākṣara gīta* (songs with meaningless words). There were fixed hand signs of clapping (*sañjā*, *tāla*, *sannipāta*) and counting of time beats during this ritual.]

The first nine items of the preliminaries belonged to the instrumental music—predominantly, that of the *vīṇā*. The *vīṇā* music was differentiated on the basis of *dhātu*, i.e. the stroke by a finger or a plektrum producing tones similar to short (*laghu*) and long (*guru*) letters. Dramatic songs—Dhruvā-s—when sung, were dominated by set patterns of *laghu-guru* syllables in each of the line (*pada*) with fixed *tāla* patterns. They were called *nirgīta* or *nirarthaka gīta* (meaningless syllables) because of the predominance of instrumental music. Also, the vocalists imitated the instruments with sounds which had no meaning. These types of songs went under various names like *nirgīta*, *bahirgīta*, *śuṣkagīta*, *śuṣkākṣara*, etc. As mentioned earlier they were songs or *tāla* patterns made of collection of meaningless syllables strung together like a *tarānā*. According to *Nāṭyaśāstra*, they were added in the preliminaries to please the *asura*-s because meaningful songs could only praise the gods.

The procedure of the first nine rituals, in this manner, mainly consisted of: (1) Occupation of the special seats by the orchestra, (2) Tuning of the musical instruments and (3) Beginning (*āram bha*) with a variety of *nirgīta*.

Pūrvaraṅga Ritual Performance on Stage (Antargīta)

(10) The song in praise of a deity (*gītavidhi*)

After the removal of the curtain, the actual singing of songs with meaningful words began. From this stage onwards the rituals which were to be performed on the stage started. These songs in praise of gods were sung in *vardhamānaka*[20] style wherein the *gāndharva gīta*-s with instrumental music and complex *tāla* structure built on many smaller *tāla* units with the syllables (*varṇa*), tempo (*laya*) and the gradual increase in the number of female dancers featured.

[*Vardhamānaka* has been associated with *Tāṇḍava* in *Citra* variety of preliminary rites by Bharata. There, the female dancers appeared one after another performing the pure dance (*nṛtta*) embellished by 32 *aṅgahāra* (a combination of six to nine hand and body movements called *karaṇa*), 4 *recaka* (graceful movements of the foot, waist, hand and neck) and 4 *piṇḍibandha* (pattern formations). The dancers were dressed as goddesses and performed the *puṣpāñjali* or the rite of scattering flowers all over the stage through their pure dance.]

Pure dance (*nṛtta*) was employed in the preliminaries of all Sanskrit plays to produce sheer aesthetic joy. With decorative pleasing patterns made by the body movements of dancers with the accompaniment of pure rhythmic music dependent mainly on tempo and rhythm, it created in the spectators the right receptive mood for the drama which was to follow.

(11) The commencement of the enactment on the stage: *Utthāpanā*

It was so styled because from here, the reciters of nāndī prayer (nāndīpāṭhaka) began the performance on the stage. The musical accompanists sang a song in slow, medium and fast tempo (*laya*) and with caturasra or trayasra *tāla* (rhythm).

Details of Performance of Utthāpanā

When the singing of songs in medium tempo started, the *sūtradhāra* clad in white, with white flowers in his hands, entered the stage after removing the curtain. He entered with his two assistants, one on each side. They, the *paripārśvaka* and another assistant or jester (*vidūṣaka*) were also clad in white. One had a water-filled golden pitcher in his hand and the other had the *jarjara*—Indra's banner staff. Bharata says that before entering the stage, these actors had to purify themselves and acquire charms to counter the evil eye.[21] While the song *utthāpanī dhruvā* was being sung they assumed the standing postures of *vaiṣṇava sthāna* with *sauṣṭhava* of the body and the wondrous (*adbhūta*) glance.

Annotation

(a) *The Jarjara*

It was a piece of bamboo with five joints. The first top joint was covered with a white cloth, the colour of Brahmā. The second joint was covered with a blue cloth which was Rudra colour, the third with a yellow cloth which was the colour of Viṣṇu, the fourth with a red cloth was *Skanda* joint, and the fifth with a variegated cloth was a Pannaga (Śeṣanāga) joint.

The jarjara was an essential consecrated item representing Indra's banner staff capable of destroying all obstacles. Indra is supposed to have used it to destroy the obstacles at the first ever *nāṭya* performance enacted by Bharata and his hundred sons. It was believed that the *jarjara* remained on the stage all through that performance. It was presented to the troupe later on as a gift by Indra.

The commencement of a performance, in ancient times, was marked by the assessors when the *sūtradhāra* ritually put down the jarjara on the stage. This ceremony was known as *jarjara-mokṣa.*

(See the sketch no. 3 of the *Jarjara* on page 389.)

(b) *Vaiṣṇava Sthāna*

The feet two and a half tāla (1 tāla - 12 *aṅgula*-s or fingers) apart. One foot in natural placement. The other obliquely placed (*trayasra*) with the toes pointing sideways and the shank bent. The other limbs are in *sauṣṭhava* posture. Two hands moving above the waist and the navel together with the chest raised.[22]

(See the sketch no. 2 on page 139.)

(c) *Wondrous (adbhūta) glance*

Eyelashes slightly curved at the end with eyeballs raised in wonder. The eyes widened with the feeling of wonder.[23]

The three performers, then, came forward five steps in a sūcīcārī, with left foot moving first three *tāla*-s apart, towards the Brahmā circle (*maṇḍala*) in the down stage centre of the stage. The *sūtradhāra* scattered the flowers there, and afterwards bowed to Brahmā with *lalita hasta* while touching the ground thrice with his hands. This was the item of scattering of flowers—*puṣpāñjali*—done in a medium tempo which according to *Abhinavabhāratī* denoted the time measure of thirty-six *kalā*-s.[24]

Annotation

(1) *Sūcīcārī*: One *kuñcita* foot thrown up and brought above the knee of the remaining foot, the raised foot allowed to fall on the other foot's forepart.

(2) *The Method of the Stage-walk*: The feet slowly to be placed three *tāla*-s apart; one foot to be raised on each side, at a time, then in the front, in the manner of *sūcīcārī.*

(3) *Lalita Hasta*: Two *alapallava* hasta-s—with all fingers turned towards the palm to be moved above the head.[25]

(4) *Utthāpani Dhruvā*: had eleven syllables in each line (*pada*) and consisted of four lines. The *dhruvā* was sung in *caturasra* or *cāccatpuṭaḥ tāla* with three *laya*-s, three *yati*-s, four *parivartana*-s and four *sannipāta*-s.[26]

After the third *āvartana* of the *dhruvā*, the *sūtradhāra* went round (*pradakṣiṇā*) the Brahmā circle, sprinkled the water from the pitcher and then took the *jarjara* in his hand. This rite was performed with the beginning of the last *sannipāta*. The entire movement was to be executed in quick tempo. Before doing the *pradakṣiṇā* the *sūtradhāra* occasionally joined in the singing of the *dhruvā* songs sung in a fast tempo. The movement of going around was done with *sūcīcārī*—with right foot put forward first and the *nalinī padmakoṣa* hand gesture done in *vyāvartita* and *parivartita* movements.

Annotation

(a) *Vyāvartita and Parivartita hands*

These hand gestures are two of the four *karaṇa*-s of the hasta gestures. In the former, the fingers beginning from the little finger gradually point inwards with the *hasta* movements; while in the latter, the movement is reversed.

(b) *Nalinī Padmakoṣa hasta*

The hands are to be moved in tune with *vyāvartita karaṇa*.

After taking the *jarjara*, the *sūtradhāra* went in five steps, in *sūcīcārī*, in a quick tempo to the *kutapa*, muttering *mantra*-s to ward off evil. The time taken for this movement was twenty-four *kalā*-s.

In the *caturasra* type of preliminaries, the movements of the hand and feet were to be of sixteen *kalā*-s. In the *trayasra* type, the movement occupied twelve *kalā*-s (a kalā was a specific unit of time forming the basis of measuring rhythm in a *tāla*.[27] One *kalā* is equal to either eight seconds or forty-eight seconds to one minute, according to Dr. M. Ghosh, NS, Vol. 2, p. 53.)

(12) *Worship of the Guardian Deities* (*Parivartana*)

In this ritual the guardian deities of different worlds were saluted with the accompaniment of *Parivartanī dhruvā* song, which had caturasra *tāla*, medium tempo and eight syllables. During the singing of this *dhruvā*, the *sūtradhāra* went five steps in *atikrāntā cārī* and bowed to different deities in the following order. First in the eastern direction to Śakra (Indra), then in southern direction to Yama, then in the west ruled by Varuṇa and finally in the north to bow to Kubera. After this—while performing *sūcīcārī* and keeping his face towards the east (i.e. towards the spectators) he bowed to Rudra (Śiva), Brahmā and Viṣṇu. He did this by going three steps forward.

At this moment, a fourth actor (*caturtha kāra*) entered with flowers in his hands and offered worship to the *jarjara*, the musical instruments and the *sūtradhāra*. During his worship, no song was sung except the drum accompanying the meaningless syllables which were chanted (*stobhakriyā*). After the worship, the fourth actor made his exit. This was the end of second *puṣpāñjali*.

After his exit, avakṛṣṭa dhruvā was sung in caturasra tāla and slow tempo.[28]

(13) *The recital of the nāndī* (*Nāndī Pātha*)

A *nāndī* verse has generally eight to twelve lines. It was recited in the *madhyama svara* by the *sūtradhāra*, with the two assistants loudly and distinctly saying *evamastu* meaning 'May it be so'. The *nāndī* prayer prised the gods, the king or the patron and the brahmins. From here the rite of *jarjaramokṣa* commenced covering at the same time the following four rituals.

(14) *The Verses which praised the Jarjara* (*Śuṣkapkṛṣṭa Dhruvā*)

They were formed by meaningless words.

(15) *The Raṅgadvāra*

For the first time *vācika* and *āṅgika abhinaya* started from this juncture with words and gestures. That is why the ritual is called *Raṅgadvāra*—the gate of the performance. The *sūtradhāra* in this ritual recited, in a loud tone, one *śloka* for the deity in whose honour the performance was being held. He also sang praises of the king, brahmins and the *jarjara*.

(16) *Cārī*

With the *jarjara* in hand, the *sūtradhāra* while doing an appropriate *cārī* stepped backwards with the two assistants. Then the *aḍḍitādhruvā* song in medium tempo, *caturasra tāla* and four *sannipāta*-s[29] was sung and enacted. After assuming *avhittha sthāna*, placing the left hand in *kaṭakamukha* gesture with palm downwards on his navel and the right hand holding the *jarjara* loosely, the *sūtradhāra* took five steps. With his left hand in *pallava hasta* he performed *sūcicārī* after which he recited a verse with erotic *rasa* as its subject matter. Then after doing a *parivartana* he went backwards all the while facing the front.

Annotation

(a) *Avahittha Sthāna*: The left foot in *sama*, the right foot *trayasra* and the left hip raised up.
(b) *Pallava Hasta*: The two *patākā* hands joined at the wrist.
(c) Abhinavagupta says that the *sūtradhāra* should portray here the state of love of Śiva for the Devī (Pārvati).[30]

(17) *Mahācārī*

After placing the *jarjara* in the hands of one of the assistants, the *sūtradhāra* again moved forward in the *sūci cārī* taking five steps of five *tāla*-s. He moved backwards and forwards. During this the *dhruvā* song was in *caturasra tāla* and in quick tempo.

Then he recited a verse of furious *rasa* after going three steps forward and bringing his feet together. After this he called for his two assistants.

(18) *The Three Men's Talk*: *Trigata*

The three men's talk or *trigata* had an occasional entry of the jester. It was executed in the verbal style (*bhāratī vṛtti*) with controversial topics (*vitaṇḍa*), abrupt remarks (*gaṇḍa*), enigmatic utterances (*nālikā*) and questions leading to the plot of the play. (These are the sub-divisions of the *vīthī* genre.)

(19) *The Laudation*: *Prarocanā*

The *sūtradhāra*, here, praised the spectators as members of the learned assembly and enumerated the merits of the playwright, the play and the performing troupe.

The preliminary rituals in ancient times were inordinately lengthy which provoked the playwrights to commence their plays with a set pattern of sentence by the *sūtradhāra* saying: "We have had enough of prolixity" (or '*alam ati vistareṇa*').

Pūrvaraṅga rituals as performed in the existing traditional theatres in India remain true in form and spirit to the seeds sown in the ancient times, albeit with variations. The ritual worship of the stage and the musical instrument has continued. Only the manner of sacrificial rituals is changed to the worship of idols like Ambā, Gaṇeśa, Śiva-śakti, etc. Rigorous drumming suggesting the commencement of a performance has continued in most traditional forms where the consecrated drums are played in the beginning.

Nāndī—The Prayer

In the post-Bharata period, the preliminaries gradually got abridged or at least got over-shadowed by the importance given to the *nāndī śloka* as the *bodhaka* or the indication of the entire performance. *Nāṭya Darpaṇa*, *Sāhitya Darpaṇa* and *Bhāvaprakāśa* give elaborate details regarding the *nāndī* prayer as an auspicious verse and state that after the *nāndī*, the playwright takes over the proceedings. These texts skip over the preliminary rituals by referring to them as essential but elaborate performance of ritual worship by the drama troupe for the success of production. The recitation of *nāndī* prayer ended the preliminary rituals at the point after the rite of *jarjara mokṣa* and began the actual performance of the play.

Nāndī Prayer and Its Enactment

It is an auspicious verse of eight to twelve lines (*pada*-s) written by the playwright in praise of his deity (or the deity of the king or the patron). It also pleased the spectators with a subtle reference to the germ idea of the play with similes to propitious objects like the moon, the conch, the *cakravāka*, the night lotus and so on.

It was recited in a medium note (*madhya svara saptaka*) by the *sūtradhāra* who delineated each of its *pada*-s through *abhinaya*. At times, even the basic word and its suffixes (*prakṛti* and *pratyaya*) were so expressed. The commentary of Kallinātha on *Saṅgīta Ratnākara* describes in detail the *padārthābhinaya* of the *nāndī* of Kālidāsa's *Vikramorvaśīyam* in such a way.

The Prologue—Prastāvanā or Sthāpana or Āmukha

The rituals after the *nāndī* prayer gradually came to be considered as parts of the prologues of the play-text. These got written by the playwrights and included the three men's talk (*trigata*), the laudation (*prarocanā*) as well as the final introduction of the dramatis personae with the induction of the play proper. It is believed that with the commencement of the prologue, the actors who performed the preliminary rites gradually vacated the stage.

Sthāpanā Sūtradhāra

It is quite possible that an actor other than the *sūtradhāra* of the preliminaries conducted the prologue. This actor—*sthāpaka* as he was named—entered the stage after the *jarjara mokṣa,* and began the proceedings with the recitation of the *nāndī* prayer. The *sthāpaka* or *sthāpanā sūtradhāra* resembled the *sūtradhāra* of the preliminaries in looks, posture and proficiency in *abhinaya.* However, he wore the costume in keeping with the presentation mode *(pravṛtti)* of the play to be enacted so that his introduction *(sthāpanā)* could appropriately build the atmosphere, style and the mood of the play. The prologue was conducted by him with emphasise on the verbal style with an occasional song and dance in the company of his assistant, the actress and the jester.

It is interesting to note that while the *sthāpaka* and *sūtradhāra* are mentioned separately in the dramaturgical texts, all playwrights, including Bhāsa, refer to the conductor of the prologue as a *sūtradhāra* and not as a *sthāpaka.* Apparently the earlier tradition of referring to him as *sthāpaka* had ceased during the course of time and the one who featured in the prologue was simply called a *sūtradhāra.*

The Song in the Prologue

Most of the prologues had a song of the *gāna* variety which was sung to please the audience. It was usually sung by the actress *(naṭī)* with the *sūtradhāra* occasionally joining in. It was often delineated with the *abhinaya* and the dance. The theme of the song generally described the season, the timing and the mood of the play.

Thus, the production began with the atmosphere of music. The *gāndharva* music predominating in the preliminaries and the *gāna* variety employed in the introduction of the play. In a way, the prologues in Sanskrit plays served the purpose of programme notes of the modern theatre. They praised the connoisseurs in the assembly, introduced the author, the play and the drama troupe. The germ idea of the play was suggestively presented with pleasing songs, dance and witty conversation.

It should be noted here that this style of introduction of the play with songs and witty dialogues after the auspicious worship of the stage (*raṅga-pūjā*) and the prayer by *sūtradhāra* is preserved in parts or in essence, in almost all traditional forms of Indian theatres to this day.

Section 3

Dhruvā Songs

Besides the songs in the drama texts, the leader of the drama troupe (*nāṭyācārya*) incorporated another set of songs in the play, "which supplied the mood of the situation over and above that created by dramatists."[31] These were called *dhruvā* songs and were part of the performing tradition. The *dhruvās* were so called because, as Bharata says: "the words, tempo, *jāti*, notes and time beat" in them "were regularly (*dhruvam*) connected with one another."[32] Abhinavagupta emphasised this by saying that they stabilise, so to say, or form a firm (*dhruvam*) foundation of the production or their themes, and hence are called *dhruva*-s.[33]

They were written in Prakrit (mainly composed in Śauraseni Prakrit) although some *dhruvā*-s are found in Sanskrit also.

Table no. 6

Five kinds of Dhruvā Songs

No.	Dhruvā Songs	Situation of Employment
1.	*Prāveśikī*	Sung at the entrance of important character/s.
2.	*Naiṣkrāmikī*	Sung at the exit of important characters.
3.	*Prāsādikī*	Sung to enhance the mood of the situation.
4.	*Ākṣepikī*	Sung to change the mood of the situation.
5.	*Antarā*	Sung to cover the faults or mishaps.

The analysis of the performance of Act IV of Kālidāsa's Vikramorvaśīyam gives the illustration of number 1, 2, 3 and 4 *dhruvā* songs mentioned above. Dāmodaragupta's *Kuṭṭanimātam Kāvyam* while describing the performance of Act I of Śri Harṣa's *Ratnāvalī* mentions specifically a *prāveśikī dhruvā* at the entrance of the *sūtradhāra*. The evidence of surviving practice in the traditional theatres and folk plays also indicate the popularity of singing *dhruvās* (which are called *Dārus*) especially at the entrance of a character.

The *dhruvā* songs were always sung by the vocalists of the musical orchestra with the performer sometimes joining in. *Nāṭyaśāstra* enumerates many situations, tempos, metres and syllables evoking a particular rasa which a *dhruvagāna* employed. The content, language, melody and rhythm of *dhruvā* songs were minutely worked out and so also the style of their rendering. An illustration of the application of a *dhruvā* song—an *ākṣepikī dhruvā*—in a play to suit the occasion, usage, tempo, note and *rasa* is given below.

Table no. 7

Dhruvā song	*Rasa*	*Tempo*	*Note*	*Occasion*
Ākṣepikī	Pathetic	Slow	Gāndhara or Niśāda	To indicate capture, fall, attack, illness, swoon, on seeing someone killed, etc.
-do-	-do-	Fast	-do-	To show impatience, dissimulation, anxiety, lamentation, weariness, depression, despair, calamity, etc.

Content of Dhruvā Songs

In this manner, each of the five types of *dhruvā*-s were graded to suit the themes, places, times, seasons, the characters and their basic states and natures (superior, middle, inferior). The content of the song had appropriate language, tempo and *tāla*. Two vīṇā-s which accompanied the singing also enhanced the suggestive elements of the songs.

Suggestive Elements in Dhruvā Songs

The characters were generally symbolised by comparable objects in the poetry of a *dhruvā*. For example, a rutting elephant and a swan symbolised superior characters and clouds, mountains, seas—demon characters. While moon, fire, sun and wind suggested gods and kings. Cranes, peacocks, geese and lakes with lotus flowers were suggestive of middle character types. The cuckoo, bee, crow, osprey, owl, pigeon and *kadamba* signified the inferior characters. The movement suggesting different activities were also conveyed through appropriately composed *dhruvā*-s. Chariots, horses, arrows, heavenly cars, swings, birds, animals were suggested by *dhruvā-s* composed with words and syllables chosen with a view to emphasise their movement and other qualities.

The meaning of the *dhruvā*-s, therefore, was to be of prime importance in their rendering. The musical instruments had to harmonise and the drum accompaniment to join only after the meaning of the song was conveyed to the spectators.

The *dhruvā* songs, in this manner, were an additional means to bring out and suggest the inner meaning or the latent *rasa* of the play. They formed an integral score which highlighted different states and situations of the dramatis personae.

Song and Dance Situations in Sanskrit Plays

Playwrights from Bhāsa onwards incorporated songs in the body of their written texts also. These songs were composed by the playwrights themselves. Most of them were called *catuṣpadī* for they had generally four lines. Mostly they were sung and not recited. They were sung by the vocalists who formed the part of the musical orchestra. The song was sung first, then the instrumental music followed, after which elaborate *padārthābhinaya* was enacted by the actor on stage who also accompanied the singing. Bharata says: "Just as a well-built dwelling house does not become beautiful without any colour, without any song (with dance) the drama does not attain (the capacity of giving) joy."[34] And he adds with practicality of a practising performer that, "the song and the playing of musical instruments when well-executed, the performance of the drama would not encounter any risk . . ."[35] He also instructs that "the song should be taken up first, then the instrumental music and the dance will be taken up afterwards because only a combination of song and instrumental music (with dance) is called a performance (*prayoga*)."[36]

Sanskrit play-texts have songs and dance—both pure dance (*nṛtta*) and expressive dance (*nṛtya*)—situations. Playwrights either mention a song sung by a character on the stage (Śakāra sings a song in *Mṛcchakaṭikam*.) Or mostly, a character sings a song in the background over which the characters on the stage comment.

Employment of the Pure Dance (Nṛtta) in Sanskrit Plays

Hallīśaka

Bhāsa, in two of his plays, provides situations where the cowherdesses are dancing a dance called *Hallīśaka* with the cowherds playing flutes and drums, 'all singing together and gaily attired.' It is a circular dance, in the manner of Kṛṣṇa's *rāsa* with *gopī*-s which according to V. Raghavan may have formed a part of the later dance tradition under the sway of Kṛṣṇa and his legends superseding *tāṇḍava* and *lāsya* associated with Śaivism. In *Bālacaritam*, Kṛṣṇa himself is one of the dancers. A fresco painting of *Hallīśaka* nṛtta can be found in Bagh caves (Gupta period, 5th century A.D.).

Kanduka Nṛtta

Kanduka nṛtta or the dance with a ball was a popular form of dance. It was a group dance in which women made many patterns in dance formation (*piṇḍībandha*) called lotus, wavy line, serpentine, a circle (*padmabandha*), *gomutrikābandha*, *nāgabandha*, *cakrabandha* and so on. In Act II of *Svapna Vāsavadattā*, princess Padmāvatī enters playing with a ball (*kanduka*) surrounded by her retinue suggesting a situation for the dance with the ball.

Songs-cum-Expressive Dances with Abhinaya-Nṛtya in Sanskrit Plays

Lāsyāṅga-s

Lāsyāṅga-s were poetic song compositions set to music and enacted with *nṛtya abhinaya*. They were incorporated, in most cases, in the main body of the play-texts and through them the performer expressed the *bhāvāvasthā*-s of the characters singing and enacting the *abhinaya* of each word (*padārthābhinaya*) of the poetry. *Lāsyāṅga*-s were performed in the *sukumāra* (delicate) mode dominated by the graceful style which enhanced the presentation of the erotic mood. These expressive songs-cum-dances were enacted mostly by one person even when they described feelings and incidents relating to the others through the technique of *ekāhārya abhinaya*. They were intended to be relished in the style of a solo recital for the enjoyment of the poetry and the music while simultaneously helping the progression of the plot and the process of *rasa* realisation.

Twelve varieties of *lāsya-lāsyāṅga-s* are mentioned in *Nāṭyaśāstra*.[36a] They are:(1) A song sung in a seated posture, with the aid of a musical instrumen; (*Geyapada*) (2) A Prakrit song sung by a lovelorn heroine (*sthitapāṭha*); (3) A dejected song in separation (*Āsina*); (4) A Sanskrit song and dance by a woman taking a man's role for the pleasure of her female friends (*Puṣpagandhikā*); (5) A taunting song of a neglected woman (*Pracchedaka*); (6) A dance by men who also sings songs with regular metres and beats (*Trigūḍha*); (7) Prakrit recitation expressing disappointment when the lover fails to keep the tryst (*Saindhavaka*); (8) Dance in circular movement with songs expressive of inner feelings (*Dvimūḍhaka*); (9) Dance with sportive movement of joyous feelings accompanied by songs (Uttamottamaka); (10) A song by a heroine separated from her beloved before her lover's portrait (*Vicitrapada*); (11) Song and dance with dialogue of coquetry and sarcasam (*Ukta-Prayukta*); (12) Heroine expressing her love after seeing the beloved in a dream (*Bhāvita*).

Lāsyāṅga-s with other forms of expressive dances like *Chalita* or *Chalika* were often employed in Sanskrit plays. A few examples of the expressive dance situations from Sanskrit play-texts are given below.

Kālidāsa

In Mālavikāgnimatram, Act II, there is a dance performance by the heroine in which she makes her appearance with proper *sauṣṭhava* and posture and expresses through her dance a composition named *catuṣpada chalika* in a medium tempo. *Chalika* was a type of a dance, where the dancer expressed her own feelings while assuming the role of another. In the play, the heroine utilises the technique of *sūcā* and *śākhā* method of fourfold *abhinaya* to denote the love-lorn state before the union. She sings the song first and then does the *nṛtya*. The dance situation enables the lovers to see each other and thus serves the main purpose of the sequence. *Chalita* dance is mentioned in *Harivaṃśa* also.

Act IV of *Vikramorvaśīyam* contains a visual recital of songs and expressive dances to delineate extreme states of love in separation (*vipralambha śṛṅgāra*) of the hero. There is a northern recension of this play in which Act IV becomes a virtuoso performance of *ekāhārya abhinaya*, with music and dance, by the actor playing Purūravas. This revised text has thirty-two Prakrit and *Apabhraṃśa dhruvā* songs in it. These *dhruvā* songs were probably sung by the musicians from behind the curtain with the actor also joining in.[37] *Prāveśikī* and *ākṣiptikā dhruvā*-s are mentioned by name in the stage directions. Apart from that a number of technical terms indicative of dance, dance-like movements, tempo and rhythm of music are also referred to in the stage directions of this act. This suggests that the expressive dance (*nṛtya*) and stylised *abhinaya* accompanied recitations of the Prakrit and *Apabhraṃśa dhruvā*-s.

In Act III of the play *Abhijñāna Śākuntalam* the heroine in a love-lorn state (*ayoga śṛṅgārāvasthā*), writes a love letter (verse 19). The *sthitipāṭhya* variety of *lāsyāṅga* is indicated here where the heroine expresses her feelings through *abhinaya* while reciting a Prakrit verse in a sitting position.

Śrī Harṣa

Śrī Harṣa's play *Priyadarśikā* has a 'play within a play' sequence in Act III. The heroine sings a song in it while playing on the *vīṇā*. She sings with appropriate *abhinaya* so that her friend coaxes the jester to watch the heroine's dance (*nṛtya*). This situation is suggestive of the *lāsyāṅga* named *Geyapada*.

His *Ratnāvalī* opens with an atmosphere of songs and dances on the occasion of a spring festival. The minister *Yaugandharāyaṇa* indicates this in the beginning of the play itself when he says that "the sound of *carcarī* of the town's people with sweet songs and dances fill the air." After some time, the king and the jester are shown watching the spring dance of the people, especially that of the two maids who are singing and dancing *Dvipadī Khaṇḍa* which depicts the states and situations of love.

Damodaragupta in this *Kuṭṭanimātam Kāvyam* describes the performance of this sequence like this: "Then as indicated by the jester, the two maids enter, a little intoxicated, enacting and staggering while at the same time dancing. . . ." "The king sees the two maids enacting and gesticulating the lotuses by the revolving of the two hands (*karaṇa*-s of hands) and suggesting the arrow by taking the *muṣṭi śikhara* and *kaṭakamukha* hands (hand gestures) at the back, with the *vīra* (heroic) glance..." The two maids entertain the king with *dhīra*, *uddhata* and *lalita* steps for a long time...[38] etc. In this way the play *Ratnāvalī* more or less opens with an expressive dance *nṛtya* which has both the *nṛtta* and *abhinaya*.

The first entry of the heroine, Malayâvatī, in the play *Nāgānanda* is presented by a song and expressive dance situation. She is shown sitting on the floor, playing a *vīṇā* and singing a song in the praise of the goddess Gauri in the *geyapada* variety of *lāsyāṅga*.

The Chinese traveller I-tsing mentions that he had witnessed a musical version of *Nāgānanda* with dancing, stringed and piped music and action.[39]

Śūdraka

The Act V of Śūdraka's *Mṛcchakaṭikam* has the heroine, Vasantasenā, as an *abhisārikā*, arriving to visit hero Cārudatta in the company of the gallant *viṭa*. There are a number of verses, twenty-four in all, describing the rainy season, the clouds, the wind, the thunder, the croaking frogs, the cranes and fulfilment of love affair which are recited or sung by the heroine and the *viṭa*. Later, when the heroine meets her lover Cārudatta, he also recites eight verses describing the rains and the union in love.

Even though there are no specific stage directions indicating the manner in which the verses were supposed to be rendered by the actors the clear traditional dictum of the delineation of situations depicting the lover's union by a delicate (*sukumāra*) variety of songs and dance, gives a definite suggestion that the large number of verses were either sung or chanted one after another with appropriate *abhinaya* of expressive dance.

Bodhāyana

Bodhayâna's *Bhagavadajjukā* has the heroine and her maid singing two songs with appropriate *abhinaya* in a pleasure garden. The songs and the *abhinaya* can be categorised as *lāsyāṅga* type, namely, *sthita-pāṭhya* where a love-lorn heroine sings a Prakrit song.

An Actor's Benedictory Verse: Bharata vākya

Sanskrit plays usually end with a verse which expresses an invocation for peace, prosperity and goodwill for all. The verse comes at the end of the play which depicts the successful accomplishment of the desire of the *adhikārī* hero; and is invariably preceded by more or less similar sentences like:

A character :	What other agreeable service should be done now (for you)?
Adhikārī hero:	Is there anything further that I can wish for? Still let there be this—(*Tathāpi idam astu*).

The benedictory verse known as Bharata vākya usually follows this dialogue.

Not much is known about the traditional rendering of this verse. Curiously, *Nāṭyaśāstra*, *Abhinavabhāratī* or *Daśarūpaka* make no mention of a Bharata vākya. The nearest that they come to such a reference is in the context of the 'conclusion' juncture stage of the *nirvahaṇa sandhi*. Benediction forms a part of the subdivisions (*sandhyāṅga*-s) of this juncture of the plot and expresses more or less the same purport as the actor's benedictory verse. *Daśarūpaka* describes this subdivision as a prayer for good things.[40] Very likely, *Bharata vākya* originally might not have formed a part of the composition of the playwright and might have belonged to the repertoire of the drama troupe.[41] It might have even been composed and recited by the *sūtradhāra* as a leader of the drama troupe.[42] We get a reference to *Bharata vākya* as an actor's sentence—*naṭa vākya*—in Rāghavabhaṭṭa's *Arthadyotanikā*, which implies that it was rendered at the end of the play by the main actor in his capacity as a leading member of the drama troupe and not as an *adhikārī* hero.[43]

Taking into consideration the still prevalent style of it's rendering by the present-day Indian traditional theatres, it is possible to conjecture that the actor's benedictory verse—Bharata vākya—in the ancient Sanskrit theatre was sung by the entire *nāṭya* troupe in their capacity as actors (*naṭa*-s and *bharata*-s) with full accompaniment of the musical orchestra.

Before concluding this chapter, it is necessary to note that the incorporation of music and dance is one more area where the ancient Sanskrit play production pointedly differed from the modern west-oriented naturalistic-realistic theatre with its weighty emphasis on the spoken dialogue. The song, music and dance were never separated from the *abhinaya* of the Sanskrit dramas or the indigeneous theatre. Actually as V. Raghavan says: "It is most natural for its poetry to heighten into a song and its action into a dance. Leave alone a drama, even a poem cannot be read even today by the Indian without a rāga."[44] In the ancient Sanskrit theatre also, one could not separate the music from the spoken word or rhythm from its acting. Poetry dissolved into a song and the chant merged into the dialogue quite unobtrusively in a play performance. The note (*svara*), the musical instruments (*ātodya*) and the songs (*gāna*) were so intermixed with the spoken words of the play text that each became inseparable from the other at the moment of performance. As a result, in the words of Abhinavagupta, "The music—*sangīta*—became the soul of a play production."[45]

Notes

1. Kau. Bra. 19/5.
2. SR (1210–47), 1 1.21.
3. NS, XXXIII, 7 (tr. M. Ghosh).
4. Ibid, 406.
5. *Kutapa*: Raghavan V., "Music in Ancient Indian Drama" p. 4, suggests that the term may signify 'rugs' on which the musicians sat. Abhinavagupta (Abh. II, 84, L-10) takes 'ku' as '*nāṭyabhūmi*' and the place which makes it shine (*tapati*) as *kutapa*.
6. NS, XXVIII 15 (tr. M. Ghosh).
7. NS, XXXIV, 270 (Kashi ed.).
8. Abh. XXXVIII, 1 (GOS), p. 394.
   Lath Mukund, A Study of Dattilam, Chapter V, 91–96 [f. Tarlekar G.H., Bharatiya Saṅgita (Marathi)]
9. NS, XXXIII, 226.
10. Ibid, 227.
11. NS, V, 7.
12. Abh. I, p. 291.
13. *Caturasra tāla*. It had eight mātrās. It was a jāti of the *Cañcūtpuṭaḥ tāla* which was composed of various combinations of 'Sañjā', 'tāla' and 'Sannipāta' (the latter three are the variations in which the right and left hands are used to beat the time). *Cañcūtpuṭaḥ* tāla is an *yathākṣara* variety. That is to say it is formed by the long and short syllables that the term has like *cañ* + *cūt* + *pu* + *ṭah* = *Guru* (2) + Guru (2) + *Laghu* (1) + *pluta* (3) = 8. It is an eight *mātrā tāla* (NS, XXXI, 10-11).
14. *Trayasra tāla*. It was another variety of *tāla*, a *jāti* of *Cāpapuṭaḥ*. It had

six *mātrā*-s and was also *yathākṣara*. It consisted of *ca* + *pa* + *pu* + *ṭaḥ* = *Guru* (2) + *laghu* (1) + *laghu* (1) + *guru* (2) = 6.

Cañcūpuṭaḥ and *Cāpapuṭaḥ* were basic tāla prototypes or *yonidvaya* (NS, XXXI, 11-12).

Mātrā—A metre in Sanskrit prosody is measured in terms of a mātrā (i.e. the time taken in uttering a short vowel). A *laghu* is a syllable containing one *mātrā*. A *guru* is equal to two *mātrās*. A *pluta* is equal to three *mātrā*-s (from Mukund Lath, Op. cit. p. 322-23).

15. NS, V. 155-60.

Aṅgahāra.	Refer	Glossary	page	no. 415
Recaka	,,	,,	,,	,, 424
Pindibandha	,,	,,	,,	,, 423

16. Abh. V, 11-15, L-1.
17. *Nirgīta*—It is a technical term. It means singing with meaningless syllables, imitating the sounds produced by different musical instruments. It is supposed to be sung first in the preliminaries, because 'such songs pleased the *asura*-s in the audience.' *Śuṣkagīta, bahirgīta, śuṣkākṣara gīta, nirarthaka gīta, śuṣkāpurṣṭā dhrūvā* mean the same type of singing.
18. *Vṛtti*—The style in music where the singing is more prominent than the musical instrument and vice-versa (Abh. V, 31-32, Madhusudan Sastri's comments, Vol. I, p. 528).
19. Bh. P. VII, 94.
20. Vardhamānaka or Vardhamāna has been associated by Bharata with *Tāṇḍava* in *Citra* variety of *pūrvaraṅga* where female dancers appear one after another and do the *nṛtta* embellished with 32 *Aṅgahāra*-s, 4 *Recaka*-s and 4 *Piṇḍibandha*-s (Lath Mukund, Op. cit. p. 417).
21. NS, XXXI, 485 and V similar practice is to be found in Kudiyattam.
22. NS, XI, 92-93. This is also called *caturasra* position
23. NS, VIII, 48 (tr. M. Ghosh).
24. Abh. V, 75, L-1.
25. NS, IX, 197.
26. Thakur Jaidev Singh, *Nāṭyaśāstramen Pūrvaraṅga Naṭyavarta* (Hindi), Anka 41–44, Feb–May, 1980, pp. 59–71.
27. NS, XXXI, 2–4 (Kashi ed.).

    Kalā was measured in terms of *nimiṣa*—the time required for a twinkling of an eye. Abhinavagupta (Abh. XXXI.4) demarcated 1 *kalā* = five *niniṣa*-s or five short syllables. The five *nimiṣa* time measure was standardised in *gāndharva* music. But, again, this time was not uniform and differed in duration as per the *mārga*-s or *gharāna*-s in the opinion of Lath Mukund, Op. cit. pp. 317-18. Ordinarily one *kalā* can be identical to one *mātrā* of music.
28. Thakur Jaidev Singh, Loc. cit. p. 69.
29. Ibid, 70.
30. Abh. V, 122-24.
21. Ibid, 88, L-10-11.
32. NS, XXXII, 8.
33. Abh. Ibid.

34. NS, XXXII, 482 (tr. M. Ghosh).
35. Ibid. 493.
36. Ibid, 435.

36a. NS, XX, 133. Dr. M. Ghosh suggests that *lāsyāṅga* section in the NS may probably have been a later interpolation. Some m/s of NS exclude them altogether. Post Bharata commentators (DR, BHP, SD) give ten types of *lāsyāṅga*-s.

37. Raghavan V., Loc. cit. p. 9. According to him "the musical fittings—or *dhruvā*-s in this version are in the technique of post Bharata period through Kohala and other writers".
38. Damodaragupta, Kuṭṭanimātam Kāvyam, 896-7 and 905 (p. 176–78).
39. A record of the Buddhist Religion as practiced in India and the Malay Archipelago (A.D. 671–95) by I. Tsing (Tr. by J. Thakaknsu), Oxford, 1896, pp. 163-64.
40. DR, I, 110.
41. Chakravarty C. "A Note on Bharata Vākya", IHQ 129, pp. 549–52.
42. Ghosh M, "The Bharata Vākya" IHQ, 1930, pp. 485-86.
43. Artha Dyo., p. 131-32.
44. Raghavan V., Music in Ancient Indian Drama, p. 6.
45. Abh. V, 88, L-10-11.

PART FOUR

EVIDENCE OF SURVIVAL

"Here sit the drummers in a delightful mood
Here the audience, to clap
Here the bhungal (long blow-pipe) men to blow

Near them stand the comedian (Rangalo)
The connoisseurs have assembled
Let the spectators be quiet

The show (Vesha) will commence now. . . .
Those who attend with devoted concentration
the mother goddess will fulfil their wishes . . . ."

The troupe leader during the preliminaries of a performance of Bhavai, a folk theatre of Gujarat

CHAPTER 9

EVIDENCE OF SURVIVAL IN INDIA

Section I

Traditional and Folk Theatres

The design of the Sanskrit play production analysed and examined in the previous chapters was fully evolved and flourishing by the time of Bharata's *Nāṭyaśāstra* (200 B.C.—200 A.D.). By the time of Abhinavagupta (A.D. 875—1015) and later dramaturgists and commentators, a long period of rich and sophisticated Sanskrit theatre tradition with different emphasis on the styles of presentation had reached its peak and had subsequently entered a phase of decline.

The gradual deterioration in its continuity came around 12th century A.D. with the emergence of the regional languages causing the decline of Sanskrit language. At the same time the political upheavals also resulted in the loss of royal patronage for the sophisticated Sanskrit theatre.[1] Consequently, the development of ten major *rūpaka*-s and eighteen minor *uparūpaka*-s which had evolved out of the rich intermix of the court and temple theatres and popular dramas was affected in the process. The Sanskrit *rūpaka*-s relying on the well-defined scripts gradually lost prominence with the decline of the Sanskrit language. And the *uparūpaka*-s with emphasis on dance, song, *abhinaya* and lesser stress on speech and the written texts got adopted into the regional requirements.

However, regardless of the decline of the Sanskrit theatre the techniques and conventions of its production did not disappear altogether but persistently continued in other newer forms of regional theatres. In the wake of the Bhakti movement, a new form of art (*harikathā*) was generated in most regions in India. *Harikathā* was a form of performing art where devotional episodes of the epics, *purāṇas* and the *Bhāgavata* were communicated to the people through songs, narration, *abhinaya* and other *nāṭya* conventions. There were special groups of theatre performers of distinct caste who performed them. A. Rangacharya refers to them as, "a professional *cāraṇa* caste, descendents of the *sūtas*, the bards of the epic days."[3] This hereditary caste of theatre artists toured, spread themselves and settled in different parts of the country. They even succeeded in getting patronage of minor feudal kings and rich landlords of various regions who allowed them to have their performances in the palaces or in the temple precincts and, at times, even at the village or town cross-roads.

The *cāraṇa*, who is called either a *sūtradhāra* or a *bhāgavata* or a nattuvar or a *nāyaka* or a *pāṭhaka* in some folk drama forms, enacted epic stories through his art of *nāṭya abhinaya* by adopting it to the distinctive regional varieties. Thus, the techniques and conventions of a Sanskrit play production reached larger sections of the people of India. This interaction had specific repurcussions.

Some of the present-day regional theatre forms, which retain the ancient Indian drama traditions, can be traced back to this period. And in almost all of them, a uniformity of a design of production is found with rich variation of local characteristics. From Kashmir to Kerala and from Assam to Gujarat, a number of forms of the present-day traditional regional theatres and folk dramas offer insight into a persistent survival of the ancient Sanskrit theatre framework. Apart from that, forms like Kudiyattam in Kerala, Kuchipudi in Andhra Pradesh and Ankiya Nat in Assam have Sanskrit plays in their repertoire which are performed with the regional variations of the style of ancient play production.

When we probe consciously into these forms and their techniques we realise that the framework that governed the *rasa*-orientation of the ancient Indian theatre is retained by most of them albeit in a scattered and broken condition. They exhibit distinct similarities of performance in the fusion of prose, poetry, music, dance, intoned speech, colour symbolism, gestures and facial expressions, in episodic representation-narration style and the pattern of interpretation (*anukīrtana*) rather than the sequential dialogue-oriented imitation (*anukaraṇa*). Even the stage structures, with special use of the *javanikā* (curtain); the continuous rhythm and tempo of the musical accompaniment from the stage area itself and above all, the unconscious rapport of the Indian audiences at large to these techniques of performance is seen to be surviving at most levels of appreciation in our country till today.

It is not possible to survey all the numerous traditional theatre forms prevalent in different regions in India today and hence a few representative forms from different regions of India have been examined in this chapter to present some of the basic facts about their staging practices which are comparable to those of the ancient Sanskrit theatre traditions.

The forms taken are Bhanda-Jashana and Manch from Kashmir and Malva in the northern region, Yaksagana, Kuchipudi, Bhagavathamela, Kathakali from Karnataka, Andhra Pradesh, Tamilnadu and Kerala respectively from the southern region, Ankiya nat from the Assam and Chhau from Bihar, Orissa and West Bengal from the eastern region and Bhavai from Gujarat in the western region. All of them have the following common features in the frame-work of their production:

The Occasions and Places of Performance

The occasions of the performances are usually fixed at the time of seasonal and religious festivals—mostly after rains in the autumn and in the spring. They are generally performed on demand of a patron wanting to propitiate a deity. The places chosen for the performance are usually a temple precinct or a village road or a fair ground or patron's courtyard. These are indicated below with respect to each theatre form from different parts of India.

Ankiya nat (*Assam*)

In *Vaishnava* monasteries (Satra), seasonal, all night performances after rains.

Yakshagana (*Karnataka*)

In celebration of *Shivaratri* or arranged for a patron's thanks-offering for fulfilment of a vow. Begins at seven in the evening and terminates in the early hours of the morning.

Bhagavathamela (*Tamilnadu*)

On occasions of Narsiṃha Jayanti festival near a temple in the months of May and June.

Kathakali (*Kerala*)

Night long open air performance at fairs, maidans and temple premises. Seasonal.

Bhanda Jashana (*Kashmir, Himachal Pradesh*)

Open air performances—Seasonal.

Bhavai (*Gujarat*)

Performed during Navaratri festival in front of Ambaji temple, or in a village maidan.

Chau (*Bihar, Orissa, West Bengal*)

In April-May in Chaitra parva (March-April) during spring festival; also at the Dashera time (September-October) in front of a Śiva temple.

Mancha (*Malva*)

After Holi, five-day festival.

The Stage Structure

The stage structures are either temporarily erected, open air or permanent. They retain the basic design of *raṅgamaṇḍapa*—a four-pillared structure with a roof or a canopy.

Ankiya nat

60 yards long and 20 yards wide, fully covered theatre with a double roof on large wooden pillars called Nama-ghar or Bhaona ghar in which the stage area is marked as a *raṅgasthalī*.

Bhagavathamela

A temporary square stage of 15′ × 15′ × 2½′ erected in a 20′ wide street adjacent to a temple main gate (gopuram) where the temple deity is placed. The performers face the deity. The stage is covered with a cloth canopy.

Yakshagana

A temporary stage of 16′ × 16′ square area on the ground level with poles on each corner in a temple courtyard or at village grounds. Large plantain leaves are tied to the poles holding a canopy. It is sometimes performed on a raised platform also.

Kuchipudi

A raised platform in any corner near a temple.

Kathakali

Open air performances on the ground level in an open maidan where a pandal is raised with four pillars.

Mancha

A 10′×12′ stage with a canopy resting on four pillars is erected a week before the performance ritually with a flag staff fixed at a proper place.

Bhavai

Open air stage on ground level. A sacred consecrated circular area of 10′ radius called *paudha*, is demarcated for it. This area can be entered only by the performers.

Chau

Ground level consecrated area in front of a Śiva temple.

The Audience—Performance Juxtaposition

The audience sits on all the three open sides or at times on two sides as in Ankiya nat. Mostly the performer confronts the audience frontally. In Yakshagana this is very evident. At times the performer faces all the three open sides where the audience is seated and performs frontally.

Musicians on the Stage

The musicians sit on the stage itself, mostly in the upstage area during performance. In some forms, they sit on the side of the stage also.

In Ankiya nat of Assam, the musical orchestra is called gāyan-vādan and sits on the pedestal opposite to that where the sacred text is placed. In most forms, the musicians sit or stand during the performance. Often the actors sit with the musicians and wait for their entries. This is reminiscent of Abhinavagupta's dictum of a character resting near the *kutapa* area in the ancient playhouses.

In all these forms, the performance begins and ends with rhythmic drum beats.

No Drop Curtain but the use of a Javanikā (Curtain)

None of the traditional forms have a drop curtain. Instead, a mobile *javanikā* (curtain) is brought on the stage by assistants and used dramatically for three purposes: (a) in the beginning as a part of the preliminary rituals; (b) during the performance to indicate the entries of important dramatis personae (*pātra praveśa*) and (c) in a situation when a character is supposed to be dead or wounded, for his inconspicuous exit from the stage.

Ankiya nat

Two curtains are used—red in the preliminaries and white during the performance. The curtains are starched pieces of cloth held by two assistants. The curtains are called *Aar Kapar*.

Yakshagana

A red piece of cloth is used for entrance of important characters and in the preliminaries. It is called There or Parade.

Bhagavathamela

The curtain is used at the time of the preliminaries. It is called *Javanikā*.

Kuchipudi

Used for an entrance of an important character. Satyabhāmā's braid plait is first seen over this curtain in *Bhāmā kalāpam*.

Kathakali

The curtain is used in the preliminaries and for the entrances of important characters. It is called *Therisila*. The character dances behind the curtain. This dance is called *Todayam*. When the character peers over the curtain, it is called *Thiravatam*. The lifting of the curtain is called *yavanikā utthāpana*. Seated and reclining characters enter behind such a curtain. Some scholars think that the term *Therisila* is derived from the Sanskrit word *Tiraskariṇi*.

Bhanda Jashana

The curtain is used for the entrance of important characters. For a king's entry, the curtain is held up as a canopy over the head of the king. It is called *Kanat*.

Bhavai

A curtain is held by one assistant and used for the entrance of main characters. It is called *Raṅgapati.*

Dressing Room (Nepathyagṛha)

The preliminary ritual worship of the troupe is performed in the dressing room where the characters get ready for the performance. In some forms there is a special place in the dressing room where the crowns are kept.

Ankiya nat

A special room in the main building of the monastery. The costumes are stored in this room. It is called *Cha ghara.*

Yakshagana

An area 10 yards away from the stage. It is consecrated with rituals. It is called *Chawki.*

Bhavai

A verandah of a house near the place of the performance. Generally the house is situated at some place behind the musicians of the stage.

Bhagavathamela

In a nearby thatched hut.

No Settings—Only One Piece of Stage Property

There are no settings on the generally bare stages. At times a seat or a stool or an ordinary chair is used in a performance. It is the only piece of stage furniture. The seat is used symbolically to represent different settings by the manner in which a character sits, leans or reclines on it. Only the royal and exalted characters make use of the seat. The other characters mostly remain standing. In forms like Bhavai, Manch, Chau, Kuchipudi there are no seats.

Bhagavathamela

An ordinary stool or a chair is used.

Yakshagana

A wheeled cart on the stage represents a throne, a chariot or an elephant to suit the situation.

Kathakali

An ordinary stool or a chair is used.

Lights

Generally huge brass oil lamps are placed frontally to light the stages. Torches are also used. In some forms like *Bhavai*, the character himself uses small hand-held torches to light up the face. The actors make an imaginative use of the flickering light of the oil lamps and the torches to heighten the mood of the *abhinaya.* Stage groupings, the gorgeous costumes, the body paint and the play of strong light, shade and darkness are cleverly manipulated. Recently, however, patromax and electric lights are also utilised in some forms.

Bhagavathamela

Nowadays electric lights are used.

Yakshagana

Brass lamps and torches are generally used. Two brass oil lamps are placed on the middle of the north and south sides of the stages. In the olden days a yellow orpiment was mixed with coconut oil and smeared over parts of the uncovered body of the actors which made the body shine in the yellow flickering light. At present, with the introduction of patromax lights, a whitish shade with slight reddish colour is used instead.

Kuchipudi

Brass lamps and torches are used.

Kathakali

Actor is seen here as a controller of light. He reveals his face directly over the light of the centrally placed lamp. At times, he turns away from the light or at other times he fans the flame of the lamp with either the curtain or his dress. The flickering but strong lighting is used most dramatically in this form.

Ankiya nat

Two persons hold a wooden arch lit by five or six small torches on the top of poles for the entry of an important character. This arch is called *agnighera*. Another kind of continuous diffused lighting is achieved by placing small earthen lamps in the trunks of plantain trees which surround the acting area.

Bhavai

A barber sits all the time with a burning torch in his hand in the stage area. He rushes with the torch and places the light in front of an important character to light up his face when the situation demands it. These small torches are called *kakda*-s. The *kakda*-s are lit from the flame of lamps which burn in front of the idol of Amba. Sometimes a character lights up his face and body dramatically by having two small *kakda*-s in his hands.

Chhau (Purulia—West Bengal)

In olden days stage assistants carrying torches moved around the performers and lit their faces and bodies at appropriate moments. Nowadays, electric lighting or patromax is used as stage fixtures.

Costumes and Body Paint

The costumes and colours of the body paint are not realistic but are traditionally handed down in most of the forms.

Body Paint

The *aṅgaracanā*, the body paint or the make-up uses colour patterns which are traditionally fixed to suit the types, ranks, states and the situations of the characters. The colour designs are symbolic and familiar to the spectators. The headgears are gorgeous, slightly heavy and are kept in the dressing room at a very special and auspicious place. They are sprinkled with holy water before being ceremoniously placed on the heads of the actors. It is believed that the spirit of the character enters the actor after this ceremony.

The start of the make-up itself is done with chanting of *mantra*-s. The actor ritually starts the make-up by dipping the right finger of the right hand in the oil or ghee and by dotting his face with that finger. In some forms he is helped in painting of his face and body by other assistants.

Costumes

The stage ornaments are not real or heavy. They are light and made up of lac, mica and glittering tinsel. The designs are fashioned to suit the regional preference.

The *Chhau* and *Ankiya nat* forms have masks symbolising various characters, such as animals, birds, gods, serpents, demons, Rāvaṇa, Subāhu, Mārīca, Brahmā, Garuḍa, Jaṭāyu, etc.

Even when contemporary dresses are worn in forms like *Bhavai*, the traditional, *pagha* (special turbans) or caps and shawl are always worn.

The Performance

The Preliminary Rituals—Pūrvaraṅga

This sacred pre-performance ritual is a must for every type of drama troupes. The long duration of the original ceremony has subsequently got curtailed in most forms these days, but some of the necessary rituals of the *Nāṭyaśāstra* tradition are invariably performed. These rituals are: the prayer in the dressing room, sanctifying of the headgear, purification of the stage, recitation of *nāndī* prayer or *sūtradhāra*, the worship of *jarjara* followed by pure dance (*nṛtta*) items, music with *tāla* patterns accompanied by meaningless syllables (*śuṣka vādya*), the entry of the jester in the item of 'three men's talk' and his irrelevant chatter, the prologue (*prastāvanā*) and the laudation (*prarocanā*) by the *sūtradhāra*.

Ankiya nat

The preliminaries last for forty-five minutes or more starting with the rhythm of the drums called *dhamali*. The *sūtradhāra* is called *pāthaka* or a *sūtrādhikārī*. He sings, dances and introduces the story and each principal character in the company of his assistant who is called a *saṅgi*. The *sūtradhāra* purifies himself by fasting on the day before the performance. The laudatory verse is recited throughout in one note.

Musicians enter behind a white *javanikā* curtain in two groups. The arched lighting with the aid of torches on poles light up their entries. A jester in a mask also enters with the musicians.

There are long, short and different kinds of *dhamali*-s.

Kuchipudi

It starts with rituals like sprinkling the stage with holy water, worship of the stage and Indra's staff (*raṅga pūja*, *Indradhvaja pūja*) *nāndī* by the *sūtradhāra* who keeps the crooked stick (*kuṭilaka*) in one hand. An assistant accompanies him. After the prayer called *puṇyavācana* another actor decorates the stage with coloured powders (*raṅgālaṃkaraṇa*). Then two other actors follow one after another with incense and flowers. Finally, the *jarjara* is planted on the stage. Then an actor as *Gaṇeśa* comes and blesses the troupe. The Bhagavatar sings and the main character who enters behind the curtain enacts the abhinaya. In this manner the performance starts.

Yakshagana

It lasts for three hours. Gaṇeśa prayer is done in the dressing room. The ritual of lighting and worship with lamp (*ārati*) is followed with only percussion instruments accompanied by meaningless syllables (*śuṣka vādya*). There is a *raṅgapūja* where the stage is worshipped. *Konangi* (the jester) enters after this. After that the *sūtradhāra* (*Bhagavatar*) chants the verses from the main action. The principal character then enters behind the curtain.

Bhagavatha Mela

Nāndī called *Todiamangalam* is sung by the *sūtradhāra* (*bhagavatalu*) leading the musicians. After that, the *konangi* (jester) enters. After *konangi*'s exit and musicians' invocatory singing a young boy donning a mask of Gaṇeśa enters. The characters are introduced one by one from behind the *javanikā* curtain by the *Bhagavatalu* with a stick—*kuttiakarana*.

Bhavai

Artists perform their prayers before Ambā in the dressing room. The deity is symbolised by a coconut kept on a small wooden board behind which a trident is drawn on a wall. A small lamp is lit in front of it. The artists start their make-up and don their costumes only after this prayer.

The *sūtradhāra* called *nayaka* draws a circle *chachara* on the ground where the performance is to be held. There is Gaṇeśa *pūjā* and ritual prayer to Ambā symbolised by the form of a light in a pot with holes or a *mandavi*. The invocation to *garabi* or the earthern pot with the holes is sung by the *nayaka*, the musicians and the actors. A barber holds a torch during the ceremony. After this, the actors go back to the dressing room.

Then, the musicians sing *avanu*, the song heralding the entry of the main character of the first *veśa*. After the completion of the song, the character enters and the *bhavai veśa* starts.

Bhanda Jashana

It begins with an invocation called *pooza pātha*. But the invocation is to Allah and expresses the desire for his *dīdāra* (glimpse). The manner of the recital in pace and accent is similar to *nāndī pātha* of a Sanskrit drama.

Chhau

Each day of the five day performance is devoted to preliminary rituals when the temple priest ceremonially hoists a red banner staff tied with mango leaves. This is done at a bathing place (ghāt) at some distance from the place of the performance. The banner staff is taken in a procession with rituals and dancing by a special worshipper on each day of the performance. The banner is then placed at the temple courtyard where the performance is to take place. This ceremony resembles the *jarjara pūjā* of Sanskrit *nāṭya* to a certain extent.

Before the actual performance commences in *Mayurbhanj Chhau* (Orissa), there is a ceremony of raṅgabāja behind a curtain where the musical instruments are tuned and the characters appear in their stances and gaits but without masks. This is called *chalis* or walks. After this, two characters called *Kaji-Paji* appear in the tradition of the jester in the 'three men's talk' (*trigata*) of Sanskrit play preliminaries.

Mancha

A water carrier (*bhisti*) appears on the stage during the preliminaries. He sings a song about his origin and acts as if he is sprinkling water on the stage. A female sweeper (*farrasan*) enters and starts sweeping the stage. The exchange through songs between the *bhisti* (water carrier) and *farrasan* (sweeper) is part of the preliminaries.

Dramatis Personae As Types

Two most important and familiar characters in these plays are that of the *sūtradhāra* and the jester—*vidūṣaka*. These characters are found in all forms.

Sūtradhāra

Sūtradhāra is the leader and the trainer of drama troupe and sings or recites the *nāndī* prayer. He introduces the play and the characters. He has a dialogue exchange with them but still remains an impersonal observer. In fact, the whole performance takes place under his expert supervision.

He continues the tradition of the *kathākāra* and is known as *pāṭhaka* or *sūtradhārī* in *Ankiya nat*, *bhagavatha-lu* in *Bhagathamela*, *Bhagavathar* or *prathamaveśa* in *Yakṣagana*, *sūtradhāra* who appears with a *kuṭilaka* in *Kuchipudi* and *nāyaka* in *Bhavai*.

Vidūṣaka or the Jester

The jester or *vidūṣaka* is the second most important actor of the troupe, providing the links, adding touches of humour and sense of contemporaneity to the play by his dialogues.

He is known as *konaṅgi* in *Bhagavathamela*, *hanumanayaka* or *hāsyagāra* in *Yakṣagana*, *pragativeshalu* in *Kuchipudi*, *sheramarakhan* or *bedhab* in *Mancha*, *kajipaji* in *Mayurbhanj Chau* and *rangalo* in *Bhavai*.

Hero and other characters

As the stories of these plays are mostly based on epics, *purāṇa*-s and other popular folk tales, the characters are known types. They exhibit qualities and characteristics which are familiar to the audience. The characters fall in the categories of divine, saintly and worldly heroes, heroines, gods, demons, sages, brahmiṇs, attendants and so on.

Unlike the traditions of Sanskrit *nāṭya*, the female roles are acted by men. In recent times, however, females have been taking part in *Yakṣagana*, *Kuchipudi* and *Kudiyattam*.

Abhinaya

The four aspects of *abhinaya* are employed with emphasis on interpretation (*anukīrtana*) rather than imitation (*anukaraṇa*), where through the process of suggestivity and improvisation subtle shades of states of being are presented to evoke the eight *nāṭya rasa*-s. However, the *abhinaya* varies according to the regional peculiarities. For example in *Bhanda Jashana* of Kashmir and *Yakṣagāna* of Karnataka[4] the emphasis is on music. (Music of *Bhanda Jashana* is known by the Persian name *māgam* which according to some corresponds to the Sanskrit term *rāgam*.)[5] In other south Indian drama forms, the dance with the gestures of hands, stylised walks and facial expressions of the *āṅgika abhinaya* are accentuated. In the *Bhavai* of Gujarat, rhythmic speech and dialogues dominate. In *Chhau* the stances of the body, the walk (*chali*) and the neck movement are stressed; while in *Kudiyattam* the hand gestures and expressions of the eyes (*netrābhinaya*) are emphasised. All these variations notwithstanding, there is nevertheless a commonality in the style of performance in all these forms. The artistic communication is done through the fourfold *abhinaya*, rather than naturalistic or realistic style of acting. The stylised stage walks (*cārī*-s), gaits, *parikramā*, zonal divisions, stances, postures and other features of Sanskrit play performance are recognisable even in their regional variations.

(a) *Entries*

Main characters enter with a series of special gestures and steps, mostly accompanied by drum beats and at times by songs and dances. There is a deliberate attempt to prepare the spectator by an elaborate introduction of the state and situation of the character. The style of self-introduction and reporting of one's intent by characters is reminiscent of the convention of *ātmanivedanam* (reporting of one's intent) of ancient Sanskrit theatre. As also the introductory song (*prāveśikī dhruvā*) by musicians which accompanies the entry and the introduction of a character behind a *javanikā* curtain (as in *Kuchipudi*, *Yakṣagana*, *Bhagavathamela* and *Kathakali*). At times, the character also joins in singing. At other times, the character remains behind the curtain and reveals himself first with his voice alone. This is specially so in the case of demon characters who let out unearthly shrieks.

In *Ankiya nat* this entry is in the form of a special dance of the actor and is called *bhavaricara nāc*. In *Bhavai*, this entry is known as *avanu*. In *Yakṣagana* it is called *vaddolaga*.

(b) Journeys and change of locations are indicated by going around the stage with a stylised walk in a *parikramā*.

(c) Battle scenes are choreographed movements with rhythm and music.

(d) Death scenes are generally avoided in enactment. But when shown, the character who dies on the stage is covered by the *javanikā* curtain. This enables the actor to quietly walk away to the dressing room.

(e) Erotic and heroic *rasa*-s are presented in the traditional stylised manner.

Music (Saṅgita)

Music is an essential element of the traditional Indian theatre. Musicians remain on the stage throughout the performance. They control the tempo, rhythm and pace of the proceedings. They also emphasise special movements, gestures and speeches.

(a) *Musical Instruments*

The musical orchestra includes persussion drums, cymbals and wind instruments. Stringed instruments are rarely used. These days the use of a harmonium is frequent. Drums are believed to be sacred instruments. In *Kudiyattam* and *Ankiya nat*, drums are specially worshipped. Cymbals (*ghana*) are predominant in most of these forms.

Kudiyattam has special female vocalists, in other traditional forms the orchestra has generally male vocalists.

(b) *Songs*

Dhruvā songs or dramatic songs are sung at various junctures of the play. In essentially operatic forms like *Yakṣagana* and *Bhagavathamela*, a special kind of chanting precedes every song. In *Ankiya nat*, the *dhruvā*-s are called *bhaṅgi*-s while in South Indian forms they are generally known as *dāru*-s.

(c) *Dance*

Both pure and expressive dances (*nṛtta* and *nṛtya*) are employed in the traditional theatres in their regional varieties. *Kuchi-*

pudi employs its own techniques of both *tāṇḍava* and *lāsya*. So does the *Yakṣagana*, where the characters enter dancing. Dance movements are used for battles, journey and water sports in this form.[6]

Chhau has steps for war dance (*parikhaṇḍa*) and different *chalis* (stage walks) symbolic of daily routine.

Nṛtta in its regional variety is mainly employed in the preliminary rituals.

Styles of Representations

Unlike Sanskrit plays, these plays are not tautly written pieces. They are episodic in style and present an amalgam of narration, songs, dances, dialogues *abhinaya*, movements and colours. The dialogues are often extempore. Even the written dialogues are spoken with a lot of improvisational interpretation with asides, soliloquies and monologues.

Timings of the Plays

Usually the performances are nightlong affairs often spreading over more than one night. The indication of an end of the day's proceeding is abruptly done by suddenly displaying a light in the dressing room. This custom is found in *Ankiya nat* as well as in *Kudiyattam*.

Actor's Benedictory Verse: Bharata Vākya

Ankiya nat

Bharata vākya is indicated by a song called *mukti mangala* sung by the *sūtradhāra*. This song is for the well-being of the chief guest, who usually receives the gift of betal leaves offered in a brass container.

Kathakali

A religious dance by a god who showers blessings on all.

Troupes, Training, Casting

Generally the troupes consist of not more than fifteen members. The performers belong to specific castes of actors, singers and other craftsmen who may be either professionals or semi-professionals but who form a group around the chief teacher (*guru*). The *guru* is the main actor-stage manager (*sūtradhāra*). In *Bhavai*, the drama troupe is known as a *naṭamaṇḍalī* and is called *toli* or *tolun*. In *Chhau*, the 'guru' is called *ustād*.

The Actor

The actor is called *bhavariya* or an impersonator in *Aṅkiya Nat*, and a *naṭa* in Kudiyattam. He is trained from the young age in all aspects of *abhinaya* and the rules of rhetorics specially dealing with divisions of heroes and heroines (*nāyaka-nāyikā bheda*) pertaining to the character type in which he specialises. All through his training, his exercises, massages, diet and so on are rigorously supervised. He imbibes his art mainly in the process of the performance itself.

There is a tradition of teacher-student transmission of the art in these forms. There are actor's manuals in the forms of treatises hereditarily handed down which are preserved as palm leaf manuscripts such as:

Kudiyattam	:	Aṭṭaprakāra, Kramadīpikā
Yakṣagana	:	Sabhālakshṇam (Yakṣagāna prasaṅga-s)
Kuchipudi	:	Bhāmā cult and Śabdam-s
Kathakali	:	Aṭṭakathā (Kathakali stories)
Bhavai	:	Veṣa-s.

Section II

Kudiyattam—Sanskrit Dramas as Presented in Temple Theatres of Kerala

A Field Study

Kudiyattam is a surviving regional variety of Sanskrit drama presentation in Kerala which can be traced back to the 9th or early 10th century A.D.

In the manner of the surviving remnant of the ancient southern regional mode (*Dākṣiṇāṭya pravṛtti*) the form appears in the tradition of the *sūta* or a kathākāra's attempt to represent the known repertoire of Sanskrit dramas in the Kerala temple precincts. The form has maintained a number of traditions and conventions which demonstrate their uncanny resemblance to the staging practices of ancient Sanskrit play production. At the same time, it must be said that it retains the flavour of an art expression of Kerala.

The Background and History

Epigraphic and literary evidences indicate that this form is nearly 1000 years old.[7] The *chakyars*—the hereditary temple actors—are exponents of this form. One finds reference to *Chakyar Koothu* in the famous Tamil work *Silapaddikaram*, dating back to 2-5 century A.D.[8] The *chakyars* acknowledge their descent from a *sūta* (or a *kathākāra*) who was brought with his family into central Kerala by the Perumals of Chola-Pandya kingdoms. In the 9th or early 10th century, the form was institutionalised and improvised by the Chera poet king Kulashekhara Varman with the help of a brahmin scholar called Tolana.

In this style of performance of Sanskrit plays, the actor goes beyond the words of the playwright and improvises to a large extent so that the main text of the play remains only the basic core of the actor's presentation.

Repertoire

Thirteen plays of Bhāsa, Śri Harṣa's Nāgānanda, Kulashekhara Varman's *Subhadrā-Dhanañjaya* and *Tāpati Svayaṃvara*, Mahendra Vikram Verma's *Maṭṭavilāsa* and *Bhagavadajjukā prahasana*-s, Nilakanṭha's *Kalyāna Saugandhikā* and Śaktibhadra's *Aścarya Cuḍāmaṇi* form the drama repertoire. Only a single act of a Sanskrit play known by its individual name is performed. It may take as many as twenty-one nights to perform the act as in the case of *Mantrāṅkam* of Bhāsa's *Pratijñā Yaugandharāyaṇa*. *Prahasana Bhagavadajjukā* takes as long as thirty-three nights. The languages of the plays are Sanskrit and Malayalam, the latter replacing the Prakrit of the original. Most of these plays belong to the group which was discovered by T. Ganapati Sastri.

The Place and the Occasion of Performance

Kudiyattam is essentially a temple theatre and the plays are mostly enacted in the temple precincts on occasions of religious festivals. They are performed in specially built temple theatres called *Kuttambalams*, which are built according to the traditional *śilpaśāstra* texts of Kerala namely Śri Kumara's *Śilparatna* and

Tantra Samucchaya. (These texts can be traced back to the 16th century.)

The Troupe

The troupe is formed by the hereditary temple actors and artists called *ambalavasi naṭa*-s. The actors belong to a community called chakyars. The drummers belong to nambiar community, who play drums with bare hands and hence are known as *Pāṇivādaka* also. In addition, the nambiars narrate the introductory story in the local Malayalam language. Another hereditory caste of nanyiar women keep rhythm with cymbals and do the chant-like singing which accompanies the performances. Occasionally, they play female roles.

Originally there were eighteen chakyar families performing in various temple theatres in Kerala. But today only seven families survive to carry on the tradition. And of them, only ten to twelve chakyars are actually engaged in the art.

The Theatre (Kuttambalam)

The similarity with Bharata's medium rectangular theatre is apparent in the structure and construction of these temple theatres of which there are nearly twenty-five medium and small sized play houses strewn all over Kerala. These theatres are located in the temple complexes. They are constructed in front of the sanctum sanctorum on its right side.

The basic framework of the ground plan is divided into: (i) Stage area, (ii) Auditorium, (iii) Dressing room. They are built with their plinth constructed of earth and their walls constructed of wooden grills. The roofs of the theatres are very low giving them a cave-like appearance from inside and outside. There are many pillars forming corridors on either sides of the east-west directions in the interior of the theatre. The interior is cool and dark. Gentle breeze blows through the grilled walls. The audience sits on the shining, polished floor. The audience-performance juxtaposition is intimate and informal. A theatre can accommodate not more than 200 to 400 persons. The acoustic quality is perfect.

These theatres were patronised by royalties of Malabar till India's independence. There is a *praśasti* (eulogy) of royal patronage on the first main pillar on the right at the Kuttambalam at the Vaddakanātha temple at Trichur which this author visited as part of the field work.

Stage

The Kuttambalam stages present several links with Bharata's theatres.

The stage is a *raṅgamaṇḍapa*-like structure with rows of teak-wood pillars, lacquered in bright orange and red.

It has an ornate roof with the inside ceiling usually carved with nine guardian deities in bas relief forming a protective sacred *maṇḍala*. At the Trichur Kuttambalam, nine lotuses are carved instead of the deities.

There are two doors on the upstage back wall leading to the rectangular dressing room behind them. Between these stage doors, a permanent place is reserved for the musicians. Two huge copper drums called *mizhavu*-s (pronouced miḷāvu) are permanently kept in a railing like wooden framework. These drums belong to the temple authorities and are held sacred.

Two narrow strips of passages, reminiscent of the *mattavāraṇī*-s as described by Bharata, are on both sides of the stage beyond the stage pillars. These narrow passages are not used as acting areas in the performance but spectators often sit there. In olden times important dignitaries used to sit there.

The stage is a wooden structure constructed with rituals and sanctified by ceremonial rites at the time of the preliminaries. It is a raised platform, a colourful focal point, in the dark interior of the temple theatres.

Auditorium

Audience-performers juxtaposition is generally frontal. Female spectators sometimes sit on the left side of the stage in the passage. The other spectators generally squat on the polished floor in the front.

Dressing Room

Dressing room is a dark, narrow, rectangular room just behind the stage. The actors get made-up there after the ritual prayer to Gaṇeśa. The costumes hang on a string ties on either side of the walls. There is a back door for the actor to enter from outside the theatre.

Musicians on the Stage

The nambiar musicians sit on the centre of the upstage area between the two doors of the stage back wall during performance. A white cloth is spread on the right side of the stage floor for the nanyiar women to sit with cymbals for their chant-like singing which accompanies the performance.

Curtain

There is no drop curtain on this stage. But a *javanikā* called *purapattu*, made of a 6′ × 9′ red cloth is used for the following purposes:

(i) At the time of preliminary rituals some of the ceremonies are performed behind this curtain held by two assistants.
(ii) Entry of an important character is staged behind a *javanikā*.
(iii) Death scenes need a *javanikā* curtain.
(iv) On certain occasions, a character indicates a temporary *javanikā*, by simply keeping the flower like end of his upper loose garment (*uttarīya*) in front of his face. By this symbolic practice, the character indicates that he is temporarily hidden behind the *javanikā* and is not seen by the audience or other characters.
(v) Sometimes an actor fully covered by the *javanikā* speaks or "feeds the lines" to a character on the stage. This convention is called as *Muti Cholluka*.

A Seat—Pīṭham—the only Stage Furniture

There is no setting. A seat (*pīṭham*) is used as an only one piece of stage furniture. This seat is a carved wooden stool with three legs made by carpenters of *asari* caste. The seat can suggest different locales like an upper storey, a tree, a mountain top or a cave by the *abhinaya* of the actor assuming different postures on it. During the performance the actor himself moves the seat.

In *Vālivadhāṅkam* of *Abhiśeka nāṭaka* (Bhāsa) it was turned down to give support to the dying Vāli. And after the death of Vāli, the royal insignia of Vāli were placed on it and covered by the *javanikā* curtain to represent his dead body.

Lighting

A metre-high traditional bronze lamp-stands on the down

stage centre. Three bright flames face the audience and two flames face the actor. This is the only source of light in the dark interior of these stages and theatres.

The Performance: Preliminaries (Pūrvaraṅga)

Prior to the main performance there are long preliminary rituals which are sanctioned by the temple authorities and last for one night. The *mizhavu* drums are sanctified and consecrated by rituals. The bronze lamp is lit with the sacred fire from the sanctum sanctorum for each evening's performance.

The stage is ceremoniously decorated with *toraṇa*-s of palm leaves and coconut shoots. The front pillars of the stage are decorated with plantain trees. On each side of the lamp, eight auspicious items like paddy, fruits, betal nuts, leaves and so on are placed in a cylindrical measures. They are called *aṣṭa maṅgalam*.

Playing of the Consecrated Mizhavu Drums

The preliminaries begin with the playing of *mizhavu* drums. A combination of rhythms is played on them by a nambiar which is reminiscent to *śuṣka vādya* of ancient Sanskrit theatre. The nambiar community alone has the traditional right to play the *mizhavu* drums which are two huge copper pots sanctified by rituals. They are not supposed to touch the ground but are supported by wooden frames. They are temple-based instruments and considered *deva-vādyam* or self-manifested. They are supposed to have the power to destroy evil spirits. The size and dimensions of these drums are determined by the principles of temple architecture and iconography and are prescribed according to *Dakṣiṇa Mārga Tantra* texts.[9]

(1) The preliminary rituals on the stage start with the playing of the *mizhavu* drums.

(2) Then the chant-like songs are sung by the nanyiar ladies. They are called *Vandana śloka* which refer to Gaṇeśa, Sarasvatī and Śiva.

(3) The next item is—*Nambayaste Tamil*—where a nambiar tells the summary of the story of the performance in Malayalam.

(4) Then the nambiar sprinkles water on the stage to purify it.

(5) He then recites the *maṅgala śloka* which is not the *nāndī śloka*.

(6) Then a *javanikā* curtain is held before the drums by two stage assistants. The *nāndī sūtradhāra*, a *chakyar* actor who has had a ritual bath and has offered a prayer at the main shrine, stands behind the *javanikā* with flowers in his hands. With the beating of the drums and rhythms, he lowers the curtain and does *Sabhānirīkṣaṇam* (observation of the assembly) by his posture of standing and expressions of his eyes. This is also called *stobham*. By this process of *stobham*, on his first entry an actor who is portraying an important role establishes his character by his stance, facial expressions and the *abhinaya* of *sāttvika bhāva*-s alone. The *sūtradhāra* stands in *stobham* for the duration of this ritual.

(7) Thereafter he introduces the story through various gestures and *cārī*-s. This is a pure dance (*nṛttam*) called five steps (*pancapadam*).

(8) After reciting the *nāndī śloka* the *sūtradhāra* leaves the stage.

(9) Then the *sthāpanā sūtradhāra*, the main *chakyar*, enters. He does a series of pure dance steps (*nṛttam*) with invocatory songs in praise of Viṣṇu and the eight guardian deities.

(10) A final description of the divine forms of Śiva-Pārvatī is executed in gestures, *nṛtta* and chant-like songs.

The invitation to the deities, with Brahmā as their leader, to protect the performance is a stylised choreographic ritual ceremony enacted according to the tradition by the *sūtradhāra*, his assistants and the musicians. The entire ritual is called *nāṭya kriyā* or *sthāpanā*. The entrance of the *sūtradhāra* from behind the *javanikā* is called *purapaḍḍu*.

The Style and the Abhinaya

The fourfold aspects of *abhinaya* with the *dharmī*-s are employed in their regional variations and emphasis.

Āhārya

The plays that the chakyars enact fall in the *nāṭaka*, *prakaraṇa* and at times, *prahasana* categories. The character types are thus divided into divine, saintly, heroic, or erotic heroes, heroines, gods, demons, characters like Hanumāna, Vāli, Sugrīva, sages, brahmins, attendants, etc. The character of the jester—*vidūṣaka*—is very important.

The physical get-up (*āhārya*) of these character types is far removed from reality and strictly follows the instructions given in the traditional treatises like *Kramadīpika*-s of Kerala chakyars. (Different chakyar families have their special "family"—*gharānā*—manuals).

The Body Paint—Aṅgaracanā

The first item on the make up list of the actor is tying of the band of red cloth (*cuḍapaṭṭam*) round the head just above the hairline. Then begins the ritual of dotting of the face with the right finger of the right hand with ghee taken from the sacred lamp in the dressing room. The actors are assisted by the nambiars in their body painting.

The materials of the body paint constitute the paste colours made up from indigenous forest-found ingredients like:

Red	:	from red earth,
White	:	from rice paste and lime paste,
Yellow	:	from turmeric and yellow mineral,
Black	:	from coal powder, or lamp black mixed with ghee,
Blue	:	from indigo,
Red	:	from *sindūra* and *kumkum*,
Glitter	:	from mica powder,
Śyāma	:	is made from a paste of yellow mineral, rice paste, and blue and results in a shiny deep green shade.

Self-controlled (dhīra) heroes like Rāma, Mitravasu, Udayana are painted in *śyāma* tints, while the vehement (*uddhata*) types like Rāvaṇa, Vāli, Sugrīva have reddish and black tints. Vāli sports a red beard. *Asura*-s or demons have black make-up. Śūrpaṇakhā has a gruesome black make-up with a hideous head dress.

The characters are broadly divided into (1) White—*Sattva* types, who are virtuous like Hanumāna; (2) Red—*Rajas* types, who are passionate or violent like Sugrīva, (3) Black—Tamas types who are ignorant and indifferent like Vāli.

Important characters have red eyes which is managed by placing a seed of a plant (*cantappuk*) in each eye. Rose red eyes are for the heroes and the deep red are for vehement (*uddhata*) types.

The painting of the face and the entire body is called *teppu* which literally means painting. A golden yellowish orange (*gaura*) colour is for the *sūtradhāra* and the exalted self-controlled human hero like *Jīmūtavāhana* (*Nāgānanda*). White with red dots and lines is the make-up for the jester. He has big black moustache drooping on one side.

Costume

Costumes consist of (1) huge crowns—*kiriṭam*-s which are heavy and decorated with flowers, (2) a jacket (*kañcuka*) and a loose garment (*uttarīya*) for upper part of the body, (3) *dhotī* covers lower part of the body. It does not, however, cover the entire rear part where a heavily folded cloth is prominently projected and seen.

Colour combinations are traditional and differ according to character-types. The jester wears a white *dhotī*, an upper garment and a flat cap. He has a flower in one ear and a betal leaf tucked in the other.

Ornaments

Ornaments are ingeniously made from wood and covered by mica and gilt. They are made by the traditional carpenters called *asari*-s.

False Hair

These are made from fibre plants.

The spirit of the character is supposed to enter the actor's body after he ritually dons the head dress (the *kiriṭam*). This process is called *Prameya Puruṣa*.

Vācika Abhinaya

Kudiyattam has a unique style of intonation of a verse. The actor attempts to maintain an even intonation of a note (*svara*) throught the verse. There are twenty notes (*svara*-s) with individual names which sound "mid way between *ṛk*, *yajur* and *sāma gāna* notes with *udātta*, *anudātta* and *svarita* (raised, unraised and intra tones notes. . . .)"[10] These *svara*-s have nothing to do with musical notes but are tonal intonations which are used according to the mood, the states and situation in a play. The intonation resembles the chanting of Veda-s by nambudiri brahmins.

The jester—*vidūṣaka*—speaks in normal Malayalam frequently indulging in asides, mologues and speech in the air technique.[11]

Noises off: Nepathye

The voices off stage come from either the musical orchestra or the dressing room.

Āṅgika Abhinaya

The *bhāva abhinaya* through the hand gestures, the facial expressions with emphasis on the glances of the eye movement, gaits and stage walks (*cārī*-s) are employed with the emphasis on the twenty-four hand gestures which are derived from an anonymous manual called *Hastalakṣana dīpikā*. The actor establishes his character first by *stobham*, his basic stance. After that, he starts suggesting ideas and detailed explanations and interpretations of ideas which are represented by his hands, body, voice and eyes (*kaye*, *meiye*, *śabdam* and *kannu*).[12]

The flight in the air, the ride in the chariot, the playing of *vīṇā* or plucking of flowers are accomplished by specific hand gestures and body movements. The change of locales is shown by various stage walks (*cārī*-s) in varying tempos in the movement of going round the stage (*parikramā*).

Entries

The main character emerges from behind the curtain (*purapaḍḍu*) accompanied by an introductory verse (*pravēśika śloka*). General entries are made from the left door of the stage with exits through the right door. Characters like *Śurpaṇakhā* enter from the back of the audience accompanied by torches and shrill cries.

Battles

Combats are choreographed martial (*nyāsa*) movements accompanied by the rising tempo of the beating of drums.

Erotic Rasa

The states of love (*ratibhāva*) are traditionally depicted.

Death Scenes

Death is delineated in a combination of *lokadharmī* and *nāṭyadharmī* practices. When the character dies on the stage the *javanikā* hides him from the audience. The actor takes his exit stealthily leaving his costume on the stool, which is then covered by the *javanikā*. This symbolises his dead body.

Sāttvika Abhinaya

In *kudiyattam*, the *sāttvika abhinaya* is indicated by the actor's *stobham* and *sabhānirīkṣaṇam*. An actor establishes his character by standing in a fixed stance with appropriate facial and eye expressions. *Sūcā abhinaya* is important in this form. First comes the *sāttvika abhinaya*, then *vācika* and then the elaborate *āṅgika* in a deliberately slow order. The *abhinaya* through the eye expression (*netrābhinaya*) and hand gestures (*hastābhinaya*) are the two elements on which the entire *Kudiyattam* performance rests.

The Stylisation of Extended Abhinaya

There is no attempt at realism in presentation of *Kudiyattam* plays nor is there an endeavour to adhere to the written Sanskrit text in its linear, narrative pattern. On the other hand, a unique style of "flash forward", "flash backward" and "an incident viewed from two or three different angles" is adopted. The scenes of the plays are performed by only three or four performers, or by a single main actor assisted by one or two other minor actors. The stylisation of *abhinaya* rests on the main actor's skill in monoacting in the pattern of the *ekāhārya abhinaya* technique. The solo actor is aided in this by a line of a dialogue occasionally fed by another actor, who enters just for that purpose fully covered by the *javanikā*.

Each evening's performance is devoted to the presentation of the background of the dramatis personae with the aid of such a solo *abhinaya* by the actor enacting the role. At times he is assisted by other actors also. He recapitulates the story by leading up to the incident which is to be presented in the act from his point of view. He does this recapitulation by:

(1) A method of delineation in a backward action, in a reverse chronological order leading up to the verse (*śloka*) or the incident which he has to depict—*anukrama*.

(2) Depiction of the story from the beginning up to the incident or the *śloka* in chronological order—*saṃkṣepam*.

The entire process is called the character's self introduction—*nirvahaṇam*. The background of the character and the incident of the situation of the play is given in elaborate detail by such a process. When the hero and the jester (*vidūṣaka*) both perform the *nirvahaṇam* the hero does the *abhinaya* while the *vidūṣaka* extemporises in Malayalam. The solo *nirvahaṇam* of the *vidūṣaka* is called the jester's treatise on the four *puruṣārtha*-s. He does this in Malayalam with satire, jokes and anecdotes with many contemporary touches. The spectators often become the butts of his ridicule.

The performance of a play falls into following pattern :

(1) Preliminary rituals.

(2) Entrance of the main dramatis personae.

(3) His self-introduction (*nirvahaṇa*) or telling of the background of the character leading up to the *śloka* from his point of view.

(4) The jester's self-introduction or the *vidūṣaka's nirvahaṇa*.

(5) The enactment of the act where the main characters enact the scene with hand gestures and controlled facial expressions (glances). Chanting of *śloka*-s or speech on a fixed note are aided by the female vocalists.

(6) The actor's benediction: The *Bharata vākya*.

Vālīvadhānka at Trichur Kuttambalam

The *vālīvadhānka*, an act from the *abhiśeka nāṭakam* of Bhāsa was presented by the great Ammannur Madhava Chakyar and his troupe, which this writer witnessed at Trichur, Kuttambalam. Although the act had seven characters (Rāma, Lakshmana, Hanumāna, Aṅgada, Sugrīva, Vāli and Tārā) in the Sanskrit text, only three of these (Rāma, Sugrīva and Vāli) appeared on the stage. The other roles were enacted by these three actors by taking recourse to the *ekāhārya abhinaya* technique. The performance lasted for five nights. The previous four nights were devoted to the delineation of self-introduction (*nirvahaṇam*) of Rāma and Sugrīva.

Madhava Chakyar appeared as Vāli, the king of the monkeys, on the last day and the battle between Sugrīva and Vāli was enacted in choreographic movements. A haunting death scene of Vāli was delineated most vividly with the intricate slow rhythm of the beating of the drums and the *bhāvābhinaya* emphasising the pure inward concentration (*sāttvika abhinaya*) by this great actor.

Music

Musicians accompany the performance by providing rhythm, tempo and the chant-like music. No instrument accompanies the verses when they are chanted. Musical instruments are of five types:

(i) Mizhavu drums (avanaddha): Two huge copper drums as already explained.
(ii) Iddaka drum (*avanaddha*): A small but sensitive drum played with a small stick by a nambiar drummer standing on the left of the *mizhāvu*-s.
(iii) *Kompe*—trumpet (*suṣira*) played by the nambiar from the left of the mizhāvu-drums.
(iv) *Kazhle*—a wind pipe (*suṣira*) also played by nambiars from the left of the *mizhavu* drums.
(v) *Kuzitula* cymbals (*ghana*) played by nanyiar women seated on the right side of the stage.

Pure Dance (Nṛttam)

Pure dance (*nṛttam*) is utilized in the preliminaries and in the dance-like choreographic movements representing the battle scenes.

Spectators

Three distinct classes of spectators are to be witnessed watching a *kudiyattam* performance:

(i) Connoisseurs and scholars who relish the nuances of the skill of the delineation of the inner states and situations (*bhāva*) by the actor. They come accompanied by copies of *Aṭṭaprakara*-s in their hands and are seen slowly rustling the pages of the book and enjoying the performance.
(ii) Women devotees and children who are familiar with the story and the characters and who come to watch the epic tales.
(iii) The nambudiri brahmins who stay on to witness the performance after their daily visit to the temple.

Training

Kudiyattam is a hereditary art. In the matriarchal system which still persists in Kerala the three great chakyar actors of Kerala, Mani Madhava, Madhava and Rama chakyar were all trained by their maternal uncles. In purely family surroundings the art of *abhinaya*, language and literature of Sanskrit and Malayalam, the epic, the *purāṇa* and *kathā* lore as well as *dharmaśāstra* and *arthaśāstra* are taught and imbibed in ten to twelve years of rigorous teacher-disciple tradition. The pupil does the various body exercises (separate for each major and minor limbs of the body) daily for many hours in a rigorous regime. He makes his debut in the role of a *sūtradhāra* which he has learnt to enact by observing his *guru*—the principal chakyar. When an important role is assigned to him, he enacts the character with his imaginative and creative capacity to improvise and select for performance the techniques taught to him by his *guru*. This is called the performer's *manodharma*. But, always, the performance is conducted under the watchful eyes of the *guru* who is usually the main actor and the manager of the troupe. The number of acts for which the chakyars are trained are seventy-two. These acts are selected from only twenty-four Sanskrit plays.

Treatises

Kuṭṭe is a Dravidian word meaning a drama or a dance and *chakkian* means an actor or a dancer.

Actual texts dealing with stage craft and the traditions of *chakyar* performance are handed down from generation to generation of performing families. They are written in simple Malayalam and interspered with Sanskrit verses. They are of two kinds:

(i) *Aṭṭaprakāra*, detailed choreographic notes on the *abhinaya* aspect of different traditions for the actors to delineate each gesture, movement and stance in a continuous performance.
(ii) *Kramadīpikā*, detailed instructions regarding stage-craft, costumes, make-up, songs, dances, svara, *raga*-s and stage directions.

Actor's Benediction: Bharata Vākya

The end of the performance on each night is announced by a sudden light in the dressing room and the ritual drumming of the *mizhavu* drums. The end of the act or the whole *kudiyattam* performance ends with a final benediction sung by the nanyiar women. There is drumming by the nambiars on the *mizhavu* drums. The chakyar washes his feet on the stage and extinguishes the wicks of the bronze lamp.

The end of the play sees the troupe with the leading chakyar actors, nambiars, drummers, nanyiar women chanters and others marching off in a procession to the sanctum sanctorum of the main temple for a prayer.

NOTES

1. The quality of the court culture and arts generating from it, had in the course of time, deteriorated to the extent that individual genius was restricted by slavish adherence to rules and mechanical repetition of what was achieved before. Commentaries and sub-commentaries and manuals and sub-manuals on *Nāṭyaśāstra* convention had become the rule of the day. De. S.K., History of Literature, pp. 26-28. Dr. De has discussed this aspect elaborately in the context of Kāvya literature.
2. Dramaturgists after NS have listed a variety of *Uparūpaka*-s. Bh. P. lists eighteen. Abh. lists ten. Bhoja's *Śṛṅgāra Prakāśa* lists twelve. This goes to show that newer *Uparūpaka* forms were evolving in post-Bharata period up to 10–12 century A.D.
3. Rangacharya Adya, The Indian Theatre, p. 56.
4. Karanth, K.S., "*The Yakhsagana of Karnataka*", JNCPA, Vol. III, No. 3, Sept. 74, p. 2.
5. Mathur, J.C., Drama in Rural India, p. 4.
6. Karanth K.S., "*Yakshagana*" Marg, Vol. XIX, No. 2, March, 1966, p. 28.
7. Nair D. Appukuttan, "*Kudiyattam: Fantacy and Poetry in Dance*", Marg, Vol. XXXII, No. 2, p. 66.
8. Silapaddikaram, (Eng. tr. V.R. Dikshitar), pp. 28, 68-78, 144, 318.
9. The information about the Mizhavu drums is collected in an interview with the noted Kerala scholar L.S. Rajgopalan.
   Similar convention regarding the percussion instruments in *Yakṣagāna* is described by Karanth K.S., Loc. cit. p. 2 ff.
10. Rajgopalan L.S. "*Music in Kootiyatam*" Sangit Nāṭak, 10 Oct-Dec. 1968.
    c.f. When asked the reason for the elongated vācika abhinaya, the great performer—Madhav Chakyar explained that Kudiyattam heavily relied on interpretative *aṅga-sattva* (specially *hasta* and *netra*) *abhinaya* which demanded time to enact.
11. The manner of performing "speech in the air" in Kudiyattam is special. The actor stands in the natural stance of the character. Nanyiar ladies chant the verse. After this the actor turns his face in both the sides

to indicate that he has heard. Then, with *hastābhinaya*, of each line (*pada*) of the *śloka* he interprets it. In the end, he asks by a hand gesture: Is this what you said? From an interview with Kalamandalam Raman Chakyar.

12. Rajgopalan, L.S., "Eloquent Eyes—Netrābhinaya in Kudiyattam", MAM, Madras, Vol. XIV, parts I–IV (1974), p. 93.

Chapter 10

IN SOUTH EAST ASIA, CHINA, JAPAN

A clearly recognisable similarity is noticed between most of the traditional drama forms of South East Asia and Sanskrit *Nāṭya* production as reflected in the *Uparūpaka* and as continued in the later centuries by the *Sūta Kathākāra*-s. Traditional theatres of South East Asia show strong Indian influence on the local theatre forms and the design of the play production. The *nāṭya* style pervades the framework of production and appears as a distinctive style of Asian theatres, different from that of the West.

Similarities of the Style of Production

India is acknowledged as "a source of most of the theatres in Asia".[1] In the first thousand years of the Christian era, the Indian culture penetrated into Burma, Thailand (Siam), Cambodia, South Vietnam (Champa), Malayasia, Indonesia (Sumatra, Java, Bali) and China. Travelling Indian traders and priests took with them, among other things, their language, epics, *purāṇa*-s and *jātaka* lores and also their dance and drama forms. The beginnings of many South East Asian classical performing arts like dance-dramas, puppet theatres and the shadow plays can be traced to Indian influence. The ritual dramas performed by the Buddhists around their monasteries and the narrative representative style of Indian epic recitals conducted by *sūta pūraṇika*-s at the dictates of South East Asian royalties were two major influences.

The *Rāmāyaṇa* stories (indicated by words like Roma, Lāma, Rāma respectively in Malaya, Thailand, Cambodia and Laos), the *Mahābhārata* (called *Bratt Yuddha* in Indonesia) and the *jataka* stories (called *Zat Pwe* in Burma)[2] along with local stories and legends provided the material for South East Asian theatres. Their production design bears unmistakable Indian influence which is reminiscent of the ancient Sanskrit *nāṭya* tradition.

Resemblance in Production Techniques

Occasion and Places of Performance

History of the theatre performances in these countries shows two distinct patterns of places and occasions of staging:

(i) The court performances in royal theatres,

(ii) The popular theatres.

Court Performances:

These were complex and sophisticated dances, recitations and drama performances presented by troupes employed by the royalty. The performances were held on special occasions like religious festivals, birth of a royal heir, weddings, victory celebrations or simply for amusement. The performing troupes were retained exclusively by the court and the performances were held only for the invited gatherings.

In Thailand (Siam), there is *Khon*, a masked pantomime, depicting *Rāmāyaṇa* battle, performed solely by men. This is the oldest theatrical form with highly Sanskritised text produced infrequently nowadays.

Then, there is *Lakon*, a dance-drama form, with dialogues, music, chanting and dance. Till recently it was performed by female dancers in the royal harem.

In Cambodia, there were dance-dramas of the female dancers of the royal harem in which the princesses took part. Sculptured friezes in the ruins of Angkor Vat have enough evidence of this.

In Sumatra, there were many varieties of palace dance-dramas depicting epic tales of the *Rāmāyaṇa* and the *Mahābhārata*. One such piece is Arjuna-Semdra (Subhadrā).

In Java, in the relief of the temples of Java (Borobudur—800 A.D.) and the Hindu Prambanam temples (915 A.D.) a number of scenes of dancing girls, actors and musicians are found in the *āṅgika abhinaya* and *nṛtta* (*Karaṇa*) postures in the style prescribed in *Nāṭyaśāstra*.

Popular Theatres

The city and town based popular theatres were run by professional troupes for the entertainment of the people. Spectators were charged an entrance fee. Similar performances are given in the present times at regular intervals in temporarily erected village stages. The shows are for the benefit of local sponsors. Other villagers also attend the show.

The Structures of Theatres and Stages

The palace theatres are held in specially erected *maṇḍapa*-like structures inside the palace complex. They are called *Peṇḍapa* in the Javanese language. They are open on all sides with polished floor space, with or without a height to the stage. The royalty and the invited guests sit in raised seats. The audience-performer juxtaposition is direct and intimate without any drop curtain or proscenium arch dividing them.

In Java, Wayang Orang, an actor, performs on all the four open sides of the stage like a human puppet.

The theatres in villages and towns are simpler in construction. In villages, open air performances are held on a ground level of an open maidan in temple courtyards. The stages are made with rough planks of bamboo and roofed over with palm thatch.

No Drop Curtain

There is no front or drop curtain dividing the continuous stage action from the audience. A hand-held rectangular curtain reminiscent of an Indian *javanikā* is brought on the stage by two assistants. In Ardja, an operetta type of *Balinese* theatre, such a curtain is brought for special entries of a character.

No Settings

The traditional classical forms have a bare stage without any settings or elaborately painted sceneries. At present, there is an attempt to have different sceneries for different scenes.

No Stage Furniture

None of the forms have complicated furniture settings except for a chair or two.

Lighting

Coconut oil lamps and torches traditionally lit the stage. This method is in practice in different village theatres even to this day. However, patromax and electric fittings also light the stages in the present times.

The Character-Types and the Genres of Plays

Gods, noble heroes and heroines, religious ascetics, clowns, servants, peasants, workers or town dwellers and other known types from local legends, the Indian epics and the *jātakas* form a conglomeration of 'good' and 'bad' characters-types.[3] The drama genres are known by the types of hero portrayed in them.

Costumes and make-Up

Costumes and make-up are conventional, colourful and symbolic. They are not realistic. They have evolved out of designs transferred through generations of performers.

Masks

Certain types of characters use traditional masks. The spectator is familiar with the costumes and make-up of the character types and recognises them on their entrance.

Style of Presentation

Presentation is not naturalistic. Poetical dialogues and intoned speech interspaced with coloquial speech, dance-like movements and constant musical accompaniment exhibit a style which is more suggestive rather than realistic.

Musicians on the Stage

Music is an essential feature of the performance, so much so that the classical theatre in Siam is referred to in intellectual circles as *saṅgīta*.[4] Drums, stringed instruments, pipes, gongs, etc., form the necessary minimum orchestra which sits on the stage and continuously accompanies and emphasises the dramatic movements.

Dance

Suggestive gestures and stylised movements with pure dance is the most popular element of South East Asian theatre which is enormously influenced by the Indian dance-dramas. As mentioned before, the common word connoting dancing in Malaya, Thailand, Cambodia and Laos is Rāma, Roma or Lāma. This popularity of Indian style dancing must have induced Rabindranath Tagore to remark that "Lord Śiva gave his dance to Indonesia and left his ashes for India."[5]

Conventions of Performance

Conventions of performance are similar to ancient Sanskrit play production in many respects. A few examples are given below:

(1) Conventional entries and exits accompanied by music and tempo.
(2) Zonal divisions are indicated by stylised going around the stage.
(3) Battles and combats are executed by choreographic movements.
(4) An army is represented by suggestion. In Thailand (Lakon Not), a boy represents a regiment.

Preliminary Ritual (Pūrvaraṅga)

It is an elaborate ceremony in Thailand (Lakon) called Prelang'. The rite is performed by two masked actors, holding peacock feathers in their hands. There is no singing but only drums and music (*śuṣka vādya*?) during the ritual. In *Khon* Pantomime (Thailand) ritual worship of Gaṇeśa and Vairavana (a god of dance) is held before a performance. Actors pray before the Indianised mask of *Khon* in the dressing room. The text of the prayer has Sanskrit influence.

Troupe and its Training

A drama troupe generally consists of a fixed number of actors, musicians, dancers, specialists in female roles, clowns, stage assistants, stage artisans and the troupe leader who is usually the main actor and the stage manager. A troupe is generally formed by hereditary and family groups around a play genre which it is specialised to perform. The play genres are epic dance dramas, war plays, civil plays and so on. Each troupe performs only one of these play-genres.

Training

Training requires rigorous discipline and starts at a young age. The main actor who is also a drama teacher transmits the hereditary techniques in rigorous regime of exercises and practice. The teacher—*guru* in Sanskrit—is known as a *kru* or *gru* in Thai. The role types and different ways of enacting them constitute the principal training. Training is usually acquired by constant observation and imbibing of the nuances of the performances of the elders' enacting the role, over and above the discipline of exercises.

Audience

The spectators watch the performance at their own level of appreciation. Knowledgeable connoisseurs enjoy the subtleties of the actor's skill; some others enjoy the didactic message and moral of the known stories; some appreciate the colourful costumes and dance; and yet others, the music.

The Chinese Opera

A Field Study

The Chinese theatre, especially the Chinese or Peking Opera, combines many common characteristics which probably may have evolved out of interrelations and exchanges with other Asian countries. Nevertheless, there are certain aspects which are undeniably similar to the ancient Sanskrit theatre.

This writer witnessed two Chinese Operas, "The Monkey King" and "The Story of a Run-Away Nun" at the Shanghai Opera Theatre in Shanghai and a number of Peking operas in Beijing and could observe some similarities with the Sanskrit theatre techniques.

The performance started early in the afternoon and lasted until well after midnight. In fact, the main actor made his entry only around midnight. The spectators sat in front of the stage on seats surrounded by tables. There was continuous coming and going of the audience. Tea and refreshments were served on little tables adjoining one's seats all through the performance and the atmosphere in the theatre was that of a cafe theatre. But the audience suddenly perked up and became tense at the time of staging of battles or at the entrance of the main actor.

Stage

The plays resembled Sanskrit theatre production design in many respects. The special stage in a characteristic Chinese Opera theatre is 5 feet high square with red lacquered 20feet high columns on each corner for support of the stage roof. There are two doors on either side of the stage back wall through which an actor goes behind in the dressing room. These doors are curtained and the stage is open to rest of the three sides. Musicians have a special place to sit on the left side of the stage. The entire stage with a roof is housed in a theatre building. This writer has seen many such stages on different floors of a theatre building in Shanghai.

(The sketch No. 5 of the stage with auditorium on p. 66.)

No Drop Curtain

No drop curtain divides the stage from the audience which sits facing the stage frontally. An ornate back drop drapes the back wall of the stage. On occasions symbolic curtains (*javanikā* type) indicating different locations are held by two assistants but they are held behind the character. For example, a piece of black cloth held behind a character symbolised a castle wall.

No Setting

The stage is a bare stage without any sets and sceneries. A simple table and a few ordinary chairs serve the multipurpose of a throne, a garden bench, a tower or a mountain (when the character stands on it) or a prison (when the actor appears from behind the chair).

Character Types, Costumes and Make Up

The Chinese Opera divides itself into genres of military (*Wu*) and civil (*Wen*) plays according to the subject-matter and the types of the main hero. The characters are usually warriors or civilians and they constitute hero (*Shenga*), heroine (*Tana*), clown (*Chu*) and painted faces (*Ching*). The female roles are played by males. The famous Chinese actor, Mai-Lang-Fan was internationally known for his female roles.

The costumes are colourful, gorgeous and elaborate. Their colour significance is symbolic, suggestive and traditional.

The main male and female leads wear heavy make up accentuating their basic features. The clown has white make up with two dots of red on each cheek. The 'painted faces' (*ching*) are conventionally painted with different symbolic colours giving them a mask like appearance. There are 250 designs for standard roles.

Style of Presentation—A System of Conventions

The presentation is stylised with different pitched intonations of speech, conventional movements, singing and music, all of which have a number of suggestive conventions. Here are a few examples of stage conventions which are very similar to the ancient Sanskrit theatre:

(i) All the entries on the stage are done through the left stage door and exits through the right door. The entry-exits are accompanied with music.

(ii) The circular movement (going round on the stage) with various gaits are done to indicate changes of location (*parikramā*).

(iii) Two yellow silk flags with paintings of wheels on them suggest a chariot. The flags are either carried by the actor himself or by two stage attendants preceding him.

(iv) A river or a sea is suggested by a banner with fish and waves painted on it. A character committing suicide in a play jumps behind this curtain from a chair after which the two stage assistants carrying the banner fold it around the actor and the group makes a quick exit.

(v) The battles are choreographic movements. The first actor to make an exit is supposed to have been defeated.

(vi) The death or a swoon is acted by extremely raised eyes and falling backwards into the arms of the stage attendants.

(vii) White bits of papers are thrown on the head of a character to indicate snow. A lantern held in the hand of a character suggests night.

Formerly, the troupe and its training used to be traditional. But now, there are government schools imparting training in the Chinese Opera.

The Noh Play of Japan

The Style of Presentation and the Playhouse

A Field Study

The *Noh* play of Japan is considered to be one of the oldest living drama forms in the world. Its true origin is lost in antiquity and perhaps it would have been entirely lost but for the team work of a father and son who restructured the form by moulding the essential elements of the *Noh* plays of their time. The father, Kisanami is credited with introducing the impersonation while his son Zeami (1363—1440 A.D.) made many innovations in the *Noh* writing and presentation. Thanks to them, the *Noh* theatre traditions, since then, have been handed down unchanged to the present day.

Scholars have recognised a strong but indirect Indian influence upon *Noh* play's assimilation of Japanese imperial palace entertainment called *Bugaku* which is said to have been imported from India some time in the 7th century A.D. With its magic rituals, dancing, music, costumes and masks, *Bugaku*, performed by palace troupes, is said to have been preserved to this day in its pure rendering.[6] Even the Sanskrit names of many melodies are preserved. Certain essential similarities with the Sanskrit theatre tradition, noticed by this writer while witnessing the *Noh* plays are detailed below with specific illustrations.

The Theatre Building

A *raṅgamaṇḍapa*—like stage with a roof supported by four square pillars and a passage way on one side with three potted pine trees dotted on either side gives the theatre and the stage an appearance of a temple sanctuary within a house garden. In fact the shape of the roof is said to be resembling a Japanese shrine.

The Stage

The stage is a 18 feet square platform of polished wood open on all sides except the rear portion of the stage which is walled. The backstage area is behind the wall. It connects the right end of the stage and the make up room called 'the room of the mirror'. There is a wooden passage way called *hashigakari*. A curtained door connects the make up room with this passage. This curtain can be rolled up and let down. The passageway is primarily utilised for the entrance of the actors. At times some scenes are also enacted in the passage. It is said that *Noh* plays were originally performed on austerely platformed stages in the buildings belonging to the holy shrines where such passageways led the priest-actors to the stage from the dressing room. A small door on the left hand corner of the stage is used for inconspicuous entries of the stage assistants and the musicians.

A huge pine tree is painted on the back wall of the stage. As mentioned before, huge pots of pine are also placed at regular points in front of the passageway.

The four pillars on the stage have special names where the actors assume conventional positions suggestive of different meanings.

The Musical Orchestra

The musical orchestra consists of a flutist, three drummers and six to eight singers who sit on the stage all through the performance. They have fixed places to sit on the upstage centre. The vocalists, six to eight in number, sit on the stage at the left.

The audience-performer juxtaposition is intimate and direct with the former sitting facing all open sides of the stage.

(Sketch of the *Noh* stage and Theatre on page 66 sketch no. 6.)

Acoustics

The acoustic quality of these theatres is perfect. No microphone is ever used.

Lighting

Formerly candle lights and daylight sufficed but nowadays, electric lighting is used. However, there are no footlights.

The Style of Presentation

Masks

It is said that the masks which were once exclusive to the *Bugaku* are utilised in the *Noh* plays also. Significantly theatrical make up is not resorted to and the main actor dons a *Noh* mask. Masks are considered sacred and an actor is supposed to be pervaded by the spirit of the character after he dons the mask. Some masks cover the full face while others only half the face. The *Noh* masks are carved out of wood.

Costumes

The costumes of *Noh* are gorgeous and are based on the 15th century fashions of high society. Wigs and headgears are elaborate and picturesque.

Settings

The stage platform is devoid of any settings or sceneries. The stage is bare and can be turned into any locale. There is no drop curtain either.

The Property

Symbolic frameworks made up of bamboo and cane bound by cloth strips represent a boat, a chariot, a rock, a house, a well, a gate, a pine tree and so on. These properties can be easily made. They are symbolic and suggestive and not realistic. They constitute mere outlines of the objects.

So also small hand-held properties like a fan, a cane, a stick, a lute, a rosary or a hand basket which can suggest a variety of meanings by the way in which they are used.

The Preliminary Ritual—Okina

This ritual has an uncanny resemblance to the preliminary—*pūrvaraṅga*—ceremonies of the ancient Sanskrit theatre.

Okina is recognised by the Japanese scholars as a survival of an earlier theatre tradition. Certain sentences during its ritual resemble the Sanskrit language. In earlier period, every *Noh* performance was preceded by elaborate *Okina* rites. When performed now, it still precedes the main performance[7] and has following features:

There is a private worship of the mask in the dressing room by the troupe. Then the principal actor enters the stage unmasked, holding in his hand the same mask which was previously worshipped in the dressing room. The actor comes to the singers and starts a dialogue with them with sentences closely resembling Sanskrit, the meaning of which is now lost.[8] He also does a number of dances.

Then the second actor enters and joins the dance. And then enters the third actor, who is the comedian of the troupe (*vidūṣaka*?). He joins in with an energetic dance. Significantly, the third actor has white face with red and green dots and lines on it. He wears a tall cap on his head. Then the three actors pray for the well-being of the patron and invoke God's blessings for the success of the performance.

The Genres and the Character Types

The *Noh* plays centre around the main actor. The genres of the plays are also known by the main character types and his actions form the main bulk of the plot. For example, the *Noh* plays are classified as (i) god plays, (ii) warrior plays, (iii) guest plays, (iv) demon plays, (v) plays of insanity, (vi) women plays rather than tragedies, comedies, farces, etc. No matter how the individual contents of the plays differ, the outline of the framework of the plot structure and the hero-types remain the same. All plays have, for example, the same list of dramatis personae.

The main actor is called *Sh'te*—meaning the doer or the agent. There is a parallel to the *netānāyaka* concept here. He wears a mask and enacts the key role. Then there is the secondary actor called *Wāki* who always appears in a subordinate role. In some plays child actors appear either in children's roles or in the roles of emperors or high personages. Each role type is played by an actor who belongs to the hereditary school which specialises in that role-type only.

The Style and Conventions

The acting as performed by the *Noh* actors is called *Mai*. It consists of movement patterns, theatrical stances, rhythmic chants, singing and dancing. There is a conventional language of techniques handed down hereditarily which is meaningful only in the *Noh* theatre context. Its understanding requires knowledgeable spectators and connoisseurs. In fact, the *Noh* acting is not realistic or imitative of the ways of the world but like ancient Sanskrit theatre it has to be understood in the framework of its strict conventions.

Here are some instances of the *Noh* staging conventions which show marked similarity to Sanskrit theatre traditions:

(1) Long journeys and changes of location are shown by *parikramā* type going around the stage.
(2) Simultaneous scenes on various stage areas indicating different locales are reminiscent of Sanskrit drama's multi-focal scenes. The stage area of the wooden passage is also used in *Noh* theatre for such scenes.
(3) An actor enters this passageway after the curtain on the make up room door is lifted up. He takes an appropriate stance, stands near the nearest stage pillar and introduces his character and his intention which is very much like a Sanskrit theatre's 'self report' or *ātmanivedanam*.

(4) The movements and music are in complete harmony; the orchestra emphasises each situation, mood and feeling.
(5) Tears are suggested by a *Noh* actor by bowing his masked face while weeping by lifting a hand to the eyes. Joy is conveyed by his uplifted face and smile with a lift of the mask.
(6) The outlines of symbolic framework of stage properties are brought on the stage by the assistants in full view of the audience.
(7) A *kimono* lying on the stage suggests a sick person.
(8) A battle is represented by choreographic movements. A journey or a battle may be compressed into seconds but a single recitation may be prolonged for long duration according to its dramatic value.

The Trainer and the Troupe

The *Noh* troupe consists of the main actors, supporting actors and their assistants, musicians and the technicians. Each group belongs to the hereditary school of specialised performers.

Training starts from a young age of seven. It is intensive and rigorous, demanding constant practice and discipline. An actor is supposed to be reaching his peak form at the age of forty or forty-five. For, it is only then that he is believed to be matured and experienced enough to intuitively improvise and create fresh performances.

Teachers belonging to different family or group traditions are responsible for keeping their particular performing traditions alive.

All roles are played by males.

The word *Noh* itself means 'talent'. And yet, in the *Noh* theatre, talent is not an end in itself. *Noh* drama aspires to higher quality of awareness for which Zeami uses the word *Yogen*.[9] It is a Zen term suggesting the beauty of reverberation, which we may compare to *dhvani* or the 'essence' beneath the ripple of presentation.

The examination of the surviving features of ancient Sanskrit theatre leads to a fairly strong supposition that even in a mutilated form, the various components of the production framework have percolated in the traditional and folk theatres in the length and breadth of India—and even South East Asia, China and Japan. And it is not difficult to suggest that a measure of continuity has been found even in our own times.

Notes

1. Bowers F., Theatre in the East, p. 3.
2. Ibid, p. 122.
3. Brandon James R., Theatre in South East Asia, p. 122.
4. Bowers F., op. cit. p. 150.
5. Brandon James R., op. cit., p. 142.
6. Bowers F., op. cit. pp. 328-29.
7. Arnott P., The Theatres of Japan, p. 62.
8. Data collected in talks with the manager of the Noh Company at Sadler's Wells Theatre, London.
9. Keene D., No the classical theatre of Japan, Introduction. Also, Arnott P., op. cit., p. 92 ff.

PART FIVE

VISUALISATIONS

Bhāsa	:	*(Ūrubhangam*
Kālidāṣa	:	*(Vikramorvaśīyam)*
Śūdraka	:	*(Mṛcchakaṭikam)*
Śri Harṣa	:	*(Ratnavālī)*
Viśākhadatta	:	*(Mudrārākṣasam)*
Bhavabhūti	:	*(Uttararāmacaritam)*
Mahendra Vikrama Varmā	:	*(Mattavilāsā-Prahasanam)*
Vararuci	:	*(Ūbhayābhisārikā-Bhāṇa)*

The lord of the gods, together with the guardians of the quarters, desires to witness today the graceful enactment of the play containing all the eight rasa-s, which the sage Bharata has taught you.

Kālidāsa. Vikramorvaśiyam. Act II, Sh. 17

VISUALISATIONS OF SCENES / SEQUENCES OF SANSKRIT PLAYS

Introduction

After exploring the Sanskrit play production theoretically and testing the clearly visible remnants of their survival in the present day traditional drama forms, one gets a glimpse of different bits of the keleidoscopic pattern of the style in which the Sanskrit plays of Bhāsa to Bhavabhūti must have been produced in ancient India. It is, however, true that the evidence gathered from the surviving traditional forms are mutilated, much changed and fragmentary, but with the help of cross references to the details of techniques enumerated in the works on dramaturgy like the *Nāṭyaśāstra* and the later works it is possible to visualise the production of the Sanskrit plays as well as to explore various sets of practices that must have evolved in the course of the period covering Bhāsa to Bhavabhūti.

It must be stressed at the outset that the conjectural visualisations of these scenes/sequences are attempted from the point of view of their production only. The details of performances, i.e. the details of elaborate, improvisational *abhinaya* are merely hinted at. In Sanskrit theatre it is the performer alone who chooses and improvises from the known parameters of *abhinaya* techniques according to his own ability and understanding and creates the performance. Here, only the mood and the spirit of the situation are indicated.

In each of the selected sequences, only one aspect of production technique is elaborately emphasised and discussed. For example, in the sequence of Bhāsa's *Ūrubhaṅgam*, *Vāc-sattva-aṅga* abhinaya is emphasised, while in the scene of Śri Harṣa's *Ratnāvalī* or Kālidāsa's *Vikramorvaśīyam*, the *nāṭyadharmī* technique of zonal division (*kakṣyā vibhāga*) is stressed. In the same way, in Śūdraka's *Mṛcchakaṭikam*, the question of the usage of the cut-outs (*pusta*) is explored; while in Vararūci's *Bhāṇa* the style of *ekāhārya* abhinaya in a play is examined.

While visualising the productions, the following considerations were constantly kept in view:

1. The *rūpaka* genre of the play.
2. The *sandhi*—i.e. the juncture in the plot (*vastu*) progression that the scene/sequence belongs to.
3. The *rasa* presentation of the scene/sequence as well as that of the play.
4. The style (*vṛtti*) of the scene/sequence as well as that of the play.
5. The regional mode (*pravṛtti*) of the scene/sequence as well as that of the play.
6. Whether the particular scene/sequence demands a *nāṭya-dharmī* or *lokadharmī* performance or both.
7. The dramatis personae featuring in the scene (*netā*). Their place in the *rasa* scheme as supports (*ālambana*) of the principal, subsidiary, concomittant or contradictory *rasa/bhāva*.
8. *Abhinaya*:

   (a) The responses (*anubhāva*-s) with the employment of transitory (*vyabhicāri*) states represented by the body (*āṅgika*).

   (b) Representation of the voice and the speech (*vācika abhinaya*); possible employment of the note (*svara*) dominating the line (*pada*) and the *kāku* to suggest the meanings and implications of the playwright's words.

   (c) *Sāttvika abhinaya*—the responses (*anubhāva*-s) and the transitory states (*vyabhicāri*).
   Very general suggestions are given regarding the above three aspects of *abhinaya*.

   (d) *Āhārya abhinaya*:

   (i) The body paint (*aṅgaracanā*)—the colour employed by the characters.
   (ii) The costumes—the ornaments, the headdresses and the hairstyles of characters.
   (iii) The small property—hand held props (*upakaraṇa*).
   (iv) The use of the seat.
   (v) Small, light cut-outs of sceneries or stage props (*pusta*) used in *lokadharmī* style of presentation.

9. The use of the stage:
   The suggestions regarding the types of the stage (rectangular, square and triangular as described by Bharata) best

suited for presentation of a particular play and the audience-performer juxtaposition. Manner of using the stage area. Design of the zonal division of the stage. Stage groupings.
Entries-exits and the use of the stage doors. Use of *javanikā*; also, processional entries.

10. Lighting: The use of the lamp and torches wherever applicable.
11. Musical orchestra (*Kutapa*):
    The use of music from the musical orchestra—instrumental, dramatic songs (*dhruvā*-s), songs and dance as well as the use of the voices or the noises off from the *kutapa*, and the dressing room.

It is taken for granted that when a reader has come to this point in the study, he is by now fairly familiar—theoretically at least—with most of the important and essential production techniques and the methods of their application in a performance. Explanatory details regarding them given in the first three parts are not repeated here. Sometimes, the Sanskrit technical terms are also freely used to denote various hand gestures, stage walks, eye expressions, accented speeches, voice modulations, etc. For the practical answers of the unavoidable questions regarding their execution, necessary notes are provided. The texts of the sequences and scenes visualised in these chapters are in English rendered by eminent Sanskrit scholars.

It is hoped that the perusal of such conjectural visualisations may give a reader a basis for his own deliberations by revealing, in a purely practical way, one of the methods by which the style of the ancient Sanskrit theatre performance may be applied to a Sanskrit play production today.

The part is divided into two chapters.

It should be noted that in these chapters, the *raṅgapīṭha* is abbreviated as RP, *raṅgaśīrṣa* as RS, *śatdāruka* as SAT and mattavāraṇi-s as MAT/s, *Nāṭyaśāstra* as NS, *Abhinaya Darpaṇa* as AD, *Bhāvaprakāśa* as Bh.P, *Daśarūpaka* as DR.

Chapter 11

SCENES/SEQUENCES FROM: ŪRUBHANGAM, VIKRAMORVAŚĪYAM (I), MṚCCHAKAṬIKAM (VI), RATNĀVALĪ (IV)

Section 1

Bhāsa's Ūrubhaṅgam

(*A sequence in Nirvahaṇa Saṅdhi stage with Aśvatthāmā's entry up to the end*)

1. **Rūpaka**

Bhāsa's *Ūrubhaṅgam* belongs to the *utsṛṣṭikāṅka* variety. The play depicts the atmosphere of the last phase of the great battle of Kurukṣetra after Duryodhana's defeat at the hands of victorious Bhīma who breaks the former's thighs in a combat.

2. **Saṅdhi**: (Juncture in the plot [*vastu*] progression)

Being as *aṅka* variety, it has two *saṅdhi* s (junctures) *mukha* and *nirvahaṇa*. The sequence which is visualised belongs to the last stage of the *nirvahaṇa saṅdhi* featuring Duryodhana's death.

The sequence begins with the entry of furious Aśvatthāmā who is angry at the news of the fall of Duryodhana at the end of the deceitful duel with Bhīma. The mortally wounded Duryodhana is already on the stage in the company of sorrowful queens, the prince, his parents as well as Baladeva who is also in the state of anger. The sequence ends with the death (*svargagati*) of the hero Duryodhana and with the *Bharata vākya* spoken by Baladeva.

3. **Rasa**

Pathetic (*karuṇa*), furious (*raudra*) and heroic (*vīra*) *rasa*-s predominate. The pathetic *rasa* however dominates as a concomitant of the preceding furious *rasa* and yet the play ultimately evokes the heroic *rasa*.

4. **Style** (*Vṛtti*)

Sublime and verbal (*sāttavatī* and *bhāratī*).

5. **Regional Mode** (*Pravṛtti*)

Pāñcālī.

6. **Dharmī**

Nāṭyadharmī presentation: No scenery or even a small cut-out (*pusta*) need be used to indicate the locale of a battlefield. In the beginning of the play itself graphic description of the battlefield of Kurukṣetra has been given through the *vāc-sattva-aṅga abhinaya* by the three warriors. The locale of the last phase of the Kurukṣetra battle has been, thus, imaginatively established.

7. **Netā**: (*Hero and Other Dramatis Personae*)

As discussed in the Part Two (p. 97) Bhāsa intended to evoke the heroic *rasa* by establishing the ultimate achievement of the state of wholeheartedness in the hero, Duryodhana, who is the main support (*ālambana vibhāva*) of the heroic (*vīra*) *rasa*. He is a renowned king, vanquished in the final battle of Kurukṣetra. In the beginning of the play he is shown in acute state of pathos, despair and despondency. The emergence of a serene state of equipoise of the hero from the pathetic depression of the initial stages is the theme of the *rasa*-presentation of the play. The strong but finally subsidiary pathetic *rasa* is all pervading, however, and is also supported by the presence of the sorrowful queens, the prince and the tragic figures of Dhṛtrāṣṭra and Gāndhārī. This shade of pathetic is clearly indicated as resulting from the state of fury (*raudra rasa*) which led to the great battle. Angry Baladeva and furious Aśvatthāmā represent the manifestations of lingering furious *rasa*.

8. **Āhārya**

The Body Paint (*aṅgaracanā*)

(a) Duryodhana—Being a *dhīroddhata* hero, he should be painted with reddish yellow colour (*gaura varṇa*). The entire body is to be so painted. A *rājatilaka* on the forehead and the marks on the face and arms should be painted. Eyes should be elongated.

(b) Aśvatthāmā—Being a brahmin, he should be painted in *gaura varṇa*, with a *tilaka* and marks on the forehead.

(c) Baladeva—*Gaura varṇa.*

(d) Dhṛtrāṣṭra—*Gaura varṇa.*

(e) Durjaya—*Gaura varṇa.*

(B) Costumes

(a) Duryodhana: He is the main support of the heroic and the pathetic with a tinge of the furious *rasa*. His costume—*dhotī*, armour and upper garments would therefore be dominated with reddish yellow and the grey with reddish hues, symbolising the heroic, the pathetic and the furious. He is a superior type of hero (*uttama prakṛti nāyaka*). He would wear a reddish yellow armour, steel grey *dhotī* and a darkish grey upper garment, streaked with red which may also suggest the gushing of the blood from his wounds. He does not have a crown. His hair is ruffled and streaked with blood (red paint). He will wear golden and pearl ornaments—in his ears, neck, arms and wrists. Also he will have weapons.

(b) Aśvatthāmā: His armour would be reddish golden yellow colour, symbolising heroic. His upper garment which may be tied around his waist should have red colour to symbolise his fury (*raudra*). His *dhotī* would be in a different shade of red. He is a superior type of character. He would have a topknot with a prominent crest jewel. He is appropriately ornamented with a few *rudrākṣa* ornaments also. He would have an armour with quiver attached, a bow and a sacred thread.

(c) Baladeva: Yellow *dhotī* with red design and vermillion coloured upper garment partially covering the bare upper body. Prominence of reddish hues suggest furious *rasa*. Moderately jewelled, with a sacred thread, he would have a mace in his hand. He is a superior type of character.

(The sketches of above costumes designs on p. 385).

(d) Durjaya: Should have a *dhotī* dominated with pale grey colour. Appropriately bejewelled as a prince, with a sacred thread.

(e) Dhṛtrāṣṭra: White dhotī and grey upper garment with black design. His grey hair should be in a *śikhā*, a sacred thread with a necklace of *rudrākṣa* beads signifying the stage of his *vānaprastha*.

(f) Gāndhārī and two queens: Gāndhārī in white and the two queens in different shades of greyish green. The lower garments draped in *sakaccha*—dhotī-style with bodices and upper garments.

The style of wearing the *dhotī*-s and the draping of the upper garments can be varied and are visualised from the line drawings of *Gāndhāra*, *Kushana* period sculpture (100 B.C.—100 A.D.) as well as the sculptures of Sanchi (200 B.C.) which is nearer to the time of Bhāsa.

(See sketches and notes on pp. 385 and 387)

9. **The Use of the Stage Area**

The zonal division is designed to accommodate the resources available in the medium rectangular playhouse, as described by Bharata. Accordingly, the stage areas consists of RS, RP and two MAT-s with four rows of pillars (three in each row) on either side of the stage.

Interior Zone

A zone in the centre of the RP would be a position where Duryodhana is seated on the stage, with a group of the two queens and Gāndhārī and Dhṛtrāṣṭra standing on his right somewhere near the line dividing RP and RS. The prince Durjaya is kneeling on his left. Baladeva is standing near a pillar on the extreme right of the RP. This group has established a separate, interior zone in the battlefield.

Exterior Zone

Aśvatthāmā who has entered from the extreme southern side door, (as per the rules of *pāñcālī pravṛtti*) may establish at first a separate zone in the battlefield, which can be termed as exterior. This zone can be established in the extreme downstage in the right MAT.

Thus, he is separated from the other group visually also by the pillars.

10. **Lighting**

The main light source would be the lamp placed in the centre of the downstage edge. The interior row of pillars dividing the MAT from RP can throw added light on the group in the centre with two torches attached to the pillars.

11. Kutapa (Musical Orchestra)

Use of chanting, singing with accompaniment of all instruments specially percussion.

Visualisation

[The zonal division of the stage with the positions of characters on the stage before Aśvatthāmā's entry is already described.

In the visualisation, only the performance—*abhinaya*—is envisaged, with special emphasis on the *vācika abhinaya*.]

Text[1]

(Enter Aśvatthāmā)

Aśvatthāmā: (Repeats the verse, 'As a priest', etc., verse 55). Oh, hearken me, ye kings renowned in war, though few survive and life is slowly ebbing with every breath, though your bodies be mutilated by those crocodiles, the weapons, upraised when the two oceans of opposing forces flowed together in the battle storm, hearken, I say, to me.

'T was the Kuru king had his thighs shattered by

fraud, not I

....

Here today I stand alone. Droṇa's son

......................with sword drawn in eagerness (Verse 57)

But to me too what boots the glory of battle without the praise of victory? (goes round)...The Kuru king.....was tricked... Who will believe it? For,

Verse 58

Now where is Gāndhārī's son? (going around and looking) Ah, here is the king of the Kurus......Here he is,

With the netted beams of his hair fallen dishavelled from his crest, with limbs bleeding from blows of mace, he sits on the stony seat of his last home...

Verse 59

(going up to him) O king of Kurus, what is this?

King: O son of preceptor, the result of insatiable ambition.

Production Notes

The sequence begins in *nirvahaṇa* sandhi stage with Aśvatthāmā's entry. Before his entry Aśvatthāmā's voice has been heard from the dressing room (verse 55.) During verse 56, enacted and sung by Baladeva (with the vocalists accompanying), the introduction of the state of fury of Aśvatthāmā has already been made. After that, Aśvatthāmā enters from the southern side door behind a *javanikā* held by two stage attendants who set it up in the extreme downstage in the right MAT, thus, establishing a separate exterior zone in the battlefield.

Verse 55 is sung again by Aśvatthāmā, from behind the *javanikā*, with the musicians accompanying him. At the end of the verse the *javanikā* is drawn aside and taken back to the dressing room by the attendants. With the rise of percussion, Aśvatthāmā is revealed, in a state of fury, separated from the king's group by the pillars.

He is in *maṇḍala sthāna.*[2]

The prose lines before verse 57 are enunciated by him with head register and extra high pitch (*tāratāra*),[3] with maximum of anger (*krodha*)[4] with transitory states of agitation (*āvega*),[5] indignation (*amarśa*),[6] anxiety (*cintā*)[7] and shame (*vrīḍā*).[8]

Verse 57 is enacted by him with full *bhāvābhinaya* and is sung by him with *ṣaḍja* (sā) and *ṛṣabha* (ri) notes dominating. The speech before verse 58 is presented with utmost fury and anger as well as shame and agitation with *sāttvika bhāvas* like change of colour (reddened face), choking voice, etc. Walking with raised feet of four *tāla*-s high and of three *tāla*-s wide[9] in a gait suggesting his furious state he conducts his going around (*parikramā*) from the left. Drum beats appropriate to the gait accompany the walk around.

After this, Aśvatthāmā, while mainly remaining in *Vaiśākha sthāna*[10] in the downstage RP, chants verse 58 with elaborate exploratory *bhāvābhinaya* in *uddāta kampita* notes[11] in medium fast tempo.

At the end of the verse 58 he goes around (*parikramā*) again in the RP for a number of times accompanied by the rhythm of the percussion. This is to suggest the distance he has to walk to reach the location of the king's group. The rhythm stops when he starts his speech before the verse 59. When he looks at the fallen king, he stands at the extreme left of the group.

Verse 59 is again chanted by him in extra low pitch starting with a chest note raised to head register and brought down to notes of the throat at the close.[12] It is enacted with minimum of *āṅgika* movements and maximum of *sāttvika* and transitory states of anger and shame.

The king, during this time, remains seated in a state of utter despair (*viśāda*) with his head slightly bent on the side[13] and with his hand, at times, supporting his chin. He is sitting on the stage seat[14] which symbolises a rock in the battlefield. Dhṛtrāṣtra, Gāndhārī, Prince Durjaya and the queens are in a state of sorrow. Baladeva is in a state of anger as a result of the foul play committed in the righteous law of fighting.

Aśvatthāmā's state of fury and shame continues when he goes up to the king and joins the interior zone with, "O king. . .What is this?"

King Duryodhana's speech is intoned in a grave low (*nīca*)[15] pitch with a slow note in a state of repentence and remorse with transitory states (*vyabhicāri*-s) of shame and despair.

Text

Aśvatthāmā: King. . .I am about to abandon the root of righteousness.

King: What will you do?

Aśvatthāmā: Listen.

Kṛṣṇa is ready for the fight..........

....

him I will wipe out..... ....

And the sons of Pāṇḍu with him. . . (Verse 60)

King: Nay, say not so.

The whole host of anointed kings now lies in the lap of the mother earth

....

............................I am brought to this plight.

Preceptor's son, unstring thy bow. (Verse 61)

Aśvatthāmā: O, King of Kurus,

When the Pāṇḍava in the fight today. . .cast his mace. . . He broke thy spirit with thy two thighs. (verse 62)

King: Kings have pride incarnate. For pride's sake I accepted war...

How Draupadī aforetime was dragged at the gambling match...how young Abhimanyu....was slain in battle, how the Pāṇḍavas...had to dwell in forest...those have done to break my spirit. (Verse 63).

Aśvatthāmā: I take an oath...

...I will make a raid by night
and destroy the Pāṇḍavas in fight
....
....(Verse 64)

Production Notes

This sub-sequence indicates the saṅdhyaṅga (unit of a juncture) of *granthanam* or the intimation of denouncement. Aśvatthāmā reveals here his intention of taking revenge for the foul action of Pāṇḍava by adopting similar means. He announces that he will slay the Pāṇḍavas by a raid at night.

Verse 60 is intoned by him in *udātta kampita* tone with fast tempo. With energetic resolve it is enacted with the transitory states of anger and arrogance (*garva*) predominating.

The king is in a state of dejection and sorrow. Verse 61 is recited by him in grave, low and deliberate tone with *bhāvābhinaya* of *sāttvika* and transitory states of despair, agitation, shame, depression and despondence presented through heavy deep sighs, tears, choking voice etc. Through non-*sauṣṭhava* of his bent body, hand gestures, and facial expressions (*hasta* and *mukhaja abhinaya*) he elaborately recounts the loss of his brothers, friends and revered elders and attempts to dissuade Aśvatthāmā from his resolve.

The states of pathos and despondence of the king are continuously contrasted by Aśvatthāmā's states of fury and anger in this sequence thereby presenting the pathetic and furious *rasa*-s as going together. Aśvatthāmā chants the verse 62 with notes of the throat. The last line rebuking the broken hearted king is intoned by him with raised chest note.

In the *sandhyāṅga* (unit of a juncture)—*nirṇaya*, the dejected king recollects his experiences and preaches reconciliation with destiny. In verse 63, he enumerates his sinful actions against

Draupadī, Abhimanyu and others in the manner of *ekāhārya abhinaya* where he impersonates the characters whom he is describing as well as his own past behaviour which is represented mainly with transitory states of recollection (*smṛti*),[16] shame as well as *sāttvika*-s like perspiration, change of colour and change of voice. The verse is intoned by the king with notes of *dhaivata* (dha) and *niṣāda* (ni). Finally he advocates acceptance of consequences of his misdeeds.

Aśvatthāmā's oath of revenge and verse 64 are recited with exited determination in a high pitch. The verse is delineated with transitory states of cruelty (*ugratā*), arrogance and anger while maintaining the standing position of *Vaiśākha*.

Text

Aśvatthāmā: Durjaya, come here.

Be thou king.........
.........of a kingdom
inherited through the valour
of thy sire..................... (verse 65)

King: Ah! my heart's desire is now fulfilled. My life is slipping away. Here are my revered ancestors.......................................

Death has sent an aerial car, the wain of heroes, drawn by thousand swans to fetch me. Here I come (Expires).

[They cover him with a cloth (*javanikā*)]

Dhṛtarāṣṭra: I'll depart for the penance grove so rich in pious folks.. . .

Aśvatthāmā: Now do I depart. . .for the slaughter of the sleepers.

Baladeva: May the king destroy all enemies and protect the earth. (Verse 66)

[Exeunt omnes]

Production Notes

This is the sandhyāṅga *ānandi* which denotes the attainment of the desire of the hero.

Aśvatthāmā calls prince Durjaya and declares him heir to the kingdom. With the others joining him and the dying king looking on, the consecration ceremony of the prince is enacted in the down stage centre of RP with elaborate citrābhinaya.[17]

Verse 65 is sung by Aśvatthāmā, with the vocalists and musicians joining him, in a medium pitch with the main notes of *ṣaḍja* (sā), *ṛṣabha* (ri) in *ṣaḍjī* and *ārṣabhi* with transitory states of assurance (*mati*), deliberation (*vitarka*) and a resolution of purpose.

After a moment of sudden silence which follows the completion of enactment of the consecration ceremony accompanied by the crescendo of percussion instruments, the king, looking on from the seat in the centre of the RP, intones the words: "Ah, my heart's desire is now fulfilled." He utters them in an exultant state with a glimmer of enthusiasm (*utsāha*), contentment (*dhṛti*) and emerging confidence but in a low pitch. A pause follows his utterance.

Then the *abhinaya* of death is enacted by the king in a very slow, broken and yet deliberately enunciated low pitched death speech indicating his ultimate contentment at the fulfilment of his desire and a buoyant state of self-assurance that he is dying a hero's death and going to heaven (*svarga gati*) from where his revered ancestors, brothers and friends are beckoning him. This is done with all the eight *sāttvika* and transitory states utilised in the traditional depiction of death in all its stages.[18]

After the king dies, two stage attendants enter from the right side stage door with a *javanikā* and stand in front of the dead king. Percussion music, wailing of the queens, tears of the old parents and sobs of the prince accompany their action after which there is a sudden cessation of all stage activities including music.

Verse 66 is recited, then, by Dhṛtrāṣṭra, Aśvatthāmā and Baladeva (who comes forward and recites the last line of the śloka as an actor proper—i.e. *bharata*—indicating that the line is the Bharata vākya of the play).

The first line is recited by Dhṛtarāṣṭra with sorrow, weakness (glāni) and *vibodha* signaling his resolve to enter a penance grove.

Next two lines re-emphasising his firm determination of taking revenge are recited by Aśvatthāmā with states of arrogance (*garva*), assurance (*mati*) and anger (*krodha*).

The fourth line is recited by Baladeva (as an actor proper)

with *vibodha* and *dhṛti* (awakening and contentment). The play is over at this point.

The fourth line is the *Bharata vākya*—actor's benediction—of this play. It is sung by all the actors including the *sūtradhāra* who enters the stage with the rest of the troupe and also by the musicians from the *kutapa.* (It is quite possible that in ancient times, the drama troupe might have incorporated an added verse of *Bharata vākya* from its own repertoire.)

After the singing of *Bharata vākya* is over, the actors go behind the *javanikā* and exit with it from the left side door of the stage with a crescendo of percussions. After that, the musicians from the *kutapa* also take their exits.

On the bare stage remain the ensigna and the upper garment of Duryodhana, the Kuru king (which symbolises his dead body).

NOTES

1. The text translated in English and edited by A. C. Woolner and Lakshman Sarup (13 Trivendrum Plays Attributed to Bhāsa, Vol. II, Oxford University Press, 1931, pp. 56-58).
2. NS, XI, 65-66 (tr. M. Ghosh).
3. NS, XIX, 45.
4. NS, VII, 16.
5. NS, VII, 63.
6. Ibid, 78, 79.
7. Ibid, 50.
8. Ibid, 58.
9. NS, XIII, 48-54.
10. NS, XI, 65-66 (tr. M. Ghosh).
11. NS, XIX, 43.
12. NS, XIX, 42-43.
13. NS, XIII, 197-98.
14. For details about the stage seat, see Chapter 6, pp. 181-82
15. NS, XIX, 45-50.
16. NS, VII, 53.
17. It connotes varied representation of different activities through hand gestures, facial and eye expressions as well as body movements. For details, see Chapter 6, pp. 139-40
18. NS, VII, 86.

SECTION 2

Kālidāsa's Vikramorvaśīyam

(**Sequence**: The beginning of Act I, after the prologue, up to the re-entry of King Purūravas with rescued heroine Urvaṣī with her friend Citralekhā)

1. Rūpaka

It is a *toṭaka* genre[1] of rūpaka, because here the love and the union of a divine heroine (celestial nymph Urvaṣī) and a human hero (King Purūravas) is depicted.

2. Sandhi: (Juncture in plot [*vastu*] progression)

Act I establishes the *mukha sandhi*, the sowing of the seed (*bīja*) of the love between the king and the divine nymph *Urvaśī*. The initial sprouting of attraction (*abhilāśā*) or *pūrvarāga*, the first state of the love (erotic), is depicted in a succession of happenings in a quick tempo. The cry of *apsarā*-s in distress, the entry of the king in a chariot somewhere in the aerial regions, the meeting with the *apsarā*-s the return with the rescued heroine and her friend on the peak of the *Hemakūṭa* mountain and the germination of love between Purūravas and Urvaśī are some of the fast moving incidents in the sequence.

3. Rasa

The *rasa* presented is erotic, with marvellous as subsidiary *rasa*, with a slight tinge of the terrible.

4. Style (Vṛtti)

Kaiśikī (graceful).

5. Regional Mode (Pravṛtti)

Āvanti.

6. Dharmī

The play is a perfect *nāṭyadharmī* expression with the characters from heaven and earth intermingling. They move about in the sky or collect on a top of the Hemakūṭa mountain in this continuously progressing sequence of Act I. The *āṅgika, vācika, sāttvika* as well as *āhārya abhinaya* would be extremely stylised with maximum use of symbolism.

7. **Netā**: (Adhikārī hero and other dramatis personae)

The hero and the heroine are the chief supports (*ālambana vibhāva*) of the principal erotic *rasa*. The other *apsarā-s* and specially the heroine's friend, Citralekhā, are the assistants (*kāmasahāyikā*-s) performing the task of female messengers (*dūtī*-s), helping the progress of love.

All characters are superior types except the charioteer who is an inferior type.

8. **Āhārya**

(1) The Body Paint (*Aṅgaracanā*)

(a) Purūravas: He is a *dhīralalita* hero. And so he is to be painted "reddish white (lotus) colour".[2]

(b) Apsarās: (Urvaśī, Citralekhā, Rambhā, Menakā, Sahajanyā) being celestials are painted in reddish yellow (*Gaura varṇa*).[3]

(c) The Charioteer: Darkish blue colour.

(2) The Costumes and accessories:

(a) Purūravas wears a half *dhotī* of mauve colour, with dull magenta yellow half armour. His upper garment (*uttarīya*) is variegated[4] with mauve, grey, green and tawny colour predominating. He wears a conical crown (*kirīṭa*).[5] His feet are in a *pādaveṣṭanika*. He is tastefully bejewelled in pearl and golden ornaments.

(b) Urvaśī: In the sequence of the Act I, the heroine is to be dressed in green colour of the shade of a parrot's tale,[6] dominating with lower garment of parrot colour worn in a *dhotī* fashion. And short colaka in deep emerald green with a loose acquamarine green coloured upper garment (*uttarīya*) studded with precious stones. She would have elaborate hair style and ornaments depicting pearls and jewels[7] covering her from the 'head to toes' (*nakhaśikha*).

(c) Apsarā-s: The other *apsarā-s* would have bright coloured clothes like pale yellow, pale blue and reddish yellow and variegated. They would have elaborate coiffures; Citralekhā would don a turban. They would be decked with ornaments resembling jewels.

(d) The Charioteer: He would be pompously dressed in *dhotī* of dull olive green with half jacket of dull tawny colour with red print, cummerband and turban.

The style of draping the dresses: The style of wearing the *dhotī*, lower garments and draping of the upper garments as well as their accessories are based on Ajanta cave paintings (caves 2, 17) and sculptures of about the Gupta period.

(The sketches of costumes designs with notes on p. 384-99)

9. The Use of the Stage

The zonal division for the sequence is worked out on the basis of resources available in the medium rectangular play house as described by Bharata.

The Zonal Divisions of the Stage

(a) The entrance of the three *apsarās*, Rambhā, Menakā and Sahajanyā is visualised behind a *javanikā* held by two stage assistants in the upstage area in the centre RS, right in front of the *kutapa*. The *javanikā* would be brought by them on the stage when the *sūtradhāra* finishes reciting the second verse of the prologue. The first cry of the *apsarās*: "May he protect us, may he protect us. . ." etc. would come from behind this *javanikā* after the introductory song (*prāveśikī dhruvā*) is over. After the end of the *dhruvā* singing, the *javanikā* would be drawn aside by the stage assistants revealing the three *apsarās* in a visually attractive grouping.

(b) The king's entry, with the charioteer preceding him would be from the stage northside door as per *Āvanti pravṛtti*. Both of them would enter and go straight to the group of the *apsarās* in the aerial *apakrāntā* cāri[8] in the middle of RS.

(c) After the conversation with the *apsarās*, the king and the charioteer, enacting "the speed of the chariot" would take a curve round the stage during the recitation of the fourth verse and take the exit by the northern side door of the stage. This they would do in *atikrāntā* aerial *cārī*.[9]

(d) After the *abhinaya* of the descent from the sky on the top of the *Hemakūṭa* mountain, the group of *apsarās* would establish a zone in the right MAT of the stage in the extreme downstage area.

(e) The re-entry of the group of the king with Citralekhā and the unconscious Urvaśī, as well as the charioteer is visualised behind the *javanikā* brought on the stage by two stage assistants from the north side stage door right in the centre of the RP after Rambhā says: "Here is in sight the chariot, Somadatta. . ." etc. After her speech the curtain is drawn aside to reveal a pictorially composed unit of the kings's group. This entry would be made more effective with the accompanying music.

10. Lighting

The main source of light is the lamp on the downstage centre edge.

11. Kutapa

Full use of instrumental as well as vocal music.

Visualisation

Text

(Then enter the nymphs of heaven)

All (nymphs): Help! Help! He who is a friend of the gods and who can move in the region of the sky. . . .

Production Notes

Zone: As said before, the zone is in the RS centre exactly before the *kutapa*.

Stage grouping: Before and during the removal of the *javanikā*, the introductory song (*prāveśikī dhruvā*) for the nymphs is sung by the vocalists from the *kutapa*. The *dhruvā* chosen is in *ramyā* metre in Prakrit. The meaning of the text would be:

> "The terrific black clouds which are roaring and covering the world are creating an alarm."[2]

Traditionally the 'clouds' symbolise the demons (*daitya* and *rākṣasa*) as per *Nāṭyaśāstra* XXXII, 408, which is quite appropriate for the situation in the play.

After the *javanikā* is drawn aside, we see Rambhā in *āyāta sthāna* in the centre of the group.[3] Her hands are in *dola hasta* indicating hurry and excitement,[4] with *bhayānvitā* glance[5] with *unnata* neck.[6] Menakā is on her right in a profile, and is turned towards Rambhā so that only her side view is seen. She is in *avhittha sthāna*,[7] with her hands covering half of her face, her glance is *trastā*.[8] Sahajanyā, on Rambhā's left, is in *aśvakrāntā sthāna*,[9] with *dola hasta* and *bhayānvitā* glance looking in the distance. She is slightly behind Rambhā.

The entry of king Purūravas.

Text

(Then enter suddenly king Purūravas in a chariot and charioteer.)

King: Away with cries. Come to me, Purūravas, who am just returned after having attended upon the Sun, and tell me what your ladyships are to be protected from.

Rambha: From the violence of the demons.

King: And what offence has the violence of the demons given to your ladyships?

Production Notes

The king Purūravas enters with a toss of the north side door curtain and his entry is unannounced (*nasūcitasya pātrasya praveśa*)[10] preceded by his charioteer. Both are enacting the gait of the riding of a chariot, with short steps,[11] as per the gaits of their own character types (*prakṛti*). The king moves with short steps and he imitates the movement of being carried in a chariot with a bow in one hand and the pole of the chariot in the other. The charioteer precedes him with quick and simple steps and remains busy with the whips and the reins.[12]

The speeches between the king and Rambhā are executed with the king remaining on the left side of the RP and the apsaras in the centre RS.

Text

Rambhā: May your Majesty hear. She, who is the tender weapon of the great Indra whenever he is alarmed by unusual austerities, she who shamed Lakṣmī, proud of her beauty, and who is the ornament of heaven—she, our dear friend Urvaśī, while wending her way was taken captive, along with Citralekhā, by Keśin a demon living in Hiraṇyapūra, who was seen all of a sudden, while we were on our way back.

King: Do you know in what direction the miscreant has gone?

Shanjanyā: In the north-east.

King: Banish your sorrow then. I will try to restore your friend.

All: This is worthy of one who is removed one degree from Soma.

King: Charioteer, turn the horses towards the north-easterly direction, and urge them to swift light.

Charioteer: As your Majesty of long life commands. (Does accordingly).

King: Well done! Well done . . . Verse 4 (Exit king in the chariot with charioteer).

Production Notes

Rambhā in her speech describing the captivity would describe with accurate hand gestures and facial expressions the *bhāvāvasthā* of all the suggested implication of Urvaśī's captivity by demon Keśin and the reaction of the *apsarās* to the episode. For her *abhinaya* she will come forward, and take the centre of the RP and take all the available light from the central lamp. The other two *apsarās* will be partially seen in the play of light and shade.

Rambhā will indicate Urvaśī with *Sūcī hasta*[22]—to describe her as a "tender weapon . . . of Indra", she will use *Haṃsāsya*[23] in a creeper form with *Śukatuṇḍa*[24] *hasta* near the eyes to indicate the piercing weapon. Lakṣmī is suggested with two *Kapittha*[25] *hasta*-s near the shoulder and Kubera with two *muṣṭī hasta*-s with right hand up and left one down, as per *Abhinaya Darpaṇa*[26] Keśin with two *śakata hasta*-s near the mouth. While Hiraṇyapūra is suggested by the left hand stretched out and up with *alapadma hasta*; while the right hand with a finger pointing towards it.[27]

The *mukhajā abhinaya* would suggest fear by delineation of transitory states of fright, agitation, depression, anxiety in quick succession. The *sāttvika bhāva*-s used at appropriate places would be tears, change of colour, choking, horripilation and tremor.

The king and the charioteer are on the left of the RP. His speeches are to be spoken from there.

When the nymphs indicate the peak of Hemakūṭa on the extreme right MAT on the downstage, the king with his charioteer again resumes the movement of the chariot, by repeating the same gaits of riding in a chariot.

Verse 4 is recited in *śārdūlavikrīḍita* metre conjuring up images of wind and clouds of dust produced by the speeding wheels of the chariot and the banner cloth resting evenly between the points of the staff in the chariot. The musicians from the *kutapa* would provide the accompanying rhythm and music to give an appropriate effect of the speeding chariot. In this atmosphere, the king and his charioteer would take their exit from the stage southern door. The *apsarās* would be in the back of RP.

Text

Rambhā: Friends, the royal sage is gone, therefore, let us also repair to the spot as appointed.

The Rest: Let us do so.

(They all represent descending on the mountain and wait.)

Rambhā: Will the royal sage extract the dart (of anxiety) from our hearts?

Menakā: Friends, do not doubt. Even the great Indra, when a war is at hand, invites him with great honour from the middle world and appoints him at the head of his army which is (then) always victorious.

Rambhā: May he be quite victorious in this adventure too. (After a moment's pause). Be of good cheer, friends! Here is in sight the chariot Somadatta of the royal sage, with its flag bearing the sign of the deer, streaming on high. He cannot have returned without accomplishing his object. (All look with upturned eyes).

Production Notes

The representation of the descent of the *apsarās* on the top of the Hemakūṭa mountain can be executed by three of them in different ways.

Rambhā can descend in the *gaṅgāvataraṇa karaṇa*[28] (as suggested by Rāghavabhaṭṭa in his Artha Dyo., in another context[29]) or she may employ *vṛścikarecita karaṇa*.[30] Menakā can descend in *viṣṇukrāntā karaṇa* and *tripatākā hasta*-s held over the uplifted foot to represent the descent.[31] Sahajanyā can perform *atikrāntā cārī* with one foot, the other foot in the *añcita* movement, with her body slightly bent.[32]

After establishing a zone on the mountain summit in the right downstage MAT with these movements, the *apsarās* would do *bhāva abhinaya* of the speeches; at the end of which all three should look with upturned eyes.

Text

(Then re-enters the king seated in the chariot, the charioteer and Urvaśī supported by Citralekhā with her eyes closed in terror.)

Citralekhā: Take cheer, dear friend, take cheer.

King: Take courage, fair nymph, take courage.

Verse 5

Citralekhā: Alas! How is it that she, the only sign of whose life, is her hard breathing, does not regain consciousness?

King: Her ladyship is terribly frightened.

Verse 6

Citralekhā: Dear Urvaśī, compose yourself. You don't seem (to act like) a nymph of heaven.

(Urvaśī revives.)

King: Ah, your friend is coming to herself.

Verse 7

Citralekhā: Friend, take courage. The wretches, the enemies of Gods, have very certainly been defeated.

Urvaśī: (opening her eyes) What, by the great Indra who sees by supernatural power?

Citralekhā: Not by the great Indra; by this royal sage Purūravas, whose power equals that of great Indra.

Urvaśī: (looking at the king herself—speaking to herself [ātmagatam]) The demons have indeed obliged me.

Production Notes

The re-entry of the king in a chariot, with the rescued Urvaśī who is unconscious, and who is supported by Citralekhā is visualised behind a *javanikā*. The *javanikā* is brought by two stage assistants from the northern side door right up to the centre of the RP after *Rambhā* utters the words: "Here is in sight the chariot, Somadatta . . . etc." After her speech with the percussion music, *javanikā* is drawn aside to reveal a pictorially composed unit of the king's group.

The charioteer should be shown to be drawing the reins of the chariot, with *kaṭaka-mukha hasta*, and thereby halting the chariot. The chariot itself is suggested by the *āṅgika abhinaya* of both the actors. Physical aids like reins, whips or flag staff are not used. The position of the chariot as depicted is somewhere near the skies of the Hemakūṭa summit which is delineated by the *āṅgika* movement of the watching *apsarās* with their heads upturned and by the king's group with their eyes looking down, executing an *atikrāntā* aerial *cāri* ending in samapāda sthāna. The king's group consists of *Urvaśī* who appears as if she is leaning on the arms of the king, in an unconscious state with her eyes closed in terror. She is also supported by Citralekhā. All the three are standing.

The king recites verses 5, 6 and 7[33] by looking at the heroine longingly in the first stage of love (*pūrva rāga*) showing the beginning of love which is called as sprouting or an attraction (*abhilāśā*). He does this with *kāmyā* and *lalitā* glances and *sāttvika bhāva*-s like horripilation.

At the same time, in the style of *nivṛtyāṅkura* he describes by his *vācika* the minute *āṅgika* movements that Urvaśī enacts. The unconscious, terrified state of Urvaśī is represented by the actress through the *sāttvika bhāva*-s which accompany the swoon; namely inaction, imperceptible breathing and responses (*anubhāva*) of fear and transitory states of weakness and apprehension like tremor, palpitation, tight lips, loose limbs, weak voice, and dryness of mouth, etc.

Urvaśī opens her eyes, comes to full consciousness and when she realises the true identity of her rescuer, she enacts the two stages of *bhāva* and *hāva*[34] depicting the emotion of the kindling of love (*icchā* or attraction) through the movements of eyebrows, the *recaka* of the neck, turning her head in bashfulness with shy glances before uttering her sentence to herself (*ātmagata*).[35] The utterance of her first words is her graceful verbalisation of her feelings (*bhāva*) in a definite expression (*helā*).

Thus, in the beginning of the play the seed of the state of love (*rati*) is sown and sprouted. The first stage, namely the attraction (*abhilāśā* or *pūrvarāga*) is established in this particular sequence.

Notes

1. Bh. P. VIII, 115, also 113-14 (For definition and description).
2. NS, XXIII, 90 (tr. M. Ghosh) 90-100.
3. Ibid.
4. NS, XXIII, 131-32 (tr. M. Ghosh).
5. Although Nāṭyaśāstra lays down that only divine heroes wear crowns (*kirīṭa*), Dr. Motichandra gives evidence of Tamil literature to substantiate the claim that many of the crowns of the kings and princes in Ajanta frescoes (Gupta period) are *kirīṭa*. (Dr. Motichandra, op. cit. p. 45.) So I have given *Kirīṭa* (crown) to Purūravas and Rāma (Uttararāmacaritam).
6. NS, XXIII, 59.
7. Ibid, 53.
8. NS, XI, 31. *Valana* position of the two thighs, a *kuñcita* foot raised and thrown sideways (tr. M. Ghosh).
9. NS, XI, 30: A *kuñcita* foot thrown up, put forward and caused to fall on the ground (tr. M. Ghosh).
10. Text translated into English and ed. by M. R. Kale (Rev. and enlarged), pub. by A. R. Sheth & Co., Bombay-2, pp. 13-21.
11. NS, XXXII, 91-92 (tr. M. Ghosh).
12. NS, XIII, 160-64 (tr. M. Ghosh) (fig. No. 7 on p. 139).
13. NS, IX, 141.
14. NS, VIII, 58.
15. NS, VIII, 167-71.
16. NS, XIII, 164-67 (Fig. No. 8 on p. 139).
17. NS, VIII, 80.
18. NS, XIII, 167-69 (Fig. No. 9 on p. 139).
19. Kale M.R., Commentary in Sanskrit on VIK p. 14-1-1 also Supra, p. 210
20. NS, XIII, 88-92, tr. M. Ghosh (gait of one riding in a chariot).
21. Ibid, 92-95 and 88-92.
22. AD, sl. 128.
23. AD, sl. 156.
24. AD, sl. 116.
25. AD, sl. 208.
26. AD, sl. 215.
27. AD, sl. 148.
28. NS, IV, 169 (tr. M. Ghosh).
29. Vatsayan K., Classical Indian Dance in Literature and Arts, p. 228.
30. NS, IV, 107 (tr. M. Ghosh).
31. Ibid.
32. NS, XIII, 96-98 (tr. M. Ghosh).
33. Verse 5 in Upajāti metre; verse 6 may be recited as a prose piece an verse 7 in Mandākrāntā metre.
34. NS, XXIV, 7.
35. DR, II, 10; also Bh. P. I, 43-46, also SD, III, 93, 94, 95.

Section 3

Śūdraka's Mṛcchakaṭikam (VI)

(A sequence dominated by realistic [laukika] dramatis personae mainly of the middle and inferior types in the act named 'The Interchange of the Carts'.)

(1) Rūpaka

This is a well-known *prakaraṇa*—a genre of *daśarūpaka*. It is a *saṅkīrṇa* or mixed type of a *prakaraṇa* which has a courtesan as a heroine and a *dhīrapraśānta* brahmin nobleman (Cārudatta) as a hero.[1]

(2) Sandhī

The sequence appears in the *garbha sandhi* stage of the plot progression where the germ of the state of love (*rati bhāva*) between the hero and the heroine has been fully unfolded. However, its perfect fruition is hampered at this stage by temporary obstacles which themselves suggest the possibility of a permanent solution. In other words, the hero and heroine have united in love and yet a divine obstacle appears in the episode of the exchange of carts whereby the heroine gets separated from the hero. At the same time, the ultimate solution which can result in their marriage is also introduced in the character of Āryaka, who is the leader of the episode (*prakarī nāyaka*).

(3) Rasa

The erotic *rasa* is the principal *rasa*. All the other *rasa*-s except marvellous, furious and odious are inter-sprinkled.

(4) Style (Vṛtti)

Verbal (*bhāratī*) with a sprinkling of graceful (*kaiśikī*).

(5) Regional Mode (Pravṛtti)

Āvanti.

(6) Dharmī

Lokadharmī presentation.

This sequence contains a number of realistic and common

types of characters in a milieu which depicts the worldly (*laukika*) happening in a busy, bustling street in the city of Ujjain culminating in the exchange of carts. An attempt is made here to present it in a *lokadharmī* convention because this is one sequence where the usage of *pusta*, in the form of a cut out of a bullock cart, can be definitely visualised.

(7) Neta

Adhikārī hero and other dramatis personae:

(i) *Vasantasenā*: The heroine—the support of the principal erotic rasa. A superior type.

(ii) *Āryaka*: The leader of the episode who appears for the first time in the play and proves to be the ultimate helper of the lovers. He offers the final solution-marriage; so that the germ of love (*rati*) which has sprouted between the lovers and which is seen and lost by turn because of obstacles, can find its final frutition. A superior type.

(iii) *The Two Ceṭa-s*: Cart drivers, both of whom finally help the lovers.

(a) *Sthāvaraka Ceṭa*: The driver of the cart of Śakāra, the *pratināyaka*. He is a simple soul, godfearing and honest, who desperately attempts to save the innocent hero—Cārudatta. Inferior type.

(b) *Vardhamānaka Ceṭa*: The driver of the cart of Cārudatta, who makes a faux pas in mistakenly carrying away Āryaka instead of the heroine in his cart. Inferior type.

(iv) *The Two City Guards*: Both are inferior types with their independent loyalties. They perform their duty of inspecting the vehicles on the street, searching for the escaped prisoner, Āryaka. Of them:

Vīraka is a loyal servant of the autocracy represented by the king's brother-in-law, Śakāra. *Candanaka* is a conscentious officer, who refused to be bullied and is obviously sympathetic to the revolting elements of the city with Āryaka as its leader.

Thus, we have, in this sequence not only the introduction of the leader of the episode, but two sets of character types who are almost individualistic and who are cleverly connected together. They help and hinder the fulfilment of the main aim of the play which is the evocation of erotic (*śṛṅgāra*) rasa. The *adhikārī* hero—Cārudatta —is absent in the sequence.

(8) **Āhārya**

(a) The body paint (*Aṅgaracanā*):

(1) *Vasantasenā*: She is courtesan heroine, the main support of erotic *rasa* of the play. She belongs to the Ujjain city and would thus fall into *Āvanti* category of the regional behavioural pattern.[2]
She would be painted reddish yellow, with a design (*pattrāvali*) drawn on the forehead and the cheeks, with an elaborate *tilaka* on her forehead and the sandal wood paste on her arms and body.

(2) *Āryaka*: He is a cowherd—a *śudra*. Accordingly, he would be painted dark deep blue.

(3) *Ceṭī*: The maid servant of the heroine. She would be painted in a deep shade of dark brown colour with a *tilaka* on her head.

(4) *Two Ceṭa-s and two city guards*: Painted in various shades of deep dark blue or brown.

All characters would have elongated eyes drawn with lamp black. The women would have red lips. The *ceṭa*-s, the city guards and Āryaka would have moustache (also beards) of various shapes.

(b) The Costumes and the Accessories:

(1) *Vasantasenā*: In this sequence, she is shown as setting out for a tryst with her lover, the hero, in a city garden. Her costume, however, would be the same as *abhisārikā veśa* in which she had come to meet the hero, Cārudatta, at his house, the previous evening. She would be without any ornaments which she has given away to the son of Cārudatta in a previous scene. Her costume is described in the text itself as "an exceedingly gorgeous dress".[3]
She would wear a lower garment, tucked in a *lūṅgī* fashion, with variegated coloured stripes with *śyāma* and yellow colour predominating, a breast cloth of yellowish white colour, an upper garment of light violet blue loosely held on one shoulder, with the other end covering the face in an *avaguṇṭhana* (or veil) style. She would have elaborate

coiffure with flowers. She would also wear garlands of flowers around her neck, arms and wrists.

(2) *Āryaka*: He has escaped from the city jail. So he would have a dirty, torn half *dhotī*, and a tattered upper garment. The colour of both the garments would be *malina*—dirty -greyish dull brown. He would have a growth of beard and a broken chain in one leg.

(3) *Sthāvaraka Ceṭa*: The cart driver of the king's brother-in-law would be more foppishly dressed than the other *ceṭa*. He would wear a blue coloured half *dhotī* and a dark red *paṭṭa* as a head band—binding his hair. He would have a whip in his hand.[4]

(4) *Vardhamānaka Ceṭa*: The cart driver of Cārudatta would have a slightly faded mustard printed half *dhotī* with a dull green upper garment tucked around his waist band and a red band binding his hair. He would have greyish moustache and hair. He would also have a whip in hand.

(5) *Vīraka and Candanaka*: Both in pale mustard and reddish brown *dhotī*-s and contrasting turbans. Vīraka would have a half jacket (*kañcuka*) of printed cloth with a belt. Both would have weapons tucked in the belts of their waists.

(6) *Ceṭī*: Vasantasenā's handmaid would be dressed in a gaily printed half *dhotī* in maroon printed design and a half sleeved bodice (*colaka*) in blue stripes. Her hair would have a top knot on one side of the head; with flowers tucked in them.

(The sketches of the costumes with notes are on pp. 388-89).

Men's costumes are based on the styles of draping of *dhotī*'s, waist cloths (*Kamarbandha*-s) made of cloth pieces, ropes and leather, and head bands (*paṭṭa*-s) seen from sculptural friezes found from Mathura Ajanta Cave No. 17 (Gupta period) and Buddhist sculpture from Goli Stūpa (Gupta period). The costumes of women are approximated from Ajanta (Cave No. 17).

Pusta: A framework of a cart, made of cane-pieces bound by colourful stripe of cloth. (See the sketch No. 9 on p. 400). In such a cut out the characters like Āryaka and Vasantasenā are fully seen by the audience, and their *abhinaya* can be relished by the spectator when in fact they are meant to be concealed inside the carts. In this way the style can intermix with the *nāṭyadharmī* tradition. The model work of the cart can be categorised as *ceṣṭima pusta* depicting moving objects.[5]

9. The Use of the Stage

The zonal divisions are worked out on the basis of resources available in the medium rectangular playhouse, as described by Bharata. Cārudatta's house is established in the RS centre region just in front of the *kutapa*. The interior zone is established there.

The zone for the street scene is established in the RP and the two MAT regions.

10. Lighting

The light source is the lamp placed in the centre of the down-stage edge of the RP.

11. Kutapa

Full use of musical orchestra.

Visualisation

The sequence starts with Vasantasenā seen decorating herself with flower garlands with the assistance of the *Ceṭī*. The actress is fully adorned with flower ornaments. Here they enact the decoration with *abhinaya* alone. They are standing in the upstage centre of RS. The Sthāvaraka *Ceṭa*, with a framework of the cart, and with a whip in hand, enters through the right stage door.

Text[6]

(Entering, mounting the cart)

Sthāvaraka Ceṭa: I have been ordered by the king's brother-in-law Sansthānaka, "Sthāvaraka, taking the cart, come quickly to the old garden Puṣpakaraṇḍaka. Well, I shall go just there. Lead on, bullock, lead on.

Production Notes

In the interior zone established previously as Cārudatta's house, the heroine is standing in *avahittha sthāna*, decorating herself. This is done with *kaṭakāmukha* and *arāla hasta*-s. The former represents holding a mirror. She is assisted by the *Ceṭī*.

Enters the *Ceṭa*, from the southside stage door.[7] He is in front of the framework of the moving bullock cart and has a whip in hand. He enters with a gait consisting of short, quick simple steps.[8] The movement of riding the cart and the presence of bullocks are established by his suggestive *āṅgika* and *vācika abhinaya*. The *Ceṭa's* body movements would be broad but he would not walk in a *cārī*; his gait of short quick steps in fast tempo would establish his low prakṛti.

The first speech as his report of self-intention (*ātmanivedana*) would be done by him while going straight to the right MAT area.

Text

Sthāvaraka Ceṭa (Moving about and beholding): The way is blocked up by the village carts! What shall I do now here? (arrogantly) Aye, you, get out of the way! (listening) what do you say? Whose cart is this? . . . I shall park this cart at the side door of the grove of the trees belonging to noble Cārudatta. (parking the cart) Here am I coming (exits).

Production Notes

Through his speech the *Ceṭa* has to establish a busy city road jam-packed with moving carts and pedestrians opposite the house of Cārudatta. He does this through appropriate *āṅgika* and *vācika* enactment and also by the technique of the speech in the air. He moves about from the front of the right MAT and goes downstage towards the left MAT area with his gait of short steps.[9] While enacting his 'speech in the air', he faces the invisible pedestrians and drivers in front (i.e. in the audience) and carries on his conversation with them. At the end of the speech he attaches the framework of the cart to left side front pillar dividing the MAT and RP. He would take his exit from the stage door on the right.

Text

Ceṭī: Madam, some noise of the rims is heard. So the cart has arrived.

Vasantasenā: Ceṭī, go, my heart hastens me on. So direct me to the side door.

Ceṭī: Come, madam, come . . .

(till the exit of Ceṭī).

Production Notes

The *Ceṭī* would indicate the zonal side door by keeping both her hands in *tripatākā* facing each other.[10] At the same time she would gesture hearing of the sound of the noise of the cart at the side door by bending her head sideways with a sidelong glance and putting the hand near her ear.[11]

Till *Ceṭī*-s words "come, madam, come . . ." etc. the conversation takes place in the centre of RS in the interior zone established as the hero's house in a quick tempo.

Text

Vasantasenā (indicating the throbbing of the right eye and mounting the cart): Why possibly is this right eye throbbing? Or rather, the sight of Cārudatta himself will wipe off the evil omen.

Production Notes

The heroine has come up to the centre left side front pillar of the RP on the downstage, where the framework of the cart is tied. When she speaks the lines, the spoken words are dominated by the *sattva* and gestures in the manner of *sūcā* abhinaya.[12] The throbbing of the eye is indicated by quivering of the eyes. Various transitory states are to be enacted to suggest śaṅkā[13]—sudden apprehension; *cintā*, anxiety, *harṣa*, joy. Thus dryness of the mouth, licking of the lips, change of facial colour and tremor would indicate *śaṅkā*;[14] deep breathing, downcast face etc. would suggest *cintā*; brightness in the face and the eyes, horriprilation, perspiration, etc. would indicate joy *harṣa*[15] and, at the end, the state of love (*ratibhāva*).[16] This is a speech where Vasantasenā has full scope to improvise on the *bhāvābhinaya* to express the inner states and stages of her love. She would do this by coming near to the light source on the downstage centre RP.

For mounting the cart, Vasantasenā would get into the framework of the cart in *atikrāntā cārī*, with her body held up high.[17] She would do that after first assuming *sampāda sthāna*. Once inside the framework, she would imitate the movement of the cart with short swift *sampāda* steps when the cart starts moving. While walking up to the cart Vasantasenā would assume the gait of a passionate woman in love.[18] This would serially include movements from *avahittha sthāna*, a walk forward in *sakāṭasya cārī*[19] with *udveṣṭita* movement of the left hand with the other hand in *latā* gesture with head gracefully held in *udvāhita* posture.

Text

(Entering) *Sthāvaraka Ceṭa*: The carts have been got out of the way by me. So, I shall go (gesticulating mounting and driving, to himself). Heavy is this cart . . . Move on, bullocks, move on.

Production Notes

The *Ceṭa* enters from the right stage door, speaks the first lines walking with quick and simple steps. He moves his body with his face looking up[20] and mounts the cart and begins to pull it. The heroine in the framework imitates the movement of the cart.

The speech and the movement of driving the cart is in the *lokadharmī* style. The heroine is fully viewed by the spectator.

Text

(Words from behind the curtain) : You gate sentries!

. . .today the cowherd boy. . .has slipped away. . .so capture him, hold him up :

Production Notes

These words are heard from the dressing room. Percussion instruments would play at the beginning and the end of the sentences which also announces the entry of the leader of the episode (*prakarī* nāyaka), Āryaka.

Text

(Entering, tossing aside the curtain, excited, with the chain clinging to one foot, and veiled, Āryaka moves about.)

Ceṭa: (To himself) A great commotion has started in the city! So I shall go very quickly (exit).

Āryaka: Verse 1

Oh, I was indeed. . .bound down with a chain in dungeon. . . by king Pālaka. . .I slipped away through the favour of dear friend Śarvilaka (shedding tears).

Verse 2

So where shall I go, luckless that I am?
(looking) Here is the house with a side-door open, of some good man.

Verse 3

So entering just here, I shall stay on.

Production Notes

The *Ceṭa* with Vasantasenā in the framework of the cart, moves on after his speech, and exits from the stage door left (northside).

From the right stage door, behind a *javanikā* held by two stage assistants, Āryaka enters. They establish a zone in the front of the right Mat during the singing of the verse 1. The singing is done by the vocalists with musical accompaniment. At the end, by tossing aside the *javanikā* (which the assistants take back to the dressing room) Āryaka suddenly shows himself as veiled with his upper garment and the chain clinging to his one foot.

Verse 2 is chanted when he is moving about. The verses are chanted and intoned with proper *kāku* and accents in a slow and fast tempo alternating to show pathos and anger. In between the chanting, the rhythm is excelerated with percussion instruments from the *kutapa*. The actor playing Āryaka may join in a line or two of chanting but his *bhāvābhinaya* will have more accent on *sāttvika*; suggested by transitory states like weariness (*śrama*)[21] indicated by tired gait, heavy breathing, etc.; agitation (*āvega*)[22] indicated by hurry, a sad look etc.; indignation (*amarśa*)[23] indicated by shaking his head, perspiration, thinking, looking for ways and means and allies and finally determination; dissimulation (*avahittha*)[24] indicated by an attempt to conceal the appearance, looking down, having a break in speech.

Shedding of tears would be represented by the *abhinaya of sāttvikabhāva* and would be realistic. After Verse 3, the lines are spoken by Āryaka while moving about in the external vicinity of the interior zone of the hero's house. This he would do by crossing from MAT (right) towards the RP in front. Āryaka can lean against the front MAT pillar and take recourse to it for hiding also.

Verse 3

After enacting the *bhāvābhinaya* of the verse, Āryaka would enter the hero's house by making the *nāṭyadharmī* hand gesture of entering the zonal side door.[25]

Text

(Behind the curtain): Move on bullock, move on.

Āryaka: (Listening) Ah! The cart is coming just here.

Verse 4

(Then entering with the cart.)

Vardhamānaka Ceṭa: Ha! I have brought the cart cushions. . .let madam proceed. . .etc.

Āryaka: (listening) This is the courtesan's cart. . .Well, I shall mount it. (approaches slowly).

Ceṭa: (hearing) What, the noise of the anklets. . .(Āryaka mounts the cart). . .Move on bullocks. (Moves about)

Production Notes

The speech behind the curtain is to be spoken from the dressing room by the actor playing Vardhamanaka. Āryaka's speech before the verse 4 is delivered by Āryaka from the inbetween (*madhya*) zone between the interior and the exterior zones. The latter zone is somewhere near RS. Verse 4 is enacted by him with extensive *bhāvābhinaya* ending with a gesture of veiling his face with the upper garment. The verse is sung by the vocalists from the *kutapa* with full music.

Vardhamānaka enter from the stage door right with short swift gait carrying the same *pusta*—framework of cart which was used previously by Sthāvaraka *Ceṭa*. He deposits the cart on the right side of RP. Āryaka approaches stealthily from behind the pillar and enacts mounting the cart frame as soon as the *Ceṭa's* speech is over. The Ceṭa speaks facing the audience.

Just as the *Ceṭa* turns the cart leftwards and comes in the centre downstage in the RP, Vīraka enters from the right stage door.

Text

Vīraka: (Entering) Oh you, you Jaya. . .come, Candanaka come, just this way.

Candanaka: (Entering with excitement) Oh you foremost among whom are Vīraka. . .when Candanaka is alive who would carry off the cowherd boy?

Vīraka: Soldier Candanaka. . .I swear by your heart that the cowherd boy broke loose. . .

Ceṭa: Move on, bullocks, move on.

Candanaka (Seeing): Aye you! See. . .A closed cart is passing. . . just investigate this...

Vīraka (beholding): O cart-driver! To whom does this cart belong? And who again is seated there? and where is it going?

Ceṭa: This indeed is the cart of Cārudatta, Lady Vasantasenā is seated.

Production Notes

Vīraka enters from the stage left door and comes up to the MAT (left) on the front stage. He addresses the other officers by the *nāṭyadharmī* 'speech in the air' technique of conversation, i.e. addressing an imaginary character somewhere in front of the stage. Candanaka enters from the stage left door and comes up to Vīraka. Their dialogues are spoken in a lively manner in fast tempo with broad gesticulations and body movements (*āṅgika*) as befitting their inferior status. The *Ceṭa*, while saying, 'move on bullocks'. . .etc., takes the framework of the cart on the centre downstage edge of RP. He places the cart in such a fashion that Āryaka who is inside the framework is clearly visible to the spectators and the lamp light is fully on him. Candanaka and Vīraka are on either sides of the cart.

Text

Vīraka: This cart driver says that the cart is noble Cārudatta's. Vasantasenā is seated up. . .

Āryaka (to himself): This Vīraka was my enemy in my last birth. Verse 16.

Production Notes

The lively dialogue of the city guards with maximum *lokadharmī āṅgika* gestures contrasts with *sāttvika mukhaja abhinaya* of Āryaka in the centre. Āryaka's speech is in extra low pitch and his subtle *bhāvābhinaya* of transitory states during the chanting of the verse 16 should be distinctly seen by the spectators.

The episode of the exchange of carts is very important for the progress of the play where the unintended exchange comes in the path of the lovers as an obstacle (*vighna*). At the same time, because of the exchange, the leader of the episode, Āryaka, gets introduced who finally resolves all the obstacles in the path of the union of the lovers. The sequence is audio-visually interesting because of the use of *ceṣṭima pusta* and the Prakrit dialects spoken to create *lokadharmī* atmosphere of a busy city street.

Notes

1. DR, II, I-6, also Bh. P. VIII, 141.
2. NS, XXIII, 100-102 (tr. M. Ghosh).
3. Mṛcchakaṭikam, V, Sh. 11-L-100.
4. NS, XIII, 88-92.
5. NS, XXVIII, 5 and 7. Such a framework was seen by the writer in a *Noh* play. In Indian folk forms like *Bhavai* such frameworks of *jharokha* and beds are utilised and such a model work can also be employed.
6. Text by R. D. Karmarkar, 2nd ed. 1950 (pub. Arya Bhushan Press, Poona-4) p. 180-91.
7. NS, XIV, 51—the Āvanti regional mode dictates that entries and the going about on the stage will be from the right.
8. NS, XIII, 88-92 (tr. M. Ghosh).
9. NS, XIII, 88-92.
10. NS, IX, 32-37 (tr. M. Ghosh).
11. NS, XXIV, 81.
12. NS, XXIV, 43 (tr. M. Ghosh).
13. Ibid. 32-33.
14. Ibid. 45-50.
15. NS, VII, 60-61.
16. NS, VII, 8-9 and XXIV, 163-65.
17. NS, XIII, 96-98 and 88-92.
18. NS, XIII, 171-76.
19. Sakāṭasya cārī—The body held upright, one *agratāla-sañcāra* foot put forword, the breast being *udvāhita* (tr. M. Ghosh).
20. NS, XIII, 88-92.
21. NS, VII, 46.
22. Ibid, 62.
23. Ibid. 77.
24. Ibid. 79.
25. NS, IX, 32-37, Two *tripatākā* hands facing each other represent a zonal door.

Section 4

Śrī Harṣa's Ratnāvalī

(*Fire in the King's Harem, Sequence from Aindrajālikāṅka*)

1. **Rūpaka**

This play belongs to the *nāṭikā* genre of *Daśarūpaka* as it depicts the love affair cf the king hero Udayana with Sāgarikā, a young lady from the harem and their final union. The sequence of 'the fire in the King's Harem' is selected from Act IV.

2. **Sandhi** (Juncture in the plot [vastu] progression)

The sequence features in *vimarśa sandhi* (the pause before the final denouement). The fire which is produced by an illusory trick of a magician provides the final climactic scope for bringing the hero—king and the heroine—Sāgarikā together. It also gives enough scope to the actors for *nāṭyadharmī aṅga-sattva-vāca abhinaya* so that a fire scene can be depicted on a bare stage.

3. **Rasa**

Erotic (*Śṛṅgāra*)

The sequence depicts mainly marvellous and erotic *rasas* with a sprinkling of terrible, pathetic and heroic.

4. **Style (Vṛtti)**

Graceful (*Kaiśikī*).

5. **Regional Mode (Pravṛtti)**

Pāñcālī.

6. **Dharmī**

Nāṭyadharmī presentation

The rescue of the heroine from the flames of fire by the king with the other characters reacting to it as if they are standing away from the fire on the same bare stage, can best be depicted with *nivṛtyāṅkūra*[1] method of *abhinaya*. Effective evocation of the marvellous *rasa* can then be achieved.

7. **Netā** (*Adhikarī* hero and other dramatis personae)

As with the genre of *nāṭikā*, the play presents a tale of a king hero and his love affair in the harem. In this sequence, the hero-king Udayana-who is the main support of erotic *rasa* is seen with the jester-Vasantaka representing comic *rasa*, as his assistant in pleasure (*narma*) and love (*kāma*). There are also other dramatis personae like the chief queen Vāsavadattā, ladies in waiting and the heroine Sāgarikā (who, in fact, is a princess in disguise, serving as the handmaid of the chief queen). The chamberlain of the harem, Bābhravya and the minister of the Siṃhala King Vasubhūti also feature in this sequence. The last two characters indirectly act as assistants in the love affair of the king.

8. **Āhārya**

(1) **The Body Paint (aṅgaracanā)**

King Udayana: The dhīralalita superior type hero, the support of the erotic, would be painted lotus blue[2] with a *rājatilaka* on his forehead, sandalwood marks on his arms and chest and long drawn eyes.

Vāsavadattā: The superior type chief queen would be painted in reddish yellow. The face would have a *tilak* and a *patrāvali* design on the forehead and cheeks; the eyes long drawn and curly hair.[3]

The Jester: Reddish yellow colour of a brahmin with many white marks on the face, forehead, nose and cheeks.[4] He is the middle type of character (*madhyama prakṛti*).

The Chamberlain : would be painted in a darkish hue. He is a middle type of character.

The Minister of Siṃhala King: In dark brown shade, middle type.

Sāgarikā: She is a princess from Siṃhala Deśa and so she would be painted in dark blue lotus colour with faint design of *patrāvali* on her forehead and long drawn eyes. A superior type of character.

(2) **The Costumes and Accessories**

King Udayana: A half dhotī draped in a pleasing delicate fashion in magenta colour of a deeper shade with an upper garment of variegated colours of amber, pink and pale orange. Fittingly bejewelled with golden and pearl ornaments with a crown of *mastaki*[5] variety—with bare upper torso adorned with a sacred thread and ornaments. The variegated upper garment dominated by pink, amber and orange colour is to signify flame of the fire which the actor playing the king will recreate mainly with his *āṅgika abhinaya* enhanced by his *āhārya*.

Vāsavadattā: One ruby red coloured garment draped in a *lūṅgī* fashion. Another red and blue bordered garment worn as a *gātrikā*. The curly hair elaborately coiffured. Suitable ornaments. She acts as an obstacle (*vighna*) in the love affair of the hero and the heroine in this play. The red colour of her costume symbolises her state of anger.

The Jester: Vāsantaka is a court jester, the king's companion in pleasure. He would wear a white half jacket with red and gold star design on it with a belt over a white short *dhotī*. Tightly strapped shoes would be worn over the *dhotī* as well as a colourful cap on his head (*Triśrīkhaṇḍaka* cap).[6] [For evidence of such a dress of a jester see Ajanta Cave No. 2, Yazdani, Ajanta, Pt. II, pl. 24, p. 22.]

The Chamberlain: In a long, loose dark red tunic (*kaśāya kañcuka*) with a staff in his hand, he would have a *pratiśīrṣa* with a dull olive green coloured piece of cloth tied round his head to appear like a turban. (Based on a frieze of Vakataka, 5th century A.D., Ajanta.)

Vasubhūti: The minister would wear a dull mustard half *dhotī*, a pale designed brown jacket and a mustard printed turban. He would have an armour with quiver attached with other weapons in his waist band. Golden jewellery. And beard.

Sāgarikā (the heroine): She is rescued from the palace prison so her dress would consist of a lower garment of dirty ash grey colour with splashes of scarlet, red, ochre and white, worn in a loose *dhotī* fashion, darkish grey-pink breast cloth (*stanāṃsuka*) with loose upper garment of dull orangish-pink colour. To indicate her *virahotkaṇṭhitā* stage she would have one plait and sparse ornaments. Her fetters would be strips of orange coloured cloths. The grey colour of her dress can be suggestive counterpoint to the orange magenta hues of the king's dress, in creating the effect of the fire spectacle.

All costumes are based on Ajanta frescoes Cave No. 17, 2 (See sketches and notes on p. 387).

9. The Use of the Stage

The stage groupings and the zonal division of the stage is conceived on the resources available in the rectangular medium play house, as described by Bharata. The fire sequence and the rescue of the heroine is established in the centre of the RP.

The group representing the palace onlookers will establish a separate zone near the right hand side pillar of the stage in the downstage MAT area.

10. Lighting

Strong central focal light from the lamp placed on the downstage edge of RP. In addition, torches held by two stage assistants near the RS pillars on either sides.

11. Kutapa

Full use of the musical orchestra in the SAT area of the NS region.

Visualisation

(The sequence starts with an announcement of the fire in the palace harem and ends with the safe rescue of the heroine by the King.)

Text[7]

(Behind the scene a great noise.)

Verse 14—describes the fire.

(All behold in confusion)

King : How, the fire in the harem? Alas, Queen Vāsavadattā is burnt to ashes (hurriedly rising)

Verse 15

Vāsavadattā: My husband, help, help!

King : Oh, how is it that I did not observe the queen, though she stands by my side? (Holding the queen's hands and embracing) . . . Oh my consort. . .

Vāsavadattā: Let my husband rescue Sāgarikā who is detained in the fetters by me, a cruel woman.

King: What, Sāgarikā is perishing? I am going.

Vasantaka: Of friend, don't carry out a thoughtless deed.

Production Notes

The king's group, with the king seated on a seat, is established in the right MAT in the beginning of the sequence (The sketch on facing page 387 gives a bare idea of this composition.) The jester Vasantaka is standing near the extreme right hand side down-stage pillar of the right MAT. The Chamberlain is standing in front of the king but behind the left side pillar, while, Vasubhūti, the *Siṃhaladeśa* minister is standing in front of the left-side pillar. The queen on the left side, is standing behind the king. The announcement of the fire is at first heard as an off-stage voice from the *kutapa* itself. Verses 14 and 15 are sung as *dhruvā*-s (*ākṣepikī* style) with full musical accompaniment by the vocalists. The dialogues between the king, queen and the others in right MAT are in *lokadharmī* style with appropriate *kāku* and *abhinaya*. When queen Vāsavadattā mentions that the heroine Sāgarikā is detained in prison by her and after exchange of dialogues with the king another *dhruvā* in quick tempo—an antarā dhruvā (appropriate to the situation from the NS repertoire) in *capalā* metre and in prakrit—is sung by the vocalists. When translated it expresses the following suggestive meaning:

> "Here have appeared in the sky terrible clouds, which are like mountains, which make sounds like drums and which look like (large) birds of blue and black colours."[8]

After the singing of the dhruvā is over, with full beating of drums, a *javanikā* is brought on the stage by two stage assistants who have a torch each in their hands. The *javanikā* is held in front of the *kutapa*, covering it from the view of the audience. Sāgarikā is supposed to be behind it. The percussion instruments create an appropriate mood of the approaching danger to the heroine caught in the fire. The group in the right MAT makes minor changes in their positions suitable to the mood and import of the song and the dialogues. The king finally gets up from the seat.

Text

King: (Pulling his upper garment). . .Sāgarikā is dying. How do I care about my life at this juncture? (entering into the fire, he is overpowered by smoke).

Verse 16

Vāsavadattā: Then, I too must follow after him.

Vasantaka (The Jester): (walking in front of her), Oh Lady, I too must become guide to your path.

Vasubhūti: I. . .must sacrifice myself.

The Chamberlain: (shedding tears). . .I will also. . .

King (observing throbbing of his right arm. . .looking in front with extreme joy): Oh, Sāgarikā is near the fire. . .Let me help her swiftly.

(Then appears Sāgarikā bound in fetters.)

Production Notes

Udayana pulls at his amber-orange coloured upper garment. Keeping one end in his hand, he makes the other end trail loosely on the ground. He suggests his entry in the fire and being overpowered by smoke, by his elaborate *abhinaya* of eyes as if troubled by smoke, running with quick steps, narrowing down of all limbs and, at times, shaking them.[9] Gestures of *hasta*-s denoting quivering *tripatākā*-s accompany this *abhinaya.*[10] His upper garment of amber-orange-reddish colour with its flowing trailing, swishing movement by the āṅgika actions of the king would help create the mood of the situation. The others who follow him attempting to enter the fire will remain in the zone of the extreme right side MAT pillar demarcating it with RP in the downstage edge.

The āṅgika choreography depicting fire is accompanied by the music, specially the percussion, as well as the swishing of the torches in the hands of the stage assistants standing in RS in extreme upstage corners. The king employs the transitory states and sāttvika bhāva-s indicating apprehension (*śankā*),[11] fear (*bhaya*)[12], anxiety (*cintā*)[13], agitation (*āvega*)[14] and assurance (*mati*)[15] for the heroine's safety as well as joy (*harṣa*)[16] at the sight of his beloved finally. Sāgarikā's entry is announced in this manner and then the javanikā is drawn aside to reveal Sāgarikā in a grey costume with orange fetters. The two stage assistants then go and stand behind the upstage pillars on either side and throw up light of the two torches to light up the interior zone.

The audience first gets a side glimpse of Sāgarikā standing in a aśvakrāntā sthāna with *karuna* (pathetic) *bhayānvitā* (fearful), *vibhrāntā* (confused) and *trastā* (frightened) glances. She is trying to cover her face with two patākā hands.

Text

Sāgarikā (looking all around):. . .Nearly on all my side the fire is spreading. . .

King (quickly approaching): Why are you 'indifferent' to me even now?

Sāgarikā (looking at the king, to herself):· . .(aloud) My lord, help me. . .

Verse 17

King: Just for a moment, endure this thick outburst of smoke. (seeing in front) Ah fie, this silk cloth dropped from your breast is burning. (Looking) Why do you repeatedly stumble? How, you are bound by fetters (tying his belt).

Verse 18

I will lead you out quickly from here; lean on me, my dearest. (holding her, expressing the joy of her touch, with his eyes closed.)

(Opening his eyes and looking) Oh, it is a great miracle, where is the burning fire now? This harem retains the same state as before. . .

Vāsavadattā (touching the king's body with joy): Fortunately my husband is unhurt.

Chamberlain: Victory to the King! Felicitations!

Production Notes

The rescue of Sāgarikā is represented by elaborate rendering of verses 17 and 18. The verses would be sung by the vocalists from the *kutapa* with the actors playing the king and Sāgarikā also joining in. The detailed representation of each 'pada' of the verse would be enacted by extensive *sāttvika-āṅgika abhinaya*. Some of the lines may be depicted in the style of *nivṛtyāṅkura abhinaya* with the king expressing with *vācika* the *āṅgika* movement of Sāgarikā. The expression of joy of touch (*sparśa sukha*)[17] is enacted by the *sāttvika* response of horripilation and tears. The sequence should be executed with a sense of balance of a choreographic piece emphasising all the four facets of *abhinaya* to suit the situation by the two performers.

The producer would aid the performance with the arrangement of the swirling movements of the flames of the torches held by the two stage assistants at appropriate moments. The rest would depend mainly on the elaborate delineation of *aṅga-sattva-vāc abhinaya* piece by the two performers in a *nāṭyadharmī* practice of performance.

Notes

1. For explanation of terms see Part Three, Chapter 6, p. 136.
2. NS, XXIII, 99-100.
3. NS, XXIII, 63-66 describing women of Avanti.
4. See Part Three, Chapter 7.
5. Mastaki crown—adopted from Ajanta Cave XVII. Herringham, Ajanta Frescoes, Pl. XXV, p. 27.
6. Agrawal V., Harsacarita, eka Sanskrutiya Adhyayana, p. 17.
7. The translation of Ratnâvali, Act IV, from the text of Bak Kun Bae, I ed. Asia Pub. House, New York, pp. 384-90.
8. NS, XXXII, 239-40 (tr. M. Ghosh).
9. NS, VII, 62-63.
10. NS, IX, 32-37.
11. NS, VII, 32.
12. Ibid. 23.
13. Ibid. 49.
14. Ibid, 62-63.
15. Ibid, 81-82.
16. Ibid, 62.
17. NS, XXVI, 50-51, also XXIV, 82.

CHAPTER 12

MUDRĀRĀKṢASA (VII)
UTTARARĀMACARITAM (III)
MATTAVILĀSA-PRAHASANAM
UBHAYĀBHISĀRIKĀ-BHĀṆA

Section 1

Viśākhadatta's Mudrārākṣasa (VII)

(*A sequence of Candanadāsa's processional walk to the execution post*)

The sequence selected for visualisation starts with Candanadāsa's processional walk to the execution post. It starts on the main street of the city and ends with the episode where the two antagonists, Cāṇakya and Rākṣasa meet for the first time in the play. It includes the sequence of the latter's surrender to the former's proposal of accepting the chief ministership of king Candragupta.

1. Rūpaka

This play is unique among the classical Sanskrit plays. It adheres to the precise conventions of traditional *nāṭya rūpaka* structure and yet creates doubts over its exact *rasa* design. While it has many characteristics of a *nāṭaka* genre, it is exceptional in its omission of *kaiśikī vṛtti* or a heroine or any other important female characters. As a result, contemporary opinions differ sharply about the genre of the play, the hero, the *rasa* and so on. Perhaps some of the confusion may be solved if we take this play as one of the series of plays dealing with the exploits of king Candragupta Maurya.

We have two plays of Bhāsa which provide examples for such an assumption. *Pratijñā Yaugandharāyaṇa* and *Svapna Vāsavadattā* are two plays of Bhāsa which are considered by some researchers[1] as a set of two dramas (duology) written on the legend of king Udayana.

If the present play is taken with 'Devī Candragupta' of Viśākhadatta (a play which is unfortunately lost, but the extracts and description of which are available in other works) as forming a part of a duology, the play *Mudrārākṣasa* can be taken to present Candragupta Maurya as the *adhikārin*—phalabhoktā hero[2] who attains the fruit of his desire (*artha*) at the end. That it is Candragupta himself who enunciates the beginning of the *Bharata vākya* of this play, with the sentence, "What can be dearer than this?" substantiates this view.

Both Cāṇakya and Rākṣasa, although powerfully delineated characters, can be then considered merely assistants in the design of *netā* presentation, whose efforts for the cause of the hero finally benefit the king Candragupta.

When viewed from this angle, the play, definitely presents heroic *rasa*. The presentation of the *rasa* is, however, not traditional,[3] but there is an innovative emphasis on 'discourses on state craft' and a possible message of loyalty and sacrifice for the king and friends.[4] Nevertheless, the ancient spectator might certainly have identified with the king hero alone and relished the efforts of the minister Cāṇakya and his men on his behalf.

Thus, this play, taken as a part of a series on Chandragupta Maurya, satisfies the conventions of *nāṭaka* genre with having all the four *vṛtti*-s including *kaiśikī* with a *dhīroddhata* king as the *adhikārin* hero.

2. **Sandhi** (Juncture in the plot [vastu] progression)

Climactic episode, beginning in the *vimarśa* sandhi and ending in the *nirvahaṇa sandhi*.

3. **Rasa**

Predominant heroic (*vīra*) *rasa*. Subsidiary *rasa*-s pathetic and furious (in this sequence).

4. **Style (vṛtti)**

Verbal (*bhāratī*)-in this sequence-.

5. **Regional mode (Pravṛtti)**

Oḍramāgadhi.

6. *Dharmī*

Lokadharmī.

In accordance with the plot and the characters found in the milieu of the intrigues governing state craft, the practice of presentation ought to be vigorous, direct and *laukika*. The sequence, thus, is mainly a *lokadharmī* presentation.

7. **Netā** (Adhikārī Hero and other dramatis personae)

Cāṇakya and Rākṣasa are superior types. They are able ministers and strong assistants for the achievement of the main desire (*artha*) of the king-hero. They finally come face to face in this sequence. Cāṇakya ultimately proves to be more able and successful in statesmanship in the service of his king. With a small device of the acquisition of a signet ring (*mudrā*) of his antagonist Rākṣasa, he manipulates him to a position of his choice. Rākṣasa, on the other hand, excels in being more human and loyal in friendship and thus a little weaker in statecraft.

Candanadāsa, a middle type, represents another facet of a loyal friend who can be very successfully manoeuvered by a clever and ruthless statesman.

Candanadāsa's wife and son (middle types) represent the loyal family and emphasise the pathos underlying Candanadāsa's sacrifice.

The two executioners (*Siddhārthaka* and Sammiddhārthaka) —Cāṇakya's spies in disguise. They are inferior types who show their individual traits of being loyal in the service of the king

8. **Āhārya**

(1) *Body paint*: *Aṅgaracanā*

(a) *Candanadāsa*—being a vaiśya, will have dark or deep brown colour.

(b) *Two executioners*: Deep dark colour.

(c) *Candanadāsa's wife and son*: A light shade of brown.

(d) *Rākṣasa*: A dark colour.

(e) *Cāṇakya*: Reddish yellow of a brahmin.

(2) *Costumes and Accessories*

(i) *Candanadāsa*: In deep red (*kaśāya*) coloured *dhotī* with a cloth in pale cherry red with stripes as a cummerband—with red flowered garland around his neck and red sandalwood marks.[5] His head is bare. He carries a symbolic executioner's pole (*vadhastambha pusta*) on his shoulder.

(ii) *The two executioners and the drummers*: Dirty multicoloured short lower garment, worn in a short *dhotī* style. A reddish headband (*paṭṭa*) in the hair. Bilvapatra would wear a short, half sleeved jacket in cobalt blue shade. Vajraloma would wear a short striped *dhotī* of nile blue and olive green. Both executioners have weapons (*daṇḍa*) tucked in the waist-bands. The drummer, in dirty skin coloured cloth, has a drum.

(iii) *Candanadāsa's wife*: A multicoloured striped *lūngī*-like lower garment with dull olive mauve and dull orange. A jacket (*colaka*) of grey with long sleeves. An upper garment of mauve covering the head and well tucked.

(iv) *The son*: A striped greyish blue mustard and white short *dhotī*. The grey colour is to symbolise the pathos.

(v) *Rākṣasa*: A striped grey *dhotī*, pale reddish orange turban and red upper short jacket (*kañcuka*) with dull white upper garment. Red is to symbolise his fury. The grey to symbolise his overpowering pathos. The reddish orange to suggest his heroic temperament. Grey moustache.

(vi) *Cāṇakya*: In white *dhotī* and upper garment. A sacred thread. Rudrākṣa necklace. A loose *śikhā*. The reddish *javanikā* covers him in the beginning.

The costumes are based on Ajanta (cave No. 17, 1) and Goli sculptures—around 4th to 7th century A.D.

(See the sketches and notes on p. 393)

9. The use of the stage

The zonal divisions are designed to accommodate the resources available in the medium rectangular playhouse, as described by Bharata.

Being presented in *Oḍramāgadhi Pravṛtti*,[6] the processional entry of Candanadāsa with one of the executioners (Bilvapatra), his wife and young son, would commence from southern stage door. It would take a circular slow route to RP middle. The other executioner (Vajraloma) is already standing in the centre of RP, creating an interior zone of the execution area. Cāṇakya later enters with a reddish *javanikā* covering his body through the stage right door. He goes straight to the right side MAT, and establishes a separate zone as part of the interior of his house on the downstage edge of the MAT.

10. **Lighting**

The lighting is from the central lamp on the RP downstage edge.

11. **Kutapa**

Use of percussion and chanting.

Visualisation

Text[7]

(Then enters Candanadāsa, accompanied by another executioner Bilvapatra, wearing the dress of a condemned criminal with the stake on his shoulder; and followed by his wife and son)

Candanadāsa (with tears): Alas, fie! Alas, fie! . . . A bow to death that there should be a death fit for thieves.

Verse 3

(looking all around) O dear friend Viṣṇudāsa, how do you not give me even a word in reply? (moves about).

Bilvapatra: (*Caṇḍāla*) You have reached the place of execution, so dismiss your family members.

Candanadāsa: Dear wife, return now with son . . .

Wife (with tears): My lord has started for another world.

Candanadāsa: Lady, this death is due to duty towards a friend, not again due to a personal crime . . .

Wife: (speeches in the same mood) . . .

Candanadāsa: . . . . . .

Boy (falling prostrate at the feet): Father, what should be done now by me bereft of my father?

Vajraloma: Oh, take hold of him.

(Both the *caṇḍāla*-s take hold of Candanadāsa.)

Wife (bearing her bosom): Gentlemen! Help:

(Rākṣasa enters tossing aside the curtain—apaṭikṣepeṇa.)

Production Notes

Processional entry (as described in Part Three, Ch. 7, pp. 215-16) can have a few added characters, not described in the text. As such the *Nāṭyaśāstra* tradition prefers a small number of characters on the stage at the same time.[8] So only a drummer heading the procession is visualised. The executioner (Bilvapatra) follows him. Candanadāsa then follows. This group is followed by the wife and the son.

The gait of each character would vary in tempo, beat and style to suit individual character type.[9] The drummer and the executioner walk in quick tempo[10] with eyes looking around.[11] Candanadāsa walks in medium slow tempo of two or four *kalā* beat.[12] As befitting the pathos of the situation, he would be patient, tearful, heaving deep sighs, and would sometimes be looking upwards. His gait would have no regular measure. At times, he would bend down his head on his chest in dejection and become senseless due to grief and walk with dragging feet.[13] The wife and the son walk in slow gaits with tearful eyes. At times the wife may weep loudly, and throw up her arms. Both would have drooping bodies.[14] The son would express fear with wide open moving eyes, *vidhuta* head, awe-stricken look.[15]

The speech of Candanadāsa before Verse 3 would be enunciated and intoned in slow tempo and low pitch to indicate lament with *gāndhāra* note predominating. The *sāttvika abhinaya* accompanying the *vācika* will depict sorrow,[16] with the *vyabhicāri*-s of despair (*viṣāda*)[17] indicating loss of energy, deep breathing, etc., dejection due to weakness of body (*glāni*)[18] indicated by weak voice, lustreless eyes, pale face, slow gait, etc., anxiety (*cintā*)[19] indicated by deep breathing, sighing, agony, thinking with a down cast face etc.

Verse 3 is chanted in *āryā* metre.[20] The verse is chanted when Candanadāsa's procession takes a longish left hand curve[21] after entering from the southern door of the stage and stops at the down stage right MAT pillar. The conversation between the wife, son and Candanadāsa occurs in this zone (down stage right MAT and RP pillar); with the wife and the son enacting greater *āṅgika* movements of anxiety, agitation, distraction and shame.[22] When both executioners finally take hold of Candanadāsa, the wailing wife and the weeping son move up to the left MAT. They hide behind the left MAT RP pillar and watch the proceedings.

Rākṣasa enters at this stage, with the toss of the right door curtain, and goes straight to the group in the middle RP.

The executioner's pole is suggestive and symbolic *pusta* (it is in fact, a longish bamboo stick). During the ensuing sequence, it is carried by Vajraloma who stands with it in the RP centre. He takes the pole from Candanadāsa when he is brought to the RP centre. (This is done by moving round in the centre of the stage twice to indicate the distance of the location.)[23]

Text

Rākṣasa (Entering, tossing aside the curtain): Lady, fear not. Oh you, hangman, you shall indeed not kill Candanadāsa . . .

Verse 4

Verse 5

Vajraloma: O Bilvapatra, you just take hold of Candanadāsa, wait a while under the shade of this tree in the cemetry, while I report . . . that Rākṣasa has been captured.

(Bilvapatra exits with Candanadāsa, accompanied by wife and son)

Vajraloma: This way minister (moving about with Rakṣasa). Is there anybody here? Report to revered Cāṇakya that . . .

Rākṣasa (himself): Even this, indeed, have I got to hear.

Vajraloma: Here is the captured minister Rākṣasa . . . etc.

Production Notes

The entry of Rākṣasa with a toss of right door curtain, up to Verse 5 should be depicted with angry and sorrowful *bhāva*-s and should have appropriate *sāttvika* and *vyabhicāri*-s.

Verse 4 is chanted in *Śārdūlavikrīḍita* metre.[24] It begins with a fast tempo and higher pitch to indicate anger but gradually slows down to an even tempo and lower pitch to indicate Rākṣasa's state of utter despair. The chanting should have *ṛṣabha* (ri) and *niṣāda* (ni) dominating. Verse 5, again in *Śārdūlavikrīḍita*[25] exhibits despair but at the same time a firm resolution of the superior nature *(prakṛti)*[26] of Rākṣasa to take a determined and courageous stand to save his noble self-sacrificing friend. It can be recited with *ṣaḍja* (sā) as the main note. Vajraloma's speech after verse 5 is spoken in his original character of the spy Siddhārthaka. Bilvapatra's exit with Candanadāsa is executed by going around the stage and finally taking the exit by left door of the stage. The wife and the son follow him by the same door.

After that, Vajraloma (Siddhārthaka) conducts Rākṣasa in another going around (parikramā) which ends in establishment of a new zone of the exterior of Cāṇakya's house. While walking around, Rākṣasa suggests pathos (*śokabhāva*) by his gait in a slow tempo of no regular measure and without the *sauṣṭhava* of his body. He can be looking upwards, occasionally heaving deep sighs and yet trying to remain patient,[27] befitting his superior nature. Vajraloma (in his original character of Siddhārthaka) will walk with quick short steps.

At the end of the walk around (*parikramā*) Rākṣasa stands at the left MAT pillar on the extreme downstage; with Vajraloma in the middle of the RP.

Text

(Then enters Cāṇakya, only his face visible, the rest of the body being covered with a *javanikā*)

Cāṇakya: My friend tell, tell . . .

Verse 6

Vajraloma: Surely by the revered one with intellect proficient in statesmanship.

Cāṇakya: No, not so, say by fate leaving Nanda family.

Rākṣasa (to himself): Here is Kauṭilya, a villain or a nobleman.

Verse 7

Cāṇakya (beholding with joy to himself): . . . .

Verse 8

(Removing the screen of mantle—*javanikā*—and approaching): Oh, minister Rākṣasa, I, Viṣṇugupta salute you!

Production Notes

Cāṇakya's entry is theatrically most powerful. His body is fully covered by the flaming red *javanikā* except his face which registers the *sāttvika* and *vyabhicāri bhāva*-s of pure joy and triumph at the successful completion of his objective of capturing

Rākṣasa. Cāṇakya enters from the right side stage door and takes a frontal position on the downstage right MAT. Verse 6, in *śārdūlavikrīḍita*,[28] is an aprastuta *praśaṃsā*—an indirect praise[29] —of Rākṣasa by Cāṇakya when he compares the former with fire, wind, powerful lion and ocean. The high compliments are paid in a deliberate quick tempo and medium pitch with excited tone. So also his conversation with Vajraloma is to be in a fast tempo. Rākṣasa, who is near the pillar on the right side, is still dejected but reluctantly admires crafty Cāṇakya and his different stratagies to manipulate him. Verse 7 in *Anuṣṭubha*[30] is chanted in medium tempo and an even pitch with an undertone of admiration and overtone of despair at his own plight. Rākṣasa delineates the verse with full *bhāvābhinaya* occasionally joining in the chant. After the chanting is over, Cāṇakya removes the *javanikā* which he leaves on the right MAT and steps out. He comes on the centre of RP and offers his salute to Rākṣasa.

The rhythm of the drums as well as other percussion instruments accompany the processional entry, all the other entries, the walking around and Cāṇakya's stepping out on the centre of RP. There is no music or rhythm accompaniment when the verses are chanted or the words are spoken.

Notes

1. Smt. Gandhi Shanta, *A Sanskrit Play in Performance* (A background note on the performance of vision of Vāsavadattā at Kennedy Theatre in Honolulu, March, 1977. A paper read at the Seminar on a Sanskrit Play in performance.)
2. DR, I, 19, Phalaswāmi.
3. DR. IV, 79, Yuddhavīra, Dayāvīra, Dānavīra, etc.
4. The text translated in English by R. D. Karmarkar (1st ed. 1940), Introduction to MR, pp. xviii and xxi.
5. From the text translated and edited by R. D. Karmarkar, Notes, p. 381.
6. NS, XIV, 52.
7. Text translated by R. D. Karmarkar, Lat. ed. 1940, Pub. by Aryabhusan Press, Poona, p. 195-204.
8. NS, XX, 44.
9. NS, XIII, 12-14.
10. NS, XIII, 13.
11. NS, XIII, 150.
12. Ibid, 35-37.
13. Ibid, 63-66.
14. Ibid, 61-63.

15. Ibid, 70-75.
16. NS, VII, 10 (M. Ghosh).
17. Ibid, 67.
18. NS, VII, 30.
19. Ibid, 49.
20. MR, Tr. and Ed. by R. D. Karmarkar, notes on VII, p. 382 (1949 ed.).
21. NS, XIV, 51.
22. NS, VII, 49, 62, 51, 57.
23. NS, XIV, 17.
24. NS, Mudrarakṣasa, tr. by R. D. Karmarkar (op. cit.) p. 385.
25. Ibid, p. 386.
26. NS, VII, 14.
27. NS, XIII, 63-66.
28. MR, tr. R. D. Karmarkar (op. cit., p. 387).
29. *Aprastuta* Praśaṃsā is a figure of speech in which a reference is made to passing circumstances to bring out something latent in the mind of the listener.
30. MR, Tr. R. D. Karmarkar, p. 388.

Section 2

Bhavabhūti's Uttararāmacaritam (III)

(A short sequence where Rāma in the company of the forest spirit Vāsantī evokes the pathetic *rasa* [karuṇā] generated by love in separation [*vipralambha śṛṅgāra*] with invisible Sītā and Tamasā watching)

1. **Rūpaka**

Nāṭaka. The play depicts the meeting of the exalted, celebrated hero Rāma with the noble heroine Sītā after a long separation (*vipralambha*).

2. **Sandhi** (juncture in the plot [*vastu*] progression)
Garbha sandhi stage.

3. **Rasa**

Pathetic *rasa* born out of love in separation with a sprinkling of heroic and marvellous (without the other four *rasa*-s).

Bhavabhūti has expressed the pathetic (*karuṇā*) *rasa*, in all its facets in this play. Each act revolves around the basic statement of the playwright that it is the pathetic *rasa* alone which reigns supreme in the scheme of the eight *naṭya rasa*-s. '*Eko rasaḥ* karuṇa eva" declares Bhavabhūti and the play reverberates with that *rasa-dhvani*.

This sequence depicts a meeting and yet a non-meeting of Rāma and Sītā. This, again, after a long separation. The presence of the invisible Sītā is only felt in the atmosphere of Pancavatī forest by Ramā who cannot see her.

4. **Style (Vṛtti)**

Verbal, graceful and sublime (*bhāratī*, *kaiśikī sāttvatī*).

5. **Regional Mode (Pravṛtti)**

Dākṣināṭya.

6. **Dharmī**

Nāṭyadharmī presentation.

In visualisation, I have tried to explore various ways in which the playwright has achieved his objective of depicting the pathetic *rasa* while at the same time keeping a high degree of aesthetic distance and abstraction, to avoid any sentimentality. For this, a *nāṭyadharmī* presentation is preferred, where the actors keep a conscious and controlled distance from the characters to be portrayed and depict the inner states of love in separation in its utmost universal, impersonal and super sensual format.

7. **Netā** (Adhikārī hero and other dramatis personae)

(1) Rāma: Superior type, who is the main support of the state of love in separation. A *dhīrodātta* hero (*mahāsattva*)

(2) Sītā: Superior type, *pragalbhā virahotkaṇṭhitānāyikā* — A *bhavatī*.

(3) Tamasā: Superior type, a female personification of the spirit of the river Tamasā. A helper in love (*kāmasahāyikā*) and a friend of the heroine. A superhuman character.

(4) Vāsantī: Superior type. A female personification of the spirit of the forest of Janasthāna. A friend of Rāma and Sītā and a helper in love. A superhuman character.

8. **Āhārya**

(a) The body paint.

(b) The costumes and accessories.

Rāma

(a) He would be painted in śyāma colour. (This is a mixture of dark blue and yellow ochre which results in a shade of brownish dark green)[1] with a *tilaka* on the forehead and long drawn eyes; with sandalwood paste on arms, cheeks and chest.

(b) He would wear a pearl greenish grey *dhotī* with a reddish yellow cummerband. He would have a white orange and grey striped upper garment loosely draped. And a shaded grey armour with a quiver of arrows attached to the back. He would be adequately jewelled, with his long sacred thread showing with a conical (*kirīṭa*) type of crown slightly triangular in shape (as worn by a king in Ajanta fresco, cave No. 17).[2]

Sītā:

(a) She would be painted in *gaura varṇa* with a *tilaka* on the forehead.

(b) Her costume would consist of a ochre-yellowish grey coloured *ekavastra* (one piece of cloth draped round the body). She would have one long plait as a hairstyle to show her state of *virahiṇīnāyikā* (Heroine separated from her beloved.) She would be sparsely ornamented mostly with forest flowers.

The colour grey predominates in the costumes of both Rāma and Sītā to emphasise their states of sorrow.

Tamasā :

(a) *Nāṭyaśāstra* has suggested specific white colour for the Gaṅgā river. In accordance, river Tamasā would be painted white with a shade of pale blue to suggest water.

(b) She would be attired in two pieces of loose and shimmering cloth with the lower garment draped as a flowing *dhotī*. The upper garment would be loosely left at the back with one end tucked on the shoulder of her pale blue coloured jacket. The colours of the two loose garments would be bluish white (*kāraṇḍava*) dominated by white. The upper garment would be pure white with a blue border. The ornaments would resemble the shimmering mother of pearl and pearls. She would have coiffure of flowing loose hair.

Vāsantī:

(a) She would be painted pale brown with red lips and long drawn eyes, with patrāvalī design on her forehead and cheeks.

(b) Her two pieces of dress and jacket would be dominated by different shades of green. She would have elaborate coiffure adorned with flowers and leaves.

The costumes for Rāma and Sītā have been determined from Ajanta (Cave No. 17). Tamasā's dress design is conceived from various reliefs of river goddess like Gaṅgā and Sarasvatī at Ellora (8th century A.D.). Vāsantī's dress is visualised from the Śālabhañjikā figurine—6th century A.D. Assam.

(The sketches and notes on p. 389).

9. The Use of the Stage

The zonal division is planned on the design of the medium rectangular play house of Bharata.

Rāma is seated on a seat—symbolising a stone slab in the centre downstage position in the RP, taking the maximum light from the centrally placed brass lamp on the downstage edge.

Sītā and Tamasā, in the right MAT on the extreme downstage, make a separate zone. Both of them are supposed to be invisible to the other characters on the stage, and yet they should be in such a position that their subtle *sattva-aṅgābhinaya* can be distinctly seen by the spectators. At times, they can make use of the MAT pillars to literally disappear from the view; at other times, they can even be partly seen. Their *vācika abhinaya* should be executed near the downstage edge of right MAT so that their voices are always audible. Vāsantī makes her entry from the stage left door.

10. The Lighting

The central lamp on the down stage edge of the stage RP and two other lamps on down stage centres of two MAT-s.

11. Kutapa

Full use of musical orchestra.

Visualisation

Text[3]

Vāsantī: (Aloud) Let your Majesty honour these spots of Janasthāna of long familiarity by a look at them.

Rāma: Just as you say (with these words he rises and walks around).

Sītā: I think the remedy thought of by my dear friend to divert his grief will simply inflame it.

Vāsantī: (Pitifully) Sire, Sire.

Verse 37

Sītā: You are cruel Vāsantī, you are cruel, since by thus constantly shaking the dart (of grief) thrust deep into the vital part of the heart you torture me, an unlucky woman and my lord, again and again.

Rāma: O ruthless Jānakī, you appear to be present here and there, and yet you do not take compassion on me.

Verse 38 (faints)

Sītā: Woe, Woe! My husband has swooned again.

Vāsantī: Compose yourself Sītā, compose yourself.

Sītā: My dear, alas, I am undone on account of me. . .its endangering your life (faints).

Tamasā: . . .the touch of your hand alone is the remedy for reviving dear Rāma.

Vāsantī: . . .Restore to consciousness the lord of your life (Sītā hurriedly approaches Rāma and touches him on the heart and forehead).

Vāsantī: O joy, dear Rāma has regained consciousness.

Verse 39

Rāma: (his eyes still closed in felicity) Dear Vāsanti fortune now smiles upon you.

Vāsantī: How Sire?

Rāma: Friend, what else? Jānakī is again with me.

Vāsantī: Of lord Rāma, where is she?

Rāma: (shows that he experiences her felicitious touch) Lo, here she is before us.

Production Notes

Rāma is in the sitting posture indicating sorrow with one of his feet slightly stretched; the other foot resting on the seat, and his hand supporting the chin. (See sketch 12 on p. 140). At times, his head would be bent forward on one shoulder.[4] He is to look with a sorrowful glance (*śoka dṛṣṭi*) with reciprocal changes of expressions of the eyes like vacant, pale, tired and dejected glances. Vāsantī is standing on his left in *avahitha sthāna*. (See fig. No. 8 on p. 139)

Sītā and Tamasā are near the MAT pillar at downstage right.

When the characters go around the stage, their stylised walk—the parikramā—would be accompanied by the rhythm of the percussion instruments in medium slow tempo. Their going around would be done from the right as per the *dākṣiṇātya* local usage.[6] Rāma's gait would be in a slow tempo. At times he would heave deep sighs while looking around. His gait would, at times, have no regular measure. He would not have *sauṣṭhava* of the body.[7] The gait of Vāsantī would be in *aśvakrāntā* cārī. She would walk with her body slightly bent and head gracefully held in *udvāhita* position.[8]

After Sītā's speech and after Verse 37, which are enacted with full improvisational *bhāvābhinaya* of the state of sorrow with appropriate *sāttvika* and *vyabhicāri*-s in medium tempo, Sītā and Tamasā would follow the first two in going around the stage. They would walk with their feet not raised very high, and Sītā would have *asauṣṭhava* of the body.[9]

Verse 37 is sung by the female vocalists from the musical orchestra with Vāsantī accompanying them. While singing, Vāsantī expresses through her *aṅga-sattva abhinaya* the *bhāva* content of each word and phrase of every line of the verse in elaborate *padārthābhinaya*.

Verse 38 is chanted by Rāma after Vāsantī's description of 'the bower of the creepers' in verse 37 and the ensuing speeches are over. He again sits on the same seat (which now suggests another location in Janasthāna).

Verse 38 is enacted by him improvisationally on the theme of *vipralambha śṛṅgāra*. At the end, Rāma faints, by representing the three main stages of inaction such as imperceptible breathing, motionlessness and finally falling in a swoon.[10] Vāsantī arrests Rāma's fall with the words 'Compose yourself' etc. The chanting of the verse by Rāma would gradually become indistinct with heavy and slurring syllables and faltering voice.[11] Sītā swoons in her zone, with Tamasā holding her limp body. Sītā can also take support of a pillar.

There is a complete dramatic silence when Sītā swoons. A sudden cessation of all stage action including music is maintained till Sītā recovers from her swoon.

The coming forward of Sītā and touching Rāma's heart and cheek even when done in *lokadharmī* style, the actress would not touch Rāma physically; but come near him and make a demonstrative gesture of touch. Rāma recovers when Sītā comes forward and enacts in a slow tempo the gesture of touching him. The deliberate silence on the stage which is maintained till then is broken at this point after Vāsantī's words by the music.

Rāma chants Verse 39 and rest of the few lines after the

musical interlude is over with his eyes half closed (*kuñcita*)[12] and enacts the thrilling touch of the beloved (*sparśasukha*). He does this by narrowing down the eyes, raising the eyebrows and touching the heart and cheeks where Sītā's hand was placed.[13] This is accompanied by the movement of the other limbs such as horripilation, change of colour, change of voice and a brightness of face.[14] The *bhāvābhinaya* of joy, wonder and pathos (depicting love in separation) is to be enacted with corresponding transitory states.

The Invisibility of Sītā and Tamasā

They would exhibit their invisibility by touching the head with the right hand raised from the side in the gesture of the *arāla hasta* where the fore-finger is curved like a bow, the thumb is also curved with the remaining fingers separated and turned upwards.[16] Both of them can also, at times, conceal themselves behind the pillars of MAT and establish their invisibility.

Notes

1. There is as yet no consensus on the exact shade of colour which śyāma suggests (Supra part three, chapter 9, p. 172). However, the traditional theatres of South in the present time depict the colour 'as deep brownish green'. The play is visualised in *dākṣiṇātya pṛravtti* and hence the colour *śyāma* is taken as per the *śyāma* colour in kudiyattam.
2. Herringham, Ajanta Frescoes, 1 cave xvii, Pl. xxvi, 28.
3. Text ed. and trans. by Kale M. R. (4th ed.), p. 934, pp. 36-37.
4. NS, XIII, 197-99.
5. Bh. P. V. 85.
6. NS, XIV, 51.
7. NS, XIII, 63-64.
8. Ibid. 171-76 (tr. M. Ghosh).
9. Ibid, 63-66.
10. NS, VII, 106 (M. Ghosh).
11. NS, XXVI, 101-02 (M. Ghosh).
12. Bh. P. V., 167, also NS, XXIV, 78 (Kashi ed.).
13. NS, XXIV, 82 (M. Ghosh).
14. Ibid, 88-89 (M. Ghosh).
15. NS, XXVI, 70-71.
16. NS, IX, 46-52.

Section 3

Mahendra Vikram Varma's Mattavilāsa—Prahasana

(A sequence from a farce named 'Drunken revelry')

1. Rūpaka

This is a pure (*śuddha*) type of *prahasana*—a genre of *daśa-rūpaka*.

Prahasana, as we have seen previously, is a farce or a ridicule in the form of mimicry and mockery of the hypocracies of ancient society. The locale of this farce is Kāñcī, the important city centre of South India in 7th century A.D. The farce revolves round the exploits of a Kāpālin, a Śaiva mendicant of a skull-bearing order and his female disciple, named Devasomā, who have lost their begging bowl (a skull) in a drunken brawl. The play depicts their search for it. In the course of their search they meet a number of characters belonging to other religious sects; like Nāgasena, a degenerate Buddhist monk, Babhrukalpa, a Pāśupata and a lunatic. In the end, the skull is found from a dog who had dragged it away. Each character in the play portrays a caricature of the current religious sectarians and their behaviour. This contributes to the general mood of hilarity[1] of the play and evokes *hāsya rasa* by provoking excessive laughter (*atihāsa*)[2] among the spectators. *Atihāsa*, as we have seen in earlier chapters, is one of the traditional vocal manners of appreciation signifying the success of a play. A short sequence depicting a hilarious situation of this farce is visualised here.

2. Sandhi (juncture in the plot [*vastu*] progression)

Mukha sandhi stage.

3. Rasa

Predominant rasa comic (*hāsya*) with odious (*bīdhatsa*) as a subsidiary.

4. Style (vṛtti)

Verbal (*bhāratī*). It employs all the ten subdivisions of *prahasana* and thirteen divisions of *vīthī* which is dominated by *bhāratī vṛtti*.

5. **Regional mode (Pravṛtti)**

   Dākṣiṇāṭya.

6. **Dharmī**

   Lokadharmī presentation.

   A play presenting inferior worldly characters suggests a *lokadharmī* presentation.

7. **Netā**: Dramatis Personae (in the sequence)
   - (i) The Kāpālin: Satyasoma, a drunken Śaiva mendicant of a low order carrying a human skull as an alms bowl. Inferior type. Support of comic as well as odius.
   - (ii) Devasomā: His temporary female companion who was a former paramour of the Pāśupata sectarian named Babhrukalpa. She is the only female character in the farce and is very colourfully delineated. She is an inferior type who is presented in various stages of intoxication throughout the play. She is the support of comic and odius.
   - (iii) Nāgasena: A Buddhist monk, a degenerate hypocrite, covetous of wine, women and good food. Inferior type. Support of comic.

8 **Āhārya**
   - (a) Body Paint.
   - (b) Costumes and Accessories.

The Kāpālin: Satyasoma:

- (a) The skin paint would be dark brown[3] and dirty with ash marks on chest, arms and forehead.[4] He would have matted locks and bushy beard.[5]
- (b) His costume would be of tattered pieces of rags, barks and skins of undefined dirty (*malina*) colour,[6] with streaks of white (suggestive of comic) and blue (suggestive of odius).[7] He would wear a *muṇḍamālā* (a necklace of skulls) and others made with beads around his neck, wrists, arms and feet respectively. He also would have a cow's horn tucked in his belt. From the text it is gathered that possession of a human skull is essential for a Kāpālin.

Devasomā, the female disciple:

- (a) She is described by the text as "a bawd, an attractive damsel belonging to a Śaivaite order who shifts her alliance to a number of different sects".[8] She would be painted dark (aśita which literally means not white) or pale brown[9] with tatoo marks on the forehead[10] and would have loose unkept hair.

(b) She would wear an *ekavastra*, one piece of soiled cloth of muddy tawnish colour draped round her body with a dirty olive breast cloth. She would also wear many necklaces and other ornaments made of beads. She would have tattered brownish dirty sack with her.

Nāgasena, a buddhist monk:

(a) His skin colour would be dark brown.[11] He would have a clean shaven head.[12]

(b) He would wear two pieces of dark red (*kaśāya*) cloth[13] with the lower garment, a *cīvara* worn in such a way that many folds would cover his upper body. The text describes him as carrying a begging bowl in his hand. He should appear spruse, clean and rich in comparison with the other two characters. (See the sketches and notes on p. 390).

9. The Use of the Stage

The zonal division is designed on the resources available in a small square play house, as described by Bharata.

Accordingly, the stage areas would consist of RP (12′ × 12′), RS (a square block of 12′ × 12′ behind the RP), two MATs (of 12′ × 12′ each on either side of RP) with the dressing room behind the stage proper (See the sketch on p. 59). The spectators would sit on three sides of the stage in a tiered seating arrangement.

10. Lighting

Three open sides of the *raṅgamaṇḍapa* would have three lamps placed at the centre of the edges.

11. Kutapa

The musical orchestra in SAT zone of RS region. Use of music where the percussion predominates.

Visualisation

Text[14]

(Behind the curtain)

Revered Sir! Here are alms! Pray accept them, Sir.

Kāpālin: Here I accept. Dear, where is my skull?

Devasomā: Me too could not find it.

Kāpālin: (thinking) Ah! I guess, that it was left forgotten in that liquor shop. Well, let us go back and look for it.

Devasomā: . . . It is sinful not to receive the alms offered with respect.

Kāpālin: . . . . take it in the cow's horn.

Devasomā: So be it (accepts).

(Both walk around and search)

Kāpālin: . . . . I am undone! My penance is lost. By what shall I now become a Kāpālin? Oh, misery.

Verse 11

(Falls down and beats his head). . . It is just a token. I am not stripped off the title Kāpālin.

(Stands up)

Devasomā: Let us go about the city of Kāñci in search of it.

Kāpālin: Yes, my dear.

(both walk around)

Production Notes

The sequence begins with a voice from behind the curtain which comes from the *kutapa*, in this case.

The Kāpālin who is in the centre of RP with Devasomā responds to it as if the voice is coming from the front, in the 'speech in the air' technique. He would come nearer to the lamp in the downstage centre for this. Their search for the begging bowl is enacted in all the three open sides of the stage. The Kāpālin starts his first walk around the stage before Verse 11 with Devasomā following. Then he would fall down. Devasomā would stagger and fall too. The walk around would be accompanied by drums and percussion instruments. Being *dākṣinātya* local usage the going around would be executed from the right.[15]

Abhinaya

The farce, with inferior types of characters, would have emphasis on *āṅgika abhinaya*, with the minimum of *sāttvikā*.[16] Enactment would mainly depend on the proficient skill of actors in the verbal (*bhāratī*) employment of many *prahasana-vīthī* subdivisions. Body movements (*āṅgika*) would be mainly *lokadharmī*—expressing literal meaning of the spoken words—often taking recourse to exaggerated gestures and movements. The gait of the intoxicated Kāpālin would be enacted by unsteady staggering steps and occasional slant of the body (*vidhūrṇita śarira*).[17] The gait of Devasomā suggesting her intoxicated condition would have a reeling movement of the body with feet going forward and backward with staggering faulty steps. At times her walk would be distracted (*udbhrāntā*). She would walk with slightly raised body and flourishing of arms, after assuming *aśvakrāntā sthāna*.[18] Both the characters would continue these gaits in their stylised going around (*parikramā*). Being a square stage the foot movements of the gait would be squarish (*catura-sra* type).[19] The bigger walk around for the search of the skull in the city of Kāñcī would be delineated by *citra abhinaya* depicting different sites of the city. They would enact these sites by their *abhinaya* in different areas of the stage by frontally facing the spectators sitting on the three open sides.

Text

(Then enters a Buddhist monk with a bowl in hand)

Buddhist Monk: Wonder indeed, is the bounty of . . . Merchant Dhanadāsa . . . from him, I obtained alms—meal with a rich variety of fish and meat of agreeable colour and smell and taste (walking about, to himself) Ha! the venerable Tathāgata has favoured the . . . monks with palatial buildings . . . sleep in couch . . . eating in the forenoon . . . savoury beverages . . . fragrant betel leaves . . . (wearing of) soft fine garments . . . but why is it that possession of women and drinking of liquor is not prescribed to us? . . . I am sure that these lazy wretched elders must have blotted that out from the canonical books . . . I shall do service to the Buddhists (by favouring the original texts).

Devasomā: Look! Look! Here is a man in red garments hurrying .... with stealthy steps.

Kāpālin: ... (approaching) O monk! You stop.

Buddhist Monk: .... I should not become the target of his drunken brawl (hurries along).

Kāpālin: ... (runs forward and blocks his way) Ha! Rascal! Where will you go now?

Buddhist Monk: What is this? (to himself) Ha! What a beautiful sister!

... (Dialogues between Buddhist monk and the Kāpālin. In the end the Kāpālin seizes the end of the robe of the Buddhist Monk.)

Buddhist Monk: Reverence to Buddha.

Kāpālin: Rather reverence to 'Karapaṭa' who promulgated the science of theft. Or perhaps, the Buddha may be superior to Karapaṭa in this field, Why?

He, ere the very eyes of Brahmins,
Has built a treasure of cannons.
Gathering the ideas from Mahābhārata,
As also from the texts of Vedānta. (Verse 12)

Production Notes

The Buddhist monk would enter from the northen side stage door as per the rules of the dākṣināṭya regional mode. His entry would find the former group in the uppermost corner of the upstage RS area. During the long speech of the monk, this group would freeze into an unobtrusive formation suggesting a state of drunken stupor.

The monk would enact his long 'self-reporting' (ātmanivedanam) by first turning on his left side and establishing a zone on the downstage RP near the region of the left MAT pillar. His speech contains humour,[20] wit, play on words and many subdivisions of *vīthī* and *prahasana*. For example, his reference to the virtue of enjoyment of wine and women displays *mṛdava*[21] division of *vīthī* where the vice is considered virtue and vice versa and, *nālikā*[22] where the humour is concealed within the deadpan enigmatic remarks like 'the need to reform the Buddhist canon' etc. These remarks would be skilfully enunciated by the actor with *madhyama* note,[23] *svarita* and *uddāta* accents[24] and tonal variations from medium to slow.[25]

The scuffle between the monk and the *Kāpālin* would take place in the downstage RP centre. The scuffle would be enacted with exaggerated *lokadharmī āṅgika* movements accompanied by drumbeats and percussion. *Devasomā* would watch it leaning drunkenly against the extreme upstage pillar in the RS right.[26] The dialogues between them would be enunciated in *lokadharmī* style with full play of repartee.

The verse 12 by the *Kāpālin* clearly shows the subdivision *prapañca* in which the double meaning exaggeratedly conceals the real thought. The Kāpālin would enunciate that with a verbal punch in excited (*dīpta*) note, (*svarita*) accents, (*vicceda*) pause and separation before the pivotal words like "Buddha may be superior to . . . (*vicceda*). . . *Karapaṭa*".

The audience of that period must have had a good laugh with all the three traditionally acknowledged responsive laughters viz. silent smile (*smīta*), smile (*ardhahāsa*) and excessive laughter (*atihāsa*).

NOTES

1. It is curious that a portion of this farce—namely, the dance of Kāpālin—is regularly enacted, to this day, by the chakyars of Kerala in Kudiyattam tradition. However, the part is performed to project the sanctity and supremacy of the Śaivaite tradition where the Kāpālin is none other than Lord Śiva in disguise. The portion is performed in answer to the wish-fulfilment of the devotees.
2. NS, XXVII, 4.
3. NS, XXIII, 100-02.
4. In Kudiyattam presentation a third eye is painted on his forehead. This is to symbolise that he is the incarnation of Lord Śiva himself.
5. NS, XXIII, 109-10.
6. Ibid, 123-27.
   Mattavilāsam description by the playwright.
7. NS, VI, 42-43.
8. Unni N. P., English tr. of Mattavilāsa Ist ed. 1974, Introduction, p. 18.
9. NS, XXIII, 104-05.
10. Ibid, 66.
11. Ibid, 104-05.
12. Ibid, 106-07.
13. Ibid, 127.
14. Text by Unni N. P., op. cit. pp. 77-80

15. NS, XIV, 51.
16. NS, IX, 165.
17. NS, XIII, 120 (Kashi ed.), 122 (M. Ghosh).
18. NS, XIII, 158-59.
19. Ibid, 20.
20. Bh. P., III, 50.
21. Bh. P., VIII, 82.
22. Ibid, 79.
23. NS, XIX, 38-40.
24. Ibid, 43.
25. Ibid, 72.
26. For the sitting posture in intoxicated state, See p. 140 fig. 12.

Section 4

Vararuci's Ubhayābhisārikā

1. Rūpaka

This single actor play belongs to the *bhāṇa* genre of *Daśarūpaka*. It is one of the four *bhāṇa*-s known as *Caturbhāṇī* which were found at the same time from Trichur in Kerala.[1] Though authored by different dramatists, the Caturbhāṇī manuscript is considered the earliest specimen of this genre that we possess. Dr. Motichandra dates it to 5th century A.D.[2]

Bhāṇa, as a genre of the ten major types of Sanskrit plays provide us also with a continuing link with one of the earliest varieties of rudimentary one-actor drama form[3] which appears to have persistently maintained its independent popular appeal, even when many of its commonly accepted features got assimilated in the later more evolved forms of *nāṭyarūpaka*-s. For example, the *ekāhārya abhinaya* technique adopted in the depiction of long verbal passages with a single character describing his own or the other's experiences and exploits by assuming various characters without any change of costume or get up.

In the long period of its existence, the *bhāṇa* genre, even while maintaining its basic structure and the technique of performance, had narrowed down to the depiction of one subject only. The content had mainly remained pleasure oriented (*krīḍāpradhāna*).[4] *Bhāṇa*-s that we possess also reflect this aspect of the pleasures of the ancient man in his social environment. The expertise in the affairs with the courtesans (*veśyopacāra*) or the specialisation in gallantry by an expert rake and the knowledge of sixty-four arts and crafts[5] were some of the requirements of a citizen (*nāgaraka*) as a member of assemblies of the experts (*goṣṭhi-sabhā*-s). The gallants or the rakes (*viṭa*), the courtesans and their messangers (*dūta* and *dūtī*) were some of the personae belonging to this environment and they are faithfully portrayed in this genre.

All four plays in the *caturbhāṇī*, including this *bhāṇa*, exhibit similarity in the following basic *rasa-vastu-netā* structure:

(1) They are all one-act plays with a single actor, *viṭa*, who is an expert gallant—a man about town. The plays describe his experiences when he sets out to help a friend (the absent hero) in his love affair with a courtesan.

(2) The plots constitute a journey of a *viṭa* towards the prostitute's quarters of a city where, as a messanger (*dūta*) of his friend, the absent hero, he presents a graphic description of the life of pleasure (*krīḍā*) of the citizenery of ancient India. In a vivid monologue consisting of wit, jokes, anecdotes, descriptions, impersonations and songs, he portrays the atmosphere of the areas of the prostitutes and various characters he comes across. In a presentation which is at times comic, at times vulgar, at times erotic and on a number of occasions also poetic, he ridicules the foibles of the hypocritical pleasure seekers in their dealings with the courtesans.[6]

(3) The techniques and conventions of *abhinaya* adopted by the single actor to present a *bhāṇa*, are:

(a) The six aspects of histrionic representation (*samānyābhinaya*) through the body to enact the monologues written mainly in Sanskrit, comprising of prose and verse.

(b) Dialogue representation with imaginary characters with the use of 'speech in the air' technique.

(c) Impersonation of other characters with *ekāhārya* technique whereby a sole actor impersonates more than one characters without the change of costume or get up (*āhārya*).

(d) Incorporation of an occasional *lāsyāṅga* (song with *abhinaya*) and/or a song to enhance the *bhāva* presentation.

2. **Sandhi** (*juncture in the plot* [*vastu*] *progression*)

In this *bhāṇa*, the *viṭa*, Vaiśikācala by name, sets out to reconcile a courtesan named Nārāyaṇadattā—who is enraged and separated from his friend Sāgardatta in a lover's quarrel. Sāgardatta, a merchant's son in the city of Kusumpura, is the hero and the courtesan is the heroine, the *viṭa* is only an assistant and a messanger in the love affair. However, it is the actor playing *viṭa* alone who depicts the entire episode without the presence of hero, heroine or other characters. He does this by bringing to life with his monoacting a number of vignette characters such as young courtesans returning from their trysts, a wandering nun, an old hag, a pauperised son of a caravan chief and many others. A small sequence of this *bhāṇa*, in the concluding juncture (*nirvahaṇa sandhi*) has been selected for visualisation. The sequence indicates the point where the *viṭa* comes to know from the maid of the heroine, Nārāyaṇadattā, that the separated lovers have already been united.

3. **Rasa**

Erotic and comic.

4. **Style: (Vṛtti)**

Verbal (*bhāratī*).

The styles and the *rasa*-s of a *bhāṇa* genre appear to have passed through long phases of change and development which should be noted here. *Nāṭyaśāstra*, in its description of *bhāṇa*, does not mention any specific *rasa*, but says that the graceful style (*kaiśikī*) generating the erotic *rasa* does not feature in a *bhāṇa*.[7] Abhinavagupta in his commentary considers comic, marvellous and even pathetic as its chief *rasa*-s but not erotic.[8] It is only in Dhananjaya's *Daśarūpaka* (974-95 A.D.) that we get a reference to heroic and erotic *rasa*-s in connection with *bhāṇa*.[9] Bhāvaprakāśa mentions Kohala's view and says that a *bhāṇa* evokes erotic and heroic *rasa*-s because it describes auspicious and valourous episodes (*saubhāgya* and *śaurya*) in mainly verbal style.[10] *Sahitya Darpaṇa* includes both graceful (*kaiśikī*) and verbal (*bhāratī*) styles with the erotic and heroic *rasa*-s emanating from it.[11] Dr. Motichandra includes comic *rasa* also.[12] This reflects a wide variety of change in emphasis of *rasa* presentation that the *bhāṇa* genre must have undergone in the long history of its existence.

So far as the chosen sequence is concerned, the chief style is *bhāratī* (verbal) and the *rasa*-s are erotic and comic.

5. **Regional mode (Pravṛtti)**

Oḍramāgadhī.

6. **Dharmī**

Nāṭyadharmī presentation.

Although the subject-matter and the characters represented in the play suggest worldly happenings, the basic concept of a single actor representing a variety of characters commend a *nāṭyadharmī* theatre of imagination where a number of conventional stage practices are made use of.

7. **Netā**—*Adhikārī hero and other dramatis personae*

The *viṭa* (Vaiśikācala) a medium type. The *viṭa* as an only actor on the stage brings to life the following characters with his expert *abhinaya* in this small sequence:

(1) Kanakalatā—the maid of Nārāyaṇadattā.
(2) Her friends.
(3) A love-lorn youth singing a love-song on his lute.
(4) The lover Sāgaradatta, the *adhikārī* hero.
(5) The courtesan, Nārāyaṇadattā, the heroine.

8. **Āhārya**

(a) The body paint and
(b) Costumes and accessories.

Viṭa—Vaiśikācala

(a) Blue body paint, with artistic designs of *tilaka* on the forehead; arms and chest are smeared in designs with saffron and sandalwood.
(b) Fashionably draped *dhotī* in a pale green colour, with a mauve coloured jacket with full sleeves (half kañcuka). Foppishly tied multicoloured turban. A pale magenta coloured upper garment modishly draped on shoulders and arms according to the situation. Stylishly ornamented with golden ornaments covering the neck, waist, forearms, fingers, ears and waist. Also a garland with perfumed flowers.

This costume is based by combining the elements of the dress of a *viṭa* as seen in Kushan Mathura frieze (1st century A.D.) at the National Museum, New Delhi, with the style of dressing of men about town as seen in Ajanta frescoes (Vakataka, 5th century A.D.).

(See the notes and sketch 396 on p. 398)

9. The Use of the Stage

This one actor performance would ideally require a small, intimate gathering to be able to communicate the nuances of various impersonations. The zonal division is designed on the resources available on the small triangular playhouse, as described by Bharata, where the spectators would surround the stage on all the three open sides.

The entire stage, with all its area divisions of RP, RS, two MATs and the stage pillars are used by the actor to display his skill of many impersonations. However, most of the action would be frontal with the actor facing the spectators seated on the three open sides of the stage. This would be either in the middle of the RP or in the new zones created by the two MATs.

A seat placed in the middle of RP would be the only stage furniture on the otherwise bare stage.

10. Lighting

The lighting source would be the lamplight placed in the middle of the downstage edge of the RP and the torches tied to the MAT pillars.

11. Kutapa

With full use of the musical accompanists in the upstage centre area of SAT in RS.

Visualisation

Text[13]

Viṭa (Rake): (Walking on)

Oh, but this surely, is Kanakalatā, Nārāyaṇadattā's maid. I see, she has profusely dusted her two breasts with scented powder, and worn bunches of flowers round her hair, and wrists; she must be a little drunk the way she is walking, looking particularly merry. I must talk to her but why is she coming so close to me to bow?

Yes, my woman, what are you saying?
"My salutation to you, Sir"
May you always be your lover's sweetheart!
Now, why have you honoured our street with your lotus feet?
What is this?

"You always say such nice things, Sir"
No, no, I don't mean to flatter you.
"I am much obliged to you, Sir."

That is all right; tell me now, why have these two lovers—two *cakravāka* birds—separated? Tell me, quickly.

"Consumed with jealousy my mistress had thrown off all her jewellery, and was sitting on a rock under a small Aśoka tree in the Aśoka grove. The moon (was) in the clear sky. . .All these increased her longing and added (to) her misery. The friends tried to comfort her with soothing words. Just then, someone as if he too was smitten with love, passed by the grove, humming some songs in *vaktra* and *apavaktra* metres to the soft liquid music of his viṇā. He sang:

What's youth, beauty, wealth? Alas, Alas!
If you don't frolic with your young love,
When the spring is here.

And then, another song:

Life is sadder still if the moon shines brighter in the sky,
And the cuckoo's calls fill the air,
Yet you don't court your love.

The song soothed her, cooled her anger, and suddenly she just could not wait, not even for you; Sir, she called me and left on foot for the master's house. He too, finding the spring tormenting, was coming to my mistress to beg for love. And they came, face to face, at the door of the Vīṇā player, Viśvavāsudatta. . ."

Production Notes

The above sequence is divided into the following sub-sequences:

(a) *The viṭa sees—Kanakalatā, the maid's approach*:

(Oh, but this surely is Kanakalatā. . .etc.)

(Line 5, p. 143).[14]

When the sequence begins, the *viṭa* has finished his conversation with Priyaṅgusenā regarding a musical play-*saṅgītaka* -to be performed in the palace, and is moving around the stage. As the production is planned in *auḍramāgadhī* regional mode he would move around from the left. His gait would be graceful. He would put forward a *kuñcita* foot with one *tāla* while holding the *kaṭaka vardhamāna* hands with proper *sauṣṭhava.*[15] Suddenly halting in the centre of RP; and standing in *Vaiṣṇavasthāna,*[16] he would look intently with eyes and face turning on the right side of the front part of the stage with a *patākā* hand held on his head, with quivering fingers[17] to indicate the sight of a person. He would speak the above line, after this.

(b) *Kanakalatā, the handmaild's approach*:

The lines describing Kanakalatā's approach would be spoken by the *viṭa* while enacting the role of the maid through *ekāhārya abhinaya.* His gait would change into that of a tipsy, merry walk of the maid. He would walk with slightly raised body and flourishing arms.[18] To indicate intoxication, his steps would be occasionally uneven.[19] His eyes would have liquid *madirā* glance.[20] All the walks and the moving around would have medium triangular (*trayasra*) foot movements,[21] which would be accompanied by *trayasra* rhythm on the drums and the percussion instruments. The *viṭa* would walk with time beat of two *kalā*-s in his own character and with the time beat of one *kalā* while impersonating the maid. The percussion instruments would accompany the walks and the moving around.

As a maid, the *viṭa* would establish an independent zone in the downstage area near the right MAT pillar.

To show the beauty of her form, he would assume a definite standing posture of *avahittha* stance[22] and with two *padmakoṣa* hands held in front of the chest (to represent the beauty of breasts), with *haṃsapakṣa* hands moving over them to suggest gentle massage with unguent.[23] This will be done with *ardhapatākā* hands. After which in quick succession he would use *mukula*[24] and *padmakoṣa* hands to indicate the placing of flowers in the hair.

(c) *Their Dialogue—In Ekāhārya abhinaya*:

From the line "I must talk to her"...to "Tell me now, why have these two lovers, (two *cakravāka* birds) separated"?

(Lines 6-15, p. 143)

The speech of the *viṭa* would be depicted in his original *prakṛti* (i.e. in his original character type). He would stand in the centre RP in a *vaiṣṇava sthāna*. His dialogues would be conducted with a *sahaja* (natural) expression in a *lokadharmī* style accompanying the spoken words which would be enunciated in grave and low pitch[25] and medium tempo.

Turning the body to face the place where he, as a *viṭa*, stood, the *viṭa* would now assume *avahittha sthāna*, in his impersonation of the maid, and would enunciate the spoken words in a quick tempo intoned in grave and high tone. The *viṭa* would use *sākānkṣa kāku*[26] before starting the last line.

(d) Description by the maid of the courtesan sitting on a seat under the Aśoka tree in the Aśoka grove in a jealous love lorn state.

(Lines 16-18, p. 144)

Āṅgika abhinaya of each stage:

(In *śākhā-aṅga-upāṅga abhinaya*, accompanied by the music from the *kutapa*)

(i) The *viṭa* would sit as the courtesan on the seat in the RP. To indicate her jealous and *mānaviyogī* state,[27] he will adopt vacant (*śunya*) and pale (*malina*)[28] glances. The head would be bent on one side, with one foot resting on the seat and other foot stretched slightly; he would assume the posture of sitting in a deep thought.[29]

(ii) Aśoka tree and the rock underneath would be indicated with two hands raised with *patākā* and *svastika hasta*-s, *with udvāhita* head looking down.[30]

(iii) The moon in the clear sky would be indicated by slightly narrowing down of the eyes in *ullokita prayoga*[31] by raising the eyebrows. This would indicate the touch of the moonlight and subsequent horripilation.[32]

(iv) Humming of the bees—by the gesture of *tripatākā* hands.[33]

(v) Fragrant breeze—by *haṃsapakṣa hasta*-s.[34]

(vi) Her friends and their soothing words—by the *mṛgaśīrṣa* hasta[35] and improvisation of appropriate *sāttvika* and transitory states to indicate anxiety and agitation.

In addition, the *viṭa* would delineate the jealous and melancholy states of a medium type of a heroine by depicting stages of her jealousy like this:

(a) Depression (*vaimanasya*) represented by intense jealous face, trembling lips due to anger.[36]

(b) Disgust (*viprīya*) represented by responses of repulsing the solicitations of friends with angry laughter. Also by weeping and shaking of the head.[37]

(c) Anger (*manyu*) enacted by the responses of turning around the bangles and by apprehensive and tearful eyes.[38]

(d) And, finally, the exhibition of sorrow by weeping, sighing, striking the breasts[39] and the harmonious representation of *vipralambha śṛṅgāra* (stages of love while separated from the lover) like distress, lamentation[40] etc.

(e) The two songs will be sung by the *viṭa* here, with the musical orchestra joining him, especially the male vocalist and the *vīṇā* player.

The actor (*viṭa*) would enact the *padārthābhinaya* of each word with appropriate *bhāva* depicting in *aṅkura* pattern of delineation (i.e. where the sentence is sung (or spoken) first, followed by the improvisational *abhinaya*). Each pada (the word and the phrase) with its various shades of meaning and moods would be enacted by the *viṭa* alternatively as the love-lorn youth and as the reactions of the courtesan also.

(f) *Abhisaraṇa*:

After the songs, the *viṭa*, impersonating the courtesan, would assume the favourable mind (*iṣṭa*), represented by happy expressions.[41] He would start decorating the body—with *āṅgika* movements of donning the ornaments and unguents etc. He would also start a slow walk as if the heroine is setting out in the company of the attendants. He would express an obvious display of passion in the style of *veśyābhisaraṇa prakāra*[42] (a courtesan going for a tryst with her lover).

(g) *The delineation of impersonation of Sāgardatta*:

> The lines: "He too finding the spring tormenting was coming to my mistress. . .at the door of the vīṇā player, Viśvavāsudatta. (line 3 p. 145)

Sāgaradatta's gait: *Viṭa* would walk to impersonate hero with graceful steps in *atikrāntā cārī* with steps of two *tāla*-s wide. His left hand showing unturned *kaṭakamukha hasta* would be on the navel; and the right hand with *arāla* would be on the side. His body would be in proper *sauṣṭhava.*[43] His condition of love-lorn despair would be shown by the *vyabhicāri*-s of excessive breathing in anxiety, looking to the path or gazing vacantly at the sky.[44]

In the beginning before he starts his 'walk around the stage in the above-mentioned *cārī* to go for meeting his beloved, the *viṭa* impersonating the hero would stand in *vaiṣṇava sthāna*; with a slight *asauṣṭhava* of the body. Then when he starts to walk in the *parikramā* towards the beloved's house, he would walk as if he was being guided by a female messenger (imaginary). He would take slow, silent steps, maintaining proper tempo and *tāla.*[45] All the walks and going around (*parikramā*) would be accompanied by percussion instruments.

(h) *The Meeting*

The lines "They came face to face at the door of *viṇā* player Viśvavāsudatta."

(Line 4, p. 145)

The *viṭa* would depict this line as the maid Kanakalatā, as if she was recounting the tale to the *viṭa*. The *abhinaya* would be mostly *lokadharmī* with the facial expressions appropriate to the spoken words. The maid would be standing in *avahittha sthāna*, with hands in *catura* gestures.[46]

A Note

The *ekāhārya abhinaya* technique continues to be employed to this day in most of the classical dance styles. The *vācika abhinaya* can be approximated by observing the recitals of the present day story-tellers like *harikathākāra*-s or the *Māṇabhaṭṭakāra*-s of Gujarat where a solo reciter, with the aid of only *vācika* and *sāttvika abhinaya*, presents before the spectators an array of a number of characters and happenings.

Taking the above as practical guides as well as with the help of the minutely detailed techniques that the traditional dramaturgists from *nāṭyaśāstra* onwards have laid down the performance of *bhāṇa* sequence is visualised here. It needs an able actor who is well versed in the art of *abhinaya* (*āṅgika*, *vācika* as well as *sāttvika*) to intuitively improvise and paint a large spectrum of characterisation with a few highly suggestive strokes in a short duration of time.

NOTES

1. Motichandra and Agrawal V., Caturbhāṇi (Guptakālina Sṛngāra Hāṭa in Hindi) Ist ed. Introduction, p. 4.
2. Ibid, p. 7.
3. Dr. D. R. Mankad considered *Bhāṇa* as the earliest primitive form of Indian drama. The types of Sanskrit drama, p. 78. Also Ketkar Godavari, op. cit. p. 354.
4. Abh. I, sl. 108-15, 1-16.
5. KS, I, 3, 34—The Jain literature, however, numbers seventy-two arts and crafts (see, Amulya Chandra Sen "Social Life in Jain Literature, Calcutta, 1933, pp. 12-15.
6. NS devotes an independent chapter—Ch. XXV—on dealing with courtesans.
7, 8 and 9. Motichandra and Agrawal V., quoting Dr. De S. K. (J.R.A.S.), 1926, pp. 63-90, op. cit. p. 2-3.
10. Bh. P., VIII, 159.
11. SD, VI, 229 and after that L-3.
12. Motichandra and Agrawal V., op. cit. p. 3.
13. Rao Amiya and Rao B. C., translation of the Sanskrit text, p. 59.65.
14. The lines are numbered according to Dr. Motichandra's edited version of the original text, op. cit., p. 143-45.
15. NS, XIII, 110 (gait of a viṭa).
16. Vaiṣṇava sthāna—See fig. No. 2 on. p. 139.
17. NS, XXIV, 83 (M. Ghosh).
18. NS, XIII, 181-83 (M. Ghosh).
19. NS, XXIV, 221 (Kashi ed.).
20. NS, VIII, 81 (M. Ghosh).
21. NS, XIII, 20.
22. NS, XIII, 164-67 (M. Ghosh); see the Fig. 8 on p. 139.
23. NS, IX, 105-08 (M. Ghosh).
24. Ibid, 116 (M. Ghosh).
25. NS, XIX, 45.
26. Sakānkṣa Kāku is the one entailing expectation, NS, XIX, 44.
27. Bh. P. IV, 60-63.
28. NS, VIII, 86-93 (M. Ghosh).
29. NS, XIII, 197-98, See the fig. 11 on p. 140.
30. NS, XXVI, 5.
31. AD, 75, 76.
32. Ibid 6, horripilation is indicated by Hamsapakṣa hasta turning into Hansāsya according to A.D. 156.
33. NS, IX, 26-32.
34. Ibid, 105-08.
35. AD, 139-42.
36. NS, XXIV, 264.
37. Ibid, 268.
38. Bh. P. IV, 60-63.
39. NS, XXIV, 262-70.
40. NS, XXVI, 57.
41. NS, XXIV, 83-85.
42. Bh. P., IV, 169, also 170. NS, XXIV, 219 (Kashi ed.)
43. NS, XXIV, 40-44 and 76-78 (M. Ghosh).
44. NS, XXIV, 194-96.
45. NS, XIII, 40-44.
46. NS, IX, 96-98 (M. Ghosh).

The Costume Sketches of the Sequences

The costume sketches of the sequences of the Sanskrit dramas as well as the sketches of stage accessories (*upakaraṇa*) are visualised here by taking recourse to the following:

G. Yazdani	: Ajanta (Texts and Plates), I-IV
Herringham	: Ajanta Frescoes
Bharata's	: NS (Kashi Ed.)
Dr. Motichandra	: Prachina Bharatiya Veshabhusha
	: Costumes, Textiles, Cosmetics and Coiffure in Ancient and Mediaeval India.
Ghurye G.S.	: Indian Costume.

This is done with the objective of visualising the colour (appropriate to *rasa* presented), the styles of dresses and draping as nearer to the period of the playwright as possible. At times, certain details are also adopted and added to the costume taking into consideration the view expressed by Dr. Motichandra who says that the dancers (actors), both male and female, covered their bodies fully (op. cit., the English version p. 72). He mentions *Bṛhat Kalpa Sūtra Bhāṣya* (IV, p. 412-17) referring to a dancer who could dance in abandon having dressed properly. However, while adding the details to original fresco or sculptural scurce/s care has been taken to select a piece of apparel which was in vogue in the particular period.

Bhāsa's Ūrubhaṅgam

Figure 1. Baladeva	: Ajanta Cave 1. From line drawing in the Prince of Wales Museum, Bombay. Also from Dr. Motichandra, op. cit., p. 98, fig. 127 (Gandhara).
Figrue 2. Duryodhana	: Ajanta Cave 2. Ceiling detail of first aisle. Zimmer, op. cit. pl. 159. Also from Dr. Motichandra, op. cit., p. 85, fig. 108 (Sanchi).
Figure 3. Aśvatthāmā	: Top knot with a helmet (*Śtraṣa-kaṭāha*) from Vogel, "La Sculpture de Mathura" Mat. p. xxxvi. Also from Dr. Motichandra, op. cit., p. 76, fig. 64 (Sanchi) and p. 85, Fig. 110 (for footwear).

Costume Design of Bhā's Ūru. **Bh.**

Fig. 1.

Fig. 2

Fig. 3

Kālidāsa's Vikramorvaśīyam

Figure 1. Purūravas	:	Approximated from 1st century B.C. frieze of a Cakravartī king from Prasenjit pillar, Bharhut, stūpa.
Figure 2. Urvaśī	:	Green colour of parrot's tail, as per NS (Chapter XXIII, p. 60). Costume approximated on the figure on the wall of left corridor in Ajanta Cave No. 1.
Figure 3. Charioteer	:	Manner of draping the *dhotī* adapted from Dr. Motichandra, op. cit., p. 180, fig. 275 (3rd to 7th century A.D.).
Figure 4. Head/Hair dressings	:	Details of the king's crown (kirīṭa) with a triangular diadem—from Ajanta Cave No. 1, Harringham, op. cit., pl. xi, 13. Urvaśī's hair-style details from Ajanta Cave No. 1, Harringham, op. cit., pl. x, 12. Citralekhā's turbaned hairstyle from Ajanta, Cave No. 17, depicting an *apsarā*'s headgear.

Costume Design of Kā's VIK.

Fig. 4

Fig. 1

Fig. 3

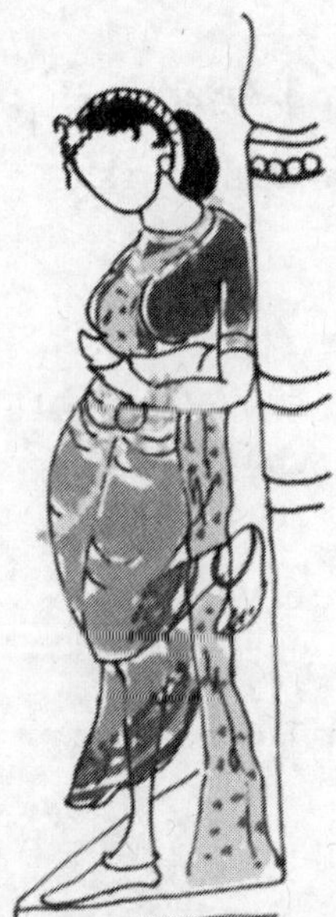

Fig. 2

Śūdraka's Mṛcchakaṭikam

Figure 1. Vasantasenā		Costume approximated on central figure in the toilet scene, Ajanta, Cave No. 17 (late sixth century) G. Yazdani, op. cit., pt. III, p. 95, pl. LXIV. Her hairstyle from the same cave, Harringham, pl. xxv, 29.
Figure 2. Ceṭī (maid)	:	Adapted from the costume of the female chawri bearer in the toilet scene referred above.
Figure 3. Āryaka	:	Costume approximated.
Figure 4. Sthāvaraka Ceṭa	:	Manner of draping the dress adapted from Dr. Motichandra, op. cit., p. 117, fig. 327 (of the same period).
Figure 5. Vardhamānaka Ceṭa	:	Manner of draping the dress adapted from Ajanta, Cave No. 17 scene of a royal procession.
Figure 6. Vīraka	:	Costume and sword adapted from the scene referred above.
Figure 7. Candanaka	:	Costume and sword adapted from the scene referred to above.

Costume Design of Sud's MRC.

Fig. 4

Fig. 6

Fig. 7

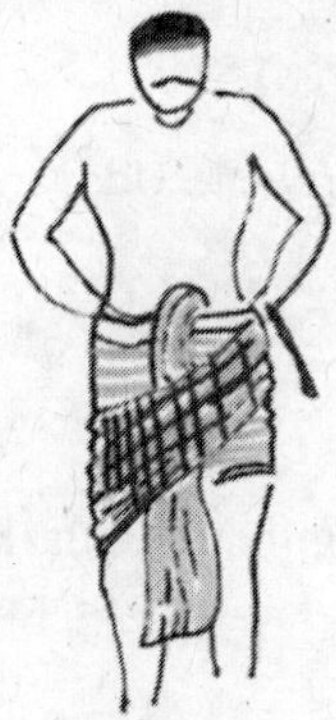

Fig. 5

Fig. 2

Fig. 1

Fig. 3

Śri Harṣa's Ratnāvalī

Figure 1. Udayana	:	Figure of king adapted from Badami, Cave III, image of Viṣṇu (c. 578 A.D.) Zimmer, op. cit., pl. 5, 126-27. His crown from Dr. Motichandra, op. cit., p. 79, No. 26.
Figure 2. Vidūṣaka (The jester)	:	Costume visualised from painting in Ajanta Cave No. 2 (7th century A.D.). Vidūṣaka's cap (as per Agrawal V.S.—Trishikhandaka) from Dr. Motichandra op. cit., p. 209, Fig. 364.
Figure 3. Kañcukī (The Chamberlain)	:	Costume visualised from Ajanta Cave No. 17 (5th century A.D.). His turban, Dr. Motichandra, op. cit, p. 67.
Figure 4. Vasubhūti	:	Costume approximated from Ajanta Cave No. 17, in the battle of Ceylon, Harringham, op. cit., pl. VIII, 10.
Figure 5. Vāsavadattā	:	The *uttarīya* draped in *gātrikā* style. Hairstyle as per Cave 1 Ajanta, from line drawing, Prince of Wales Museum, Bombay.
Figure 6. Sāgarikā	:	Costume approximated with hairstyle of one plait as per NS description (Chapter XXIII, 70).

Fig. 6

Fig. 5

Fig. 1

Fig. 2

Fig. 4

Fig. 3

Viśākhadatta's Mudrārākṣasam

Figure 1. Cāṇakya	:	Costume approximated from the painting depicting a minister, Ajanta Cave No. 17, Refer Dr. Motichandra, op. cit., p. 200 Fig. 331.
Figure 2. Rākṣasa	:	Costume visualised from Buddhist sculptures near Goli village, Maharashtra.
Group a: Candanadāsa	:	Costumes approximated from a citizen's dress, Ajanta Cave No. 17.
Candanadāsa's Wife	:	From Ajanta Cave No. 1, Dr. Motichandra, op. cit., p. 232 Fig. 422 is adapted as a base.
The son	:	From a painting in Cave No. 17 of a little boy.
Group b : Two Executioners	:	The costumes visualised from the fresco of the royal procession, in Cave No. 17, Ajanta.
The Drummer	:	From another portion of a frieze procession in Ajanta Cave No. 17. Reference in Ghurye G.S., op. cit., Photo 263.

Costume Design of Visakha's MR.

Group b

Fig. 1

Group a

Fig. 2

Bhavabhūti's Uttararāmacaritam

Figure 1. Sītā	: Visualised from a painting in Ajanta Cave No. 17. Also from Dr. Motichandra, op. cit., p. 225, Fig. 410. Hairstyle of one long plait of a *virahiṇī nāyikā*.
Figure 2. Rāma	: Adapted from a figure of a prince in Ajanta Cave No. 17. Also from Dr. Motichandra, op. cit., p. 187 Fig. 298. His crown—*kirīṭa*—(conical) slightly triangular in shape, Cave No. 17, Ajanta pl. xxvi 28 Harringham.
Figure 3. Tamasā	: Adapted from C. Sivaramamurti's "Some aspects of Indian Culture" friezes of river goddess, p. 16 (Fig. 5 and 6) also p. 30 (Fig. 22). And various reliefs of river goddesses at Ellora-Kailas temple (8th century A.D.).
Figure 4. Vāsantī	: Approximated from Śālabhanjikā figurines in 6th century A.D. Assam. Her hairstyle adapted from Ajanta Cave No. 17, Harringham, op. cit., pl. xxx (27).

Costume Design of Bhava's URC

Fig. 1

Fig. 2

Fig. 3

Fig. 4

Mahendra Vikram Vermā's Mattavilāsa—Prahasanam

Figure 1. Kāpālika Satyasomā	:	Approximated from Rawson Phillips, "The Art of Tantra" illustration No. 45 and 28 for muṇḍamālā, the same, p. 100. For cow's horn, Ghurye G.S., op. cit., pp. 243-45.
Figure 2. Devasomā	:	Adapted from Mathura pillar figures, (11th century A.D.) as shown in Zimmer, op. cit., Illustration 74-75a.
Figure 3. Buddhist Monk Nāgasena	:	Approximated from Dr. Motichandra's description of dresses of Buddhist monks in and around 7th century A.D. (Dr. Motichandra, op. cit., pp. 175, 177-78, 136).

Vararuci's Ubhayābhisārika—Bhāṇa (overleaf)

Viṭa Vaiśikācala	:	Adapted from the figure of a Viṭa in a Kushana frieze (1st century A.D.) at National Museum, New Delhi. Costume approximated from the painting of men about town as seen in Ajanta (Vakataka, 5th century A.D.).

Costume Design of Mahendra V.V.'s Matta V.

Fig. 2

Fig. 1

Fig. 3

Costume Design of Vara's Ubhaya - Bhāna

VITA

Stage Properties in Sanskrit Theatre (overleaf)

Sketch 1 : Door curtains seen in fresco painting in Ajanta Cave No. 17. Viśvāntara Jātaka. Agrawal V.S., in 'Harshacharita. ek Adhyayana' (p. 155) refers to them as "Triguṇa Tiraskāriṇī".

Sketch 2 : Hand held Javanikā curtain.

Sketch 3 : Jarjara—as per NS, XXIII, 161-71, description.

Sketch 4 : Kuṭilaka—as per NS, XXIII, 173-76, description. Also as seen in Ajanta Cave No. 17. A palace scene.

Sketch 5 : A pitcher—as shown in Dr. Motichandra op. cit., Fig. 143.

Sketch 6 : A painting board. C Sivaramamurti, *Citrasūtra* of Viṣṇudharmottara, Fig. 2 in plates Chandella 10th century A.D., Khajuraho.

Sketch 7 : A seat—one of the many designs of *āsana*-s in Ajanta frescoes—Cave No. 17, Viśvāntara Jātaka.

Sketch 8 : Yaṣṭidīpa (hand-held lamp). From Mathura (Kushana period) found in Vedisthambha, frieze at Jamalapur mount, Mathura.

Sketch 9 : A rough design of the Noh theatre (Japan) stage property of a frame work of a cart in one of the Noh plays witnessed by this writer.

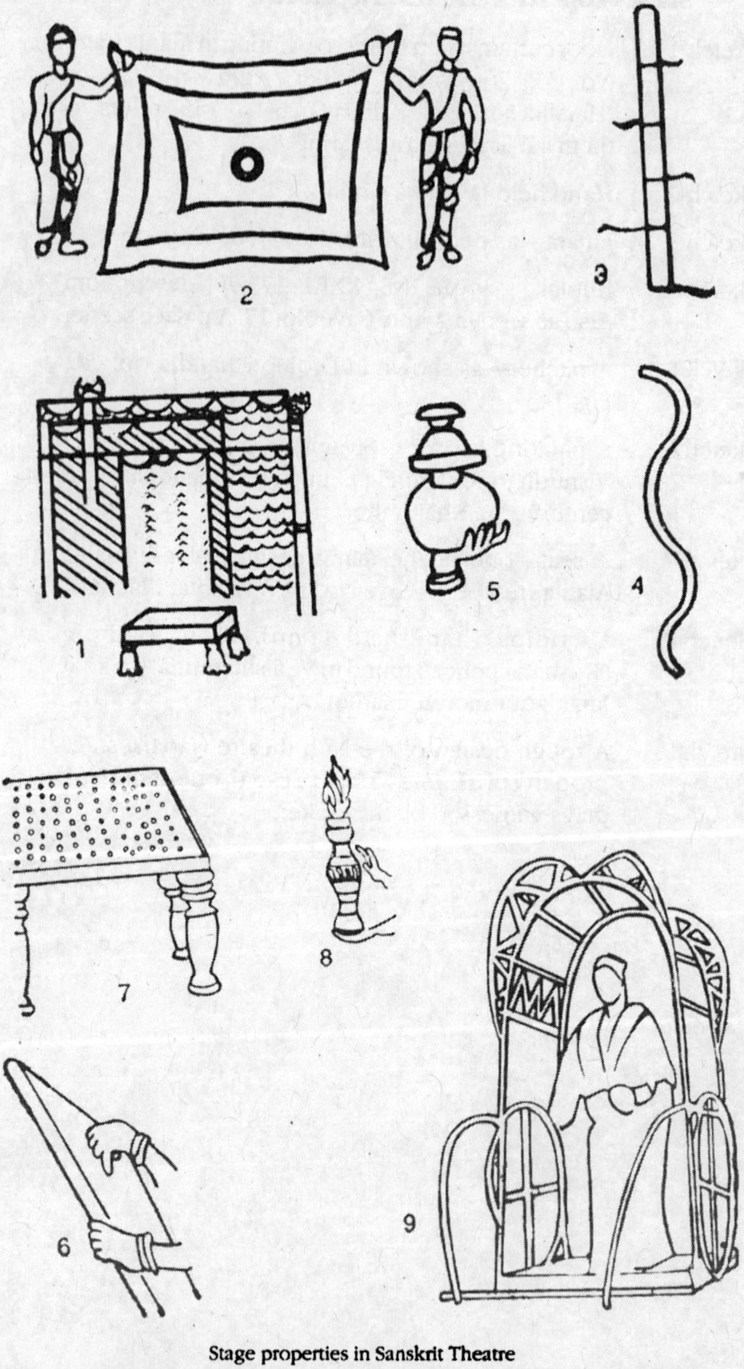

Stage properties in Sanskrit Theatre

CHAPTER 13

TASKS BEFORE A MODERN PRODUCER

The objective of this concluding chapter is very different from what has been discussed and proved so far. It is to examine and evaluate the potency of the framework of ancient Sanskrit play production in the context of our times at the hands of a modern producer. We have recognised the essential *rasa* orientation of ancient Sanskrit plays—in terms of their themes—(*vastu-netā* structure), presentations (practices of *bhāvābhinaya*) and the designs (*vṛtti-pravṛtti* music, etc.) They could very well be described as a total theatre or an all inclusive system. This system is seen to be complete in itself and does not need any addition to accomplish its objectives. It has also been emphasised that in some of the traditional village theatres, an aspect of *rasa* orientation in Sanskrit plays and its style of *bhāva* presentation can be observed. From all this, it is possible to state that the ancient style of Sanskrit play production can be recreated without any major departure from its basic elements.

Theoretical Ground Work

In the first place, detailed descriptions are available regarding each of the components and its place in the style of production in the ancient Indian dramaturgical treatises starting with *Nāṭyaśāstra*. Because of researches in the recent times, a measure of consensus has been arrived at on some of the ambiguities regarding them arising out of the *sūtra* form of writing.

In the Context of Ancient Fine Arts

When this is not the case, it has been seen in this work that the evidence regarding their use in a performance is not only limited to the field of play production, but also in other allied ancient fine arts such as dance, music, sculpture, architecture, painting, etc. In fact, all these arts constituted parts of *nāṭya* and hence the norms, the aesthetics, the objectives, the practices, etc. of the production techniques were shared by all of them. Even at present, therefore, the repertoire of these production techniques are seen, if not in one art form, then in another.

For example, a number of controversies surrounding the precise structural characteristics of the ancient play houses and stages become somewhat clarified when examined in the light of the principles of the architecture of the period (200 B.C.—800 A.D.) specially the *maṇḍapa* structures of the period. Similarly the *nāṭyadharmī* and *lokadharmī* practices of *aṅga-sattva abhinaya* become sufficiently explicit by the availability of the comparable evidence of sculptural representations of figures in repose (*sthiti*), and the present day regional varieties of classical dance as well as the recent researches on Chapter IV of *Nāṭyaśāstra* as regards postures and movements (both *sthiti* and *gati*). Features of *āhārya* can likewise be identified from the norms of fresco paintings as well as sculptural representations of the period.

It should, however, be pointed out that it is difficult to produce comparable evidence of the original state of rendering of *vācika* and the *gāndharva* and *gāna* varieties of *jāti* music of the period. However, the researches continuing at present in these fields point a way towards the explorations of *Sāma* chanting and open up new vistas which can best be explored in the process of practical performance and production.

A strong underlying current which has contributed to the survival of these components and the style of production over all these years is the society rooted in tradition. In the process of *rasa* realisation, cultivated appreciation plays a very important part. The continuity in this field is an outcome of common history, common culture, social traditions, expectations from a performance and weighty heritage of themes and mythological stories which have been woven in the social fabric of Indian people. The norms of appreciation have grown roots and have been preserved and ensured further continuity by the peasant culture. In fact, the Indian rural based audience can be described as an unidentified premise contributing to the continuity of the style of ancient theatre production.

The most natural question which arises from the above is whether or not the ancient style of Sanskrit play production, as visualised in this work, can be utilised for production of Sanskrit plays today.

I would like to examine this problem in terms of several stages through which we can visualise the reconstruction of the style of Sanskrit play production today.

Reconstruction in the Total Framework

In the first place, I would discuss the question of reconstruction of the Sanskrit *nāṭya* framework as a totality. As emphasised again and again in this work, this is a total system and a Sanskrit play can be produced only if all the components of the framework are present. This would mean:

(1) Reconstruction of designs of Bharata's play houses.

(2) Performer (or the drama troups) and the spectator (or the audience) conversant with the aesthetics, norms, objectives and practices (*dharmī*-s) of the performance (*bhāvābhinaya*).

The performer should be well trained and proficient not only in Sanskrit speech but capable of intuitive improvisional *abhinaya* covering *aṅga-sattva* and *vāca* aspects.

The spectator should be a connoisseur—a *sahṛdaya* or a *rasika prekṣaka* in a true sense. He should be a person with a cultivated appreciation who would aesthetically respond to the nuances of a play production (*nāṭya prayoga*) and become an active partner in evoking an atmosphere for *rasa* realisation.

(3) Ideally, such a performance would have an *aṅka* or an act performed in a single session—or even a scene or a sequence. This is because the *rasa* evocation demands a slow process of unfolding where a proper mood is created for extended savouring of inner states of being represented by the intuitive improvisation by the performer in the course of *bhāvānukīrtana*. Such a style of enactment would need two or three hours or more, which is our present day norm of a performance length. The single unit of representation of Sanskrit plays thus would ideally be an *aṅka* (act) even in its reconstruction in the present times.

(4) Such a style of production would come closer to an exclusive *baithak* style of performance in the manner of a classical music concert or a dance recital before an exclusive audience.

(5) It should be realised that the relationship of such a theatre to the mainstream theatre can only be exclusive. It can be

> comparable to that of the Noh theatres of Japan or Kudiyattam performed in Kerala temple theatres to the mainstream Japanese and Kerala theatres respectively. I am referring here only to the place each of these styles of production occupy in the mainstream of the respective theatres.[1]

Undoubtedly, such a reconstruction is possible in the contemporary setup based on the present state of our knowledge about the original concept.

Practical Problems

However, serious problems are likely to confront a modern producer in the course of his efforts because of:

(1) Theatre buildings with drop curtains, procenium arches and side-wings.

(2) A drama troupe—untrained in *abhinaya*.

(3) The modern urban theatre going audience and its western orientation in the area of drama forms (comedy, tragedy, etc.); a style of production purely related to either a word-based spoken drama or a musical or a dance-drama or a ritual oriented drama arising out of compartment as against comprehensive view of the theatre.

(4) Spectators without cultivated appreciation in the ancient *nāṭya* techniques, especially *rasa-bhāvābhinaya*.

(5) Limitation of a set method of conducting a production. For example, time limit of two or three hours for a whole drama performance.

The tasks before a producer for such a reconstruction is ardous, but, as explained above, not impossible. It would require a lot of preparation both on the part of the producer and the spectators.

Apart from satisfying the need for revival, it is not inconceivable that such a recreation may prove to be a germinating ground of new ideas.

Modern Approach to Revival-cum-Reconstruction

It is absolutely essential to state precisely what is meant by the term 'revival', and the context in which it is referred to here.

Revival is not used here to suggest the last resort of a traditional community. This fact needs emphasis because in many developing communities which have an ancient culture, major conflicts in the field of experience and policy are found at various turning points. Such communities have a definite choice to make regarding what they understand by revival. It is a revival which is compatible with modern progress and development. But even in such a synthesis of revival-cum-reconstruction it is absolutely necessary that what is to be revived or reconstructed is thoroughly understood. At various turning points communities with ancient heritage will confront this question but it should be made very clear that it is not 'revivalism' *per se*. In other words, the ancient Sanskrit theatre design is neither sought to be reconstructed nor revived in its original form today in order to reassure ourselves about our 'golden past' and its 'rich heritage'. Nor is it an endeavour for something that lives only in the minds of research scholars and the museum. But it is aimed to be reconstructed in order to find out whether the design is potent enough to help regenerate forces of renaissance in our contemporary theatre. Or, to consider whether it has an inherent capacity for renewal and reinterpretation to meet the requirements of modern man.

I wish to turn here to a more challenging and indeed an abiding aspect of the main findings of this work.

Contemporary Relevance

In the first place, the moot point is to determine how efficacious and engulfing *rasa* orientation is as a style of drama production in the conflict ridden nuclear age. Will the modern producer accept it as a total style of production without any addition or subtraction? Or, does it have the potency as a design of production to delineate themes which can appeal to the modern theatre goer? Alternatively, how far would a straight reproduction of a *rasa* oriented ancient Sanskrit plays satisfy the modern spectator?

In the olden times, such a play production satisfied all the levels of tastes in the audience because the spectators knew the *vastu-netā-rasa* structures of the plays based on well known stories. Therefore, the plays were staged in an environment of familiarity. The modern spectator is far removed from those times. His attitudes and approaches are bound to be influenced by contemporary reality and sensibilities. The *rasa* evocation through the vehicles of plays like Kālidāsa's *Mālavikāgnimitram* or other *nāṭikā* genres depicting the *śṛṅgāra* and the *vipralambha śṛṅgāra* (states of love and love in separation) of a much-married king in his harem or the removal of obstacles by the depiction of divine intervention enkindling the marvellous *rasa* at the end of all *nāṭaka* genres may not find an easy reciprocity in the mind of the contemporary spectator. This is because his experiences of life are different, and so are his expectations from a drama. A modern producer, therefore, will have to adapt the ancient Sanskrit play-texts with an understanding, as precisely as possible, of what will satisfy his audience.

The Universal Message of Sanskrit Dramas

At the same time, it should be emphasised here, that these ancient Sanskrit plays have not lost their relevance for the modern theatre going audience. If at all, the general message of these plays is very universal and relevant. It is the message of the celebration of attainment of homogeneous equipoise of a person in terms of his own being, his relationship with his surroundings and his access to the universal. This message was never more relevant than today for the spectators not only in India but also abroad. The basic raison d'etre of this is that the Sanskrit plays are a total expression of a theatre emerging from an ethos which portrayed every moment of life—both of pleasure and pain—as an experience to be relished as a *rasa* with a consciousness of an inner harmony of things. This is the universal element which is found in the ancient Sanskrit plays which is most relevant today.

Be it *Abhijñāna Śākuntalam*, *Uttararāmacaritam*, *Mṛcchakaṭikam*, *Mudrā Rākṣasa*, the plays of Bhāsa or even some of the *prahasana*-s, the basic structure of their form and content (*rasa-vastu-netā* structure) is always universal. The unequivocal common characteristic in all these dramas is their being woven around a principal *rasa* or a basic state of being (*sthāyībhāva*) which is universalised and impersonalised. It is this more than anything else which succeeds in evoking the similar state of consciousness in the spectators. The actors do not portray individuals but universal types. The characters are put in situations—stimuli (*vibhāva* etc.) which induce from them responses (*anubhāva*-s) which are not personal but universal. As a result, a large number of states of being are formed which become visible in the actions of mind, speech and body of the characters. These are represented by actors through their *abhinaya* which is communicated and transferred to the spectator who is not a detatched onlooker but a conscious participant. It is this framework which is capable of producing powerful theatre even today.

The contemporary producer will nevertheless feel the need for adapting these dramas when staged in our times. This question of adaption can be assessed from various standpoints. Adaption, after all, is only a generic process of which there can be several specific variations.

For example, a play like *Abhijñāna Śākuntalam* may address itself to the question of a woman's identity in the context of the prevailing social norms. *Uttararāmacaritam* may be considered an attempt to discover the true basis of abiding aspects of human relationship, as between Rāma and Sītā, Lava-Kuśa and Rāma, and Rāma's parents and Sītā. In Bhāsa's *Karṇabhāra*, the aim is to portray the conflict of values in a man's life as between duty and filial affection, as well as the non-compromising personality which comes out of it. Similarly, *Mṛcchakaṭikam* presents the tyranny and the power of the autocrat as against the life sustaining force of love found among the common people. In terms of universalised aspect of *rasa* evocation, erotic *rasa* (*Śṛṅgāra—Abhijñāna Śākuntalam*) pathetic (*karuṇa*) *rasa* associated with love in separation (*Uttararāmacaritam*), heroic *dānavīra rasa* (*Karṇabhāra*) and the erotic *rasa* as a life sustaining force (*Mṛcchakaṭikam*) can be successfully presented by bringing the *vastu* and the *netā* nearer to our own times.

At the same time the producer can do so only within the limits of the broad framework provided by *rasa* orientation. Remaining within these limits, he can execute a number of small changes, with a little more emphasis on one aspect as against another.

Scope for Adaptation

One of the most important questions, therefore, lies in the field of how one would attempt to adapt these ancient Sanskrit plays while retaining this framework in order to satisfy the needs of the contemporary sensibilities. This will perhaps point to the widest scope for adaptation. The broad suggested guidelines for this may be offered as follows:

(1) The scripts of the plays, especially *nāṭaka*, *prakaraṇa* and other genres will have to be edited, but with the total understanding of the play within its *rasa-vastu-netā* parameter. Remaining within this parameter and at the same time interpreting it with the point of view of contemporary sensibilities, more important scenes and sequences will have to be chosen with an angle of how best they can be presented.

(2) The nuances of stylisation in practices—*dharmī*-s, *bhāvābhinaya* and the embellishments such as the *dhruvāgāna* and the *lāsyāṅga* song-dance and *abhinaya* situations will perhaps point to the widest scope for adaptation.

(3) Such edited versions of *rasa* oriented Sanskrit plays would also satisfy and suit the limitations of timings as accepted by present day norms of a drama performance wherein a whole *nāṭaka*, a *prakaraṇa* or a *nāṭikā* can be performed in a single session with even one interval or more in between the acts.

(4) Such productions have all the possibilities of acquiring a place in the mainstream theatre.

However, it must be emphasised that the few areas of adaptations which a producer may try will not in any way dislodge the style of *rasa-bhāva* presentation, viz., the practice of portrayal for creating an atmosphere for extended savouring of the inner states of being of a character to stimulate in the spectator a changed state of consciousness. To the extent various sequences in a play touch the inner sensibilities of the spectators and in this way pull him in the same frame of mind as the hero, the particular act would have succeeded in its objective. Since a play has different types of experiences, sequences, happenings in the life of the hero, a successful adaptation should see to it that the spectators pass through the same sequence of events and experiences. There is a great measure of flexibility of approach as between one producer and another and between one spectator group and another.

For example, the design of ancient Sanskrit *nāṭya* and many of its techniques of productions have been adopted in varying degrees in modern Indian play productions as well as those of the West. Brechtian theatre[2] and the theatre of cruelty are two of the obvious instances. The latter has adopted a number of conventions of *nāṭya* techniques. The famous laboratory of Jersy Grotowski of Poland has been inspired by physical impulses of the body—acting which was the base of the actor's art in ancient India. Mostly in these cases, various conventions and stylisations of ancient Sanskrit theatre have been adopted without its *rasa* orientation.[3]

A distinctly different kind of proof relating to the area of the adoptation of *rasa* oriented style of production can be brought forth from the recent attempts at staging some of the foreign language plays. For example, Goethe's *Faust* has been produced very successfully in a *rasa* oriented Kathakali style of production.

There has also been an attempt to produce Shakespeare's Macbeth in the Yakṣagana style. What has been attempted through these productions is taking the *rasa*-bhāva presentation truly as a box of tools and applying the same on an altogether different soil. This only proves that it is possible to think about the style of ancient Sanskrit play production as independent of time-space-theme-language. It shows that if carefully employed, the true potential of the ancient Sanskrit theatre framework can be far more extensive than what appears on the surface.

While we have illustrated this by considering only a few ways of looking at the question, there is a very important other side. Could a modern theme be enacted within the framework and the *rasa* orientation as found in the Sanskrit dramas?

We are, therefore, searching into deeper depths of *rasa* orientation and all that ancient Sanskrit plays successfully attempted to convey through it. The doors are open for the modern producer. He has a vast set of efficient and viable tools, in fact a universal language of communication, in the design of *rasa* oriented Sanskrit play production. How best would he adapt these to the needs of the contemporary ethos needs to be seen. It is a major threshold in the adaptation of a style of a drama production which would validate whether or not the design is potent enough for renewal and reinterpretation.

Each stage will amount to an endeavour in adaptation but each will be significantly different from the other. And to this extent, unexplored potential of the ancient Sanskrit theatre framework will go on appearing and reappearing.

Notes

1. The present trend of equating Kudiyattam with the exact manifestation of ancient Sanskrit play production does not seem to be valid. It may be possible that Kudiyattam represents the present day survival of *dākṣināṭya* regional mode, especially of Kerala region. But from that one cannot surmise that the form represents the total ancient Sanskrit drama style in India.
2. Brecht evolved his style of theatre by adapting and absorbing many elements of Asian drama, especially the Chinese Opera. His attempt was to "change certain institutions from places of amusement into organs of public communication" for which he adopted techniques where:
   (a) There was no barrier between the performer and the spectator in the form of a drop curtain.
   (b) Direct communication between the performer and spectator.
   (c) Actors were not individuals but types who consciously enacted a 'role'.
   (d) Music, songs, dance and speech fused together in a performance.
   (e) No attempt at being sequential or naturalistic.

APPENDIX I

List of some important authors whose works have provided literary data for this study

Abhinavagupta	:	The Kashmiri aesthete philosopher commentator, follower of *pratyābhijña* (recognition) school of monistic Śaivism of Kashmir. Flourished at the end of the tenth century, his commentaries on Bharata's *Nāṭyaśāstra* (*Abhinavabhāratī*) and on Ānandavardhana's *Dhvanyāloka* are celebrated. He was a great exponent of Indian aesthetics. He also wrote a monumental encyclopaedic work on *tantra*, called *Tantrāloka*. He is believed to have written no fewers than twentythree works and commentaries.
Aśvaghoṣa	:	A poet dramatist in the court of Kaniṣka (*c.* 58 B.C.—120 A.D.). Three plays of his, in fragmentary form, are available. They are Buddhist plays, one of which is named *Śāriputra prakaraṇa*. They are fully developed Sanskrit-Prakrit plays, reflecting the dramaturgical rules laid down by Bharata.
Bhāsa	:	Thirteen plays of Bhāsa have come down to us which are generally referred to as *Bhāsa nāṭyacakra*. He was most probably from Southern India. Predecessor of Kālidāsa and Bāṇa. From Kauṭilya to Rājaśekhara important playwrights and critics have made a reference to him.
Bhaṭṭanārāyaṇa	:	Author of *Veṇisaṃhāra*. He must have flourished before 9th century A.D., as his work is frequently referred to by *Ānandavardhana* who lived during 855-884 A.D.
Bhaṭṭanāyaka	:	Advocate of the theory of 'universalised' *bhāva* presentation in drama as quoted by Abhinavagupta. Believed to have written a work named *Hṛdayadarpaṇa*. Contemporary

		of Ānandavardhana in the court of King Avantivarman of Kashmir (later half of 9th century A.D.).
Bhavabhūti	:	Well-known playwright of *Mahāvīra Carita*, *Mālatī-Mādhava* and *Uttararāmacarita*. A native of Vidarbha. Most probably flourished at the end of 7th century A.D.
Bodhāyana	:	Author of the *Prahasana Bhagavadajjukiyam*.
Dhanañjaya	:	Author of *Daśarūpaka*, a short manual of *Nāṭyaśāstra*. A member of the expert's assembly of the court of Munja, the king of Parmar dynasty of Malva (974-95 A.D.).
Kālidāsa	:	The renowned playwright-poet of *Abhijñāna-śākuntalam*, *Vikramorvaśīyam*, *Mālavikāgnimitram* and other works. Earliest reference to him is in an inscription dated 634 A.D. His date is controversial.
Kohala	:	One of the hundred disciples of Bharata. His work has been mentioned in *Nāṭyaśāstra* as its supplementary treatise (*uttaratantra*) which is available today in a very damaged condition and is yet unpublished. He has been mentioned in most of the later dramaturgical works. In *Bālarāmāyaṇa*, (Act III.12) Kohala appears as a *nāṭyācārya* and conducts the prologue. He wrote on music, expressive dance and *abhinaya*. His lost works are *Sangītameru*, *Tālalakṣaṇa* and *Kohalarahasya*.
Mahendra Vikram Varmā	:	The pallava king who wrote the *Prahasana Mattavilāsa*. He ruled over Kāñci (South India) in the first half of 7th century A.D.
Nandikeśvara	:	*Abhinaya Darpaṇa* is attributed to Nandikeśvara. Nothing definite is known about him, but *Abhinaya Darpaṇa*, which is a handbook of *abhinaya* is considered by scholars to be an abridged version of either *Bharatārṇava* or *Nandikeśvara Saṃhitā*. He is believed to have written on *abhinaya*, *tāla* and music—posterior to 5th century A.D.
Rāghavabhaṭṭa	:	His commentary on Kālidāsa's *Abhijñāna*

		Śākuntalam, called *Arthadyotanikā* provides illuminating insights to the *nāṭya abhinaya* of the play-text. Son of Prithvidhara of Vārāṇasi.
Rāmacandra and Guṇacandra	:	Authors of *Nāṭyadarpaṇa*, a work on dramaturgy. From Gujarat, Anhilwad Patan. Disciples of *Hemacandrācārya*—followers of Jainism. Middle of 12th century A.D.
Sāgarnandi	:	Wrote *Nāṭakalakṣaṇaratnakoṣa*. Refers to many authorities and opinions other than that of Bharata, which gives an indication to divergent schools or traditions of dramaturgy in ancient India. Early 10th century A.D.
Śāradātanaya	:	Author of *Bhāvaprakāśa*, a work on ancient Indian dramaturgy. The manuscript of his work was found in South India. He learnt about dramaturgy from his guru Divākara. He probably lived around 1250 A.D.
Sārangadeva	:	Wrote an elaborate work on Indian music called *Saṅgītaratnākara*. His work serves as a link between the ancient music tradition as described in the *Nāṭyaśāstra* and mediaeval works on music. Flourished in 1210-47. From Kashmir. The commentator of *Saṅgītaratnākara*, Kallinātha lived in 1450 A.D.
Śri Harṣa	:	King Harṣavardhana of Kānyakubja, a patron of Bāṇa. Writer of three plays. *Ratnāvalī*, *Priyadarśikā*, *Nāgānanda*. Latter half of 6th or first half of 7th century A.D.
Śūdraka	:	Celebrated author of *Mṛcchakaṭikam*. It is uncertain whether he lived before or after Kālidāsa. He is believed to have written a play on the theme of Udayana-Vāsavadattā probably called Vīṇā-*Vāsavadattā*.
Vararuci	:	Author of *Ubhayābhisārikā bhāṇa*. Dr. D.R. Mankad dates him before Bhāsa.
Viśākhadatta	:	Author of *Mudrā Rākṣasam*. His other play *Devī Candragupta* is available only in fragmented quotations. Flourished around late 7th or early 8th century A.D.
Viśvanātha	:	Author of *Sāhityadarpaṇa*, a work on poetics and dramaturgy, 1300-84 A.D.

GLOSSARY

Abhidhā : The literal power or the sense of the word, denotation.

Abhinaya : Actor's art of communication.

Ābhyantara : Interior, exclusive, for the initiated.

Ācārya : A master, a teacher or a preceptor.

Adhikārī netā : The hero who is entitled to the final fruit; also referred to as a *Nāyaka*.

Āgama-s : Sacred scripture, a traditional doctrine.

Āhārya : External, effected by decoration or ornamentation, one of the four aspects of *abhinaya*.

Ākaśa bhāṣit : 'Speech in the air', a stage technique when a character on the stage enters into a dialogue with one who is not on the stage.

Ākhyānavid : A rhapsode, a teller of legendary tales.

Akṣara : A letter of the alphabet, a syllable; a primary unit of word or a metre.

Alaṅkāraśāstra : The science of rhetorics, poetics.

Alaukika : Not belonging to the world, super sensual.

Āliḍha : One of the standing positions denoting shooting.

Ānanda : Supreme bliss.

Aṅgahāra : A measured sequence of dance movements of the body arising out of a combination of two, three or four units (*karaṇa*-s). *Nāṭyaśāstra* describes 32 *aṅgahāra*-s.

Angaracanā : Body paint, magico-decorative designs on the body.

Aṅka : An act of a Sanskrit play; an abbreviation of *utsṛṣṭikāṅka*—a genre of Sanskrit drama.

Aṅkāsya : A linking device—that part of an act wherein the subject of the act is intimated, also called ankamukha.

Aṅkāvatāra : A linking device—that part of an act when the happenings in the next act are hinted at.

Ankiyanat : Present-day traditional theatre of Assam, performed in the *vaiśṇava* monasteries called

Satra-s. It is also called Bhaona. Can be traced back to 15th century A.D. It is a Vaiṣṇava theatre using Asamiya brajaboli and scattered Sanskrit words. Mainly rural audience.

Anudarśana : A perceptive aesthetic enjoyment.

Anukaraṇa : Imitation, a reproduction.

Anukīrtana : A specific cognitive process of aesthetic expression, artistic activity and aesthetic enjoyment, a creative exploratory interpretation.

Anukramam : The technique of presentation of a character's life history by the mono acting of a Kudiyattam actor by narrating incidents backward.

Apavāritaka : Concealed speech related to some secret thought which the character conveys to the spectator by coming forward and then taking a turn—a *nāṭyadharmī* conventional speech.

Apsarās : Essence (*rasa*) of water (*ap*), water nymphs, actress-dancers and courtesans of heaven.

Āratī : Waving of a light before an image.

Artha : Inner meaning of the play or a poetic composition—its rasa content—*nāṭyārtha*;
(2) one of the four goals of human existence meaning wealth and prosperity.

Āsana : Sitting position.

Āsvādana : Tasting, eating, enjoying, experiencing.

Atharvaveda : The fourth of the ancient collections of sacred texts of Veda-s which deals specially with magic, charm and medicine.

Ātodya : Musical Instruments.

Āviddha prayoga : A play production in vigorous style.

Bāhya : Outside, external, popular, a parallel stream to the *ābhyantara* practice.

Bhakti : The adoration and devotion for a deity.

Bharata : An actor or a disciple of actor's (Bharata's) tradition as a common noun. As a proper noun the term denotes the brother of Rāma, the son of Śakuntalā and Jaḍa Bharata, the brahmin recluse mentioned in the Bhāgavata.

Bharata Vākya : An actor's benediction.

Bhagavathamela : Present-day traditional dance-drama from Melattur in Tanjore district, Tamilnadu. Can be traced back to 16th century A.D. Performed near temple for Narsiṃha Jayanti celebrations before rural audience. The themes of these dance dramas are from the *purāṇa*-s.

Bhand jashana : Regional folk theatre of Kashmir. Seasonal. Based on the local tradition of wandering singing groups of performers.

Bhāva : Being, existing, existence; Inner states of being as represented in a work of art for evocation of eight *nāṭya-rasa*-s.

Bhavai : Open-air rural based theatre form of Gujarat. Can be traced back to 16th century A.D. Word-based scenes of secular themes with stress on social satire and sharp comments.

Bhāvāvasthā : Inner states of being (of a character) in a specific situation in a play.

Bhāvaka : Having a taste for the beautiful.

Bhoga : Enjoyment, as a principle of creation.

Bhṛkuṃśa : An actor playing a female role.

Bhū : To be, to become.

Bīja-Śakti : The seed power.

Bindu : Point, seed, a drop—a part of the five *artha-prakṛti*-s of the plot progression of a Sanskrit play.

Brahmā : The first deity of the sacred Hindu trinity, the creative principle.

Brahma : The Supreme, absolute, essence from which all created things are produced and into which they are absorbed.

Camatkāra : Amazing delight which constitutes the essence of an art experience.

Cārī : A stage walk depending on the simultaneous action of feet, shanks and the hip where the movement of one foot is suggestive of different actions.

Carvaṇā : Chewing, eating, self-experiencing, relishing, enjoying.

Caturasra tāla : A musical rhythm pattern with eight time

beats. A *tāla* with eight *mātrās*-s. It is a *jāti* of *cancūtpuṭaḥ tāla*, the ancient basic *tāla*, prototype mentioned in the *Nāṭyaśāstra*.

Caturvarga Sādhanā : Four goals of human existence recognised. by ancient Indian society; also called *puruṣārtha*-s. The four goals are *artha* (wealth, prosperity), *kāma* (love and pleasure), *dharma* (righteous action) *mokṣa* (liberation).

Ceṭa : A male servant.

Cetanā : Consciousness, life, vitality, and intelligence.

Ceṭī : A female servant.

Chau : Dance drama form from Eastern India, known as Seraikela (Bihar), Mayurbhanj (Orissa) and Purulia (West Bengal) Chau. Can be traced back to 17th-18th century A.D. They are open-air masked dance forms (except Mayurbhanj Chau) where the epical and purāṇic tales and simple themes on nature are mostly danced before a largely rural audience gathered annually at *Caitra parva* (March-April). This dance form is highly stylised and sophisticated.

Cittavṛtti : Changes in the state of mind, wavering in the inward working of mind.

Citrābhinaya : Varied representation of different activities, moods, animate and inanimate objects through hand gestures, facial expressions and the body movements.

Cūlikā : A linking scene—An intimating speech in an act from behind the curtain suggesting an explanation of the matter on the stage.

Deśī : Belonging to a region, a country, a province, popular—contrasted with *margī*.

Deva : A celestial being, a divine figure.

Devī : A female deity, a goddess.

Dharmī : Practice, customary usage according to prescribed code.

Dhātu : A primary or elementary substance, a verbal root, a note made on a *vīṇā* with a special stroke of a plektrum.

Dhvani : Resonance or reverberation of sound, one of the main features of poetry where implied or suggested meaning is more striking than the expressed idea.

Dhyāna : Meditation, contemplation, one-pointed concentration.

Doṣa : Demerits or shortcomings in a work of art.

Dṛṣṭi : The expressive eye movements of *āṅgika abhinaya.*

Dṛṣṭaphala : Tangible result. A reward that can be seen.

Dṛṣyakāvya : Visual poetry, a drama.

Dūtī : A female messanger, a confidante, a go-between for the lovers.

Dvibhūmi : Two levels of a building.

Ekāhārya abhinaya : *Abhinaya* of a solo actor who enacts a variety of roles without the change of get up; also called *ekapātrahārya.*

Ekārtha Abhinaya : *Abhinaya* where an actor enacts diverse incidents and situations under one theme.

Gāna : A song; *deśī* music constituting songs where more importance is given to the words than the note or the time measure.

Gāndharva : Relating to celestial singers who wear fragrant garments; a subordinate Veda attached to *Sāmaveda*; sacrosanct exclusive *mārgī* music used in the preliminaries of dramas where nuances of notes and time measure were more important than the words.

Gaṇeśa : God of wisdom and remover of obstacles; the elephant headed god, son of Pārvatī and Śiva.

Gaṇikā : A courtesan, a harlot.

Garuḍa : A mythical bird, vehicle of Viṣṇu.

Gati : Gait.

Gātra : Limbs of the body.

Gāyikā : A female singer.

Goṣṭī Sabhā : Assembly of connoisseur citizens,

Guṇa : Merits in a work of art; attribute, characteristic of all substance or property belonging to all created things (*sattva, rajas, tamas*).

Guru : Initiated teacher belonging to an established line of teacher-disciple tradition.

Hallisaka : Pure dance in the round.

Hasta : Gestures of hands in *nāṭya abhinaya.*

Hṛdaya : Heart, soul, mind, the interior essence of anything.

Indra : The lord of the gods, Vedic god of rains. He is represented as being in constant fear of sages practising austerities and as sending heavenly nymphs to destract them.

Itihāsa : History—legendary or traditional.

Itivṛtta : The story of the plot of the drama.

Janāṅtika : A stage convention where one's private feelings are conveyed to another character in the presence of other characters who are not supposed to hear. Indicated by the use of *tripatākā hasta.*

Jarjara : Indra's banner staff, presented to Bharata and his drama troupe; essential for Sanskrit drama performance where it is installed during the preliminaries.

Javanikā : A handheld mobile curtain used in Sanskrit theatre.

Kākalī : An overlapping note between the two voice registers.

Kāku : Modulation of voice to express different emotions.

Kakṣyā Vibhāga : *Nāṭyadharmī* zonal division.

Kalā : Musical time measure; a division of time variously computed (1 minute 48 seconds or 8 seconds).

Kāma : One of the four *puruṣārtha*-s, love or desire of sensual enjoyments; pleasure of any kind.

Kāmadaśā : Convention of the ten stages of love to be portrayed in works of art.

Kañcukī : Chamberlain of a royal palace.

Karaṇa : A combined unit of prescribed positions (sthāna-s), stage-walks (cārī) and hand gestures (*nṛttahasta*-s). *Nāṭyaśāstra* describes 108 *Karaṇa*-s.

Karṇe : Conventional speech in Sanskrit drama where words are spoken in another person's ears preceded by words 'evam, evam'-like this to avoid repetition or to maintain secrecy.

Kathakali : A traditional dance-drama form of Kerala.

Kathākāra : A reciter-singer-instrumentalist-mono-actor who narrates the stories of epics and *purāṇa*-s before rural communities.

Kathā Literature: Literature consisting of narrated stories or fables.

Kavī : A seer of *ṛcās*, a poet-dramatist.

Kārya : An effect, necessary result of a cause, the motive or an object in a drama finally attained by the hero.

Kubera : The God of riches and treasure; the lord of the northern direction; step-brother of Rāvaṇa, king of *yakṣa*-s and *kinnara*-s. His kingdom is in Kailāśa. He is represented as being deformed in body.

Kulajā : A noble lady, a girl of high birth.

Kuśilava : A singer, a bard, an actor.

Kutapa : Musical orchestra, also a place where the musicians sit.

Kuṭilaka : A crooked staff with three bends, usually carried by the jester in a Sanskrit play.

Kuchipudi : A traditional theatrical form developed in Andhra Pradesh, influenced by compositions of Siddhendra Yogī.

Kudiyattam : A temple theatre of Kerala where certain acts of Sanskrit plays are enacted in regional style by temple drama troupes of Chakyars and others. Can be traced back to 11th century A.D.

Lakṣaṇā : Secondary meaning of the word which is indicated or indirectly expressed, connotation.

Lāsya : Gentle dance with *abhinaya* of the poetic compositions set to music. *Nāṭyaśāstra* describes twelve subdivisions of *lāsya* called *lāsyāṅga*-s where the state of love (*rati*) is expressed through *abhinaya*. *Lāsya* is said to

	have been created by *Pārvatī* who taught it to Uṣā.
Lokānusārī	: As per the ways of the world.
Lokottara	: Supersensual.
Māṇa	: To measure, to mark off proportionately.
Manch	: A street theatre from Madhya Pradesh. Can be traced to late 18th century. Secular themes like historical stories, contemporary romances and social satires as well as legends are performed before rural and semi-urban audience in this style.
Maṇḍala	: (1) One of the six standing positions of men; a movement formed by a group of *cārī*-s; (2) a magical, consecrated area which must be kept pure for ritual end.
Manodharma	: Actor's own judgment in selection of the conventional techniques to create a fresh performance.
Mantra	: A group of syllables used to concentrate on cosmic and psychic energies. Needs correct incantation.
Mārgī	: A tradition of art which is rigorously learnt by initiated disciples from a teacher—an exclusive system.
Mokṣa	: Final liberation or realisation—one of the four *puruṣārtha*-s.
Nāḍikā	: A measure of time equal to 24 minutes, also called a *ghaṭikā*.
Nāgaraka	: A citizen, a town-born gentleman.
Narma	: Ancient Indian system of pleasure connected with erotics.
Naisargika	: Natural, inborn, inherent, *sahaja*.
Nāndī	: A prayer recited at the beginning of the play proper, a verse or verses in praise of a deity.
Nartaka	: A male dancer.
Nartakī	: A female dancer, a nacakī.
Naṭa	: An actor.
Naṭī	: An actress or an actor's wife, a *naṭiyā* a *nartakiyā, raṅga strī* or *naṭabhāryā*.
Naṭagāmaṇi	: A leader of actors.

Naṭa vākya	:	An actor's benediction; *Bharata vākya.*
Nāṭayati	:	Enacts, a stage direction connoting enactment with four fold *abhinaya.*
Nāṭyārtha	:	The inner meaning of the play; the *rasa* content of a play.
Nāṭyācārya	:	A teacher of dramatic art.
Nāṭyadharmī	:	One of the practices of *abhinaya* presentation with a stress on stylisation.
Nāṭyaśālā	:	A theatre or a play-house, also called a *nāṭya-maṇḍapa*, *nāṭyaveśma*, *prekṣāgṛha* or *raṅga.*
Nāyaka	:	Hero.
Nāyikā	:	Heroine.
Nī-rasa vastu	:	Essential incidents in the plot without *rasa* which are lengthy or forbidden by tradition for enactment on stage. They are usually narrated or depicted with the aid of linking devices.
Nirgīta	:	Singing with meaningless syllables imitating the sounds of the instruments—employed in the preliminaries.
Niṣkramaṇa	:	Exit from the stage.
Nṛtta	:	Pure dance, dependent on rhythm (*laya*, *tāla*).
Nṛtya	:	Expressive dance to interprete a song where the meaning of each word is delineated.
Patākā Nāyaka	:	Leader of the subsidiary plot.
Parikramā	:	Technique of going around the stage to establish *nāṭyadharmī* zonal divisions.
Pāripārśvaka	:	Assistant to *Sūtradhāra.*
Paṭa-paṭi	:	Stage curtains, same as hand-held javanikā.
Pātra-praveśa	:	First entrance of an important dramatis personae.
Pekkhā	:	A show put upon a stage.
Phala bhoktā	:	Hero who is competent to enjoy the fruit of the efforts in a drama.
Phalaprāpti	:	Attainment of the fruit of one's desire.
Piṇḍibandha	:	Patterns in dance formations made by dancers.
Pīṭhaka	:	A seat.
Pīṭhamarda	:	A bachelor too poor to be a citizen, expert in the art of pleasure, hero's assistant in love.

Prakarī Nāyaka : Leader of the episode.

Prakṛti : Basic nature of all beings (superior, middle, low).

Prarocanā : Laudation, a part of the prologue.

Prāśnika : An assessor in the drama competition.

Pratibhā : Creative genius of an artist.

Praveśa : Entry on the stage.

Praveśaka : A linking device, introductory scene of an act.

Pravṛtti : Regional modes of a play production.

Purāṇa-s : Sanskrit encyclopaedic collection of myths, legends and traditional history.

Puruṣārtha : Four main goals of human existence recognised by ancient Indian Society (*Artha*, *Kāma*, *Dharma*, *Mokṣa*), also called *Caturvarga sādhanā*.

Pūrvaraṅga : Pre-performance rituals of a drama troupe; preliminaries.

Pusta : Model work denoting small, lightweight cutouts of artificial objects.

Rākṣasa : Descendent of non-Aryan seer Pulatsya, a non-Aryan clan.

Raṅga : Ancient Indian play-house.

Raṅgamaṇḍapa : The stage proper.

Raṅgapūja : Ritual worship of the stage.

Rasa : A term used to refer to 'tasting', 'enjoying' or 'self-experiencing'; an aesthetic experience.

Rasika : A man of taste, appreciator of excellence, capable of tasting the *rasa* in a work of art.

Recaka : Circular movements of limbs like the neck, hand, waist and feet in a dance.

Rūpaka : Ancient Indian dramatic compositions in Sanskrit and Prakrit languages.

Rūpayati : Represents on the stage, enacts on the stage, a stage direction.

Śabda : Sound, note, a word; sound in general.

Sabhā : an assembly.

Sabhāpati : The chief patron of the assembly.

Sādhanā : The discipline employed in learning an art; the acts and efforts of a person committed to achieve excellence in any field.

Sādhu : An exclamation of appreciation to a performance meaning 'well done'.

Sahaja : Spontaneous, natural.

Sahṛdaya : One who has the similar space in his heart for the art; a rasika, a responsive spectator.

Śailūṣa : A musician-actor.

Samāja : A gathering of people who assemble for entertainment.

Sandhi : A juncture in the plot progression.

Saṅgīta : A combination of songs, musical instruments and pure dance.

Sāṅkhya : One of the six systems of ancient Indian philosophy attributed to sage Kapila.

Sa-rasa vastu : That portion of the plot which is capable of evoking *rasa* and which can be represented through extended *bhāvābhinaya.*

Sattva : Inward concentration of pure mind, essential pure quality of a being.

Sauṣṭhava : The basic posture of a superior character.

Śayana : Reclining posture.

Śilpa : An art (fine or mechanical), skill, craft. Songs, musical instruments and pure dance have been bracketed together under this heading from olden times in India.

Sphoṭa : Sudden expansion of mind as a result of distinctly clear understanding of the inner idea of a work of art.

Soma juice : Juice of a plant; the most essential ingredient of ancient sacrificial rituals.

Sthāna : Standing posture, a stance in *āṅgika abhinaya*.

Sthāyi bhāva : The basic state of being presented in a work of art.

Sūcā : Expression of a meaning of the spoken word by delineating the *sāttvika* or subtle body vibrations (*spandana*).

Sukumāra Prayoga : A delicate production with music, dances, female artistes and erotic rasa.

Sūtra : An aphorism.

Sūtradhāra : (a) A stage manager, leader of the drama troupe, teacher and at times the main

	actor. He conducts the prologue and recites the *nāndī śloka*;
	: (b) a draftsman, holder of the string, son of Maya, a non-aryan architect of *asura*-s.
Svagata	: Soliloquy or speaking aside of one's delibera-tion and feelings—a stage convention of speech.
Svapnavākyam	: A speech during sleep; a stage convention of speech.
Svara	: A note of human voice and music.
Śākhā	: The representation through body movements of the head, face, shanks, thighs, feet and the hands of the spoken word in the manner of branches of a tree.
Śruti	: Quarter tones in music scale.
Tādātmya	: Complete self-identification of the spectator with the performer.
Tāla	: Time measure, a musical instrument made of bell-metal; canon of proportion.
Tāṇḍava	: A dance created by Taṇḍu, the attendant of Śiva. It is a vigorous dance combining *aṅga-hāra*-s, *recaka*-s and *piṇḍibandha*-s.
Tanmayibhāva	: One pointed concentration of the spectator.
Tātparya	: The unsaid implied meaning of a sentence.
Tilaka	: Decorative mark on the forehead.
Tiraskarṇī	: A hand-held stage curtain; magical art of disapprearance.
Trigata	: Three men's talk in the prologues of Sanskrit plays.
Trigūṇātmaka Prakṛti	: Three fundamental qualities pervading all aspects of the universe such as *sattva* (aware-ness) *rajas* [action] and *tamas* (inertia).
Trivarga Sādhanā	: Three goals of human existence (*artha*, *kāma*, *dharma*).
Trayasra Tāla	: A musical rhythm pattern of six time beats (*mātrā*-s).
Udātta svara	: An ascending note.
Ulkā	: Torch.
Upakaraṇa	: Stage property, material implements.
Upaniṣad	: Mystical writings attached to the Brāhmaṇa-s

the chief aim of which is to express the true knowledge of the supreme spirit.

Uparūpaka : Minor varieties of drama with emphasis on dance, song, *abhinaya* with lesser stress on spoken words.

Uṣṇīṣa : A cloth tied on the head like a turban.

Uttarīya : A loose upper garment worn by men and women.

Vaitālika : Bard, a ministrel.

Vākyam : Spoken words in a play.

Vardhamānaka : Gāndharva gīta-s where the syllables, tempo and number of dancers gradually increase.

Vāsanā : Genetic memories.

Vastu : Plot of Sanskrit plays, the subject-matter of any poetic composition.

Vibhāva : Stimuli in the form of dramatis personae placed in different situations in the plot for *rasa* evocation.

Vidūṣaka : The jester.

Vidyādhara : Bearer of wisdom, mythical figures who resemble men, have magic powers and change forms at will; generally move in pairs and shower flowers over the valiant heroes from the sky.

Viṣkambhaka : Linking supporting scenes in the beginning of an act.

Viśvakarmā : Architect of the gods, appears in *Ṛgveda*, presiding deity of all craftsmen.

Viṭa : Gallant parasite, a rake, an expert in the ways of the courtesans.

Vṛtti : The styles of play production.

Vyabhicāribhāva : Transitory states.

Vyanjanā : Suggestive power of the words.

Yajña : Ritual sacrifice.

Yakshagana : Traditional open air theatre of Karnataka with emphasis on music. Can be traced to 16th century A.D., deals mainly with purāṇic themes.

Yama : God of death or death personified; the son of the Sun.

Yantra : A machine, appliance, contraption, a diagrammatic symbol for a field of energy.

Yavanikā : A mobile hand-held curtain used in Sanskrit theatre.

Yoga : Union, deep and abstract meditation.

SELECT BIBLIOGRAPHY

PRIMARY SOURCES	*SANSKRIT TEXTS and COMMENTARIES*
Abhinavagupta: Nāṭyaśāstra with Abhinavabhāratī	— GOS, Baroda, Vol. I (2nd ed.) and Vol. II, III, IV.
Abhinayadarpaṇa of Nāndikeśvara	— Ed. by M. Ghosh, 1957, Calcutta (2nd ed.).
Abhijñāna Śākuntalam of Kālidāsa	—
(a) With Rāghavabhaṭṭa's Arthadyotanikā	— Ed. by N.B. Godbole and K.B. Parab, 1883, NSP.
(b)	— Ed. with complete trans. by R.D. Karmarkar, 1957, Aryabhushan Press, Pune.
Amarakośa	— NSP, 1920, 4th ed.
Bharata's Nāṭyaśāstra	— Kashi Sanskrit Series, 1929.
	— Vols. I and II, ed. by M. Ghosh, 1956, Asiatic Society, Calcutta.
Bhāsa Nāṭakacakram	— (a) Chawkhambha Series (b) Ed. by C.R. Devdhar, 1951 (2nd ed.), Pune.
Bhagavadajjukiyām of Bodhāyana	— Ed. by P. Annajan Achan, Trichur, 1925.
Bhāvaprakāśa of Śāradātanaya	— Ed. by M.M. Agrawal—Sankrit text with Hindi translation, 1978, Jainsons Printers, Agra-3.
Caturbhāṇī	— (a) Ed. by M.R. Kavi and S.K.R. Shastri, 1922, Shivpuri. (b) Ed. and tr. in Hindi by Motichandra and V.S. Agrawal, Hindi Granth Ratnakar Pvt. Ltd., Bombay, 1959.
Daśarūpaka of Dhananjaya with Avaloka of	— (a) Ed. K.P. Parab, 1941, NSP, 5th ed.

Dhanika — (b) Ed. and tr. in English by G.C.O. Haas, 1922, New York.
(c) Ed. & tr. in Hindi by Hazariprasad Dwivedi and Prthvinath Dwivedi, 1963, Rajkamal Prakashan, Delhi.

Kāvyaprakāśa of Mammaṭa — Ed. by H.N. Apte, Anandashrama, Granthavali No. 66, Pune (1911).

Kuṭṭanimatam Kāvyam of Dāmodaragupta — Ed. by T.M. Tripathi, 1924. The Gujarati News Printing House, Bombay.
— Ed. and tr. in Hindi by A. Vidyalankar Indological Book House, Varanasi.

Mahāvīracarita of Bhavabhūti — Ed. Todar Mall, Revised by A.A. Mcdonell, 1928, Oxford University Press.

Mahābhāṣya — Ed. NSP, 1945.

Mālatī Mādhava of Bhavabhūti (with commentary of Kātyavema) — Ed. R.G. Bhandarkar, 1905.

Mālavikāgnimitram of Kālidāsa (with commentary of Kātyavema) — Ed. (and tr. in English) by M.R. Kale 1968 (6th Revised and enlarged ed.), A.R. Sheth & Co.

Mattavilāsa Prahasanam Mahendra Vikrama Varmā — Ed. and tr. in English by N.P. Unni 1974, College Book House, Trivendrum.

Mayamata of Mayamuni — Ed. by T. Ganapati Sastri, T.S.S. 1919.

Mṛcchakaṭikam of Śūdraka — Ed. and tr. in English by R.D. Karmarkar, Aryabhushan Press, Pune, 1940.

Nāgānanda of Śri Harṣa — Ed. and tr. in English by Buk Kun Bae, 1961, Indian Council of Cultural Relations, Asia Publishing House, New York.

Nāṭaka-Lakṣana-Ratnakoṣa of Sāgaranandin — Ed. by Myles Dillou, London, 1937.

Nāṭyadarpaṇa of Rāmacandra Guṇacandra — Ed. GOS XLVIII, 1959 (Revised second ed.)

Priyadarśikā of Śrī Harṣa — Śrī Harṣa's Plays, Tr. in English with full Sanskrit text.

Ratnāvalī of Śrī Harṣa — Bak Kun Bae, Indian council of cultural relations, Asia publishing House, New York (1961).

Sāhityadarpaṇa of Viśvanātha — Ed. and tr. in Hindi, Motilal Banarsidass, New Delhi, 1961 (4th ed.).

Sangīta Ratnākara of Sāraṅgadeva with the commentary of Kallinātha. — Adyar Library, Adyar, Madras.

Saṅgīta Makarandam of Nārada — G.O.S., No. 16, 1920.

Śilparatnam of Śrī Kumāra — TSS, 1929.

Uttararāmacaritam of Bhavabhūti (with Vīrarāghava's commentary) — (a) Ed. and tr. by M.R. Kale (4th ed.), 1934, Gopal Narayana & Co., Bombay.
(b) Ed. and tr. in Gujarati by Umashankar Joshi.

Vikramorvaśīyam of Kālidāsa (with Raṅgānātha's commentary) — (a) Ed. by H.D. Velankar, Sahitya Akademi, New Delhi, 1961.
(b) Ed. and tr. in English by M.R. Kale (Revised and Enlarged); A.R. Sheth & Co.

Viṣṇudharmottara Purāṇam, 1, 2 — (a) Ed. by Dr. Priyabala Shah, Oriental Institute, Baroda, 1958, 1961.

Citrasūtram of Viṣṇudharmottara (b) Text and tr. in English by C. Sivaramamurthi, 1978, Kanak Publications, New Delhi.

Viśvakarmā Vāstuśāstra — Ed. by K. Vasudev Shastri and N.B. Gadre, Tanjore Sarasvati Mandal Series, 1958.

Veṇi Saṃhāram of Bhaṭṭanārāyaṇa — Ed. and tr. in English by A.B. Gajendragadkar, New and second hand bookstall, Bombay-28.

SECONDARY SOURCES: BOOKS CONSULTED FOR THE STUDY OF NAṬYAŚĀSTRA

Bharata's Nāṭyaśāstra Vol. I and II (in English) — Dr. M. Ghosh, 1967, Vol. I (Revissed), Manisha Granth Mala Pvt. Ltd., Calcutta-12.
Vol. II, 1961, The Asiatic Society, Calcutta-16.

Nāṭyaśāstra with Abhinavabhāratī (1 to 18 Chapters tr. in Hindi), Vol. I and II — Ed. and tr. in Hindi Madhusudan Sastri, Vol. I, 1971, Banaras Hindu University Press.
Vol. II, 1975, Banaras Hindu University Press.

Abhinavabhāratī (Chapters 1, 2, 6, 7 in Hindi) — Ed. and tr. in Hindi by Visveshvara Siddhanta Shiromani, 1960, Delhi Vishva Vidyalaya, Hindi Vibhaga.

A Monogram on Bharata's Nāṭyaśāstra — P.S.R. Apparao and P. Sri Rama Sashtri, 1967, Natyamala Publication, Hyderabad.

Bharata Nāṭyamañjarī — G.K. Bhat, 1975, BORI, Poona.

Studies in Nāṭyaśāstra — G.H. Tarlekar, 1975, Motilal Banarsidass, Delhi.

Introduction to Bharata's Nāṭyaśāstra — Adya Rangacharya, 1966, Popular Prakashan, Bombay.

Bharatīya Nāṭyaśāstra (in Marathi) — Godavari Ketkar, 1928, Aryabhushan Press, Pune.

Saṃkṣipta Bharata Nāṭyaśāstra (tr. in Gujarati) — K.K. Shastri, 1958, M.S.U., Baroda.

Nātya, Nṛtta and Nṛtya —Their Meaning and Relation. — K.M. Varma, 1957, Orient Languages, Bombay.

Seven Words in Bharata —What Do They Signify? — K.M. Varma, Bombay Orient Languages, 1958.

Theatre in India, Vols. I and II — Sylvain Levi, Tr. from French, Narayan Mukherjee, Calcutta, Writer's Workshop Publication, 1978.

Part One—Chapter 1

Ṛksūkta Vaijayantī — Ed. H.D. Velankar, Vaidika Samsodhan Mandala, Pune, 1965.

Shri Upaniṣado — In Gujarati by N. Sharma. Shri Anandasram Bilkha, Saurashtra, Sam. 2009.

Rāmāyaṇa — Akhandananda, Sastu Sahitya Vardhaka Karyalaya, Ahmedabad (3rd ed.) (in Gujarati with Sanskrit text), Sam. 1992.

Mahābhārata — Bhandarkar Oriental Research Institute, Pune.

Harivaṃśha — Akhandananda, Sastu Sahitya Vardhaka Karyalaya, Ahmedabad, Sam. 2019.

The Ancient Indian Royal Consecration (The Rājasūya described according to Yajus texts and annoted) — J.C. Heesterman, Mounten & Co., Printers, The Hague, Netherlands, 1957.

Arthaśāstra, Part II, III — Eng. tr. with Critical and Explanatory notes by R.P. Kangle, 1972—A Study (Part III) 1965, University of Bombay Studies.

Part One—Chapters 1 and 2

Kāmaśāstra — With Jayamangala's Vyākhyā, Chowkhambha Sanskrit Series, New Delhi.

India as known to Pāṇini — Agrawal V.S., 1953, Allahabad Law Journal Press, Allahabad.

The Jataka or Stories of Buddha's former births. — Vol. III, ed. by E.B. Cowell, Lusac & Co., 46, Great Russel St., W.C.1, 1957.

Jataka Tales — Ed. and tr. by H.T. Francis and E.J. Thomas, Cambridge Unversity Press, 1916.

Life in Ancient India — By Jagdishchandra Jain, 1947, New

as Depicted in Jain Canons — Book Co. Ltd., Bombay.

India—In Times of Patanjali — By B.N. Puri, 1968, Bharatiya Vidya Bhavan, Bombay.

Śilāppaḍikaram — Eng. tr. by V.R.R. Dikhshitar, 1939, Oxford University Press.

Ancient Indian Historical Traditions — By E.E. Pargiter, 1972 Motilal Banarsidass.

Harṣacarita—Ek Sanskrutika Adhyayana (Hindi) — V.S. Agrawal, 1953, Bihar Rashtrabhasha Parishad, Patna.

Concept of Ancient Indian Theatre —M. Christopher Byrski, 1974, Munshiram Manoharlal, Delhi.

Traditions of Indian Theatre — M.L. Varadapande, E-37, Hauz Khas, New Delhi, 1979.

Speaking Tree—Study of Indian Culture and Society — Richard Lannoy, 1971, Oxford University Press, Great Britain.

Part One—Chapter 3

Acharya P.K. (Ed.) — Māṇasāra Series.
— A Dictionary of Hindu Architecture, 1927, Allahabad.

Brown Percy — Indian Architecture (Buddhist and Hindu Period) 1959, Taraporwala & Sons, Bombay.

Bhattacharya Tarapada — A Study of Vāstu Vidyā or Canons of Architecture, 1948, University Press, Patna.

Ferguson J. — Cave Temples of India, 1969, Delhi Oriental Books Corp., Reprint.

Gupta C.B. — The Indian Theatre, 1954. Motilal Banarsidass,

Havell E.B. — The Ancient and Mediaeval Architecture of India (A story of Indo-Aryan Civilisation), 1915, John Murray, London.

Kramrisch Stella — The Hindu Temple, Vols. I and II, 1946, University of Calcutta.

Mankad D.R. — Ancient Indian Theatre, 1960 (2nd ed.) Charotar Book Stall.

Rai Govindrai — Bharata Natyasastramen Natyasala-aonke Roop (Hindi), 1958. Kashi Mudranalaya, Varanasi.

Shukla D.N. — Samrāṇgaṇa Sūtradhār (Pt. II), 1967, Vastu Vangamaya Prakashan Shala, Lucknow.

Tripathi Ramsagar — Bharatiya Natyashastra aur Ranga-mancha (Hindi), 1971.

Wilson H.H. (ed.) — The Theatre of the Hindoos, 1955, Sushil Gupta (India) Ltd., Calcutta.

Part Two—Chapters 4 and 5

Bhattacharya Biswanath — Sanskrit Drama and Dramaturgy, 1974, Bharat Manisha Research Series.

Bhat G.K. — Tragedy and Sanskrit Drama, 1974 Popular Prakashan, Bombay.

Butcher S.H. (M.P.) (Ed. and tr.) — Poetics. Aristotle's Theory of Poetry and the Fine Arts, 1907 (4th ed.) Macmillan & Co. Ltd., London.

Bedekar D.K. — Sahitya Vichara (Marathi), 1964, Popular Prakashan, Bombay.

Bhattacharya Vishnupad — Sahitya Mimansa (tr. in Gujarati by Suresh Joshi), 1957, Chetan Prakashan Griha, Vadodara.

De S.K. (and Dasgupta) — A History of Sanskrit Literature (Classical period), Vol. I, 1962, University of Calcutta (2nd ed.).

Dalal Minakshi — Conflict in Sanskrit Drama, 1973, Somaiya Publication, Bombay.

Gnoli R. — Aesthetic Experience according to Abhinavagupta, 1968, Series Oriental Roma. XI—Roma.

Gupta Rakesh — Studies in Nayaka Nayika bheda, 1967, Granthayan, Aligarh.

Indu Sekhar — Sanskrit Drama: Its Origin and Decline, 1977 (2nd ed.), Munshiram Manoharlal Pub. Pvt. Ltd.

Jagirdar R.V. — Drama in Sanskrit Literature, 1947.

Keith A.B. — Sanskrit Drama in its Origin, Development, Theory and Practice, 1924, Oxford University Press.

Krishnamoorthy K. — Dhavanyaloka or theory of suggestion in poetry, 1955, Poona Oriental Book Agency.

Mason J.L., Patwardhan M.V. — Aesthetic Rupture, The Rasâdhyâya of NS, 1970, Deccan College, Poona.

Mankad D.R. — The Types of Sanskrit Drama, 1936, Urmi Prakashan Mandir, Karachi.

Mainkar T.G. — The Theory of Sandhis and Sandhyanga-s 1978, Ajanta Publication, Delhi.

Pusalkar A.D. — Bhasa—A Study, 1968, Lahore.

Parekh Nagindas — Abhinavano Rasa Vichara Ane Bija Lekho (in Gujarati), 1969, Dilip Printers, Ahmedabad.

Pandey K.C. — Comparative Aesthetic, Vol. I, II, 1950, Chawkhamba Sanskrit Series, Banaras.

Shastri S.N. — The Laws of Sanskrit Drama, 1961 Chawkhambha Sanskrit Series, Banaras.

Winternitz M. — History of Indian Literature Vol. III, Part I (Classical Sanskrit Literature) Vol. III, Part II (Scientific Literature), 1963, trans. by Subhadra Jha, Motilal Banarasidass.

— Some Problems of Indian Literature, 1925, Calcutta University Press.

Warder A.K. — Indian Kâvya Literature, Vols. I, II, III, 1972, 1977, Motilal Banarsidass.

Wells H.W. — The Classical Drama of India, 1963, Asia Publishing House, Bombay.

Part Three—Chapters 6, 7 and 8

Boner Alice — Principles of Composition on Hindu Sculpture (Cave temple period) 1962 Leiden E.J. Brill, Netherland.

Barrat Douglas and Gray Besil — Painting of India, 1963. The World Publishing Co., Ohio, USA.

Cheney Shelden — Theatre—Three Thousand Years of Drama, Acting and Stage Craft, 1929/1947, Tudor Publishing Co., New York.

Coomaraswamy A.K. — The Dance of Shiva, 1965, Asia Publishing House, Bombay.

— The Transformation of Nature in Art, 1934/1956—Dover Publication, New York.

Christian and Indian Philosophy of Art, 1943, New York, Dover Publication.

— History of Indian and Indonesian Art, 1965, Dover Publication, New York.

Ghosh A. — Ajanta Murals, 1967, Archaeological Survey of India, New Delhi.

Gajjar Irine N. — Ancient Indian Art and The West (A Study of Parallels, Continuity and Symbolisms from Protohistoric to Early Buddhist Times) 1971, D.B. Taraporewala & Sons, Bombay.

Ghurye G.S. — Indian Costume, 1951, Popular Prakashan, Bombay.

— Bharata Natya and its Costume, 1958, Popular Book Depot, Bombay.

Havell E.B. Indian Sculpture and Painting, 1908, London.

Kramrisch Stella — Indian Sculpture, 1933, The Heritage of India Series.

Lath Mukund — A Study of Dattilam, 1978, Impex India, New Delhi.

Dr. Motichandra — Costumes, Textiles, Cosmetics, Coiffure in Ancient and Mediaeval India, 1973, Oriental Publishers, Delhi.

— Prachina Bharatiya Veshabhusha (Hindi), Sam. 2007, Bharati Mandir, Prayag.

Parikh R.C. and Shah Priyabala (ed.) — Nṛtya Ratnakoṣa—Pt. II of Saṁgītarāja of Mahārāṇā Kumbha, 1968 Rajasthan Puratan Granthamala, Jodhpur.

Ragavan V. (Ed. and tr.) — Śṛṅgāra Prakāśa of Bhoja, Vol. II, Chapter 12.

Sachs Curt (tr. by Bessie Schonberg) — World History of Dance, 1937/1963 The Norton Lib. W.W. Norton & Co., New York.

Saunders E. Dale — Mudra, 1960, Routledge & Kega Paul Ltd., London.

Shivaramamurthy C. — Sculpture inspired by Kalidasa, 1942.

Vatsayan Kapila — Classical Indian Dance in Literature and Arts, 1977 (2nd ed.) Sangeet Natak Akademi, Delhi.

Zoete Beryl de — The Other Mind—A Study of Dance in India, 1953, Victor Gollancz, London.

— Dance and Magic Drama in Ceylon, Faber & Faber Ltd., London.

Zimmer Heinrich (ed. by Joseph Campbell) — The Art of Indian Asia, Vol. I, II, 1955. Bollington Series, Princeton University Press.

Part Four—Chapters 9 and 10

Arnolt Peter — The Theatre in Japan, 1969, Macmillan London.

Bowers Faubian — Theatre in the East, 1956, Thomas Nelson & Sons, New York.

Brandon J.R. — Theatre in South-East Asia, 1974, Harward University Press, Cambridge, Massachusets.

Chen Jack — The Chinese Theatre, 1948, Dennis Dobson Ltd., London.

Gargi Balwant — Theatre in India, 1962, Theatre Arts Books, New York.

Keene Donald — Noh—The Classical Theatre of Japan, 1973, Kodunsha International Ltd., Revised; Paperback ed.

Mathur J.C. — Drama—in rural India, 1964, Indian Council for Cultural Relations, Asia Publishing House, Bombay.

MARG ISSUES — (a) Invitation to the Dance—March, 1966.
(b) In Praise of Bharatanatyam—Vol. XXXII, No. 3.
(c) In Praise of Kerala Heritage—Vol. XXXII, No. 2.

JOURNALS AND ARTICLES

Acharya P.K. : "The Playhouse of the Hindu Period" Dr. S. Krishnaswamy Com. Volume.

Achwal M.B. : "A Note on the ancient theatre" Natya—1959-60, pp. 21.

Athawale R.B. : "The Problem of Nāndi and Purvaraṅga" paper in AIOC, 1953.

Bloch T. : "Caves and Inscriptions in Ramgarh Hills", Archaeological Survey Annual Report, 1903-4, pp. 123-31.

Bedekar D.K. : "Primitive Society and Yajna" ABORI Vol. XXXI, 1950-51, pp. 70-99.

Balbir G.K. : "The Conception of Conventions of Speech in Sanskrit Dramaturgy" AIOC Vol. 1946, October, Part II, pp. 187-96.

Banerjee Sastri A. : "Patañjali and Bhāsa" JBORS, Vol. IX, pp. 71ff.

Chakravarti Chintaharan : "A Note on Bharata Vākya" IHQ. Vol. V, 1929, pp. 549-52.

"A further note on Bharata Vākya" IHQ, Vol. III, 1931, pp. 190-91.

Chatterjee S.K. : "Indian Synthesis" Racial and Cultural Intermixture in India, 1954. Indo-Asian Culture 4, New Delhi.

De S.K. : "The Curtain in Ancient Indian Theatre, Bharatiya Vidya, Vol. IX, 1948.

Diwekar H.R. : "Mattavāraṇi" AIOC, 1959, Vol. II Pt. 1.

Ghosh M. : "Bharata Vākya, IHQ, Vol. VI, 1930, pp. 485-86.

: "The Hindu Theatre", I.H.Q. IX.

Karmarkar R.D. : "Dramatic Terms—Janāntikam and Apavāritam, Praveśaka and Viṣkambhaka, ABORI, Vol. XXXV.

Purohit N.B. : "Apavārita Speech in Sanskrit Drama" AIOC, 1937, p. 421-35.

Khokar Mohan : "The Saraikela Chhau Dance" NCPA Journal, June 1973, Vol. II, pp. 25-32.

Panchal G. : "The Curtain in Classical Sanskrit Drama", Sangeet Natak-25, July-Sept. 1972, pp. 23-38.

: "Kootampalam—Sanskrit Stage of Kerala" Sangeet Natak—8, April-June, 1968.

: "The Curtain in Abhijñāna Śakuñtalā" Sangeet Natak—41, July-September, 1976.

: "Kuttambalam and Its Link with Bharatas Stage", NCPA Journal, Vol. VI, March, 1977, pp. 27-44.

: Bharata's Stage in Action" Sangeet Natak, 34, October Dec., 1974.

Rajgopalan L.S. : "Music in Kootiyattam" Sangeet Natak-10, Oct.-Dec., 1968.

: "Eloquent Eyes—Netrābhinaya in

Journal of Madras Music Academy, Vol. XIV, p. 93, 1974, parts I-IV.

Raghavan V. : "Hindu Theatre" 1933, IHQ Vol. IX Calcutta.

: "Nāṭyadharmī and Lokadharmī" 1933-34 JOR Madras, Vol. VII, and VIII.

: "Sanskrit Drama in Performance" 1957, Madras University Journal, Vol. XXIV No. 1, July.

: "Producing Sanskrit Plays" 1959, Natya Spring number.

: "Music in Ancient Indian Drama" JMMA, Vol. XXV, Parts I-IV.

: "Uparūpakas and Nāṭya prabandhas" 1965, Sangeet Natak-2, April, New Delhi.

: "A Note on the name Daśarūpaka" JOR, Madras, Vol VII.

: "Vṛttis", JOR, Madras Vol. VI and VII.

: "Tantras or Mechanical Contrivances in Ancient India", 1956, Indian Institute of Culture, Bangalore.

: "The Social Play in Sanskrit", Indian Institute of Culture, Bangalore, 1952.

Raja K. Kunjanni : "Kootiyattam, NCPA Journal, Vol. III, June 1974, pp. 1-12.

Richmond Farley : "Vaiśṇava Dramas of Assam" Education Theatre Journal, May, 1974; pp. 145-63.

Sivaprasad K.S. : "A note on the Popular Element in the Classical Sanskrit Drama" 1922, AICC.

Tarlekar G.H. : "Music in Sanskrit Drama", paper read at Natyasastra Seminar, Calcutta, 1980.

Thakur Jaidevasingh : "Nāṭyaśāstra men Pūrvaraṅga", Nāṭya Śāstra Viśeṣānka—Nāṭya vārta, February May 1980, Calcutta, pp. 59-72.

Shanta Gandhi : "A Background note on the performance of Vision of Vāsavadattā" a paper read at seminar on A Sanskrit play in performance, University of Hawaii, Honolulu, 1974, March, 15-24.

: "A note on the construction of the model of the rectangular theatre described in the NS", an accompanying note to a model prepared by her for the Brander Mathews Museum of theatre arts at Columbia University, New York, USA.

Richmond Farley : "The rite of passage and Kuttiattam, the Sanskrit Theatre in Kerala". A paper prepared for tenth International Conference of Anthropological and Ethnological Sciences New Delhi, Dec. 10-16, 1978.

Unni N.P. : "Mattavilāsa—on the Kerala Stage" Journal of Kerala Studies, Vol. I, Serial No. 1, July, 1973.

Wijesekara, O.H. de A. : "Buddhist Evidence for the Early Existence of Drama", IHQ, Vol. XVII.

Wells H.W. : "Eastern Dramas and Western Stage" February 11, 1962, Illustrated Weekly of India.

: "Varieties of Conflict in Asian Drama."

M.R. Kavi : "Bharata Kosha", Tirupati, 1951.

V.S. Apte : Sanskrit English Dictionary, GOI Publication.

INDEX

ERRATA

Page	Line	Incorrect	Correct
52	2	24' × 24'	24' × 48'
93	26	and	through
113	23	Prakarṇa	Prakaraṇa
121	9	Uddhāta	Uddhata
153	25	told to DR:	DR: It imparts a confidence told to
157	9	"The Apavārita speech is Sanskrit Drama"	"The Apavārita speech in Sanskrit Drama"
174	14	p. 391	p. 400
174	24	p. 387	p. 391
175	27	p. 389	p. 391
188	28	nāṭyasūtra	Naṭasūtra
223	2	5-Vinā player	9-Vīṇā player
223	4	7-Flute player	5-Flute player
223	6	9-Female vocalist	10-Female vocalist
223	7	10-Male vocalist	7-Male vocalist
308	12	pp. 385-387	pp. 384-385
318	11	pp. 384-99	pp. 386-387
340	40	p. 387	pp. 390-391
350	27	p. 393	pp. 392-393
359	38	p. 389	pp. 394-395
366	19	p. 390	pp. 396-397